LITERACY AND ORALITY IN
EIGHTEENTH-CENTURY IRISH SONG

Poetry and Song in the Age of Revolution

Series Editors: Michael Brown
John Kirk
Andrew Noble

Titles in this Series

1 United Islands? The Languages of Resistance
John Kirk, Andrew Noble and Michael Brown (eds)

Forthcoming Titles

Cultures of Radicalism in Britain and Ireland
John Kirk, Michael Brown and Andrew Noble (eds)

LITERACY AND ORALITY IN EIGHTEENTH-CENTURY IRISH SONG

BY

Julie Henigan

Routledge
Taylor & Francis Group
LONDON AND NEW YORK

First published 2012 by Pickering & Chatto (Publishers) Limited

Published 2016 by Routledge
2 Park Square, Milton Park, Abingdon, Oxfordshire OX14 4RN
711 Third Avenue, New York, NY 10017, USA

First issued in paperback 2015

Routledge is an imprint of the Taylor & Francis Group, an informa business

© Taylor & Francis 2012
© Julie Henigan 2012

To the best of the Publisher's knowledge every effort has been made to contact relevant copyright holders and to clear any relevant copyright issues. Any omissions that come to their attention will be remedied in future editions.

All rights reserved, including those of translation into foreign languages. No part of this book may be reprinted or reproduced or utilised in any form or by any electronic, mechanical, or other means, now known or hereafter invented, including photocopying and recording, or in any information storage or retrieval system, without permission in writing from the publishers.

Notice:
Product or corporate names may be trademarks or registered trademarks, and are used only for identification and explanation without intent to infringe.

BRITISH LIBRARY CATALOGUING IN PUBLICATION DATA

Henigan, Julie.
Literacy and orality in eighteenth-century Irish song. – (Poetry and song in the age of revolution)
1. Songs, Irish – Ireland – 18th century – History and criticism. 2. Oral tradition – Ireland – History – 18th century. 3. Music – Social aspects – Ireland – History – 18th century. 4. Music and literature – Ireland – History – 18th century.
I. Title II. Series
781.629162-dc23

ISBN-13: 978-1-138-66465-4 (pbk)
ISBN-13: 978-1-8489-3342-2 (hbk)

Typeset by Pickering & Chatto (Publishers) Limited

CONTENTS

Acknowledgements	vii
List of Figures	ix
Introduction	1
1 The Medieval Background	15
2 Songs of the Dispossessed: Eighteenth-Century Irish Song-Poetry	27
3 'Éirigh i do Sheasamh': Oral and Literary Aspects of the Irish Lament Tradition	65
4 'For Want of Education': The Songs of the Hedge Schoolmaster	111
5 The Eighteenth-Century Printed Ballad in Ireland	151
6 The Eighteenth-Century Irish Ballad and Modern Oral Tradition	181
Notes	207
Works Cited	245
Index	263

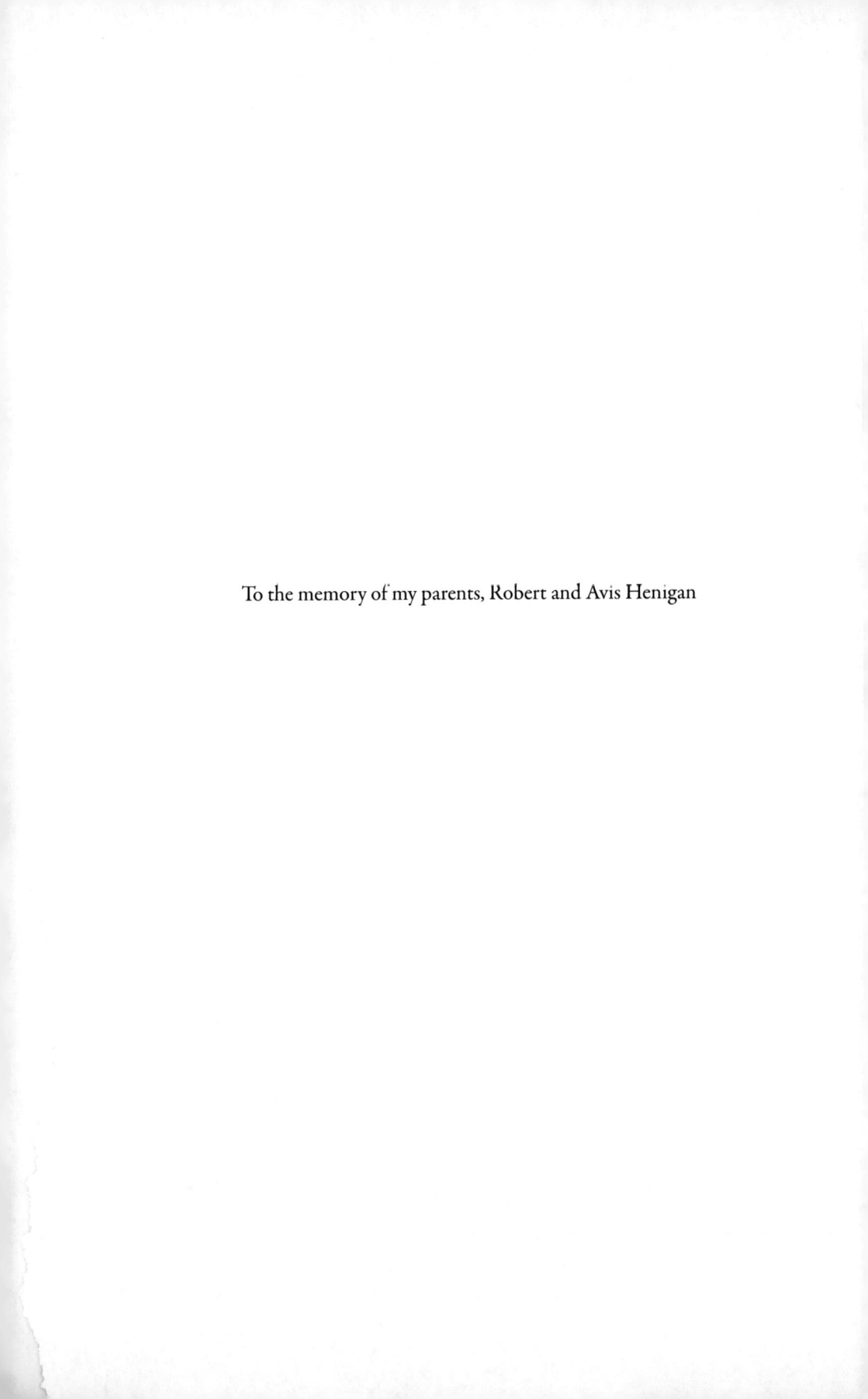

To the memory of my parents, Robert and Avis Henigan

ACKNOWLEDGEMENTS

I wish to express my gratitude to those without whom this book could not have been written: first and foremost to my teachers and mentors at the University of Notre Dame, including Drs Peter McQuillan, Christopher Fox, Patrick Gaffney, Luke Gibbons, the late James Walton and the late Breandán Ó Buachalla. I would also like to express my gratitude to my fellow folklorists, collectors and friends, including the late Tom Munnelly and Hugh Shields, Lisa Shields, Annette Munnelly, John Moulden, Virginia Blankenhorn, Pádraigín Ní Uallacháin, Len Graham, Cathal Goan, Anthony McCann, Jimmy McBride, Lillis Ó Laoire, Deirdre Ní Chonghaile, Jim Carroll and Pat McKenzie for their generosity in sharing unstintingly of their knowledge, fieldwork and enthusiasm. I am especially grateful to Michael Brown, Aedín Clements and Virginia Blankenhorn for reading and commenting on the manuscript. Finally, I wish to thank Patrick O'Neill, Daniel Patterson and Terry Zug for their guidance and support over the years.

Thanks also are due to the entire staff of the Irish Traditional Music Archives and to all the archives and libraries which have kindly given me permission to reproduce texts and images from their collections, including the British Library Early Printed Collections, the Linen Hall Library, the Ulster Museum, Queen's University Belfast Special Collections, the Royal Irish Academy and the Early Printed Books section of Trinity College Dublin. I am especially grateful to Robert Heslip and Charles Benson for their assistance with chapbook material. I conducted much of my archival research while holding a Mellon Pre-Dissertation Fellowship in association with the Institute for Historical Research at the University of London; I wish to thank Professor Warwick Gould at the University of London, who acted as my mentor for this fellowship. I conducted other archival and field research funded by a Dissertation-Year Fellowship from the University of Notre Dame and by an award from the Paddy Clancy Memorial Foundation, both of whom I wish to acknowledge.

Finally, I would like to express my profoundest gratitude to my greatest teachers, the singers (not already named), both living and dead, who have shared with me their knowledge, their memories, their songs and their friendship – among them Aodh and John Ó Duibheannaigh, Neilí Ní Dhomhnaill,

Tríona and Maighread Ní Dhomhnaill, Mairéad Ní Mhaonaigh, Sailí Ní Ghallachóir, Caitlín Nic Niallais, Paddy Tunney, Seán 'ac Dhonncha, Máire Nic Dhonncha, Tomás Mac Eoin, Bridget Fitzgerald, Sally Coyne, Packie Manus Byrne, James Callaghan, Tommy McDermott, Kitty Hayes, Vincent Boyle, Kitty McFadden, Dinny McLaughlin, Peg McMahon, Éilis Ní Shúilleabháin and Máirín Uí Lionaird.

LIST OF FIGURES

Figure 2.1: John Derricke (J. D.), *The Image of Irelande* — 28
Figure 3.1: John Barrow (J. B.), *A Tour Round Ireland, Through the Sea-Coast Counties, in the Autumn of 1835* — 71
Figure 3.2: Edward Bunting (E. B.), *The Ancient Music of Ireland* — 79
Figure 4.1: W. Carleton (W. C.), *Traits and Stories of the Irish Peasantry*, 6th edn — 114
Figure 4.2: *A Compleat New Song Called Tullymore's Fair Queen, To which are Added THE CUCKOO'S NEST and MOLLY-O* — 144
Figure 5.1: 'The Royal Blackbird' — 157
Figure 5.2: J. Hand (J. H.), 'Irish Street Ballads' — 174
Figure 6.1: Mikeen McCarthy — 187
Figure 6.2: Packie Manus Byrne — 188

INTRODUCTION

This book deals with what is usually called 'folk', 'traditional' or 'vernacular' song. While the definitions of such terms are constantly being revised, the popular (and until recently, even scholarly) image of this kind of song usually includes such traits as oral transmission, relatively simple lyrics created by illiterate or semiliterate composers, and informal performance within small communities. Although all of these traits may characterize traditional song, not all are necessary to it: for while 'folk' or traditional song tends to be transmitted orally, it has also often been circulated via the written word; and although often simple, it is not invariably so – and its creators have included well-known poets as well as anonymous local songmakers. Performance in community, on the other hand, is integral to the song tradition, a tradition I prefer to define more in terms of context than content. The following study will therefore question the first two of these assumptions specifically in the context of the Irish song tradition; for although certainly not unique in this regard, it offers a striking example of the ways in which the oral and the written, the vernacular and elite, can interact, aesthetically and socially, to create a tradition that draws on a wide range of linguistic, poetic and musical forms and conventions.

Concentrating on the eighteenth century, when many of the songs or song-genres in the contemporary Irish traditional song repertoire first appear, I argue that while differences in poetic idiom may appear between folksong and elite or 'educated' poetry, there is ultimately no absolute dichotomy between oral and written forms on the one hand or folk and 'literary' authorship on the other, either within the song tradition itself or in the realm of literary poetry. Instead, I will demonstrate that in Irish poetry continuous interaction has long existed between the vernacular and 'high' cultural spheres; that the boundaries between the two, many of which have been retrospectively imposed by scholars and commentators with little real knowledge of or affinity for the tradition, are historically fluid rather than rigid; that the distinctions are more stylistic and formal than cultural and social; and that both are driven by aesthetic as well as functional considerations. Thus one idiom (whether defined as 'oral', 'traditional' or 'vernacular') cannot be valued at the expense of the other (written, 'literary' or 'elite') on the basis of received ideas of what distinguishes one from the other. Far from being a monolithic entity, traditional Irish song encompasses a greater breadth of forms than is often assumed. Neither do written or oral origins determine either the form of the poetry or its ultimate use. Certainly within traditional singing communities songs are more subject to the aesthetic and performative values and requirements of their respective communities than to the concepts of what does and does not constitute the popular or the literary.

This dynamic interaction has deep historical roots in Irish culture, roots that can be traced to the medieval period. As Lesa Ní Mhunghaile comments, 'the connection between the oral and the written in the Gaelic tradition in Ireland has been so pervasive since the advent of writing in the sixth century that it is often difficult to say what originated as an oral narrative and what was originally literary'.[1] This connection becomes far more apparent, however, during the eighteenth century, not only with the entrance of the songs of the 'dispossessed' Gaelic poets[2] and their English-speaking schoolmaster counterparts into the popular song repertoire, but also with the spread of literacy, which both the greater availability of education and of cheap printed forms (chiefly the ballad sheet and the chapbook) helped to promote. Therefore, while some of the material in the popular repertoire during this period is arguably derived from earlier, oral models, the circulation of song via both manuscripts and printed forms, in conjunction with oral transmission, is demonstrable. So, too, is the use of 'high' poetic and thematic elements, such as the *aisling* ('vision') poem by the eighteenth-century literary poets and the Latin-derived *conflictus* conventions by the hedge schoolmasters and their imitators. Meanwhile, the shared conventions of the *caoineadh* (lament) demonstrate not only interaction between oral and literate spheres but also vernacular and aristocratic ones, contributing to a form that seems to have been common to all echelons of society. The elite and vernacular shared much other common ground: 'literary' poets from Aogán Ó Rathaille to W. B. Yeats retained a view of themselves and their art that placed them on a higher than popular level; and yet a comparable self-consciousness of artistry can be traced in the work and commentary of local song composers like Seán Bán Mac Grianna. This self-consciousness, while at least partly interwoven with the entrance of the songs of such 'literary' Ulster poets as Art Mac Cumhaigh and Peadar Ó Doirnín into the traditional repertoire, may also reflect a prior and parallel sense of the importance of poetry and the role of the poet in society.

This is not to entirely equate the two idioms. For example, orality does play a part, if not necessarily in the original composition of many traditional songs, frequently in their recomposition, especially when written aids are unavailable – arguably making variation a more aesthetically acceptable trait in the song tradition. It is also undeniable that certain genres of traditional song are characterized by linguistic, metric and imagistic conventions (including quotidian language, directness of diction and the use of repetition) that make them at least generically identifiable as 'folksong'. Whether these conventions can be strictly designated as 'oral' or even 'folk', however, is another question. Not only might simplicity of expression owe something to aesthetic preference, it could also be employed by the literate, as it was by priest-poet Uilliam English. On the other hand, even some of Eoghan Rua Ó Súilleabháin's more arcane compositions found favour in traditional singing communities; and the songs of hedge schoolmaster poets acquired much of their impact by departing from everyday language in their deliberate use of learned allusion and Latinate word constructions.

Moreover, song fashions change, a fact that is reflected in both the contents of eighteenth-century chapbook and miscellanies and in what people were actually singing – for instance, in the early nineteenth-century community Patrick Kennedy describes in his Wexford memoirs, where we find that middle-brow English-language material (including both narrative 'broadside ballads' and more sentimental lyric fare) entered the traditional song repertoire via print. In fact, the variety of song-forms and styles in the repertoire of the singing communities of the past hundred years demonstrates that aesthetic distinctions in the traditional song repertoire are much more malleable and relative than previously believed; and that, instead of a single, monolithic aesthetic, we must recognize a reasonably wide range of individual and community aesthetic preferences. Ultimately, however, defining song repertoire on the basis of its oral or literary origins or features can distract the observer from one central fact: that, while capable of being abstracted from its social contexts, it is most wholly realized in performance. This is a theme that will recur throughout this book in relation to each of the genres I examine.

Orality Studies: A Critical Overview

> 'Orality' and 'literacy' are not two separate and independent things; nor (to put it more concretely) are oral and written modes two mutually exclusive and opposed processes for representing and communicating information. On the contrary, they take diverse forms in differing cultures and periods, are used differently in different social contexts and, in insofar as they can be distinguished at all as separate modes rather than a continuum, they mutually interact and affect each other, and the relations between them are problematic rather than self-evident.
>
> – Ruth Finnegan[3]

The study of literacy as it relates to 'pre-literate' or oral modes of art and culture – now frequently termed 'orality studies' – has burgeoned in recent years, permeating not only the fields of anthropology, literature, folklore and communications, but also sociology, social work, social history, neuroscience and religious studies. Where does such interest come from? Although the term 'oral tradition' was first employed by Renaissance Catholic theologians to express the idea of an unwritten tradition, 'preserved by the Church, and of equal authority to the written Word of the Bible',[4] the concept of oral tradition as we know it today only emerged in the eighteenth century, 'shaped,' as Lesa Ní Mhunghaile notes, 'by a number of interlinked debates in antiquarian and literary circles on the nature of the literary source and the reliability of oral tradition as a means of preserving history'.[5]

One debate that became particularly heated in the seventeenth and eighteenth centuries concerned the composition of Homeric epics. Drawing upon the writings of first-century historian Flavius Josephus (who had asserted that Homer's works 'were put together just as they were remembered distinctly from songs'), François Hédelin contended that Homer did not exist – a view accepted by Perrault.[6] This notion, along with the Ciceronian tradition 'that the Homeric poems were brought to Athens in fragments by Lycurgus and there assembled into the great epics', served, by the late seventeenth and early eighteenth centuries, to discredit Homer in favour of the more 'unified' (and therefore more worthy) Virgil; it also, coincidentally, functioned 'as a useful bit of propaganda for those [like Joseph Addison] who were venturing to offer ... ballads to the serious attention of men of taste'.[7]

By the late eighteenth century, the focus on Homer-as-ballad-singer had become strongly interwoven with the long-standing interest in bardism, now come to prominence in the age of Blair, Macpherson, Rousseau and Grey – an age, notes Nicholas Hudson, of 'increased interest ... in "primitive speech and culture"'. This interest informed Robert Wood's theories about an 'unlettered' Homer, whose language 'derived from a primitive age when speech, unrestrained by writing, was passionate and spontaneous'.[8] It embodied, according to Wood, 'the passionate expression of Nature, which, incapable of misrepresentation, appeals directly to our feelings and finds the shortest road to the heart'.[9] Such a bard was well-suited to the Age of Sensibility. Although Giambattista Vico had earlier represented Homer's poems as 'the reflex' of an entire people, both Wood and Friedrich August Wolf found a more receptive audience for such ideas at the end of the century. In this, they were no doubt aided by an increasing 'fascination with the oral culture of ancient peoples' and 'the expectation encouraged by scrupulously edited, 'amended' and 'purified' publications such as Percy's *Reliques of Ancient English Poetry* (1765): namely that ancient songs were not barbarous or rude in the way that might have been expected, but rather were compatible with refined eighteenth-century taste'.[10] Ultimately, Wolf's *Prolegomena ad Homerum*, published in 1795, not only asserted proof of the oral transmission of Homeric verse, but also revived the old notion of the epics as a compendium of 'loose songs', subsequently assembled into written form. Wolf's work, which argued that the Homeric works 'had necessarily to be the creation of later redactors who joined together the primitive oral songs into the works we celebrate for their unity of design', paved the way for the nineteenth-century debates that eventually led to the oral-formulaic theories of the twentieth century.[11]

Such a glorification of oral culture was, however, a late development. A far less sympathetic view of oral society had been common in Europe since the Renaissance, when the written word, conceived primarily as an image of speech – but increasingly viewed as the principal orientation to language – had been exalted to the point where some seventeenth-century grammarians and rhetoricians imagined what Hudson describes as a 'visual language that mirrored the nature of things more accurately than any existing form of speech'. The rise of the middle classes and the scriptural emphasis of Protestantism no doubt reinforced the preeminence of literacy, and illiteracy was increasingly associated 'with ignorance, superstition and social inferiority'.[12] Commentators from Samuel Purchas to Vico and Adam Ferguson viewed unlettered cultures as essentially primitive, sometimes possessing a form of hieroglyphic representation, but mainly incapable of higher forms of thought, including abstract analysis.[13] As late as the 1770s, Edward Gibbon maintained 'that the ancient Germans had neither history nor poetry because they were without the "artificial help" of letters'.[14]

Dissenters to the view of writing as a mirror of speech arose as early as the sixteenth century, becoming increasingly numerous by the end of the seventeenth: by 1700 Conrad Amman argued that speech was a 'natural' form of expression and less 'liable to deceive' than writing. Samuel Johnson saw writing and speech as distinct forms of discourse, while Thomas Sheridan asserted that there was 'no sort of affinity' between writing and speech.[15] Sheridan, in his promotion of oratory, even accorded primacy to speech, maintaining, for example, that literacy produced a stultifying effect on sermons – a view shared by Oliver Goldsmith.[16] But these were linguistic and rhetorical concerns, not cultural ones. Nicholas Hudson connects the 'tendency of linguists and grammarians to separate the functions of writing and speech' in the mid-eighteenth century with the higher value increasingly placed upon passionate utterance by advocates of the poetry of Sensibility.[17] Yet the rhetorical perspectives, which had their own history, could well have complemented rather than arisen from the movement of Sensibility, reflecting other values of the era, including an emphasis on empiricism and linguistic pedagogy.[18] The aesthetics of vernacular literature also had complex roots in early Enlightenment thought and criticism (like Joseph Addison's), which exalted the natural above the artificial, the simple above the ornate and the 'true taste' of the 'common people' over the 'false taste' of many educated readers, well before the subsequent ascendancy of bardism among the literate classes.[19] Ultimately, it was the elevation of oral culture in the romantic and quasi-anthropological writings of Wood, Wolf, Herder and others that, as Albert Friedman notes, 'helped shape the concept of unlettered culture', in which poetry like Homer's had 'long survived without the benefit of the written word';[20] and which, closer to home, had produced the works of Ossian and the ballads of the ancient English and Scottish minstrels. Even as most of these theorists also saw oral culture as a reflection of an earlier 'primitive' phase in the development of human civilization ('that barbarous state of society which necessarily precedes the invention of letters'),[21] their claims offered a new perspective that ran counter to the view of a culture without letters as no culture at all.

Many of the issues central to the more recent debates about orality and literacy are therefore far from new. Contemporary orality studies usually traces its roots to the groundbreaking work of Milman Parry in the late 1920s through the mid-1930s. Influenced by Antoine Meillet at the Sorbonne, Parry initially focused on the formulaic and 'traditional' nature of Greek – especially Homeric – epic poetry, ultimately (following intensive fieldwork work with Yugoslavian epic singers or *guslars*) developing the theory of oral-formulaic composition. Parry's assistant and protégé, Albert Lord, continued this work, eventually publishing *The Singer of Tales* (1960), in which he described his and Parry's work and set forth the tenets of the oral-formulaic theory. This theory posits the existence of a repertoire of formulae and thematic material from which the singer draws to create his composition-in-performance, weaving these elements together according to both the aesthetic and metrical demands of the genre. Parry's definition of the formula – 'a group of words which is regularly employed under the same metrical conditions to express a given essential idea' – replaced terms like 'stock epithets' or 'epic clichés' used by Homeric scholars to describe the composition of Greek epic poetry[22] and introduced a broader conception of the mental and linguistic processes involved in oral composition. Comparing it to language itself, i.e. 'substitution in the framework of the grammar', Lord saw the formula as 'the offspring of the marriage of thought and sung verse'.[23] Bruce Rosenberg, who has convincingly applied the theory to southern American folk preaching, clarified the technique further by describing its art as 'the skillful manipulation of metrically consistent phrases, some memorized and some spontaneously composed (based on lexico-syntactic models known by the singers), which skill enabled them to spin out narratives at great length'.[24] The oral-formulaic system thus encompasses not only repeated words and phrases but also 'patterns that make adjustment of phrase and creation of phrases by analogy possible'.[25] It also ensures that, as Ruth Finnegan observes, 'There is no correct text, no idea that one version is more "authentic" than another' and that 'each performance is a unique and original creation with its own validity'.[26] Themes, or entire compositions, can be lengthened or shortened according to occasion or audience.

If Parry and Lord's theory made orality a defining feature of certain forms of literature, distinguishing oral from written poetry on the basis of formal, structural and stylistic characteristics, it also claimed that the singer must be illiterate to practise his art. This claim may have been partly motivated by a desire to raise the status of the oral singer from that of 'folk' or 'peasant' performer to that of the 'traditional creative artist', whose compositions were on a par with the best written poetry. Lord pointed out, however, that many of the *guslar*'s songs were aristocratic in origin, surviving longer in 'peasant populations ... not because it is essentially "peasant" poetry, but because the peasant society has remained illiterate longer than urban society'.[27] Yet this view also drives a wedge between written and oral cultures and their respective verbal arts. Written literature – with its notion of the 'fixed' or 'correct' text, to be memorized rather than improvised in performance – is seen as wholly incompatible with oral technique.[28] In fact – although he elsewhere qualifies this generalization – Lord proclaims the oral and written modes 'contradictory and mutually exclusive'.[29] Lord's book had an enormous impact on scholars, particularly in the fields of anthropology, folklore and medieval literature, who applied it to everything from ballads to *Beowulf*. John Miles Foley, having inherited the Parry-Lord mantle, has carried on both the work on Yugoslavian oral epic in particular and the oral-formulaic theory in general, which he has refined and qualified, while successfully straddling the fields of literature, classics and anthropology.[30]

Another major development in orality studies began with the work of scholars like Eric Havelock, Marshall McLuhan and Walter J. Ong, who, approaching the subject from different but complementary angles, made even more sweeping distinctions between the oral and literate spheres than had the oral-formulaic school. Havelock proposed that the development of the Greek alphabet reflected a revolution not only in classical Greek culture but in western culture in general, effecting a radical change 'in the way [we] think' and, by transferring the process from the aural to the visual realm, in the way we remember or 'store' information.[31] According to Havelock, 'Atomism and the alphabet alike were theoretical constructs, manifestations of a capacity for abstract analysis, an ability to translate objects of perception into mental entities, which seems to have been one of the hallmarks of the way the Greek mind worked'.[32] McLuhan, influenced by Havelock, believed that writing radically altered fundamental cognitive and psychological processes. Specifically, 'the technologies of alphabetic writing, especially print, trained the brain to process visual information linearly, and such linear thinking – implying determination, causality, logic, detachment, delayed gratification – is then applied to the rest of life'.[33] McLuhan further distinguished between visual, written (especially printed) culture and 'oral culture', as exemplified by 'acoustic man'. His primary interest, as Ruth and Elihu Katz put it, was 'in the contrast between media of "heart" and media of "mind"'. Paraphrasing McLuhan's formulation, they remark:

> In the beginning was orality, the extension of the ear, the medium of heart. Unlike print that extends the eye individualistically, word-of-mouth is sociable, pluralistic, playful, favouring generalist and operational wisdom rather than specialist and classified information. Acoustic man experiences life simultaneously rather than sequentially, and sees the world more cubistically with competing aspects in the same

single frame. Word-of-mouth favours communication in time across generations, and hence tradition and religion, whereas print pushes for communication in space, and hence towards the development of nations and empires.[34]

This distinction between the modern and the primitive is also evident in Walter Ong's work, although Ong, an expert on the rhetoric and logic of Peter Ramus, emphasizes the advances of literacy, with a nostalgic but resigned glance back at the world we have lost. Yet in spite of his recognition that 'writing can never dispense with orality' and that 'writing ... did not reduce orality but enhanced it',[35] he too posits an array of cognitive differences between literate and preliterate or 'primarily' oral cultures, basing them on the radical division between visual and auditory media and their effects upon human consciousness and thought. Writes Ong:

> The thought processes and expression of those in oral cultures are typically formulaic, redundant, conservative, agonistic, participatory rather than distanced, situational rather than abstract, additive and aggregative rather than subordinative and analytic ... [Writing] turns from oral situational thinking to increasingly abstract thinking, which moves in interlocked, sequential, linear patterns ... The mind formed by writing conducts even its orally expressed thinking in modes quite different from those of the oral mind, for it lives in a differently structured intersubjective world and a differently structured cosmos.[36]

Yet if Ong's emphasis on the evolutionary model of human development implicitly allies him with McLuhan's brand of romanticism, it also connects him with the nineteenth-century cultural anthropologists and folklorists who saw the 'primitive' as 'something to escape' rather than 'something to cherish'[37] and who (in keeping with the 'four-stages' theory first enunciated in the eighteenth century) viewed 'civilization' as a natural development from 'primitive oral roots to sophisticated literacy'.[38] Thus, while Parry and Lord viewed writing as destructive to oral poetry and McLuhan saw it as the death-knell for the world of the 'heart', Ong saw it as a 'humanizing' technology and the artifacts of the oral world, although valuable, as less highly developed:

> Oral cultures indeed produce powerful and beautiful verbal performances of high artistic and human worth, which are no longer even possible once writing has taken possession of the psyche. Nevertheless, without writing, human consciousness cannot achieve its fuller potentials, cannot produce other beautiful and powerful creations.[39]

Jack Goody and Ian Watt, although sharing many of Ong's and Havelock's views and clearly believing in some sort of cultural evolution, resisted a nomenclature 'based upon the assumption of radical differences between the mental attributes of literate and non-literate peoples', preferring to emphasize cultural and social distinctions in order to avoid the more pejorative contrast between the 'primitive' and 'civilized' *mentalité*, such as that forwarded by Lévy-Bruhl, who characterized primitive peoples as 'prelogical'. They concluded that the persistence of 'non-logical' thinking in 'modern literate societies' can be partly explained by the fact that 'in our civilization writing is clearly an addition, not an alternative, to oral transmission'.[40]

Grappling with many of the tenets of this 'literary hypothesis', anthropologists like Ruth Finnegan, socio-linguists like William Foley, Deborah Tannen and Wallace Chafe, psychologists like Sylvia Scribner and Michael Cole, and folklorists like Eric Montenyohl and Bruce Rosenberg have argued for a continuum of spoken and written culture instead of the 'great divide' posited by the 'communications' scholars. While acknowledging differences between the oral and written modes, they speak of them in terms of 'tendencies, shades, and degrees' rather than entirely discrete worlds, and find far more that is common than antithetical between them.[41] For example, in the realm of verbal art, they point to largely oral cultures that conduct their own sort of 'literary criticism' and to the use of formal and stylistic conventions like formulae, parallelism and repetition in both written and oral poetry.[42] Ruth Finnegan, whose chief concern is oral poetry, stresses the centrality of performance in 'oral' as opposed to written literature, but otherwise finds that 'oral and written literature often in practice comprise relative and overlapping rather than mutually exclusive categories'.[43] Chafe and Tannen argue for 'the inextricability of speaking and writing in even those modes of discourse that seem most exclusively a matter of writing and reading, and the inherently social nature of all discourse'.[44] Indeed, there is evidence to show that 'strategies associated with writing [can] be found in spoken language'; that, for example, 'Parallelism and intonations thought to be basic in poetry are also basic in face-to-face conversation'. Other studies, notably by Deborah Tannen and William Labov, comparing oral narratives with both factual and fictional accounts by the same person, suggest that 'written imaginative literature combines the facility of involvement of spoken language with the integrative quality of writing'.[45]

Given the fact that, as Ruth Finnegan reminds us, 'A degree of literacy has been a feature of human culture in most parts of the world for millennia', and that even historically the illiterate often had indirect access to the written word,[46] various scholars have attempted to construct meaningful 'cognitive correctives' for the orality-literacy dichotomy within literate cultures, conducting studies, for example, which show that severely dyslexic children who cannot read or write (and thus do not acquire the visual-spatial cognition McLuhan attributes to literacy) nonetheless often perform normally on intelligence tests and demonstrating that 'the transfer between [putative] written and oral competencies can occur even in the absence of reading and writing skills'.[47] Nor, according to a number of scholars, is logic the sole domain of the literate: G. E. R. Lloyd has argued that 'it was Greek oral political and legal discourse and its rules of debate and evidence which gave rise to Greek logic, philosophy and science, not widespread literacy'.[48]

A number of scholars have pointed out that the logic of the orally transmitted Vedic tradition is highly codified, abstract and reflective, the fact that it was historically limited to the realm of religious discourse indicating cultural rather than cognitive differences.[49] To counter Basil Bernstein's contention that the mastery of 'elaborated' linguistic codes (corresponding to literacy and middle-class culture) versus 'restricted' codes (associated with lower levels of literacy and to working-class society) determined an individual's ability to engage in 'abstract classification and logical reasoning', William Labov 'demonstrated that a speaker of Vernacular Black English, by any of Bernstein's metrics, a restricted code, could produce chains of logical reasoning to do honor to any academic'.[50]

Thus the 'cognitive correctives' (along with the 'ethnographic correctives') seek to vitiate the notion of the superiority of literacy over orality – and of one kind of culture over another – perpetuated by the 'literacy' theorists. They also seek to demonstrate how pedagogical and other cultural processes effect cognitive changes in individuals and the ways in which 'literate and illiterate modes of discourse complement rather than contrast one another'.[51] Many differences previously attributed to distinctions between literate and illiterate (or 'oral') cultures have been shown to be the products of a complex social and cultural picture, of which literacy is only one element. Shirley Brice Heath's study of the 'literacy practices' of three Piedmont North Carolina communities demonstrates the ways in which the development of literacy skills and the uses these skills are put to are moulded by both class and cultural norms and expectations.[52] Concludes Foley, 'Literacy is not a straightforward 'technology of the intellect' ... There are as many literacies as there are ways of engaging the world and ourselves through the written word'.[53]

Meanwhile, folklorists and literary scholars alike have argued that the oral-formulaic theory is not universally applicable, as initially thought, but limited to specific genres in specific cultures. For example, the application of the oral-formulaic theory to traditional ballads by writers like David Buchan and James Jones has been demolished by Albert Friedman, H. O. Nygard, Flemming Andersen and Thomas Pettit, who have shown that the set phrases or ballad 'commonplaces' that Buchan took for oral formulae cannot stand scrutiny as part of a system of composition-in-performance, especially in light of the remarkable stability of ballad texts in contrast to texts of *guslar* compositions.[54] There has also long been much revisionism about the applicability of the oral-formulaic theory to medieval poetry. As early as 1966 H. L. Rogers wrote:

> The term 'formula' becomes a portmanteau, enclosing within its ample capacity many different, and often undefined, sorts of lexical, morphological and syntactic similarities ... One is forced to suspect that the growing dogmatism about the oral-formulaic character of Old English poetry owes more to faith and presumed psychological insight than to reason.[55]

Scholars have also questioned another major tenet of Lord's theory: that, because of its tendency to fix texts and discourage variation, literacy is antithetical to and destructive of oral literature. A number of ethnologists, including Ruth Finnegan, have delineated oral cultures in which highly literate storytellers and other oral composer-performers function in an identical fashion to non-literate ones, employing the same strategies and inventiveness.[56] Also, as many ethnographers have demonstrated, despite the almost universal identification of variation as an essential characteristic of oral literature, verbatim (or near verbatim) memorization is actually integral to some oral traditions. For example, in Somali and Zulu poetry 'the concept of a "correct" version is locally recognized';[57] many of the Hausa-speaking Nigerians 'have memorized the Koran', yet 'do not know any classical Arabic';[58] and the Sanskrit *Rigveda* has been 'transmitted faultlessly from generation to generation through purely oral means'.[59] Written verse can also interact with oral verse in oral literatures: 'In Swahili verse there is a constant interchange and influence as between orally-composed and written verse', while in Somalia, some poets 'have used writing ... as a visual aid to their oral memory'.[60] Clearly, as Rosenberg has remarked, 'Writing co-exists peacefully with orality; it is not its executioner'.[61]

The literacy/orality debate has also engaged social historians and literary scholars. Of the historians, certainly the best-known is Elizabeth Eisenstein for her 1979 book *The Printing Press as an Agent of Change*. While avoiding (and even taking issue with) many of the claims for literacy advanced by the communications scholars (particularly McLuhan), Eisenstein argues that print culture effected far-reaching social changes, such as standardization and reproducibility of information, as well as the wider circulation of ideas – changes that manuscript, with its much more limited readership, could not achieve. Unlike Febvre and Martin, who view printing as a force for social conservatism, 'Eisenstein portrays movable type as the seed of cultural rebirth during the Renaissance', one that 'spurred the exchange of new ideas', fostered nationalism and 'inaugurated the general democratization of art and science'.[62] Subsequent historians (including Adrian Johns and Margaret Ezell) have sought to question or at least qualify a number of Eisenstein's assertions, including the supposed 'fixity' of the printed book in the Early Modern period; the accessibility of print; the sudden decline of manuscript culture; and the ability to isolate 'the technological, commercial, and legal influence of the printing press from a myriad of other social and political developments'.[63] Meanwhile, G. E. R. Lloyd has pointed to the development of writing in China 400 years in advance of Europe, which occurred without an accompanying scientific revolution.[64]

Many recent social historians have tended to represent oral and literate modalities as mutually interacting social and aesthetic spheres, with influence flowing in both directions. This is certainly the message of Adam Fox's *Oral and Literate Culture in England 1500–1700*.[65] Reassessing literacy levels of the period and examining the interaction between cheap print and everything from proverbs and nursery lore to ballads, rumours and news, Fox asserts:

> There was no necessary antithesis between oral and literate forms of communication and preservation; the one did not have to destroy or undermine the other. If anything, the written word tended to augment the spoken, reinventing it and making it anew, propagating its contents, heightening its exposure, and ensuring its continued vitality, albeit sometimes in different forms.[66]

As Barry Reay, author of *Popular Cultures in England 1550–1750*, comments, 'The bipolar or binary model of the cultural make-up of Early Modern England has slowly been replaced by a newer interpretation which stresses diversity and multiplicity'.[67]

In literary criticism an ever-increasing number of works deal with questions of orality in relation to subjects ranging from Anglo-Saxon and Middle English poetry to the works of Milton, Defoe and Conrad, the epistolary novel, broadside ballads, Victorian sermons and modern poetry. A number of these studies still draw upon dualistic concepts of writing and orality (and many of those concerned with medieval literature still involve oral-formulaic theory), evidence that the question of the 'great divide' is far from settled. On the other hand, scholars like Denis Donoghue have addressed the dichotomies postulated by Ong, McLuhan, Lévi-Strauss, Derrida and de Certeau, in order to argue for a more complex view of the relationship between the oral and written modes,[68] while Carl Lindhahl has contributed much to the lowering of barriers between the elite and the 'folk', the written and the oral, in the study of medieval literature.[69]

Folklorists, too, have modified their concepts of 'traditional' or 'vernacular' culture. Until at least the last quarter of the twentieth century, William Wells Newell's 1890 definition of folklore as 'oral tradition and belief handed down from generation to generation without the use of writing' was reconfigured but remained essentially unchanged.[70] In the 1960s, Jan Brunvand defined folklore as 'Those materials in culture that circulate traditionally among members of any group in different versions, whether in oral form or by means of customary example, as well as the processes of traditional performance and communication'.[71] The mention of groups and of performance and communication were new, but the definition retained the essential ingredient of orality. Even as late as 1972 – in spite of Dan Ben-Amos's groundbreaking formulation of folklore as 'artistic communication in small groups'[72] – Ruth Finnegan found that 'for folklorists "oral tradition" is not only the central focus of much of their interest, but is often taken to be the most important defining characteristic of "folk literature"'.[73] And in spite of the now-universal acknowledgement in the field of folklore that tradition is not strictly defined either by the medium of oral transmission or by post-romantic theories of communal creation, primitive 'survivals' and other concepts of cultural passivity associated with orality and 'the folk mind', such attitudes have changed only gradually. David Buchan, who believed that ballads were composed in an oral-formulaic manner, claimed that the traditional ballad could not survive into the highly literate, post-industrial era because the 'oral' mentality that allowed singers to compose ballads in performance would be replaced by one that relied on the 'fixed text' and rote memorization.[74] But while Elaine Lawless found that 'Buchan's distinction relied far too heavily on the anthropological confusions of primitives and peasants, illiterates and "the folk"', her own definition of folklore as 'a dynamic, living, oral form that will, by its very nature, vary', while certainly true of many genres, leaves out much that is folklore and insists too strongly on variation itself (as opposed to the latitude for variation) as a determining feature.[75]

Ideas on the relationship between variation and stability and orality and literacy have, however, broadened considerably in recent years. This is due in part to the influence of newer academic concepts such as communications and performance theories, but also to a greater emphasis in ethnographic research upon the 'tradition-bearers' themselves and to the study of 'folklore in context' – that is, on the circumstances in which tradition-bearers function as performers, creators and human beings. Such an approach, while hardly ignoring the importance of oral transmission, performance and composition in traditional societies, accords orality significance as only one factor in a complex cultural milieu which operates on multiple levels, partakes of multiple spheres of social influence, and consists of thinking human beings who make choices about the world they inhabit and the lives they live. Folksong scholars like Eleanor Long, Edward Ives and many others have emphasized the role of the singer in continuity, creation and re-creation of song repertoire in a recognition that, as John Quincy Wolf presciently remarked, 'differences in temperament, personality, and artistic judgment determine what [singers] do to their songs'.[76] The concepts of pure, orally transmitted folklore, uncorrupted by print culture, or of the passive, illiterate (or semi-literate) tradition-bearer have long been as untenable as they are unrealistic.

Meanwhile, work on the interrelationship of print and popular song traditions by numerous song scholars has opened exciting new avenues in the study of creativity and aesthetics within traditional cultures and subcultures. Study of the effects of oral transmission continues, although with greater attention to aesthetic and social considerations and less emphasis on orality as a controlling force, separable from the traditional artist or community. Thus most folksong scholars would agree with Hugh Shields that 'it is becoming clearer that the demarcation of oral and literate modes of composition is not easy to draw nor probably very precise. Features apparently characteristic of oral expression occur as well in written literature which, after all, is written by people accustomed also to speak'.[77]

While much of the following study deals with material from libraries and archives, it will also be informed throughout by both Irish folksong scholarship and ethnography, from the simple documentation of eighteenth-century collectors to the broader social, historical and contextual studies of the twentieth. For although we have no crystal ball into the past, given the extraordinary conservatism and continuity of Irish traditional culture, knowledge of this more recent, fieldwork-based work offers us far greater insight into the practices, attitudes and aesthetics of participants in the popular song tradition, past and present, than the study of texts alone can provide. My own position has thus been informed not only by such scholarship but also and – perhaps most importantly – by the time I have spent with traditional singers and in singing communities. My own field research has included singers from both the Irish- and English-language singing communities, as well as Irish song collectors – notably Tom Munnelly, whose concentrated work over a thirty-year period in County Clare gave him a unique depth of experience with the tradition. Because of my own orientation as a folklorist and ethnographer, this study will unavoidably reflect what I believe to be the central concern of that discipline: the illumination and celebration of human culture, particularly the culture of groups often left out of the historical or social picture.

1 THE MEDIEVAL BACKGROUND

The dispute about the relationship of orality and literacy in Irish literature is arguably as old as the literature itself. As Seán Ó Coileáin remarks, the debate

> has probably received more attention than any other question relating to the early literature without the achievement of anything approaching a consensus, except perhaps for the negative one of justified ignorance and bewilderment in the face of conflicting attitudes and theories, of inadequate evidence, and of inadequate examination of the evidence.[1]

Not only have recent scholars disagreed about almost every aspect of this relationship; but, as Joseph Nagy has demonstrated, medieval texts themselves acknowledge and play upon tensions between the two modes, the one old and pagan, the other new and Christian. Many of the issues in this debate relate directly to those raised in the subsequent chapters of this study; hence the relevance of a comprehensive discussion of them in connection with early oral and literate traditions, which were arguably intertwined from the introduction of a written vernacular into Ireland.

The principal genres under scrutiny are the older narratives and sagas dating from the Old and Middle Irish periods and the late medieval romances in Middle and Early Modern Irish from the twelfth to the seventeenth centuries. The former are principally in prose, though interspersed with verse passages, which are often composed of dialogue; the latter are comprised of prose narratives with incidental poems, as well as a large number of metrical 'lays', some of which have survived into recent times in oral tradition. In practice, these two categories – 'saga' and romance – are not entirely distinct, as some late romances are based on earlier narratives. The often overlapping problems most frequently raised in recent scholarly debates about these categories are (1) the nature of the relationship between the manuscript tradition of these narratives and oral tradition; (2) whether and how the written texts were derived from the oral traditional – direct transcription, summary, or simply later variant; (3) how to account for the variety of forms the texts take; (4) if orally composed, whether rote memorization or improvisational composition was employed; and (5) what the relationship might have been between the folk tradition and the elite oral tradition in connection with the surviving manuscripts. Many scholars have acknowledged the highly speculative nature of their theories on these matters. In the absence of direct testimony or documentation of performances of medieval Irish stories and poetry, there can be no definitive answer to any of these questions. The evidence is mainly oblique, coming largely from the comparative study of internal structural and stylistic features; from comparison of the tradition with other medieval (or earlier) cultures and with modern oral and later written tradition; and, finally, from the kind of reflexive references Joseph Nagy has described in his studies of Fenian literature. Yet a number of commentators have taken strong, sometimes intractable, stands at both extremes of the debate.

For example, while most scholars of medieval Irish literature have accepted the concept of an underlying oral tradition behind the various extant recensions of medieval Irish narratives – and while few of these have downplayed the role played by the medieval scribes, redactors and *literati* in the formation of the extant texts – others, including James Carney, Alan Bruford and Kim McCone, have, as Ruairí Ó hUiginn puts it, 'accorded the written form primacy',[2] arguing that, whatever the previous history of the oral narrative tradition in Irish society, the manuscripts reflect a written and learned, pan-European monastic tradition. Carney is undoubtedly the most prominent of these scholars, having accused those who emphasize the influence of a pre-existing oral tradition on the manuscript tradition of sentimental 'nativism'.[3] He argues strenuously that both the style and many of the materials of sagas like *Táin Bó Fraích* (*The Cattle Raid of Fráech*) are clearly 'literary'. These materials consist of 'certain extensive [learned Christian] elements [including classical and historical references] which could not have belonged to the native pre-literary tradition of either of the peoples concerned', and without which 'neither work can have existed in anything like the form in which we know it'.[4] Elsewhere, he states:

> I find it impossible for many reasons to believe that the form of any of the fictions or entertainments preserved in our medieval manuscripts is in any way close to the form in which they would be told when they existed (in so far as they actually did) on a purely oral level.[5]

Yet Carney also emphasizes features like repetition, variation, patchiness of composition, brevity and 'the episodic nature' of the *Táin Bó Fraích* to support his view of its literate origins, features that Nora Chadwick, Gerard Murphy, Kenneth Jackson, Edgar Slotkin, Rudolf Thurneysen and others have taken as evidence of oral composition – or at least oral transmission. In these respects, Carney can be countered with the same evidence he uses to make opposing points. Yet, as Nagy points out, Carney's analysis ultimately argues his case for literary primacy both ways:

> If the text is a poor job, or at least is so judged according to our modern aesthetic criteria, it is probably a literary production. If it is consistent, sophisticated, and sustained, according to those criteria, then too it is probably a literary production.[6]

Thus, although his theories do not preclude the possibility of oral performance, Carney leaves little room for even the medieval elite oral tradition so widely attested in the sources themselves. Nor does he allow for a dynamic, interactive oral-literate tradition of the sort discussed later in this chapter. It is well to keep in mind, however, some of the perspectives to which Carney and later scholars as diverse as Kim McCone and David Dumville are reacting – including 'naïve' notions of a static, unvarying, oral tradition, in which poets were skilled at 'memorizing and reciting and handing on a large number of traditional tales', able to pass on stories 'for centuries without any really fundamental change';[7] as well as the position held by scholars like Gerard Murphy that 'the Irish narrative tradition has on the whole been essentially oral'.[8] Many of these theories seemed to equate orality and archaism in ways that appeared to Carney (and others) as motivated by an overly insular view of the Irish literary tradition, one that ignored the 'European' nature of medieval Irish literature and the 'impact upon primitive Irish society of Christianity and of Graeco-Latin civilization' in favour of an assumption that this literature presented 'an accurate reflection of Ireland's pagan past'.[9]

Moreover, much of what Gerard Murphy and others on this side of the debate have written about the oral features of medieval Irish literature contains an implied or overt comparison to current oral tradition. While such comparison is potentially useful, this approach contains as many pitfalls and aesthetic biases as Carney's too-ready dismissal of orality, in its blanket assimilation of modern and ancient practice and vernacular and elite traditions. Yet it is one to which a number of scholars, including David Greene and Séamus Ó Duilearga, have at various times subscribed. Even Seán Ó Coileáin, despite having stated that he is 'not at all certain that close analogies should be made between such compositions as the international folktale and the keen ... and the saga literature', displays a tendency to base many of his conclusions on what we know of more recent oral tradition.[10] It is a view that far too readily leads to the simple antithesis of Carney's 'too good to be oral' formulation in favour of all things oral and 'folk'. Obviously, while it is certainly possible – even likely – that modern performance practice and oral 'texts' of prose stories associated with saga manuscripts or Fenian lays offer us significant insights into medieval oral tradition, without firmer evidence than we presently possess, both earlier performance practice and the provenance of such literature remains uncertain.

More recent forms of comparative oral-literary study have at times seemed to offer greater promise. For example, the influence of Milman Parry and Albert Lord's oral-formulaic theory has led commentators like Kevin O'Nolan to identify both the repeated 'themes' and 'formulaic passages' that Lord finds indicative of oral composition in multiple examples of saga narratives and romances in both manuscript and oral tradition. According to O'Nolan's analysis, these formulae consist chiefly of 'particular and specific noun-epithets applied to persons, places and things'; triadic constructions; and 'runs' (*cóiriú catha*), which Joseph Nagy aptly defines as 'recyclable and variable descriptions of recurring scenes or situations, such as setting out to sea, fighting, feasting and so on'.[11] Similarly, Edgar Slotkin remarks that in parts of the medieval Irish prose version of the *Aeneid* (*Imtheachta Aeniasa*), 'we find ... the descriptive formulas suggesting oral composition and the bombastic alliterative depictions of warriors in battle common to twelfth-century Irish prose style and directly engendered by the formulas' – formulas which, 'with a little editing ... would approach the metrical pattern of archaic Irish verse'.[12] Georges Zimmermann, not taking any firm stand on the issue, sanely emphasizes the uncertainty of our knowledge about the presence of these supposedly oral formulas, especially their relation to the set-piece 'runs' of contemporary oral storytelling.[13] Yet it has become almost obligatory in later criticism to make a connection between the oral-formulaic features of a prose work and its underlying poetic composition, since it is poetic composition that Lord's theory describes.

A great deal of the oral vs. literary argument, especially among oral-formulaicists, hinges upon the question of variation and, implicitly, the creativity of the individual in oral performance – an issue with obvious political and social implications. Indeed, some of the more extreme present-day arguments are coloured by an understandable desire to validate 'vernacular' culture or to resist what appears to be neo-romantic or 'nativist'. At any rate, in the wake of oral-formulaic theory, 'when the emphasis shifted from the tale to the tale teller, from memory to composition, from a set of plot elements to verbal art', variation has been taken by many to be the single most defining feature of oral literature. For Ó Coileáin, 'the question of variation involves the essential concept of what oral tradition is'.[14] Hence his opposition to the concept of the sagas as either 'plot summaries' or *hypomnemata*, since in his view such perspectives presuppose the existence of a verbal *Ür*-text, in which the ideal is one of 'exact preservation'. Such a notion runs counter to the more recent understanding of what many scholars refer to as the 'multiform', a more malleable, post-oral-formulaic concept of the story in which variation is a given (even a *desideratum*) and an *Ür*-text a chimera imposed by minds accustomed to 'fixed texts'. Memorization, however, is not necessarily incompatible with oral transmission. As Nagy and even Ó Coileáin have pointed out, 'certain contemporary storytellers have in fact memorized written texts', and both medieval written tradition and '[contemporary] oral tradition itself encourages the conceit of a memorizing storyteller'.[15] Moreover, some genres in the medieval poet's repertoire (e.g. genealogies and law) seem to have called for exact repetition.[16] Yet the use of memorization has ultimately been rejected by both the literary and oral-formulaic camps in the argument about the transmission of medieval Irish narrative.

The oral-formulaic theory can thus be just as divisive as Carney's or Murphy's theories, positing orality and literacy as two conflicting modes characterized by specific stylistic traits, by stasis vs. variation, and even by different cognitive states. Yet it has also helped to foster the concept of the 'transitional text', a more flexible literary concept, whose earliest formulation in medieval Irish literary scholarship may have been made by Gearóid Mac Eoin as early as 1964, when he wrote:

> The development of [short literary sagas] from the oral tales, may have originated in the freedom allowed the *scélaige* or *fili* in his recital. Each telling of a tale could vary in phrasing and, to some extent, in incident. It would have been pointless to record any one recital of a tale, for the next telling could have differed considerably within the limits allowed. The short sagas seem to be the result of an attempt to achieve an artistically satisfying form based on the invariable elements of the tales.[17]

Ultimately, while wholly rejecting the idea that their manuscripts represented either transcriptions of orally performed or dictated tales – or summaries of such tales – Mac Eoin goes on to suggest that scribes could have 'constructed what they regarded as a model version in the style of the oral storyteller' without recourse to dictation: 'for there were in the monasteries, from the eighth century on, men well versed in historical traditions. These could have written the sagas in the form in which we have them without recourse to a narrator'.[18] Ó Coileáin identifies this perspective as the *athláech* (that is, 'ex-layman' or 'master of two careers') theory, which proposes a moderate position between the oral and literate poles and suggests that the oral and written modes, while not identical and often in conflict, are at the same time complementary and interwoven in significant ways.[19] A number of historians have also noted that Irish poets and clerics formed alliances, collaborating, for example, on the *Senchus Mór* (the chief compilation of Irish law). Thus, in dealing with the later Middle Ages, when literacy was becoming increasingly widespread, provenance becomes more difficult to ascertain. As Bruford observes, 'Some tales ... seem to have been composed by clerics or at least graduates of the monastic schools: but since many clerics wrote poetry, and many poets were literate, the two classes cannot be rigidly distinguished, nor can scribes be distinguished from either'.[20]

Edgar Slotkin, in accord with the attempts of Joseph Nagy, Daniel Melia, Philippe Walters and Carl Lindahl to explain the often 'bewildering proliferation of variants' characteristic not only of medieval Irish literature but of medieval European literature in general,[21] speculates that many additions and rearrangements in Irish manuscripts were 'the result of the curious "transitional" state of mind between retentiveness and creativity' of the Irish scribes, who 'did not treat saga texts as fixed texts in the way in which we think of fixed texts.

They do seem reluctant to leave out anything in the manuscript before them. Yet they may add or rearrange or "correct", if they deem it necessary and the context seems proper'.[22] Challenging the theory that the use of writing automatically gives rise to the notion of the 'fixed text, a sense of the unique and original in literature', Slotkin concludes:

> Given the attitude of scribes towards their work, we can think of each one of their productions as a kind of multiform of their original. In this sense, the entire nature of a critical edition of a saga is a false concept. Surely, the 'interpolation' of a late scribe may be traditional, meaningful, and necessary to the tale or that particular scribal performance of the tale.[23]

This tendency towards 'variant reproduction' or 'multiformularity' in early Irish literature is particularly evident in the later native Irish romances, notably *Fiannaíocht*, a body of tales associated with the hero Fionn and his paramilitary band, the *fian*. Nagy, Bruford and Mac Cana, among others, have commented pointedly about the proclivity towards variation shown by the scribes of such tales, a tendency that to Proinsias Mac Cana demonstrates 'the inner dynamism of the mythic themes and structures that enables them to generate variant reflexes in response to changes in social or political circumstance or to regional appropriateness'.[24] Bruford documents such adaptations extensively in his commentary on medieval Irish romance, noting that not only did later scribes (those of the seventeenth and eighteenth centuries, arguably the last days of Ireland's 'long Middle Ages') frequently substitute names, words, poems and motifs from other stories 'or their own heads', but even wrote 'new sequels to stories they had copied, as well as composing new romances on the traditional pattern'. By the Early Modern period, such scribes, Bruford asserts, sometimes simplified the language and added adventures 'to make stories less like medieval romances and more like folk-tales, in accordance with their new, less sophisticated audience';[25] or took 'complete folk-tales from oral tradition and recast them to a varying extent in literary language'.[26] Such a flexible approach to the scribal task lends credence to Slotkin's theory of multiform vs. a single authority and to the notion of overlapping and interacting oral/literary traditions and aesthetics characteristic of Ó Coileáin's *athláech*. As Mac Cana has argued, the medieval Irish preference for the oral mode meant that

> the Irish oral tradition embraced the literature of greatest social prestige as well as the common lore of the mass of the people. And precisely because this literature of prestige was cultivated and conserved by an order of learned men specially trained to the task, it had its own separate existence, quite independent of writing, though not of course uninfluenced by it.[27]

The probability that some strands of this oral tradition were popular (though the extent of their influence is debated), others elite, and others from shared tradition makes absolute certainty on the origin of any particular work impossible, especially when we consider that, as Nagy notes, 'Particularly in a culture as conservative as the Gaelic, texts of literary origin can contain and transmit many of the same patterns and messages that we find in texts collected from oral tradition.'[28] The question of transmission is especially complicated during the post-Norman period by the 'gradual integration of the Christian monastic *literati* with the native poetic class.'[29] During this period, the 'migration of literary activity from monastic scriptorium to secular school and court occasioned a rearrangement of the traditional Irish hierarchy of verbal performers, both literate and nonliterate, with erstwhile occupants of lower rungs ascending to higher status.'[30]

The increasing interaction between oral and written culture in mid- to late medieval Ireland – as well as the ambivalent relationship of secular poets and monastic clerics – is particularly well illustrated in the *Acallam na Senórach* (*The Colloquy of the Old Men*), a 'frame story' from the twelfth or thirteenth century (though attested in manuscripts only from the fifteenth century on) in which the newly Christianized Fenian heroes Oisín and Caílte relate tales of their exploits to St Patrick. As Nagy puts it:

> This text purports very self-consciously to be a transcription of the lore, tales, and poems transmitted by Caílte to Patrick and others in the era when writing came to Ireland along with Christianity. Therefore the *Acallam* contains a series of supposedly oral performances rendered into a literary form.[31]

The encounters between Caílte and Patrick allow the author of the *Acallam* to express sympathy for Caílte's oral and pagan world while illustrating tensions between that world and the literate, Christian one Patrick represents. Thus, while Patrick receives divine permission to listen to and record the stories of the *fian*, Caílte contrasts their two worlds when, listening to clerics reciting their offices on the water, he hints at a preference for his own, saying:

> Seldom did my head's ear hear reading (*léigenn*) over a lake; there was a time when more often did I listen to the murmuring (*dordán*) of fine women. If someone had a pen, long would he be at writing them down; for, as wretched as I am now, I have experienced a multitude of wonder ... Books of learning (*liubair léighind*), rarely did I hear them read aloud.[32]

To Nagy, this passage reveals 'a penetrating awareness of the compatibilities and incompatibilities between oral and literary processes of transmission and preservation.'[33] Such self-consciousness on the part of the medieval Irish *literati*, he observes, resulted in the representation of literature as sometimes 'emerging from oral tradition; at other times ... running alongside it, intersecting with it, running counter to it, or all the above simultaneously.'[34]

Katharine Simms has commented on the 'rich hybrid culture' of medieval Ireland, in which 'Latin ecclesiastical learning and traditional bardic training had blended successfully'.[35] This 'hybrid' oral/literate culture is also evident in the persistence of the oral mode in the elite tradition well into the period of more widespread literacy and in the continued emphasis on oral performance of both bardic praise-poetry and of poetry and prose romances, whether recited 'without the book' or read aloud. The latter practice is attested widely throughout medieval Europe and in Ireland into the sixteenth century.[36] In favour of its application to Irish romances, Bruford argues that the tales are too 'ornate and academic', with runs 'too varied to have been designed to be learned completely by heart by some sort of *reacaire*, or to be either prompt-book or written record of an improvised performance'. He also makes the salient point that there would have been little sense in writing out each run if it had not been intended to be read aloud.[37] The romances, he asserts, were written on the whole to be heard rather than read silently, with the exception of some mid-seventeenth-century texts that seem to have been composed 'with the solitary reader in mind'.[38]

The practice of reading aloud – or at least oral performance – is also alluded to in the *Acallam*, when the angels tell St Patrick to let Caílte's tales 'be written by you on the tablets of poets and in the decrees of the learned, for it will be entertaining for both the masses and the nobility of later times to listen to these tales.'[39] This quotation also suggests the breadth of the medieval audience, which would have been comprised not only of the nobility in both public and private readings, but also those who attended open-air performances and fairs.[40] By the seventeenth or eighteenth century the stories could also have entered the popular repertoire through oral readings of the manuscripts that circulated in the countryside, especially in Munster, as well as through an oral tradition largely based on these manuscripts.[41] Charlotte Brooke heard a farm labourer in County Cavan 'reading Fenian prose tales aloud from a manuscript',[42] and Standish O'Grady describes such readings in farm houses at wool-cardings or wakes in the early nineteenth century.[43] Such diverse audiences could have in large part motivated the amount of variation found in the romances, reflecting not only complex interconnections between different echelons of society, but also a shared 'hybrid' culture consisting of illiterate as well as literate audiences and performers.

According to Bruford, the oral-performative bias of Irish romances is reflected textually by such rhetorical features as the use of 'runs' (formulaic, alliterative descriptive passages, 'certainly intended for oral delivery'); wordy, bombastic language; and inserted poems, especially when employed for dialogue.[44] But if such features indicate oral delivery, they do not, to Bruford, prove their oral origins. Pointing to such characteristics as the syllabic verse used for the incidental poems, learned digressions and interpolations, the use of 'literary' Early Modern Irish (with occasional archaisms), and to the sheer length and complexity of the tales, Bruford argues that the prose romances were both written *and* 'literary'. On the other hand, despite the fact that the verse lays, or *laoithe,* were composed 'probably by professional or near-professional bards, in the medieval syllabic verse known as *dán*', far fewer of them are preserved in writing, and Bruford conjectures that some Fenian lays may have survived for centuries without having been transcribed 'until they were recorded from oral tradition in the past two centuries'.[45] Both he and Hugh Shields note the less complicated structure of the lays, making a long oral life much more possible for them than for the prose tales. Again, there is some difference of opinion among scholars as to the ultimate origins – written or oral, folk or courtly – of these so-called 'ballads' (Gerard Murphy, for one, opting for their oral and folk origins), but the consensus seems to be that whatever their genesis, the history of the lays involves complex interaction between written and oral, as well as elite and popular, spheres.[46] As Shields puts it, 'the prehistory of the surviving lays is now remote and not easily accessible through their texts, which have no doubt been deeply influenced by writing, in their composition as well as their transmission'. Noting that the printing of Fenian lays began in the 1780s, he adds, 'but a manuscript tradition reflecting their popularity has existed for centuries, in which their words were available at least to some singers: those who were able to read them or have them read to them'.[47]

Yet despite an apparent split between oral and literate camps on the subject of romance, scholars as various as Murphy, Bruford, Mac Cana and Nagy seem to agree about many essentials of the question. For example, although it is true that, unlike Murphy, Bruford emphasizes the literary rather than the oral origins of Fenian stories, he does not deny that popular tradition could have lain behind many of the romances.[48] His contention is, rather, that the evidence militates against the conclusion that any given prose romance 'as it stands in the manuscripts is a written-down folk-tale' and that the majority of later folk versions of these romances are based on 'literary' manuscript originals.[49] It is the social rather than oral origins of the genre that scholars dispute. Thus, while conceding that some of the later stories 'may have been written before they were told', Murphy views the Early Modern Irish Romantic tales as 'either in whole or in part, a raising of the simple folktale ... to a form which could please' a more genteel audience, arguing that because many of the 'folk' versions, while 'unsophisticated' are well-wrought, they must represent the original versions of the tale, while the less elegant, written romances represent deliberate alterations of these originals.[50] Murphy bases much of his argument on the assumptions that the 'folk' do not consciously alter their material and that when it does change by mistelling it invariably changes for the worse – assumptions that most current folklorists would challenge. In any case, since we have no way of knowing what the originals may have been, this sort of retrospective argument is highly tenuous. As Bruford, who, unlike Murphy, believes that whatever their origins the romances as we know them were meant for the nobility rather than the masses, observes that although many of the written romances employ folk motifs, 'more accurately ... motifs which are now common in folk-tales ... there is no reason to doubt that [a particular motif] was invented by the author of the romance and passed from there into oral tradition'.[51] Of the many folk versions of both the prose and verse romances, some, like the manuscripts, display great variation and innovation, while others reflect remarkable conservatism in relation to their manuscript sources: As Bruford notes, 'In Munster at least romances used to be recited almost word for word as in the MSS. for some time after regular readings had lapsed, perhaps up to 1900'.[52] Other versions found in oral tradition feature inserted 'literary' features (such as syllabic poems), illustrating just how closely the two modes can influence and imitate each other and suggesting that the *athláech* theory may be just as applicable to the community poet (literate or otherwise) as to the monastic scribe.

To say then, as Nagy does, that Bruford lacks 'appreciation of a synergistic relationship between the literary and the oral traditions, and sets in place a tyrannical primacy of the former'[53] is to overlook his keen appreciation of the interaction between the two spheres, as well as his lack of the kind of aesthetic snobbery Carney betrays. For example, he finds that many 'folk' versions of the tales represent improvements on their written originals through such modifications as elimination of superfluous episodes, characters and repetitions: 'oral transmission' he concludes, 'can be a cleansing as much as a destructive process'.[54]

Despite *caveat*s articulated by scholars like Proinsias Mac Cana about the impossibility of devising simple answers to the question of the relationship between orality and literacy in medieval Irish literature or David Dumville's emphasis on the need for careful, objective evaluation of available evidence,[55] it is clear that scholars can still be polarized into camps on the issue, as witnessed more recently, for example, by Kim McCone's hard-line pro-literary views on the one hand and Seán Ó Coileáin's more cautious but essentially oral-formulaic approach on the other. Such polarization of opinion reflects the extent to which both sides are influenced by theories and ideological attachments that lie outside the actual argument itself. It also provides a salutary reminder of the difficulty of avoiding such influences in evaluating the debate about orality and literacy, and of the need to approach the subject with as much objectivity and sensitivity as possible. For, as we have seen, interaction between oral and written modes in medieval Irish literature is not only possible: it is demonstrable – not only in the manuscripts themselves and in the persistence of specific genres attested in medieval manuscripts and in recent oral tradition, but also in the numerous cross-influences noted by scholars like Bruford, Mac Cana and Nagy. Thus, while the origins of any particular item (whether in the written or oral tradition) may always be obscure, the subsequent interaction of these different but overlapping spheres is self-evident, demonstrating, as Bruford comments, that 'the different classes of tradition are inextricably interwoven'.[56] It is arguably this dynamic relationship that gives the Irish literary tradition as a whole its peculiar vitality and variety from the Early Middle Ages to the present time.

2 SONGS OF THE DISPOSSESSED: EIGHTEENTH-CENTURY IRISH SONG-POETRY

The ascendancy of accentual, or 'song', metres in the poetry of seventeenth- and eighteenth-century Ireland marked a new phase in the development of Irish poetry, one in which the works of literary poets became increasingly accessible both by virtue of their form as strophic song and because of the ever greater number of social nexuses through which poetry (and culture in general) was disseminated and shared during this period. In the following chapter I will examine the extent to which these 'new' song metres reflect both innovation and continuity with the poetic traditions that preceded them; the interdependence of written and oral media in recording and disseminating poetry; the relationship between works by known literary poets and the 'songs of the people'; and the profound effect that the subsequent interaction between the two spheres has had on the Irish song tradition since the eighteenth century. We shall also see that from the medieval period on, performance has been integral to the Irish poetic tradition.

I. The Bardic Tradition and Oral Performance

In the later Middle Ages and the Early Modern period, oral performance was a significant element in the communication of Irish literature, whether through public or private readings of romance manuscripts, the recitation of praise-poetry, or the narration of tales or lays – these last frequently involving musical accompaniment. Whether or not the poet himself actually performed or merely directed others in such performances is not entirely clear. Many scholars maintain the view, transmitted to us not only through contemporary accounts but also through the famous illustration in John Derricke's *Image of Ireland*, that the public performance of poetry entailed a strict division of labour between *file* (poet-composer) and *bard* (lesser poetic assistant), whose designation seems often to have been more or less synonymous with *recaire* ('reciter'), a species of *jongleur*.[1]

Figure 2.1: John Derricke (J. D.), *The Image of Irelande* (London: J. Kingston for Ihon Daie, 1581). Reproduced from the original held by the Department of Special Collections of the University Libraries of Notre Dame.

Thus, as Spenser observed of Irish poets in the mid-sixteenth century, 'Theyr verses are usually songe at all feasts and meetings by certayne other persons whose proper function that is'.² His contemporary, Thomas Smyth, described an event at which the 'Rhymer that made the Ryme' entered with his 'Rakry', who 'is he that shall utter the ryme'; and even in 1722, the Marquis of Clanrickarde described a performance at which 'The poet himself said nothing, but directed and took care that everybody else did his part right. The bards having first had the composition from him, got it well by heart and now pronounc'd it orderly'. The *recaire*, or reciter, in turn, was accompanied by the *cruitire*, or harper, with whom the bard kept 'even pace'.³

In support of the view that the distinctions between these performers were rigidly observed, Cathal Ó Háinle points to a poem that mentions a poet who is chastised for having given the harp to his *recaire*:

> Digheólad go mín ar Ó Gnimh
> a ndearna sé:
> do-bheir cláirseach a measc cháich
> a láimh a reacaire féin.
>
> I will gently chide Ó Gnimh
> for what he did:
> giving his harp in front of everyone
> into the hands of his own reciter.⁴

There is some evidence, however, to suggest that the roles of these professionals – or at the very least, their titles – were sometimes blurred, especially during the later Middle Ages, when major reordering of the poetic classes resulted in the merging of the previously distinct literate *file* and illiterate *bard* to produce the praise-poet of this period. While of relatively low status and not 'learned' (i.e. versed in Latin), the later *bard* was, however, probably literate in Gaelic; hence, even an amateur poet among the nobility could be considered a species of *bard*.[5] By the thirteenth century, there is already some confusion of the terms *file* and *bard*, which are sometimes used to identify specific roles and at other times employed more or less interchangeably. In any case, it seems that both *fili* and *baird* could at various times be expected to engage in oral performance. For instance, the late sixteenth-century poet Tadhg Dall Ó hUiginn describes 'a visit to one of his patrons where he told a story to his patron and some other visiting poets while they were all in bed'.[6] Joseph Nagy goes so far as to state that besides being a *fer légind* ('man of reading'), the medieval *file* was 'an oral performer', describing sixteenth-century poet Urard Mac Coisse as a '*fili* storyteller';[7] and some late bardic poets, including Tadhg Dall Ó hUiginn and Cearbhall Ó Dálaigh, apparently played the harp. A few late medieval poems contain phrases suggesting that their composers were musicians: for example, 'mo sheinm ar chruit cheoil' ('my playing on a harp'), 'Tabhraidh chugam Cruit mo Ríogh' ('Give to me my king's *cruit*'), and so on.[8] Although Ó Háinle dismisses many of these poet-harpers as dilettantes, the fact that they could play – and perhaps sing or chant, as well – indicates that the roles may not have been as distinct as is usually believed and that the various members of the elite triumvirate of *file/recaire/cruitire* were capable of assuming each other's roles – or at least of understanding one another's business.[9] Certainly by the late seventeenth and early eighteenth centuries, when the bardic tradition had declined, harpers like Turlough Carolan and Pádraig Mac Giolla Fhiondáin combined all of these roles by composing both the music and words of songs, reciting (or singing) them and playing their own harp accompaniment; others, like Séamus Dall Mac Cuarta, may have collaborated with composer-harpers.[10]

Whether performed by *file*, *bard*, or *cruitire*, however, it is clear that oral delivery still played a large part in elite society, especially prior to the sixteenth and seventeenth centuries, when, as Katharine Simms has observed, 'the continuing illiteracy of many patrons meant that the oral aspects of the poets' work were still important'.[11] Simms notes a long, early bardic poem by Donnchadh Mór Ó Dálaigh, which ends 'with a blessing for every one who memorizes and recites it';[12] Pádraig Breatnach quotes Paul Zumthor's observation that throughout the Middle Ages in Europe the text seemed designed to operate 'à titre de communication entre un chanteur ou récitant ou lecteur, et un auditoire [as a form of communication between a singer or reciter or reader and an audience]'.[13]

As an example of this dynamic in Irish poetry, Breatnach describes directions in a seventeenth-century manuscript copy of *crosántacht* – a 'verse/prose medley' or species of *cantefable* – 'supplied by the scribe at various stages in the text to indicate that the verse is to be "sung" and the prose "spoken".[14] On the other hand, as Simms observes, the bardic poets would have assiduously distinguished themselves from the 'genuinely oral balladeers', with whose 'cut-price competition' they had to contend in the fourteenth century,[15] for much of the status of these poets lay in their mastery of both oral and literate modes.

We cannot, however, dismiss the role of literacy in the poetic process itself. While we are told that the bardic poets of the late Middle Ages and Early Modern period composed in their heads, lying in darkened rooms, they subsequently committed their verses to parchment or paper. And, as Pádraig Ó Macháin has asserted,

> if, as the poets themselves affirmed, the spoken form was of primary importance, the written form, and therefore the written text, also had some function in what may be termed the bardic process, that is, the composition of a poem and the presentation of it to the person for whom it was intended.[16]

Indeed, by the mid-fourteenth century, as literacy became more widespread among not only the poets themselves but their aristocratic employers, *duanairí* (collections of poems transcribed by poets for their patrons) became increasingly common, as did 'textbooks' in the bardic schools, where poets were taught their craft. Genres like the letter-poem, as Simms has noted, 'could be intended for one pair of eyes only';[17] similarly, some of the medieval prose romances seem to have been designed for private, silent reading.[18] In his discussion of the sixteenth-/seventeenth-century poet Fearghal Óg Mac an Bhaird, Breatnach, while noting the importance of the 'aural/oral' dimension generally in bardic poetry, comments that in reading Mac an Bhaird's poetry 'we can have almost no sense whatever of the nature of the performance it received – or know for that matter whether it was performed at all'.[19] Elsewhere, Breatnach asserts that a great deal of seventeenth-century literary verse was composed with no musical context in mind.[20]

Yet the historical interdependence of the two modes – oral and literate – survived into the seventeenth and eighteenth centuries. Nicholas O'Kearney notes that,

> Owing to the rigour of the penal laws, several bards [at Pádraig Mac Giolla Fhiondáin's bardic contentions] could not commit their compositions to writing, but the learned and patriotic Linden corrected where necessary and copied them; hence, he was usually called *Reacadóir na mBard* (A Repetitor of Poets).[21]

Apparently, this was the rule rather than the exception: according to one contemporary source, *cúirteanna filíochta*, or 'courts of poetry' (assemblies in which eighteenth-century poets met to reinforce their craft in the absence of the by-then defunct bardic schools), were obliged to employ a *canntuire*, a sort of publicist/messenger, entrusted with a written manuscript of each work, in order to be properly constituted.[22] One poetic messenger, identified by the poet Seán Clárach Mac Domhnaill as *an reacaire mná* ('the female reciter') was a woman named Anna Prior, who seems to have functioned both as a carrier of manuscripts and memorizer/reciter of their contents, 'do bhíodh ag imeacht ó fhile go file ar fuaid na Mumhan [going from poet to poet throughout Munster]'.[23] Improvised verses composed at the meetings of such courts would have had to be committed to writing at a later time, a fact that underscores the link between the oral and written in the Irish literary tradition, as well as the concurrent necessity for accurate memorization of orally composed poetry.

II. The Decline of the Bardic Tradition and the Emergence of Accentual Metres

The picture was likely to have been similarly mixed in the seventeenth and eighteenth centuries, even as the accentual *amhrán* or 'song' metres – as opposed to the syllabic poetry which had dominated the elite poetry of previous centuries[24] – gained currency and the poets' traditional aristocratic audience declined. *Duanairí* remained important throughout much of this period as literacy became increasingly widespread; and many poets worked as scribes or tutors. Commonplace books, too, were kept by seventeenth- and eighteenth-century scribes and poets, some of which, as Virginia Blankenhorn notes, 'contain short compositions of a personal nature which were clearly not intended for a wide public audience, or literary *jeux d'esprit* intended, at the most, for the delectation of other poets who might be lent the manuscript'.[25] Meanwhile, while many (if not most) of the poems composed in stress metres were meant to be sung to popular song-airs of the time,[26] some Early Modern Irish verse genres resist a musical context. One such genre is the *barántas*, a poetic 'warrant', written in mock-legal language, calling poets to the courts of poetry. Another is *trí rann agus amhrán*, a form with three stanzas in what Seán Ó Tuama calls 'loose syllabic verse' with a final stanza in an accentual song metre.[27] A famous example of *trí rann* is Séamus Dall Mac Cuarta's 'An Lon Dubh Báite' ('The Drowned Blackbird'), a poem whose intimate content (consolation of a young woman for the loss of her pet bird) also suggests private reading rather than public performance. Pádraig Breatnach has argued that measures such as *trí rann agus amhrán* and others in which either the *amhrán* metre is variable or in which the 'alignment of stressed and unstressed vowels' is at odds with 'musical quantities and the barring of phrases' could not have been performed to the strophic song melodies we are used to hearing today. Instead he proposes that – as with several examples of eighteenth- and nineteenth-century *marbhnaí*, or elegies, composed in accentual rather than in the older syllabic metres – poems composed in *amhrán* metres for which there is no designated melody may have been performed in much the same manner as the syllabic poetry of the bardic period: that is, in a sort of chant or recitative style.[28] Patrick Dinneen's childhood recollections of his mother's 'crooning' (as opposed to singing) of Ó Rathaille's 'lays' seems to support this – although whether Dinneen was referring only to Ó Rathaille's elegies or to his songs in general is unclear.[29] Evidence concerning the professional harpers of this period also lends indirect support to Breatnach's theory: as Gráinne Yeats has commented, because of the great melodic range in most of Carolan's compositions, the words of his songs – although composed in stress rather than syllabic metres – would probably have been chanted with 'something of the old recitation style' inherited from medieval and Early Modern bardic practice; and we are told that several of the participants of the 1792 Belfast Harpers' Festival 'sang or recited' their songs.[30] Even Eoghan Rua Ó Súilleabháin's 'Dá mB' Éigs Mé' ('If I Were a Poet'), with its mixed syllabic/accentual metre, calls itself *amhrán*.[31] Thus it seems likely that by the eighteenth century a variety of approaches to performance was possible.

There has been some debate about the origins of the accentual metres. Some scholars, like Daniel Corkery and Osborn Bergin, have assumed that they were borrowed from the 'songs of the people'[32] – although Bergin, along with Gerard Murphy, also suggested that some stress forms may have developed from the syllabic metres themselves, an adaptation which Murphy and Terence McCaughey have demonstrated is at least possible.[33] Alan Bruford, in accord with Seán Ó Tuama's theories of later continental influence, has asserted that although it was probably modified by contact with native accentual forms, '*amhrán* was a novelty introduced in the late Middle Ages from England or the continent, where the kinship of some of the tunes now associated with the verses has been established'.[34] Others, however, including Murphy, Breatnach, Carney, Blankenhorn and Travis believe the metres to have been descended from earlier indigenous poetic forms;[35] and indeed the majority of scholars agree that these metres were, in Eleanor Knott's phrase, 'cultivated for a considerable period' by professional poets before their increasingly widespread use in the seventeenth and eighteenth centuries.[36] They support this argument by pointing to the assurance with which the late bardic and post-bardic poets used the forms in both Ireland and Scotland and conclude, as does Derick Thomson, that the use of such metres 'has every appearance of having a long tradition behind it'.[37] Ó Tuama concurs with this point of view, stating that the Irish aristocracy is likely to have 'encouraged a wider range of verse than [formal elegies and eulogy]. Otherwise,' he observes, 'it is hard to account for the corpus of delightful non-formal syllabic verse which survives from the same period, or for the sudden emergence of other types of verse, apparently fully-fledged, in the era after Kinsale: learned accentual verse, sophisticated folk poetry, lays and lyrics of the Fianna.'[38]

One source of the evidence of the antiquity of song-metres in the Irish tradition exists in clerical comments from manuscripts such as the eleventh-century *Irish Liber Hymnorum*, which contains a poem describing the performance of song (*amrán*) 'ri croitt': 'to a *cruit*' (see note 8).[39] Another reference occurs in a manuscript that mentions *abrān* in the context of 'clerigh ... ceallabranaigh' ('clerics skilled in church song').[40] While Breatnach admits that we have no foolproof way of knowing that the songs referred to in such texts are identical to later *amhráin*, he bolsters the connection by comparing a verse of a Marian hymn in an accentual Latin form known as *septenarius* (again from the *Liber Hymnorum*) with a religious poem by eighteenth-century poet Tadhg Gaelach Ó Súilleabháin, demonstrating a remarkable congruity of metric structure between the Latin and Irish forms.[41] However, he also argues that a distinction existed at the time between song metres and other, more prestigious forms of poetry. Quoting a Latin passage that indicates the use of *rithim* in the same hymn, he notes that the term *rhythmus* (as opposed to *metrum*) was one of contempt among medieval Latin scholars; and he speculates that there may have been competition between the purveyors of the two forms (*rhythmus* and *metrum*) throughout Europe, just as in Ireland there was competition, as E. J. Gwynn has argued, between the *filí*, who employed *mettur* (*metrum*) and the lower-status *baird*, who used *rithim* (rhythmus).[42] Derick Thomson provides an analogue in his description of accentual poetry in the Scottish tradition when he remarks that, 'Presumably [*amhrán*] comes into prominence in the seventeenth century ... because it was earlier associated with poetry by "lesser breeds" of poets – *aos-dàna* rather than *filidh* – and with the decline in influence of the *filidh* it at last got a hearing.'[43]

This is certainly the likeliest explanation of the matter; for whether accentual poetry was originally a lower-status 'bardic' medium, a mostly oral, popular mode, or a genre shared by both classes, it was arguably well-established by the late Middle Ages. Furthermore, from what we have seen of the importance of music in the composition and performance of bardic poetry, its adoption by post-bardic poets would certainly not have constituted the entirely radical departure from previous poetic practice in form, function, or quality it has sometimes been portrayed as: i.e. a sudden, cataclysmic break with tradition in response to an apocalyptic political situation, resulting in the loss of patronage. That such a sudden break did *not* occur is evidenced by the fact that, even as late as Aogán Ó Rathaille's and Séamus Dall Mac Cuarta's time, poets could find at least 'casual patrons' like the Cotters of Cork and O'Connors of Roscommon, for whom they 'sometimes wrote formal eulogistic or elegiac verse' – verse 'which, from the point of view of content, could as well have been written in the sixteenth century'.[44] Second, seventeenth-century poets produced so-called 'transitional' verse forms, which combined aspects of syllabic and stressed poetry in complex and sophisticated ways. Third, many of the intricate 'transitional' forms of the seventeenth century, as well as the later full-fledged stress metres, reflect, in the hands of poets like Haicéad, Céitinn, Ó Bruadair and Eoghan Rua Ó Súilleabháin, consummate craftsmanship and a sheer artistry that belies the popular notion that with the decline of the syllabic metres Irish poetry had lost its vitality.[45] Such poets managed to link the rigour of poetic invention with a rejection of the artificiality of the bardic rules and were, as Proinsias Mac Cana has observed, 'in a very real sense students of literature who assiduously preserved and cultivated all of the old discipline that remained viable in their altered society'.[46]

Even so, the *amhrán* forms were clearly ill-regarded in comparison with syllabic metres – not so much because they were oral, as some have implied, but because they were *déclassé*. As early as the fourteenth century, there is evidence of the contempt in which they and their purveyors were held in the 'condemnation by a professional poet of compositions in popular "song" measures, said to be by women and churls who are accused of usurping the payments rightfully due to the professionals':[47]

> Is é an t-abhrán ro fhalaigh
> a n-éadáil a n-ealadhain;
> do sgar an daghdhán re a dhath
> amhrán ban agus bhachlach.

> It's the *amhrán* that hid
> the great riches of their art;
> the song of women and churls
> that parted the true poem from its beauty.[48]

In 1603 Eochaidh Ó hEódhusa composed a wry poem called 'Ionmholta Malairt Bhisigh' ('A Change for the Better is to Be Praised'), expressing 'a half-humorous, half-apologetic fear of the displeasure his aristocratic patron, the earl of Tír Chonaill, might feel at his descent into popular and profitable "soft" poetry'.[49] Later poets like Dáibhí Ó Bruadair wrote with greater asperity about the necessity of having to 'play upon the strings' of *sráidéigse* ('street poetry') or employ the 'Guagán Gliog' ('Jingling Rattle') of the popular metres.[50] This, in spite of the fact that many of these non-syllabic compositions were often of the highest order. Ó Bruadair lamented:

> D'aithle na bhfileadh dár ionnmhas éigse is iúl
>   is mairg de-chonnairc an chinneamhain d'éirigh dhúinn:
>   a leabhair ag tittim i leimhe 's i léithe i gcúil
>   's ag macaibh na droinge gan siolla dá séadaibh rún.

> After those poets, for whom art and knowledge were wealth,
>   alas to have lived to see this fate befall us:
> their books in corners greying into nothing
>   and their sons without one syllable of their secret treasure.[51]

Yet implicit in their disparagement of the verse they employed was a lament for their lost position of privilege and respect, which was, arguably, the real point of such invectives. Elsewhere Ó Bruadair wrote:

> Os mó cion fear deaghchualaith
>   ná a chion de chionn bheith tréitheach;
> truagh ar chaitheas le healadhain
>   gan é aniogh ina éadach.
>
> Since a man is respected more
>   for his suit than for his talents
> I regret what I've spent on my art,
>   that I haven't it now in clothes.[52]

Given the association of song poetry with a decline of status, the question remains as to why the literary poets of this period chose to employ the *amhrán* forms in the first place. Many scholars point to the diminution of patronage and thus audience for the kind of poetry practised for the native Irish aristocracy before their dispersal and diminution, first after the Flight of the Earls in 1607 and later, following the Flight of the Wild Geese in 1691, when numerous poets, priests and members of the Catholic Irish aristocracy departed for the continent. They argue that with the erosion of the entire social and cultural system of which bardic poetry was an integral part poets would also have had much less opportunity for the kind of rigorous training the bardic schools had provided, making the complicated construction of bardic poetry out of range for poets after Ó Bruadair and Ó Rathaille, the last of those known to have employed syllabic forms to any great degree.

Logically, it seems likely that the more arcane diction and archaic vocabulary of the bardic schools was at least a factor in this transition. One doubts, however, that even as late and yet manifestly skilled a poet as Eoghan Rua Ó Súilleabháin would not have been able to compose in at least the less demanding syllabic forms – and indeed, one specimen of syllabic verse by Ó Súilleabháin does survive.[53] Some even believe that too much has been made of the difficulty of bardic poetry in this connection. As Eleanor Knott comments,

> Doubtless like any other literary writing [bardic poetry] was somewhat over the head of the uncultured listener, though the preservation of so many Early Modern texts in late paper manuscripts accurately transcribed long after the schools had perished, and the oral transmission of so much Ossianic verse, shows that there was a reasonably large public to appreciate literary compositions.[54]

Moreover, the decline of syllabic poetry and the adoption of *amhrán* metres during the same period in neighbouring Scotland, where the patronage system had not yet eroded to the extent it had in Ireland,[55] suggests that other influences were at work – not least the oft-dismissed but ever-present operation of literary fashion.

Undoubtedly, one of the principal reasons for the decline of the bardic system and the gradual abandonment of syllabic bardic poetry lay in the increased literacy of the poets' employers and of the Irish as a whole. Louis Cullen points out that patronage deteriorated during this period,

> in a way which reflects not simply the decline in the fortunes of archaic patrons but the diffusion of literacy which subtly altered the potential role of patronage itself. In fact, it shifted decisively from patronage of poets as such to the transcription of manuscripts and to tutoring and teaching: for the potential patron the value of poetic talent and of the skills of transcribing documents or teaching literacy had been reversed.[56]

According to Katharine Simms, the spread of literacy in the fifteenth and sixteenth centuries and 'Latin learning' of the sort that aristocratic heirs would have obtained at the recently founded Trinity College Dublin (1592) 'ultimately played a major role in transforming the nature and function of bardic poetry'. Simms also notes that at this period many of the patrons themselves were writing in the 'amateur metres, composing verse "turn about" with their literary retainers',[57] a fact that, in Declan Kiberd's view, 'signaled the end of a purely professional caste' of poets.[58] Now that the aristocrats were no longer completely reliant on semi-public performances of eulogistic poetry for literary gratification, Simms argues, they developed a taste for more personal and private poetry such as could be 'the vehicle for confidential advice, or genuine declarations of love'. Encomiastic poetry, she implies, had had its day. Meanwhile, 'the invention of printing and a wider reading public led to the fully public poem, an exhortation to patriotism, or to piety, or a lament for the changing times addressed to the population in general rather than a particular patron'.[59] This statement should be qualified, however: while the 'reading public' was wider, if it read poems in the Irish language, it would not have depended on print, since most Irish poetry during this period was disseminated in manuscript rather than in printed form.[60]

Much of the 'wider reading public' Simms refers to would have consisted of members of a new gentry, as well as of a growing middle-class, both products of the socio-economic upheavals of the sixteenth and seventeenth centuries. As early as 1541, the English system of 'surrender and regrant' replaced the Gaelic system of 'election' with primogeniture, undermining not only the role of poets as 'interpreters of rightful sovereignty' but also the foundations of land ownership. Laws prohibiting tanistry and gavelkind cemented this change in the early seventeenth century.[61] Some of the new proprietors were English planters, but others were former Irish serfs, who 'were soon outbidding the fallen noblemen or bards for rented or even for purchased tracts of land'.[62] Observes Brian Ó Cuív,

> A social revolution was taking place, the liberation of the proletariat ... Their new freedom was decried by their former rulers, so some of them found common ground with the English planters who were settling throughout the country trying to develop the estates which they had acquired ... History, in a sense, was repeating itself, for many of the settlers were willing to forget their own country and soon they took Irish wives. Before long a new generation of cross-bred Irish speakers would emerge. Since the remnants of the Gaelic aristocracy despised them, the settlers formed an alliance with the lower-ranking native population, and from this alliance a prosperous middle-class arose. They lacked the traditions and the cultural appreciation of the old upper classes and they also lacked their generosity.[63]

The anonymous seventeenth-century prose satire *Pairlement Chloinne Tomáis* (*The Parliament of Clan Thomas*) mocks the earlier members of this new class of philistines; a later version taunts the post-Cromwellian middle class in similar terms, satirizing their boorish imitations of English manners and fashions and their fabricated genealogical credentials – as well as indicting the native Gaelic aristocracy with neglect of its own and its poets' interests.[64] Declan Kiberd points out that Ó Bruadair's invectives were similarly aimed at late seventeenth-century Gaelic nobles who aped English customs – as well as at the planters, some of whom were, in Kiberd's words, 'militantly' anti-cultural, 'opposed not just to *filí* but to all forms of art'.[65] Ultimately, as Kiberd puts it, 'what the *filí* were undergoing, somewhat sooner than their colleagues in other parts of Europe, was what would much later be called the loss of aura, in the decline from aristocratic patronage to commercial conditions'.[66]

Thus, even those like Seán Clárach Mac Domhnaill (1691–1754) and Piaras Mac Gearailt (1709–91), who could still obtain patronage at this late date, often found themselves writing not only for their peers and other surviving members of the old aristocratic class but for a frankly more 'public', more general and less highly educated audience.[67] We can, however, discount the impression some commentators have conveyed that these poets began primarily 'to write for the people'.[68] Given their much-attested sense of cultural and social superiority, traces of which are apparent well into the eighteenth century, this is the least probable explanation of the situation, at least for the majority of the period under discussion. Brian Ó Cuív has gone so far as to assert that 'nearly all the ... activity [of the Early Modern literary poets] was carried on with a complete disregard for the common people'.[69] Until quite late in the eighteenth century this distinction – that is, between the culturally elite perspective of the poet and that of the peasantry, or even the middle-class – is important to bear in mind. Even Daniel Corkery, who in Louis Cullen's view greatly over-emphasized the reduced economic status of the post-bardic poets, admits that in spite of their diminished circumstances, they thought of themselves not as peasants but 'as poets, as literary men'.[70] Observes Cullen, 'The prestige of the poets was enormous and can easily be underestimated. The multiple copies made by scribes of their poetry is one dimension of this; so too is the fact that the deaths of some of the poets were even reported in the newspapers of the period.'[71] Poets represented a literate and highly specialized culture in which the written word was enshrined in the numerous manuscripts and *duanairí* that were written, copied and circulated during the period; a culture which, as Sean Connolly notes, distinguished them from their humbler, less literate countrymen in significant ways.[72]

Yet in his analysis of the divisions and commonalities between elite and popular culture in eighteenth-century Ireland, Connolly also discusses the numerous points of contact and interaction between the members of different social groups – including theatres, local festivals, religious and sporting events, and faction fights – which helped to establish and perpetuate many elements of what ultimately constituted a shared culture: 'In post-Restoration Ireland,' he concludes, 'as elsewhere in pre-industrialized Europe, the worlds of élite and popular culture were linked by the bridges of shared interest, patronage, and emulation of social superiors.'[73] Thus, for example, a number of musicians and dancing masters of the period catered to both the gentry and the peasantry; and while in some instances they performed or taught different repertoires to their respective clients (as was demonstrably the case with harpers), in others the repertoire was similar or even identical.[74] The dance fashions of the time reflect a particularly complex pattern of interaction, with 'country-dances' 'sweeping' polite society in both England and Ireland in the sixteenth century, then returning, with modifications, to the countryside itself. In the following century, elegant French quadrilles, 'cotillons' and other recent imports were adopted (and sometimes adapted) by both dancing masters and communities alike.[75] In the realm of literature, schoolmasters and clergymen were responsible for (among other things) 'the transmission down the social scale of ... fragments of the high culture of the vanished Gaelic order'.[76] Sometimes these 'bridges' were individuals: dancing masters or schoolmasters. At other times they took the form of shared social contexts, as, for example, when an entire household, from the master and mistress to the servants, danced to the music of the 'bagpipe, Irish Harpe, or Jewes Harpe'.[77]

It is probable, then, that both individuals and social contexts played a part in the wider dissemination of the songs of the seventeenth- and eighteenth-century *amhrán* poets, most of whom may not have composed their verses primarily for a rural 'peasant' audience – but managed to reach it nonetheless. Probable points of contact would have included taverns (at which courts of poetry were frequently held), hedge schools or city academies, where a number of poets taught at various times, and even Big Houses at which some poets were employed. Here, too, however, we should note that manuscripts of songs circulated widely throughout rural communities – primarily in Munster, south-eastern Ulster and Dublin, where the manuscript tradition was strongest. R. A. Breatnach has estimated that some 2,500 manuscripts have survived out of a vastly larger number, copied either by the poets themselves, by scribes, or by schoolmasters.[78] Meidhbhín Ní Úrdail argues that in the eighteenth century,

> the scribe's reading public was confined to an initiated group, those who were literate in the Irish language ... This kind of literary activity can be said to have been producer-orientated: the scribe ... wrote a text or compiled a manuscript for a patron – a fellow scribe or poet – who was already literate in the Irish language and did not need to concern himself with a wider reading public. For widespread literacy in the Irish language did not prevail and manuscripts were incorporated into the context of oral performance.[79]

This statement is particularly interesting in view of reports that by the early nineteenth century (and possibly before) manuscripts had penetrated into 'remote places' in Connacht and Munster, where, as one Bible Society teacher wrote, people were wont 'to assemble in some cabin to play cards, or to hear some of their old fabulous stories', their 'historians' proceeding 'either by heart, or out of an old manuscript, to deliver to his auditors a whole pack of nonsense'. In some cases, the commonalty perpetuated the manuscript tradition not only through oral performance but also through transcription: Pádraig de Brún cites a report from Tipperary which describes, as an example of 'the avidity with which Irish books are read and listened to', the manufacture of five copies from a single text of the Proverbs of Solomon.[80] Breatnach, noting the oral retention of aristocratic texts like the *duanaire* of the O'Reillys (600 lines of which were 'transcribed in part from the dictation of a blind man in 1620'), posits a 'synthesis' of amateur and professional scribal activity in the production of manuscripts from both written and oral sources, a synthesis that calls into question yet again the assumption that literature was restricted to a narrow elite.[81]

For even if we accept that few outside the select group Ní Úrdail describes could read the manuscripts in circulation, ultimately the orality implicit in both the form and presentation of seventeenth- and eighteenth-century poetry constituted another kind of bridge between the two classes, which, while still psychologically separate, were growing socially less disparate with the passage of time. And if most of the poets of this era did not compose their songs specifically for 'the people', they clearly intended them to be sung, as is evident from the many indications in manuscripts of tunes to which the poems are to be performed. The melodies they used were frequently well-known and eminently singable – unlike the more difficult (and no doubt less memorable) chantlike settings for syllabic poetry. Certainly in this respect – especially given the number of their songs that have remained in the oral repertoire – their art could be viewed as popular.[82] One illustration of the interconnection between the educated, scribal culture and the popular, oral culture of the period is the manuscript entitled 'An tAbhránuíghe' ('The Singer'). Compiled for theologian John Murphy in 1817–18 and consisting primarily of *amhráin*, it is described in the manuscript itself as a book 'in which are many fine songs ... from every part of Ireland'.[83] Such an anthology becomes particularly significant in light of Patrick Dinneen's description of his County Kerry neighbours singing songs from manuscripts in the early nineteenth century.[84]

The use of *amhrán* as a poetic vehicle also preserved the integrity of musical performance to the Irish poetic tradition, and was arguably even a greater part of the poet's art. According to Pádraig Ó Crualaí of Macroom, who contributed a vast fund of poetry and *seanchas* (historical background) to the Irish Folklore Commission in 1942,

> An file bhíonn sé go maith dineann sé ceol leis na focail agus leis a' gcaint: bíonn siad a' freagairt a chéile i gcónaí ... Bhí ana-cheol ag Aogán Ó Raithille, agus do bhí sé go maith ag Eón Rua. [A poet does well when he fashions the music with the words and with the speech: they always correspond to each other ... Aogán Ó Rathaille was very musical, as was Eoghan Rua.][85]

As Breandán Ó Madagáin has pointed out, this does not mean that the poets were necessarily skilled composers, but that they were practised at wedding words to music. He quotes Dinneen's description of this process, in the case of both literate and illiterate song-writers, who painstakingly corrected their words until they fit the melody, droning all the while, until the song was ready to sing 'ós árd ós chomhair sluaigh daoine nó ós comhair buidhne den éigse' ('out loud before an audience or before people of learning').[86] Yet a variety of melodies are often used for a single set of lyrics, particularly in different regions of the country. Obviously, singers along the way have also participated in the creative act of fitting lyrics to aesthetically and emotionally suitable musical vehicles. In his work in the Cork Gaeltacht, A. M. Freeman discovered that, 'If you tell [a singer] that two of his songs have the same tune, he will answer that that is impossible, since they are different songs'; for, as Virginia Blankenhorn notes, 'to a traditional singer the text and its tune are an indivisible entity'.[87]

III. Eighteenth-Century Song-Poetry and Popular Tradition

Judging by the survival of a large number of *amhráin* in oral tradition, they were indeed enjoyed by a broad spectrum of listeners and singers – this, despite what Louis Cullen has called the 'decidedly aristocratic tone of much of the poetry written even in the eighteenth century'.[88] As I have already noted, many of these *amhráin* combined popular melodies and verse metres with sophisticated, sometimes elaborate, poetry; and there is still a sense among traditional singers that songs like Eoghan Rua Ó Súilleabháin's 'Ceo Draíochta' ('A Magic Mist') and Art Mac Cumhaigh's 'Úr-chill an Chreagáin' ('The Graveyard at Creggan') exist at the more rarified end of the traditional song spectrum.

Undoubtedly the most ornate song form of the seventeenth- and eighteenth-century poets to have entered the Irish song tradition was the *aisling*, the genre *par excellence* of the period. Comments Seán Ó Tuama, 'If one is to judge by what has been preserved in oral tradition, of all the high literary work of the seventeenth and eighteenth centuries it would seem that it was the *aisling* which made most impact on the popular mind';[89] and Daniel Corkery, writing in a similar vein, observed, 'Though not the folk-poetry of the period, [*aislingí*] were the popular songs of the period.'[90] These assertions may err on the side of overstatement: actual popularity of the genre is difficult to gauge accurately in retrospect. But the form does seem to have had currency well beyond the period of its original inspiration, especially in Munster. Patrick Dinneen, for one, attests to the popularity and influence of Eoghan Rua Ó Súilleabháin's *aislingí* in late nineteenth-century Sliabh Luachra, where he describes them as having been sung at almost all 'social gatherings', arousing an almost religious fervour.[91]

Although *aisling*, or 'vision', poetry has native precursors in both the 'love' or 'fairy' *aisling* (dating back to at least the eighth century) and the equally ancient 'prophecy' *aisling*, the allegorical or political *aisling* did not emerge as a distinct genre until the late seventeenth century. To the conventions of the fairy *aisling* (in which the poet is visited at his bedside by a fairy woman who enraptures him with her beauty) and the prophecy *aisling* (in which a sleeping man receives a prophetic vision – frequently of success in battle),[92] the allegorical *aisling* adds, as Breandán Ó Buachalla has demonstrated, such independent Irish literary motifs as the allegorical personification of Ireland as a woman, her fruitful and salutary unification with the rightful king, and prophecy of the return not of an Irish military leader but of one of the members of the House of Stuart.[93] The political *aisling* also tends to be set not at the poet's bedside but more frequently in 'outdoor surroundings, beneath trees, or on a hillside, or beside a river'.[94] Later, other conventions appeared, notably a sometimes lengthy interrogation of the woman's identity, in which the poet asks whether the *spéirbhean* ('woman from heaven') is any one of a number of goddesses drawn from classical and/or Irish mythology – a convention folklorist D. K. Wilgus has dubbed 'the goddess routine'.[95] Not all seventeenth- and eighteenth-century *aislingí* are allegorical or political and, of those that are, not all follow this pattern in every respect, the various conventions being present to varying degrees according to the period and the poet in question. For example, Aogán Ó Rathaille's late seventeenth-/early eighteenth-century *aislingí* tend to be rather less sanguine about the political situation; nor do they feature 'the goddess routine', a trope which apparently only began to appear with any frequency in the songs of Eoghan an Mhéirín Mac Carthaigh and Seán Clárach Mac Domhnaill.[96] However, by the time Eoghan Rua Ó Súilleabháín was writing his own elaborate *aislingí* in the later eighteenth century, the structure had become fairly formulaic, as in 'An Spealadóir' ('The Mower'):

> Trim néal ar cuaird 'sea dhearcas-sa
> Réaltann uasal taitneamhach
> Go béasach buachach ceasnnasach
>   A' téarnamh im dháil:
> Ba dhréimreach dualach daite tiugh
> A craobh-fholt cuachach camarsach
> A' téacht go sguabach bachalach
>   Lé i n-éinfheacht go sail.
> 'N-a leacain ghil, mar cheapaid draoithe, éigse 'gus fáidhe,
> Gur sheasaimh Cúipid cleasach glic is gaethe 'n-a láimh,
>   Ar tí gach tréin-fhir chalama
>   Do thíodh 'n-a gaor do chealaga,
>   Tré'r claoiodh na céadta faraire
>   I ndaor-chreathaibh báis ...
>
> 'A rioghan bhéasach, aithris dam
> An tú an aoil-chnis tré n-ar treascaradh
> Na mílt' 'en Fhéinn le gaisge Thailc
>   Mhic Thréin thug an t-ár?
> Nó'n bhrídeach Hélen d'aistirigh
> Tar tuinn ón nGréig lér cailleadh truip
> I *siege* na Trae mar bheartaid draoith'
>   I léir-rannaibh dán?
> Nó'n mhascalach ó Alabain thug laoch leis 'n-a bhárc,
> An ainnir lér thuit clann' Uisnigh mar léightear san Táin?
>   Nó'n rioghan aerach thaithneamhach
>   D'fhúig saoithe Gaeal i n-ana-bhruid,
>   Dá druim gur phréamhuigh danair uilc
>   I réim Inis Fáil?'

While in my dream I beheld approaching / A noble and lovable lady, / Mannerly, comely, of proud mien, / Advancing to meet me. / In long plaited tresses, glossy and thick, / Her branching locks, curled and twisted, / Reached in sweeping, ringleted masses / All down to her heels. / In her glowing cheeks, as the poets, bards and seers fancy, / Playful, tricksy Cupid stood with darts in his hand, / On the point of wounding / Every hero that might venture near, / Whence warriors were laid low by the hundred / In the dread throes of death ... 'Gentle queen, tell me / Are you the fair-skinned one (Niamh) who caused the overthrow / Of thousands of the Fianna to whom Tailc Mac Treóin / Brought slaughter by his feat of arms? / Or the lady Helen that fared / Overseas from Greece through whom a troop was lost / In the siege of Troy as poets tell / In well-remembered lays? / Or the graceful one from Scotland

(Deirdre) whom a hero carried off with him in his barque / (And who was) the maid through whom fell the children of Uisneach, as we read in the saga? / Or the lightsome, lovable queen (Dervogilla) / That left the Irish nobles desolate, / Since through her the evil foreigners took root / In the realm of Inisfáil (Ireland)'?[97]

Not surprisingly, given its late arrival on the scene, there is a good deal of speculation about the origins of the allegorical *aisling*. Gerard Murphy, while not entirely dismissing its native precursors, suggests – judging by the existence of an analogous thirteenth-century Latin poem composed in France (which sounds as though it in turn could have been based in part on Boethius) – that the genre could have existed as a 'sub-literary' European song-form for some time before its emergence into the Irish literary mainstream.[98] Ó Tuama, meanwhile, believes the eighteenth-century Irish *aisling* to be derived largely from medieval French models, particularly the *reverdie*;[99] while the 'goddess routine' he views as a 'later development', reflecting medieval Latin influence from the seventeenth century on and inserted by classically influenced poets.[100] Ó Buachalla, on the other hand, while recognizing the ubiquity of 'vision' poetry, particularly in medieval Europe, emphasizes native influences on the genre. For example, he cites the *aisling*'s natural setting not (as Ó Tuama would have it) as evidence of the form's origins in the *reverdie*, but as a longstanding convention of Irish literature, with its suggestion of otherworldly encounters.[101]

Given its ornateness and often recondite quality, why would such a form have become so popular not only among the literate but also among the semi-literate or illiterate singers who perpetuated the genre in community traditions well in the twentieth century? This is probably not a question with any definitive answer; for while Hugh Shields has speculated that content seems to override stylistic considerations when political songs are in question,[102] the Jacobite politics of the *aisling* form would seem to have little to recommend themselves to labourers and peasants. Louis Cullen maintains that the peasantry were not the intended target for the political message of the *aisling*, agreeing with Daniel Corkery that they 'gave [the *aislingí*] welcome rather for the art that was in them than for the tidings'.[103] In support of his argument, he quotes a line from Eoghan Ó Súilleabháin's 'Saxaibh na Séad', as evidence that he was directing his verses not to his peasant neighbours but to his fellow-poets: 'aithris mo scéal don éigse ag baile' ('tell my news to the poets at home').[104] By Ó Súilleabháin's time, however, it is possible that poets might have had as wide an audience as possible in mind for at least some of their compositions: one of Ó Súilleabháin's Jacobite songs is written in the form of a popular lullaby.[105] And, while he does not provide any direct evidence of reception, Ó Buachalla implies – in his assessment of the evolution of the *aisling* from a patrician and royalist form to a popular and Jacobin one – that as time went on, the audience for the *aisling* broadened accordingly, especially when Jacobite conventions began to be used to promote nationalist and agrarian causes later in the eighteenth century.[106] Ó Madagáin, in answer to Cullen's statement that 'the *aisling* was a literary form, not a message for the people', has cited Ó Buachalla for 'rightly' pointing out 'that of course it was both'. Emphasizing the form's 'value as a symbol', invoked to '[reiterate] the innate sense of dignity of the oppressed and deprived and their "hankering after national freedom and religious equality"', he also notes Dinneen's comment that Eoghan Rua's *aislingí* 'had a profound influence on the social and political outlook of the people'.[107]

Whatever their motivations for learning the songs, it is clear that singers were not deterred by their sometimes abstruse diction. As Eleanor Knott's comments on the transmission of manuscripts and oral Ossianic verse demonstrate, popular tastes (see above, p. 35), even among the rural poor, were not necessarily limited to the homely and simple verse most now associate with the word 'folk'. Collette Moloney comments on the 'high proportion of praise-songs and death-laments, and the occasional epithalamium, for landowning patrons of both Gaelic and British origins and their children' in the Irish song repertoire, remarking that 'it is interesting that these had been learned by singers of such humble background and had meaning for them'.[108] Indeed, ethnographic work conducted in the past several decades has revealed that people will sing whatever is in the air, from old songs to new theatrical productions, printed broadsides, hits from the radio, and 'literary' songs like Thomas Madigan's 'Lone Shanakyle', George Sigerson's translation of 'Seán Ó Duibhir an Ghleanna' or Padraic Colum's 'She Moved Through the Fair'. Furthermore, Proinsias Mac Cana – agreeing with Corkery that 'the appeal of [the *aisling*] is primarily to an audience cultured in literature' – attributes the existence of such an audience 'among the eighteenth-century peasantry' to 'the tenacity of the oral tradition, sustained and supplemented as it was by its parallel scribal tradition'.[109] Hugh Shields's suggestion that the 'aura of respect' accorded Fenian lays through their connection with scribal and educational *literati* may have also extended to the more learned productions of literary song-poets is also highly plausible in light of the historical veneration for learning characteristic of both Irish and Scottish culture.[110] Mac Cana implies that the accident of history that caused aristocratic literature to be 'forced down to the level of the Gaelic-speaking peasantry' broadened their tastes[111] – although it is likely that the presence of cultural 'bridges', notably taverns, hedge schools and hedge schoolmasters, also played a crucial role in this process. As Louis Cullen, echoing Sean Connolly, has noted, the two classes, while by no means fusing, 'intermingled to a degree', so that 'the ordinary people acquired the cultural outlook which give this period of popular literature in Irish a particular richness and distinctiveness'.[112] Thus even drinking songs of the period could possess the elegant irony of Cathal Buí Mac Giolla Ghunna's 'An Bunnán Buí' ('The Yellow Bittern') or the satirical wit of Riocard Bairéad 'Preab san Ól' ('Drink with Spirit') – both subsequently found in oral tradition:

> A bhonnáin bhuí, is é mo chrá do luí
> Is do chnámha críon tar éis a gcreim,
>   Is chan diobháil bídh ach easpa dí
> D'fhág tú 'do luí ar chúl do chinn;
>   Is measa liom féin nó scríos na Traí
> Thú bheith sínte ar leacaibh lom,
>   Is nach ndearna tú díth ná dolaidh is tír
> Is nárbh fhearr leat fíon nó uisce poill.
>
> Oh, yellow bittern, I hate to see you lying
>   With your bones all gnawed and eaten away.
> It's not lack of food but want of drink
>   That has left you face-up upon your back.
> It's worse to me than the sack of Troy
>   To see you stretched on the naked stones,
> You who never caused pain or harm in the world,
>   And who'd as soon drink muddy water as wine.[113]

* * * * *

> Is gearr a' saol tá ag a' lili sgiamhach,
>   Cé gur buí agus gur geal a góil,
> Agus Solamh críonna ina chulaí ríoghmhail
>   Nach bhfuil baol air i n-áille dhó.
> Níl sa' tsaol seo ach mar sionán gaoithe,
>   Gath a sgaoiltear nó slám dho cheó:
> Mar sin 's dá bhrí sin níl beart níos críonna
>   Ná bheith go síorruí 'cur preab san ól!
>
> Life is as short as the fair lily's,
>   Although its raiment is gold and white,
> And Solomon wise in his royal finery
>   Could not compare with its beauty bright.
> This life is only a puff of wind,
>   An arrow loosed or a wisp of fog:
> There's no course, therefore, more wise or prudent
>   Than to be heartily drinking grog.[114]

Admittedly songs like 'Preab san Ól', despite their learned biblical and classical allusions, possess a more accessible quality than the more convoluted *aislingí* like 'Ceo Draíochta', 'Aisling ar Éire' or 'Úr-chill an Chreagáin'. They also exploit a genre – the drinking song – well-attested by both high and low throughout Europe. Yet we have some hints that even among the earlier poets popular song-forms may not have been as foreign as one might surmise from their harangues against jingly metres. For example, Dáibhí Ó Bruadair's 'Nach Iogantach É mar Theannta Grinn' ('Isn't It Wonderful How Mirth Is Embraced') is, as Pádraig Breatnach points out, 'evidently a pastiche' based on 'Thugamar Féin an Samhradh Linn' ('We Brought the Summer with Us'),[115] a song well-attested in oral tradition and which appears both in form and content to represent an Irish version of the medieval song-and-dance *carole* form. Ó Súilleabháin's lullaby is another, later, case in point, as are Jacobite songs written to well-known theatrical melodies, like Seán Clárach Mac Domhnaill's 'Rí Searlus' ('King Charles'), which is set to the tune of 'Over the Hills and Far Away', an air associated with both Farquhar's *The Recruiting Officer* (1706) and, more famously, John Gay's *The Beggar's Opera* (1728). Nor, apparently, was it beneath poets like Art Mac Cumhaigh to compose bawdy songs, some of which were censored in anthologies but many of which entered community tradition.[116] Yet while this use of such song idioms need not imply complete assimilation into popular culture, Dáithí Ó hÓgáin has argued that,

> for all their affectation, the poets themselves in the course of the eighteenth century moved progressively closer in the internal references in their compositions to the folk culture ... For instance, their references to otherworld beings tend to move away from the literary convention of the 'Tuatha Dé Danann' towards the 'sí' people of oral tradition.[117]

Pádraigín Ní Uallacháin calls Cathal Buí Mac Giolla Ghunna 'a poet of the people'; and she suggests the same of even the more highly regarded Ulster poets like Art Mac Cumhaigh and Peadar Ó Doirnín: in other words, that they were poets whose work, mostly composed without the support of patrons and meant to be sung, reflected popular 'values and beliefs'.[118] Certainly eighteenth-century song-poets seemed to embrace both popular song forms and internal references to traditional culture (e.g. dowries, wakes and fairies) with increasing frequency – and to compose macaronic songs and even a few songs wholly in English, such as Eoghan Rua's 'Rodney's Glory' and Peadar Ó Doirnín's 'The Independent Man'.

In terms of accessibility, too, we can see a progression from the more recondite *amhráin* of Ó Bruadair, Mac Cuarta and Ó Rathaille to the highly singable verses of Mac Giolla Ghunna, Ó Doirnín and (despite the frequent density of his verse) Ó Súilleabháin. This observation is more applicable still to the very late eighteenth- and early nineteenth-century poets like Antaine Raiftearaí, Tomás Rua Ó Súilleabháin and Máire Bhuí Ní Laoghaire, whose compositions, while still arguably 'literary' in flavour, reflect less poetic intricacy and are clearly addressed to a local, 'popular' audience. However, with the more accomplished poets of the eighteenth century, the adoption of various popular song forms and styles appears to reflect not a lack of training but a conscious choice of poetic mode, either to reach a wider audience (especially in the case of political songs) or from a predilection for the mode itself, as *amhráin* became increasingly acceptable in poetic circles. This holds especially true of poets like Peadar Ó Doirnín or Uilliam English, many of whose songs, like 'Mná na hÉireann' and 'Ólaim Puins is Ólaim Tae', seem to partake distinctly of what some have called 'the idiom of the people'.

IV. 'Folk' versus 'Learned' Song-Style

But just what defines this idiom? Certainly not anonymity, although most anthologists, including Ó Tuama, seem to use this as their principal classificatory tool. Since we do not know how many anonymous songs were by literary poets, this distinction seems of little practical use. In fact the ultimate origins of what many call 'folk' or 'traditional' songs in Irish are far from clear. We have little concrete knowledge of traditional Irish song until the seventeenth century and afterwards, when manuscripts and later references to pre-existing melodies have helped us to at least tentatively date a number of songs – although such references can also give rise to chicken/egg debates about the ultimate provenance of songs like 'Eibhlín, a Rúin', for which there are both conjectural 'literary' and 'folk' originals.[119]

Another possible clue lies in the relationship between traditional Irish song and international folksong-types. The presence in the Irish Gaelic song tradition of the international narrative ballad (of the type associated with F. J. Child's *English and Scottish Popular Ballads*) seems chiefly to reflect oral and popular channels – although there is still debate about its own oral vs. literary origins; and later imports may have been disseminated, at least initially, via printed ballad sheets. Irish-language variants of ballads like 'The Cherry Tree Carol' and 'Lord Randall' are derived from early – and, probably oral – imports; although who composed the translations is unknown, and the ballads themselves are few in number. It is clear, however, from the paucity of international ballad specimens in Irish (and despite the presence of ballad motifs in some Irish lyric songs) that, while this traditional narrative form had an impact on Irish song, it made relatively few inroads into what is primarily a lyric rather than a narrative poetic tradition.

The more widespread influence on traditional Irish song of medieval French forms like the *carole*, the *pastourelle*, the *reverdie* and the *chanson de malmariée* following the Norman invasion in the twelfth century is widely acknowledged, although whether these song-types became part of the Irish-language folksong tradition at that stage, whether they were used by lesser professional poets during this period and later incorporated into the oral tradition, or whether they constituted a shared idiom from the first, is not entirely clear.[120] As Ó Tuama suggests, by the time poets like Eoghan Rua Ó Súilleabháin, Eoghan an Mhéirín and Tadhg Gaelach Ó Súilleabháin were using the conventions of the *reverdie* and the *pastourelle*, such forms had probably long been absorbed into the Irish tradition,[121] although through what paths of influence is also unclear. Furthermore, while we certainly find French forms and imagery in seventeenth- and eighteenth-century Irish song-poetry, we also find interesting *mélanges* of conventions from, for example, the courtly love tradition and the native Irish tradition.[122] The picture is complicated by the fact that the ultimate origins of the French forms are also obscure, although they certainly became prominently distributed throughout Europe during the Middle Ages and subsequently figured widely in both continental and insular folksong repertoires.[123] Given these uncertainties, however, identification by continental song-type only takes us so far in attempting to assess such influences in the eighteenth century as elite or vernacular.

A potentially safer means of distinguishing 'folk' from 'literary' verse is by literary style – 'style' comprising such elements as diction, imagery, structure and the use of technical features including repetition, rhyme, metre and alliteration. But can a distinction be made on the basis of stylistic evidence alone? As an initial point of comparison, let us look at an early version of 'Eibhlín, a Rúin', a song (possibly dating from the early seventeenth century) widely accepted as 'traditional':

> Do sheólfainn féin na gamhna leat, a Eibhlín, a rúin,
> Do sheólfainn féin na gamhna leat, a Eibhlín, a rúin,
> Do sheólfainn féin na gamhna leat, amach fésna gleanntaibh leat,
> D'fhonn ag dul i gcleamhnas leat, a Eibhlín, a rúin.
>
> It's I would drive the cows with you, Eileen, aroon,
> It's I would drive the cows with you, Eileen, aroon,
> It's I would drive the cows with you, out around the glens with you,
> In hopes to make a match with you, Eileen aroon.[124]

This excerpt is obviously characterized by simplicity of diction and extensive use of repetition, both commonly associated with vernacular song. The repetition makes both the final and internal assonances easy to achieve.

By contrast, a 'later, literary version' of the song (possibly composed by Cearbhall Ó Dálaigh) runs:

> Le cúirtéis is clú bhéithe thú, a Eibhlín, a rúin,
> Dúrt bréag nó is liom féine thú, a Eibhlín, a rúin.
> Is breátha ná Vénus tú, is áille ná réilteann tú,
> Mo Hélen gan bhéim is tú, a Eibhlín, a ruin.
> Mo rós, mo lil, mo chaor is tú, mo stór dá bhfuil sa tsaol seo thú,
> Rún mo chroí is mo chléibh is tú, a Eibhlín, a rúin.
>
> All honour and renown are yours, Eileen aroon,
> I spoke a lie or you're my own, Eileen aroon.
> More fairer far than Venus you, more beautiful than a star are you.
> My Helen without stain are you, Eileen, aroon.
> My rose, my lily, my berry are you, my treasure in this world are you,
> Love of my breast and heart are you, Eileen aroon.[125]

Although this version also employs repetition, it is far less extensive; the syntax is more complex; the vocabulary and imagery – including the classical allusions – Latinate, denser, more formal and less obviously quotidian. The internal and external assonances, although simple, are maintained throughout the verse; alliteration, while not plentiful, is also present. Very few would hesitate to denominate such a song as 'literary' and educated in origin. This, however, is an extreme example. Moreover, many anonymous songs in the Irish tradition also possess a high degree of ornamental regularity and, if conversational rather than formal in diction, present striking poetic imagery:

> Thíos i dteach a' tórraimh chuir mis' eolas ar mo chailín donn,
> Bhí a gruaidhe mar na rósaí 's bhí a béilín mar an siúchra donn,
> Bhí mil ar bharraí géag ann is céir bheach ar bhun na gcrann,
> 'S bhí iasc na Finn' a' léimnigh le pléisiúir mar bhí sí liom.
>
> It was down at the wakehouse my brown-haired girl I first did meet,
> Her cheeks were like the roses and her mouth was like the sugar sweet.
> There was honey in the branches and beeswax under every tree,
> And the salmon they were leaping with pleasure that she was with me.[126]

Compare this to a verse from another song that features everyday language and even simpler imagery:

> Do tharlaigh inné orm is mé im' aonar sa ród,
> Fánach beag béithe agus éistigh lem' ghlór,
> Ba bhreá deas a béal is ba craorac mar rós,
> Is ba lách deas a claonrosc ag géilleadh don spórt.
>
> I met yesterday, all alone on the road,
> A wandering maiden, and hear now my song:
> Her mouth it was sweet and as red as a rose,
> And pleasant her fine eye, a-roving for sport.[127]

The (perhaps) surprising fact about this song, 'Do Tharlaigh Inné Orm', is that it was composed by Uilliam English, schoolmaster and, at the time of writing (c. 1760), an Augustinian priest. Lest it be objected that the song is a satirical song of seduction and therefore deliberately pitched in a lower cultural register, compare a verse from poet-schoolmaster Peadar Ó Doirnín's 'Mná na hÉireann':

> Tá bean in Éirinn a bheadh ag éad liom mur' bhfaighinn ach póg
> Ó bhean ar aonach, nach ait an scéala, is mo dháimh féin leo;
> Tá bean ab fhearr liom nó cath is céad dhíobh nach bhfagham go deo
> Is tá cailín spéiriúil ag fear gan Bhéarla, dubhghránna cróin.
>
> There's a woman in Ireland who'd envy me if I got a kiss at all
> From a girl on a fair-day, though strange to say, I love them all;
> There's one I'd take for a whole battalion and a hundred women more
> And yet this lovely girl is with an ugly, ignorant boor.[128]

Obviously, then, simplicity of diction does not necessarily indicate authorship, even if it does help to define a style that most would denominate as 'folk' or 'popular', but which could be successfully imitated by the educated and the literate. Yet there is also enough of a qualitative range in anonymous seventeenth- and early eighteenth-century Irish song to prompt some scholars to suggest that the most artistically successful of these songs were the work of 'professional poets; poet-harpists, perhaps, of slightly lesser rank than the learned bards', making some of the particularly well-wrought songs 'popular by destination' rather than by origin.[129] Gerard Murphy has ventured a more democratic belief that these superior compositions 'belonged to the broader tradition of Celtic craftsmanship'.[130] Most radically, Seán Ó Súilleabháin has suggested that Irish folksong developed from the 'semi-poetic' speech of the people themselves.[131]

Regardless of their authorship, however, it is clear from such observations that the majority of the popular songs of this period, whether anonymous or identifiably authored, are characterized by certain aesthetic and stylistic qualities that typify the repertoire as a whole. Robin Flower has spoken of 'the direct passion' of Irish folksongs;[132] Daniel Corkery of their 'frank and passionate' nature;[133] Proinsias Mac Cana of their 'breath-taking simplicity';[134] and Declan Kiberd of their 'conscious artistry'.[135] Seán Ó Súilleabháin views Irish folksong as typified by a sophisticated use of rhyme and alliteration, a naturalness and conversational quality, 'a vividness of phrase and of imagination ... with no straining after effect; sound and sense, directness and simplicity ... joined in a union which is the essence of true poetry'.[136] Ó Tuama, echoing Matthew Arnold, assigns to them a 'natural magic', finding that 'sna hamhráin is fearr, tá tuiscint do stíl atá álainn thar an gcoitiantacht [in the best of the songs, there is a sense of a style that is uncommonly beautiful]'.[137] In attempting to define this 'magical' style – which he also identifies in Old Irish poetry – Ó Tuama points to the use of imagery that conveys either the natural world itself or human emotion in terms of nature, with an immediacy bordering on epiphany. Thus, he says, 'Ní bhaineann na tagairtaí do nithe comónta – do "spré", "bá", "athaireacha" is "máithaireacha" – aon phioc ó fhileatacht an amhráin. Is amhlaidh a chuirid léi [The references to common things – to "dowry", "cattle", "fathers" and "mothers" – don't detract one bit from the poetry of the song. In fact they add to it]'.[138] Ó Tuama probably had in mind verses like these:

> Is glaise súil é ná féar is drúcht air 's ná duilliúr na gcrann,
> Is gile taobh é ná sneachta séite ar Shliabh Uí Fhloinn –
> Sneachta séite is é dhá shíor-chur nó 'tuitim go mall,
> 'S go bhfuil mo ghrá-sa mar bhláth na n-áirne ar an draighneán donn.

> His eye is greener than the dew-covered grass and the leaves of the trees,
> His skin is whiter than the driven snow on Slieve Flynn –

Driven snow that is constantly blowing or falling slowly;
And my love is like the sloe-blossom on the blackthorn tree.[139]

* * * * *

O, tiocfaidh an samhradh agus fásfaidh an féar
Agus tiocfaidh an duilliúr glas ar bhárr na gcraobh,
Tiocfaidh mo chéad-searc le bánu 'n lae
Agus buailfidh sí port suas le cumhaidh 'mo dhiadh.

Oh, the summer will come and the grass it will grow green,
And the green leaves will come upon the tops of the trees,
My true love will come with the dawn of the day,
And she'll strike up a tune to drive sadness away.[140]

Corkery found such anonymous verses 'simpler and rougher' than those of the known literary poets, comparing the difference in 'register' to that evident in the two classes of Robert Burns's poetry, those 'he wrote for the easing of his own wild heart' and 'those he wrote in emulation of the *literati* of Edinburgh'.[141] Yet the Irish literary poets could also write in two registers, and without further evidence, we might assign songs like English's 'Do Tharlaigh Inné Orm' and Ó Doirnín's 'Mná na hÉireann' to anonymous 'tradition'. Ultimately then, whatever the range of quality of the songs in this category, the overall aesthetic is common to an entire stylistic genre, typified as it is by the kind of vivid, direct but imaginative imagery and the straightforward but artistic diction we have seen in the verses quoted above. We can even see its mark on Irish translations of British imports like 'Lord Randall'. In the British variants, Lord Randall eats 'a dish of sma' fishes', 'eels boiled in brue', and so on;[142] more colourfully, one Irish variant describes the meal as 'eascainn a raibh lúb uirthi/nimh fuinte brúite uirthi' ('a coiled eel,/with kneaded and mashed poison on it') and another as 'sicíní nimhe ar phláitíní óir' ('poisoned chicken on golden platters').[143]

As in most folksong traditions – or indeed most older poetic traditions – much of the imagery in traditional Irish songs consists of stock phrases (especially common epithets and similes) that recur in different songs, although in the Irish case which phrases came from the 'learned poets' and which from earlier oral tradition is not always easy to judge. Examples include 'ógánaigh óig' ('young man'), 'a shúil is glaise' ('his eye is greener'), 'réalt eolais' ('star of knowledge'), 'fear gan chéill' ('man without sense') and 'plúr na mban' ('flower of women'). Whole lines may in fact be used in otherwise disparate songs: e.g. 'Dá mbéinnse 'mo bhádóir nach deas mar a shnámhfainn' ('If I were a boatman how nicely I would float'), 'Shiúil mise soir agus shiúil mise siar' ('I walked east and I walked west'), 'Níl mise tinn agus níl mise slán' ('I am not ill and I am not well'), and so on. Indeed, entire stanzas – what folklorists call 'floating verses' – are often 'shared among any number of discrete songs, functioning just as effectively and appropriately in each'.[144] This interchangeability is common among traditional songs generally, but because the Irish tradition is predominantly lyric, it is a more noticeable characteristic. As Hugh Shields notes, 'Variability is reinforced by the lack of a clear temporal progression and the ambiguities of real versus imagined action, so that the number, order and selection of verses, to say nothing of their reworking, are particularly subject to revision.'[145]

Also variable is the related convention of the *údar an amhráin*,[146] the background or 'authority' of the song, whose narration frequently precedes the performance of the song itself and often provides the narrative details which the song omits. The story behind the song is always present, whether related aloud or simply implied, presumed familiar to the listeners. As Donegal singer Aodh Ó Duibheannaigh commented, 'There's a story – some sort of story – attached to every song; and you must put that story across in your singing.'[147] These stories can be based either on events that gave rise to the song's composition or that were attached to the song at a later date. In the case of songs for which the composers are known, traditional singers will sometimes relate a brief biography of the poet, along with a description of the circumstances surrounding the composition of the song.[148] The fact that the narrative is implicit rather than explicit in the song itself makes its performance less a matter of imparting factual information (as in a ballad) than of expressing emotion – whether sorrow, love, grief, gaiety, or religious fervour. In this respect, songs from the Irish tradition are loosely comparable to American blues songs, whose lyrical flexibility reflects a similar emphasis on language as a primarily expressive rather than informative medium. While the lyrics of Irish songs in the present repertoire do not possess the same degree of flexibility as blues and are only rarely improvised in performance (most commonly in comic and occupational songs, e.g. lúibíní), they do exhibit a similar structural freedom.[149]

The direct emotional expression that so many have recognized in the lyrics of traditional Irish song is thus an integral part of its aesthetic – although whether this aesthetic or its concomitant stylistic devices can be attributed to a specific literary or social origin is at this remove a matter only for speculation. It is, however, the combination of the words and music of the songs in performance that gives them their greatest expressive power. Seán Bán Mac Grianna described the combination of music, emotion and poetry in song as one of the richest of human experiences;[150] and Pádraigín Ní Uallacháin quotes Douglas Hyde's description of Ó Doirnín's song-poetry as 'probably the most sensuous attempt to convey music in words ... an art between literature and music'.[151]

Hugh Shields uses the phrase 'lyric intensity' to indicate the result of the verbal and emotional compression of a song lyric to express the greatest emotion in the fewest words. Shields and other folksong scholars have suggested that while lyric songs are most prone to this kind of compression, even narrative songs, especially in the Irish tradition, have a tendency to become increasingly concentrated over time, ultimately shedding extraneous features in favour of what Tristram Coffin calls their 'emotional core'.[152] It is a commonplace that the process of oral transmission often transforms songs over time in specific ways, and the process of compression to which Shields alludes is one possible kind of transformation.[153] A comparison of songs in the oral tradition with manuscript texts may help us assess such variation and to shed light on differences – or similarities – between the two media. The manuscript tradition itself is by no means free from variation, but we often have no way of definitively stating whence the changes in manuscripts were introduced: from oral sources, from the scribes themselves, from transcriptions of altered versions from oral sources, or from the interaction of all of these – although the stability within a specific scribe's transcriptions of a particular work and our ability to trace sources from one scribe to another suggests adherence to pre-existing texts. On the other hand, as A. M. Freeman has pointed out, 'corruptions' can come into the oral tradition either through scribal errors or the misreading of manuscripts by singers who 'have cherished [a mistaken] form as "focal seanaghaoluinne" – i.e. an expression differing from those used in their own colloquial speech'. Stating that he thinks the textual garblings he encountered had little to do with 'the encroachments of English', he concludes that they were 'due, in the first place to the difference between everyday speech and the language of "Munster Poetry", and their perpetuation to the singer's reverence for his text'.[154] Comments Virginia Blankenhorn,

> We may perhaps assume that this veneration for the written word came about – among a people whom we are always encouraged to believe had a nearly exclusively oral culture – as a result of the importance of manuscript traditions at a time when writing, and the compilation of manuscript collections, were the privilege and the province of an elite determined to emphasise the cultural superiority of their own achievements at the expense of those of the common people.[155]

As Pádraig Breatnach has indicated, some errors – or at least variations, as well as 'barbarities of spelling' – may have been the products of 'enthusiastic amateur' scribes, 'who wrote texts not from a written source, but as [they] had heard them, or rather thought to have done so'. Some singers feel quite free to change unintelligible words or phrases, but this may be more acceptable at a greater remove from the manuscript tradition. On the other hand, singers like Pádraig Ó Crualaoi have been part of a chain of transmission that has remained 'astonishingly faithful to its sources'.[156] Furthermore – in contrast to the notion that variation in traditional oral culture is not only the norm but the ideal – are comments like those of song-poet Seán Bán Mac Grianna, who asserted, '[Ní] féidir focal amháin a athrú i bhfilíocht ná fuaim amháin a athrú, ná rud ar bith a chur isteach sa scríbhneoireacht de bharraíocht ar an rud a chan an file [One cannot change a single word or sound in poetry, nor add anything to what is written beyond what the poet sang]'.[157] With these qualifications in mind, while an examination of oral and written variants will not necessarily help us to distinguish oral from literary influences, it may shed some light on the process of variation itself and on the relationship between the manuscript and oral traditions.

According to northern song collector Énrí Ó Muirgheasa, 'the versions of songs found in MSS. are invariably superior to the oral versions of the same songs ... Indeed the generality of oral versions compare as poorly with a MS. version as a worn, torn, patched and mended garment does with a new one.'[158] Songs in oral tradition can indeed deteriorate in any number of ways as a result of poor memory or mishearing, especially when unfamiliar vocabulary or references are involved. In extreme cases of mishearing or confusion, garbling occurs when unfamiliar words, instead of being replaced, are rendered almost meaningless – a process especially apparent in some of the extant oral Fenian lays.[159] Another common source of variation is the abbreviation of songs: a one-verse fragment of 'Úr-chill an Chreagáin' collected by Lorcán Ó Muirí is a case in point.[160] When the abbreviation is less radical, however, the song can frequently still stand on its own. This is, for instance, the case with most of the three-verse variants of 'An Bunnán Buí', which avoid damaging the essence of the song by recombining particularly salient lines from different verses. There are, on the other hand, instances of longer versions existing in oral tradition than in manuscripts: Ó Muirí collected a seven-verse version of 'An Bunnán Buí' in Omagh early in the twentieth century and Pádraig Ua Cnáimhsí an eight-verse version from Róise Bean Mhic Grianna of Arranmore in County Donegal.[161]

One of the most common effects of oral transmission is localization, as illustrated by the replacement in 'An Bunnán Buí' of 'Loch Bhéasaigh/Vesey' ('Vesey's lake' – probably, given his geographical history, Mac Giolla Ghunna's original wording) with, variously, 'Loch Mac 'nÉan' (Loch MacNean, in Cavan), 'Loch-na-bhFiann' (possibly Loch Finn, in Donegal), and 'Loch an Léin' (which Ó Buachalla argues is not Loch Lene but, more fancifully, 'the lake of woe').[162] It is also possible that these changes were the result of unfamiliarity with the *Loch Bhéasaigh* of the song and replacement of it with another rhyming (or near-rhyming) name. A number of other variations of the lake's name have been noted in manuscript variants, occurring in scribal tradition either because they were reflecting or interacting with oral tradition, because of scribal error – or for both reasons.

Interestingly, the reference to 'Loch an Léin' occurs only in several nineteenth-century manuscripts of the song:

> Thig brón is lionn dubh ar mo chroí go hiomlán
> Tráth chím an linn ag teacht as Loch an Léin,
> Mar raibh mo Bhonnán buí ar an leic ina luí
> Gan lúth, gan bhrí, ná an guth ina bhéal;

Le sioc is gaoth agus fuacht na hoích'
Agus easpa dí go bhfuair sé bás den tart,
Bhí coin agus gadhair agas éanlaith an aeir,
Ag déanamh féasta ar a chroí's ar a chorp.

Sorrow and melancholy come upon my heart completely
When I see the water rising from *Loch an Léin*,
Since my yellow bittern upon the stone was laid
Without vigour, without strength, nor voice in his mouth;
With the frost and wind and cold of night
And for want of drink he died of thirst,
Hounds and harriers and the birds of the air
Were feasting on his heart and carcass.[163]

Despite the vivid imagery of these lines, the verse of this manuscript variant sits rather awkwardly with the melody, perhaps a sign of scribal interpolation. Compare this to a verse, not found in any of the extant manuscripts, but better versified from a musical standpoint, as well as inventive and spirited. This version of the song was transcribed by Thomas Martin in County Tyrone from a singer named Nancy Tracey:

Chuaigh mé 'n a thórraimh is mo leath-chos leointe,
Agus buidéal beorach ar mo thaoibh,
Ar nós go n-ólfadh sé braon nó dhó as,
A fhliuchfadh a bhéal is a chorp anuas.
A hum-bum-bó! sé mo mhíle brón!
Re deoir char ól sé nó go dtill mé arís,
D'fhág Cathal Buí brónach, go buartha, tréith-lag,
Ag filleadh ó thórramh an bonnáin bhuí.

I went to his wake with one foot sprained
And a bottle of beer all by my side
So that he would drink a drop or two from it,
To moisten his beak and his body down.
Hum-bum-bo! It's my thousand woes!
He drank not a drop till I returned,
And left Cathal Buí spent and sorrowful
Returning from the wake of the yellow bittern.[164]

Better still is this version collected by Ó Muirí from another Tyrone woman, Neillidh Ní Annluain, in which both rhyme and rhythm are true and the sense improved:

Fuaigh mé 'na thórraimh a's mé tuirseach brónach
Agus buidéal beorach ar mo thaoibh,
Air nós go n-ólfadh-se deoch nó dó
A fhliuchfadh a bhéal a 's a chorp astoigh

> Acht, hóm-bóm-bó! 'sé mo mhíle brón
> A'n dheor chan ólann sé a choídhche 'ríst;
> Acht bhí an buideál ólta, a's mé air leith-chois, leóinte,
> Ag pilleadh ó thórramh an bhunáin bhuidhe.
>
> I went to his wake and I grieving and sad
> With a bottle of beer all by my side,
> So that he would drink a drop or two
> To moisten his beak and his body inside
> But hum-bum-bo! It's my thousand woes
> He will never drink a drop again;
> For the bottle is drunk and I hobbling home
> Returning from the wake of the yellow bittern.[165]

Most oral variants exclude the mention of the destruction of Troy found in a number of the manuscripts of the song, perhaps reflecting the omission of an unfamiliar reference. Manuscript and oral variants of 'Moll Dubh an Ghleanna' also illustrate this process – as well as the alteration of diction from a rhetorical to a more conversational idiom typical of many oral versions of songs with manuscript precursors. One early Connacht manuscript variant runs:

> Dá bhfaighainnse bean ón bPrionnsach is bean eile ón Luinnseach
>   is bean uille ó ríogh Seórsa,
> Innighin Choirnéal Biongam is í a bheith lé funn liom
>   ná bean uille agus míle bó léith,
> Innighin óg a n'iarla is í bheith go príaclach
>   da m'iarraigh féin le pósadh,
> Mná deas an domhain dá bhfaghain orthadh mo romhain
>   sí Mall Dubh an Ghleanna thógfuinn.
>
> If I could get a wife from the Frenches or a wife from the Lynches
>   and another wife from King George,
> The daughter of Colonel Bingham and she glad to have me
>   or another wife with a thousand cows,
> The Earl's young daughter and she riskily
>   seeking me in marriage
> If I had my choice of the most beautiful women in the world
>   it's Dark Moll of the Glen I would have.[166]

The references to these members of the local aristocracy (King George aside) clearly localize the song to Connacht, probably northern Galway or southern Mayo – although Tomás Ó Concheanainn believes the allusion to Colonel Bingham, who lived in Ireland from 1805–9 and led the Cork militia in the Peninsular campaigns, to be a later and more general interpolation, although still in keeping with the other prestigious figures mentioned in the verse.[167]

A northern manuscript variant omits these specific references, replacing them with terms like 'prionsa' and 'impire' ('prince' and 'emperor'), which retain both the vowel rhymes and (in the first case) initial consonants of the proper names Frionseach/Prionnsach and Loinseach, while also preserving the idea of nobility. Another difference between the two variants is the alteration of 'Mná deas an domhain dá bhfágháin orthadh mo romhain' in the Connacht versions to ''S dá bhfaighainn-se mo roghain ar mhnáibh óga an tsaoil' in the northern one, reflecting dialectical pronunciation differences, e.g. rhyming *roghain* and *saoil* instead of *domhain* and *romhain*. The inversion of word order also makes the line more conversational:

> Dá bhfuighinn-se bean o'n bprionnsa is bean eile o'n impire
>   is bean eile o'n mór rígh Séorsa,
> Bean na n-ór-fhuilt buidhe, bheidh [i d]teanta liom san oíche,
>   nó bean eile is na mílte bó léith,
> Dá gcasthadh inghíon óg a n-Íarla is í ' bheith go ró phriaclach
>   dom iarraidh-sa le na pósadh,
> 'S dá bhfuighinn-se mo roghain ar mhnáibh óga an t-saoghail,
>   's í Moll Dubh na Ghleanna thóghfuinn.
>
> If I were to get a wife from the prince and another wife from the emperor,
>   and another from the great King George
> A woman of the golden tresses to be along with me at night,
>   or another with a thousand cows
> If I met the Earl's daughter and she seeking me
>   riskily in marriage
> If I had the choice of the most beautiful women in the world,
>   it's Dark Moll of the Glen I would have.[168]

An oral variant of the song collected in Donegal by Lorcán Ó Muirí follows the text just cited fairly closely. It retains the exotic references to foreign royalty, yet it also alters them slightly and employs somewhat simpler syntax and, in places, more natural diction than in the manuscript versions: for example, the replacement of the more formal, grammatically inverted 'dom iarraidh-sa féin le na pósadh' ('seeking me in marriage') with ''Gus í teacht dom' iarraidh le pósadh' ('and she coming to me seeking marriage') and the use of the formulaic phrase 'a chrádhfadh go deoigh mo chroidhe' ('who would break my heart forever'), which seems to be more a feature of the oral rather than the written variants of the song.[169] Another oral version from Omagh contains yet another variation of this verse, contrasting goddesses (rather than contemporary royalty) to the more desirable Moll and giving the song a more 'literary' flavour:

> Dá mbéadh Helen a's Bhénus a's Deirdre 'na dhéidh sin
> Ag teacht do mo iarraid[h] le pósadh
> Dá mbéadh an triúir sin ag teacht air a'n iúl
> 'Sí bean dubh a' Ghleanna a thoghfhainn.

> If Helen and Venus and Deirdre besides
> Were asking me to marry them
> If these three were of the same mind
> It's the dark woman of the glen I would have.[170]

The second half of the verse, however, echoes other traditional songs with phrases like 'Nuair a amharcaim 'bhfad uaim ar an áit a bhfuil mo rún/Ó, líonann mo shúile le deóra' ('When I look far away to the place my love is/Oh, my eyes fill up with tears'). Two other Donegal variants also feature a verse reminiscent of the opening lines of the well-known historic song about seventeenth-century hero 'Éamonn a' Chnoic', with its echoes of the night-visit song, i.e. 'Cé h-é sin amuigh ag fuinneogaí mo thigh?' ('Who is that outside my windows?').[171] Many oral Connacht variants include the addition of a chorus. One of these, published by Eibhlín Bean Mhic Choisdealbha in 1923,[172] contains features similar to both a Munster variant printed by John O'Daly in 1849 and a Clare variant sent to Douglas Hyde by Donal Considine and printed in 1893 in *The Love Songs of Connacht*. Hyde also prints a variant of the song which he suggests is from an oral source; however, the version of the specific verse under consideration is identical to that in the Daniel Moloney manuscript (the first example of the song, given above).[173]

As these examples illustrate, it is frequently no easy task to separate the manuscript and the oral traditions, simply because they are so intertwined. Nor can any hard-and-fast rules be inferred about change in oral transmission, although certain tendencies may be observed: a propensity towards abbreviation and compression (although, paradoxically, extension also occurs), localization, the interpolation of material from other songs (or perhaps from a scribe's or a singer's own muse), and an inclination towards more straightforward syntax and simpler vocabulary. In some instances unfamiliar 'literary' references are also dropped, although this is not invariably the case. Even admitting these simplifications and variations, however, are oral variants necessarily inferior to 'literary' manuscript versions? This view was held as early as the eighteenth century – most famously by ballad-anthologist Joseph Ritson, who declared tradition to be 'a species of alchemy which converts gold to lead'.[174] In 1786 Charles O'Conor of Belnagare wrote to fellow antiquarian Joseph Cooper Walker that 'the vulgar who always learn words by ear, are running continually into solecisms, daily more and more. This I suppose is the reason why we meet so many corrupt words in Carolan's Compositions.'[175] More recent song scholars, however, have rethought this proposition. In his discussion of the tendency of ballads towards lyricization, Tristram Coffin noted that while details of the narrative are often lost, the 'emotional core', as well as the overall aesthetic effect is preserved and even heightened by the process of compression.[176] Similarly, Alan Bruford has observed that 'folk' versions of both prose and verse romances, in omitting non-essential details, are more compact and hence frequently more effective than their manuscript sources. He concludes:

> A good many versions of Romantic tales, perhaps even the majority, far from being mere rustic imitations of their originals, are more dramatic and better constructed and so, arguably, better ... Oral transmission can be a cleansing as much as a destructive process.[177]

Speaking of the Scottish vernacular song tradition, James Ross has commented that, 'Variants of one song can individually have a completeness and a character all their own. In such cases we cannot adhere to the over-simplified viewpoint of assuming an original X and a progressive degeneration from it.'[178]

Ballad scholar Edward Ives has remarked that 'ballad variation need not be viewed as erosion or corruption, for we know of numerous ballads which have continued to develop, grow and branch out; plenty of instances where ballads have been vastly improved through the variations introduced by talented singers'.[179] The same can be said about oral versions of literary songs in Irish: compression, judicious interpolations and simplification may well improve a song which in its original form was wordy, cluttered, diffuse, or artificial; certainly traditional singers prefer songs that are, as John Ó Duibheannaigh puts it, *nadárach*: 'natural'.

Some question whether such modifications are evidence of unconscious 'oral' processes or of deliberate aesthetic choices. Eleanor Long has argued persuasively for a view of textual change in folksong 'not as representing haphazard corruptions of a once-virginal model, but as reflecting the impact of personality upon tradition.'[180] Long delineates four distinct types of singers: 'perseverating' (conservative singers who may retain even the most garbled phrases in their attempt to faithfully reproduce a song); 'confabulating' (stylistic improvisers who feel free to revise a song to their liking); 'rationalizing' (singers who also feel free to manipulate their material, but are possessed of more abstract motivations); and 'integrative' (those who, with 'the value-system of a poet', not only remake received material but also create new songs).[181] It is obvious from the last three categories that no firm line divides composing from recomposing; but the salient point, implied if not stated by Long, is that conscious alteration is often a matter of aesthetic choice. Such choice is well illustrated by song-makers like Eddie Butcher of Magilligan, County Derry, who reworked Padraic Colum's 'She Moved Through the Fair' to reduce its 'parlour' flavour and give it the styling of an older, more 'traditional' song; and Seán Bán Mac Grianna of Ranafast, County Donegal, who, besides composing numerous original songs, also deliberately recomposed such songs as 'Líontar Dúinn an Cruiscín' ('Fill Us Up the Wee Jar').[182] Several older traditional singers have told me that they have had no hesitation in changing the lyrics of a song in order to render it more meaningful; and some, like Packie Manus Byrne, have composed additional verses when either their memories or their sources had reduced to the song to one or two verses – or, like Paddy Tunney, simply in order to exercise their own poetic impulses.[183] As John Quincy Wolf remarks, such singers are 'creative artist[s] who intentionally and unintentionally [revise their] songs as a part of the art of singing'.[184]

It is thus clear that singers can remake songs, accidentally or deliberately, and it is self-evident that deliberate changes are a function of aesthetic choice. What is less clear is whether accidental changes are due merely to the vagaries of memory or to unconscious aesthetic forces. In a way, both may be at work, at least when the changes constitute an improvement or a felicitous variation; for familiarity with a stylistic idiom is enough to allow a singer to supply at need an appropriate word or phrase in place of a forgotten one, either inside or outside the context of a performance. Commenting on classical Irish love-poems, Robin Flower wrote that they have a

> peculiar edge and accent ... more to be felt than illustrated, and it cannot be conveyed to those who do not know the language, for, as with all good poetry ... the whole effect is dependent upon the deft handling of idiom and a keen sense of the history and the associations of words.[185]

To members of a singing tradition – particularly the more creative members – this sense of language, idiom and association – in other words, a poetic aesthetic – are a given; and to the degree that when they consciously or unconsciously alter a song they do so with this aesthetic in mind, they are also creative artists. Precisely defining the aesthetic that guides them, however, is a more difficult matter, especially since this will vary from person to person, community to community, and song idiom to song idiom. And even as we accept such features as compression and simplification as criteria of the oral aesthetic, we can find exceptions to it, such as the 'learned' interpolations in the Omagh version of 'Moll Dubh an Ghleanna' cited above or the use of 'oral' techniques by the eighteenth-century poets themselves. In attempting to define an oral aesthetic, Carl Lindahl has subsumed Roger Abrahams's three characteristics of oral art – 'overstatement and understatement, concrete and specific language, and translation of idea and emotion into action and symbol' – into the single term 'unglossed', by which he means that 'listeners are presented with a striking picture, but each must individually caption it and draw personal conclusions concerning the ideas and emotions implicit in the poem'.[186] Yet such an approach is also characteristic of much learned, written Irish verse, before and during the eighteenth century (indeed, it could easily be applied to lyric poetry in general). Nor is the Irish song tradition monolithic in expression, containing as it does modes ranging from the simply suggestive to the explicitly allegorical, the baldly declamatory to the purely descriptive. The manuscript (or 'literary') and the oral (or 'vernacular') traditions share far more than they differ in either style or substance. Given the absorption of so much 'learned' poetry into the Irish song tradition and the apparently 'popular' quality of many songs by recognized poets, it makes better sense to define an aesthetic that is largely shared and diverse rather than to attempt to determine its relative orality or literacy – or, as we have seen, to identify the precise origins of an individual song on the basis of style or structure alone.

It is worth noting that traditional Irish singers are often keenly aware of the literary origins of many of their songs and frequently cite their authors. This attribution of authorship is unusually common in the Irish song tradition, in which legends about the poets, accurately or inaccurately associated with specific songs, abound. Hugh Shields speculates that this practice 'is to be explained by the fact that Irish folk song absorbed traditions of earlier court poetry more than most European folk traditions', and he compares these biographical prefaces to the *vidas* of the troubadour tradition.[187] If this is so, the practice seems to have been reinforced by the influence of the eighteenth-century literary song-poets, from whom later local composers could well have inherited the idea of songwriting as poetry, poetry as *métier*, and poet as artist.[188] This influence is perceptible not only in what Seán O'Boyle has called 'the indubitable and characteristic literary flavour' of many Irish songs in current oral tradition,[189] but also in the consciousness of local song composers since the eighteenth century of their own participation in a literary tradition with deep and complex roots.

These roots are inextricably tangled, reflecting the influence of popular poetry on literary poetry and vice versa: for if the songs of the people influenced the poets of the eighteenth century in matters of style, diction and imagery, the poets also indelibly influenced oral tradition. As Seán Ó Súilleabháin has observed, 'one of the happier results' of the greater interaction of classes during the eighteenth century 'was the fact that literary talent was spread more widely at the lower levels of society than in other countries'.[190] Certainly the literary conventions of eighteenth-century song have left their mark on subsequent Irish song-poetry. Refined stock phrases (e.g. *spéirbhean* – 'skywoman', or *órfholt* – 'golden-haired'); a penchant for description – especially of women; classical allusions and other older literary conventions (including the sentiments of the elegiac and courtly love traditions), have been incorporated to varying degrees not only in eighteenth- and nineteenth-century vernacular song, but in many songs well after the mid-nineteenth century, as the following examples will illustrate:

> Is aige tá 'n spéir-bhean soinneannta séimhidh
>   A tháinic ó fréimh na ndaoine;
> Sí sgapfadh an spré ar bhochtaibh an tsaoghail
>   Sé 's aimn dí Déirdre an righ-bean.
> Sí mholfainn le féile le maise 's le méin mhaith,
>   Eadar Tráigh Éineach is Baoghallach,
> 'S a Chiottaigh Nic Daeghid, duit-se bheirim 'n réim,
>   Agus creidigidh an méid sin fíor uaim.

It's he who has the *spéirbhean* mild and serene
    Who came of the flower of the nation;
It's she who would spread wealth among the poor of the world
    And her name it is Deirdre the queen.
It's she I would praise for style and for beauty,
    Between Trá Éineach and Baoghallach,
And it's Kitty McDade, to you I give sway,
    And believe that much true from me.[191]

* * * * *

Tar chugam in mo néaltaí a spéirbhean a mhearaigh mé,
'Gus aithris domh nár chaill tú riamh a' grá orm,
Leag do cheann dubh díleas anall ar mo bhrollach
Agus codail go séanmhar go lá liom.

Come to me in my dreams, fair one who distracted me,
And tell me that you never lost your love for me,
Lay your own dark head here on my bosom
And sleep happily with me till daylight.[192]

* * * * *

Dá dtiocfá liomsa, a chailín álainn,
Aríst go brách ní bheadh orm brón,
Sheinnfinn ceol dhuit mar cheol na cláirsí,
Nó ceol binn smóilín is an drúcht gheal ceo.

If you'd come with me, my lovely colleen,
I would again be in sorrow no more,
I would play you music like the music of the *clairseach*,
Or the sweet song of the thrush in the mist-white dew.[193]

We can easily see in such songs the influence of more learned eighteenth-century song-poetry in their imagery, versification and choice of vocabulary, as well as their conventional praise of women and sentiments of romantic love. (In Mac Grianna's song, note especially the use of the phrase 'ceann dubh dílis' from the opening line of a well-known song dating from perhaps as early as 1724.) In fact, the majority of examples I have cited reflect evidence of *both* popular and literary eighteenth-century aesthetics and style, confirming Seán Ó Tuama's comment that 'the line between folksong and learned lyric is often a very fine one indeed'.[194] This sort of hybridity belies the strict dichotomy between oral and literate modes that the oral-formulaic school has in the past sought to impose upon literature of all kinds. When Albert Lord asserted that 'to become a "literary" poet [an individual] has to leave the oral tradition and learn a technique of composition that is impossible without writing, or that is developed because of writing',[195] he was presumably unaware of a tradition like Irish bardic poetry, in which writing was a late development, used primarily as means of recording poetry composed in the poet's head and meant for subsequent oral performance. Nor did he envision illiterate – and literate – local song composers profoundly influenced by earlier aristocratic poets, who themselves composed in a hybrid idiom involving a 'mixed legacy' of 'scholarly, courtly and popular' elements.[196]

Similarly, David Buchan's theory that literacy necessarily 'erodes' oral tradition by inculcating the notion of the 'fixed text' ignores a situation in which both written and oral variants exist side-by-side and in which it is sometimes impossible to tell a song composed by a literate, highly-educated poet from one composed by an illiterate or semi-literate songmaker – or to distinguish either from the many anonymous songs in the tradition.[197] The Irish song tradition is by no means unique in this, but its penchant for identifying authorial provenance as well as its cultivation of a widespread manuscript tradition makes it a more transparent example of the kind of closely woven cultural interaction that can take place in specific societies. As Thomas Crawford has observed of the interaction between popular and literary song in eighteenth-century Scotland, 'Folksong and traditional music were not pre-existent and statically 'given' from the start, but two sides of a developing medium created by individuals, known and unknown'.[198] Since we are ignorant of the precise origins of many of the songs in the Irish tradition, this interaction is particularly complex and resistant to analysis. For although in some instances we can assign different degrees of 'popular' or 'literary' influence by identifying specific songs or conventions as stylistically more sophisticated or 'aristocratic' and others as more 'popular' or 'folk-like', this amounts to little more than an academic exercise. All we can ultimately hope to do in assessing the tradition is to describe a broadly defined idiom, with the shared conventions, aesthetics and stylistic traits outlined above. This idiom reflects the interaction of two overlapping traditions, a dynamic process that has given us a unique body of song-poetry of at times striking excellence, one that displays not only individual genius but the creativity of an entire culture.

3 'ÉIRIGH I DO SHEASAMH': ORAL AND LITERARY ASPECTS OF THE IRISH LAMENT TRADITION

I. The Irish Lament Tradition

Nowhere in the debate about the oral versus the written nature of Irish literature have the lines of battle been so clearly drawn as in the controversy over the nature and function of the *caoineadh* ('keen'), or lament. The paucity of our actual knowledge about the *caoineadh* in both poetic and social-historical terms, as well as antagonistic assumptions made by proponents on both sides of the debate, have helped to ensure that the controversy remains heated – especially in connection with *Caoineadh Airt Uí Laoghaire* (*The Lament for Art O'Leary*), the well-known eighteenth-century lament generally ascribed to Eibhlín Dubh Ní Chonaill. Ultimately, however, neither side negates the other, but rather each contributes its own distinctive insights into this complex, multi-faceted phenomenon. For, as is so frequently the case in Irish literature, the *caoineadh* and its related forms reveal that the oral and the written, the elite and the vernacular, may be seen not as opposing sides of a social and literary dichotomy but as participants in a dynamic process of interaction and shared tradition.

The evidence we possess for the Irish lament tradition comes in the form of manuscripts (many of them transcriptions from oral sources), a handful of recordings of 'reconstructed' keens, and both written and oral accounts of the performance of laments in the context of wakes and funeral rituals. The dearth of first-hand scholarly descriptions and of sound recordings is largely the result of several interrelated factors: the apparent failure of most nineteenth-century song collectors to record texts of *caointe* (keens); the known reluctance of keeners to make sound recordings for twentieth-century collectors – as well as the concomitant reluctance of collectors to intrude upon wakes and funerals, occasions at which they would naturally have heard keens; and the decay into which the tradition had fallen by the time folklorists were actively seeking material on the subject. Hence, we are forced to draw tentative conclusions from a relatively small body of evidence. It is the interpretation of this evidence that has caused the current controversy.

Lack of precision concerning the terminology of lament poetry – and concerning the categorization of different forms of laments within the Irish tradition – has also contributed to the confusion. It is thus crucial to examine as broad a spectrum of the lament tradition as possible in order to determine what definitions are sound and what categories viable. It is possible, as Breandán Ó Madagáin has done, to outline several types of lament – *marbhnaí* (elegies), *caointe* (keens), and 'death-songs'; but, as we shall see, these categories are not wholly distinct from one another.

1. The Elegy, or Marbhna

Marbhnaí, or elegies, constitute the oldest lament texts we possess and represent a class of poetry practised by professional medieval and Early Modern poets to commemorate a patron, chieftain, or some notable political or literary figure after his death. The oldest such elegies known to us are written in the standard syllabic quatrains (*dán díreach*) preferred by literary poets until well into the seventeenth century and are most frequently – though not exclusively – composed in the third person. They typically employ a variety of conventional motifs, including genealogies, stylized praise (often reciting the patron's deeds, comparing him with heroic historic or mythological figures and praising his generosity and hospitality), and images of disruption in the natural world, as if it too were mourning the patron's demise. As Katharine Simms points out, there may in fact have been a range of elegiac types in addition to the *marbhna* (in which the loss of the dead patron is mourned), including the *laoidh*, which emphasizes the *caithréim*, or battle-career, of the deceased, and the *duan*, or commemorative elegy – a 'reflective ode', composed a year or more following the date of the individual's death. 'As a rule, however,' concludes Simms, 'the three elements of lamentation, commemoration and celebration of past exploits are found mingled in a single elegiac poem.'[1] The tone of *marbhnaí* is usually exalted and relatively impersonal, except when they feature the 'recurring motif, sometimes dominating the whole poem, sometimes confined to a single couplet', of 'the poet's passionate personal grieving in a quasi-feminine persona'.[2] Another motif often expressed in more personal terms in formal elegies is the poet's lamentation (perhaps as sincere as it was conventional) for the loss of his protector and benefactor. As with other bardic poems, *marbhnaí* are thought to have been performed in a sort of chant or *recitative*, with harp accompaniment.[3] The following excerpt from Fearghal Óg Mac an Bhaird's *Marbhna Aodha Ruaidh Uí Dhomhnaill*, lamenting the death of Red Hugh O'Donnell in 1602 and composed in the metre known as *deibhidhe*, is representative of the genre.

> Teasda Ēire san Easbāinn,
> do deaghladh a dīleasdáil;
>   an sēn fuair tre theasdāil thoir
>   uainn san Easbāinn do fhāgaibh ...

Laithe gruamdha, guirt tana,
dā chaoi b*h*īd mar bhrughadha;
   bīd mar ollamhna Chraoi Chuinn
   lomabhla ag caoi Í Chonaill.

Tiocfamaois tar tairthibh feadh
Aodh Maonm*h*uighe dā maireadh;
   nī 'na t*h*ráth teasda in toradh;
   gach bláth feasda ag feō*dh*ughadh ...

Tuar uathbháis treathan na dtonn;
tuar uilc ruithneadh na rēltonn;
   tuar dībheirge niamh na nēll;
   sgiamh fhífheirge ar an aiér ...

Cormac mac Airt flaith Finne
Le foillsiughadh fírinde,
   le breathaibh ríogh, le cor ccath,
   le síodh fa thol na ttreabhthach ...

D'Aodh Ō Domnhnaill, codhnach, cāigh,
d'ēis buaidh do b*h*reith mar Shés*āir*,
   caor bhuaidh ō b*h*raoinlios na bhFionn
   do chuaidh ō aoibhnios Ēirionn.

Ireland has perished in Spain; her faithful tryst has been broken; the prosperity she found, he through dying in the east has left it in Spain, out of our reach ...

A gloomy day, sparse fields – they mourn him as do farmers. Bare apple trees are mourning the descendant of Connall like the learned men of the race of Conn.

If Hugh of Maonmhagh were living we would speak of the fruits of the forests; the crop was not wanting in his time. Henceforth every flower (will be) withering ...

The fury of the waves is a portent of horror; the shining of the stars is an omen of evil; the colour of the clouds is a presage of vengeance; the sky has a look of true anger ...

The prince of the Finne is (as) Cormac Mac Airt in revealing truth, in royal judgements, in fighting battles and in making peace in accordance with the wishes of the householders ...

Like Ceasar, after the champion of all Hugh O'Donnell had won victory the victorious hero from the day of the dewy fold of the Fair departed from the enjoyment of Ireland.[4]

Along with these highly formal, conventionalized poems, there were more intimate 'personal elegies', such as Giolla Brighde Ó hEoghusa's seventeenth-century lament on his late friend Richard Nugent, or Muireadhach Albanach's lament for his wife, composed in the *rannaíocht mhór* metre:

   M'anam do sgar riomsa a-raoir,
   Calann ghlan dob ionnsa i n-uaigh;

Rugadh bruinne maordha mín
Is aonbhla lín uime uainn.

My soul parted from me last night; a pure body that was dear is in the grave; a gentle stately bosom has been taken from me with one linen shroud about it.[5]

Early post-bardic *marbhnaí* retain most of the features of the more formal elegies, as in Aogán Ó Rathaille's lament for Diarmaid Uí Laoghaire, composed in 1696:

Gliabh na ndúl is cúis a gcomhraic,
Diarmuid fionn 'san úir mac Domhnaill,
Carabuncal crú na mór-fhlaith,
Is fearachú nár smúin bheith feóllta ...

Bráthair saor Uí Néill na g-cóigheach,
Uí Bhriain Ara, Uí Chealla, 's Uí Dhomhnaill,
Mhic na Mara do radadh na seóide,
As céile cneasda na Carraige seólta ...

Monuar a thighthe go singil 'san bh-fóghmhar,
Gan ceól cláirrighe, fáidh ná eólaigh,
Gan fleadh, gan fíon, gan buidhean, gan cóisir,
Gan sgoil éigse cléir ná órd ann.

Mar a m-bíodh gasradh cearbhach cómhfhoclach,
Fíonta fairsinge a n-easgaraibh órdha,
Laocradh gaisge as buidhean mheanmnach mhodhmhar,
Ringce air hallaíbh t' athas le ceóltaibh.

There is war among the elements; and the cause of their strife is
That Diarmuid the fair, son of Domhnall, is in the grave,
The carbuncle of the blood of the great chieftains,
And a hero who thought not of being treacherous ...

Noble kinsman of O'Neill of the Provinces,
Of O'Brien of Ara, of O'Kelly and of O'Donnell,
Of Mac na Mara, who bestowed jewels,
And of the mild spouse of Carrick of the sails ...

Alas his dwellings lonely in the Autumn!
Without the music of the harp, without seers, or the learned!
Without a banquet, without wine, without company, without a festive gathering!
Without meeting of learned men, of bards, or of divines.

Where there used to be a multitude of chattering gamblers,
Abundant wines in golden goblets,
Champion warriors and a high-spirited, courteous band,
And dances to music in thy father's halls.[6]

Unlike the elegies of his predecessors, however, Ó Rathaille's composition is in a form of *caoineadh* metre, a stress or accentual metre that, as Breandán Ó Buachalla asserts, in medieval and Early Modern Irish literature encompasses a range of closely related verse forms and subject matter, all falling under the heading of 'public poetry': threnodies, political verses, hymns, 'warrants', etc. Ó Buachalla compares the *caoineadh* to some of the *amhrán* metres, in which the same pattern of accented vowels is maintained from line to line throughout each verse and frequently throughout the entire composition, and in which the verses themselves consist of quatrains, their lines comprising several regularly stressed feet. However, unlike *amhrán*, *caoineadh* metre does not require that the pattern of accented vowels be consistent from line to line – with the exception of the final assonance in each line, which tends to be maintained throughout each stanza. The more formal compositions in this metre feature three-four rhythmic feet, with three regular assonances per line (creating the pattern x-x-y), usually in quatrains, though occasionally in non-stanzaic, or 'paragraph', form.[7]

Another, later example of a highly formal elegy in accentual metre is that composed by Seán na Ráithíneach for Donnchadh Bhail' Aodha Mac Carthaigh, who died in 1739. Na Ráithíneach's elegy is again very close to the classical tradition in style, tone, imagery and poetic ornamentation – making liberal use of both alliteration and *conchlann*, a form of enjambment in which each stanza opens with the word that closes the previous one.[8] The elegy is not in *caoineadh*, but in an elegant and consistent five-stress *amhrán* metre:

> Ósna agus éacht na h-Éireann tríd an dtreóir,
> Orchra daor is créim d'fuil Mhíleadh mhóir!
> Torchartha tréith i gcré 'n-a luí fén bhfód,
> Donncha tréan Bhaile Aodha, mo mhíle brón!
>
> Is brón 's is cumha trí Mhúsgraí trasna go préimh
> Stór na ndúithchí i gclúid fí leacaibh go faon;
> Pór na bprionnsaí d'úr-chraoibh Chaisil na récs,
> I ngleó nár bh'ionntaoibh ionnsaí a phearsan le faor.
>
> Faor is fuiling is fuinneamh is fíoch nár thláth,
> Tréin-neart cuisleann is mire nár claoidheadh go bás,
> Féile, cumann is tuigsint le linn an gháidh:
> Sin tréithe an bhile', s mo mhille-sa a ghníomhartha ar lár!
>
> A sigh, a moan is heard throughout the land,
> A blow that strikes the Gaels on every hand!
> The silent tomb encloses Ireland's best,
> Brave Donough of Ballea is laid to rest!
>
> The rest of Ireland shares in Muskerry's woe,
> In grief so great a chief is thus laid low;
> A scion he of Cashel's kings and lords,
> His honour aye unsullied as his sword's.
>
> Swordsmanship, endurance, courtesy,
> These were the hero's gifts for all to see,
> With timely help to all that stood in need,
> To every such a tower of strength indeed![9]

This tradition of formal elegy lasted into the early years of the nineteenth century, as attested by Diarmuid Ó Sé's *Marbhna Mhic Fínín Duibh*. This elegy is also in an *amhrán* metre, although it features the use of *dúnadh*, a technique in which the poem ends with the same word or phrase with which it began – a convention more typical of syllabic verse. This elegy was composed as the result of a competition arranged by Mac Fínín's sister after his death in 1809, in which five poets competed for the prize of ten pounds: a reminder that the old order had not quite died. As Pádraig Breatnach remarks, 'The fact that the lament was composed with a view to obtaining a financial reward at once places it outside the general run of compositions by Irish poets in the nineteenth century, to whom material reward for poetic effort was a thing of the past.'[10] Both na Ráithíneach's and Ó Sé's elegies were noted in oral tradition: na Ráithíneach's lament by P. W. Joyce in 1851 in County Limerick and Ó Sé's lament for Mac Fínín Duibh in two different settings recorded c. 1914 and 1919, in Counties Cork and Kerry, respectively.[11] While both employ *amhrán* metres, they were apparently performed with the kind of simple, chantlike melodies associated with recent recordings of syllabic Fenian lays, whose loose rhythmic structure and melodic simplicity have led many to conjecture a possible analogy with the performance of bardic poetry. Breatnach further speculates that:

> in composing his entry for the contest the poet Ó Sé was conscious of a need to emulate what in the understanding of the judges was oldest and best in the tradition. That he chose to combine the five-stress measure with the recitative manner of delivery may therefore be an indication that for him the combination was nearest the heart of the tradition.[12]

In other words, *amhrán* metres may have historically been used for literary elegies side-by-side with syllabic metres. There is no solid evidence that this was the case, however, and there may simply have been a connection between the musical performance of elegies and keens in the Irish tradition; alternatively, both genres may have drawn on a more ancient convention of stress metres – a subject to which I shall return after a consideration of the keens, or *caointe*, themselves.

2. The Keen, or Caoineadh

The term keen, or *caoineadh*, is generally used to denote a lament 'performed in the presence of the corpse' (*os cionn coirp*).[13] Nomenclature seems to have varied according to region. For example, in Oriel (south-east Ulster), the word *tuireamh* – which in southern Ireland usually carries the general connotation of 'lament' and is frequently found in literary elegies but not usually associated with the act of keening – could mean both 'the act of reciting or lamenting' at a wake and, more specifically, *caoineadh gan bhrón*, 'a lament without sorrow', the 'dry crying' characteristic of wakes for an old person without friends or relatives.[14] While there are no actual recordings of the keen in the context of a wake or a funeral, we do possess a number of descriptions of keens from the time of

Giraldus Cambrensis through the twentieth century. Most of these descriptions date from the nineteenth century, including the following account from 1838, recorded by John Donaldson of Creggan, County Armagh:

> The rhymers or keenaghers ... are mostly women noted for that employment and are often sent for to a considerable distance to perform their funeral rites. When they arrive, the females are formed in two divisions and ranged one on each side of the dead body. One of the rhymers, after they have regaled themselves with something liquid to make them more susceptible of expressing their grief, begin their lamentations generally in the Irish language in a doleful tone of voice, expressive of either the genealogy, possessions, virtues or vices of the deceased. Or a number of absurd interrogations are addressed to the dead person, such as: 'Why did he or she die?' etc. She then raises the keenagh or cry and is joined by the whole party; the opposite keener then repeats her *gul* or lamentation and is joined in like manner, thus they continue for a considerable time together answering in opposition to each other with some intervals during the night ... The Irish cry, *caoine* or keenagh, cannot boast of much harmony as it is at present made use of in this country; but is on the contrary extremely harsh and wild in its cadences; it has however something doleful in it. There is another kind of keenagh made use of in some parts of county of Monaghan which is accounted more melodious, but the rhyming is conducted in the same manner.[15]

It is clear from nineteenth- and twentieth-century accounts that in some localities the corpse was keened not only after it was laid out but also on the way to and at the burial site, sometimes on multiple occasions.[16]

Figure 3.1: John Barrow (J. B.), *A Tour Round Ireland, Through the Sea-Coast Counties, in the Autumn of 1835*. Drawn and Etched by D. Mclise A.R.A. (London, J. Murray, 1836) (no page number given). Reproduced from the original held by the Department of Special Collections of the University Libraries of Notre Dame.

Gearóid Ó Crualaoich's synthesis of Irish Folklore Commission reports collected in the 1930s from elderly respondents in County Cork, and thus reflecting practices dating back to the mid-eighteenth century, states that the family and neighbours keened over the dead before the more formal lamentations were performed by professional keening women:

> The whole family assembles around the corpse and cries over it, talking to it and calling back the deceased. Later, when the corpse is coffined and just before the lid is put on, every member of the family must again come and cry over the corpse and kiss it. The final family crying is done outside the house just before the coffin moves off. When the family have finished their initial crying over the corpse, the neighbours cry over it in turn as they arrive at the wake house during the course of the night. The special 'keeners' also cry over the corpse from time to time during the wake. These are old women who are especially good at crying and composing extempore verses in praise of the deceased, for which they are rewarded with drink and money ... Such 'keeners' were summoned from miles away to come and perform at wakes, and it is disrespectful to the deceased not to arrange to have keening at the wake and funeral[17]

Although keening is typically thought of as the province of female professionals, male keeners, as well as relatives of both sexes, could perform the *caoineadh*. Not surprisingly, keening by relatives was recognized as producing the sincerest and most emotionally potent laments.[18] And while it is widely believed that keening was restricted to the peasantry during this period, there is evidence to suggest that such was not always the case. As early as 1751, Daniel O'Connell's grandmother was reported to have reproached a female relative (while she herself was keening her eldest son) for kneeling by the corpse in silent prayer, instead of lamenting and clapping her hands, as 'the dark women of the glens' would have done.[19] In his 1869 memoir *Evenings in the Duffrey*, Patrick Kennedy retells his godmother's story of a noble Gaelic family, displaced by the Cromwellian usurpers who murdered the family's young heir. Kennedy's account, like those of the Folklore Commission, describes the subsequent lamentation of close relatives and friends, 'whose feelings could not be restrained, approach[ing] the couch and express[ing] in a fitting kind of verse the sorrow that was uppermost in his mind at the time, the words being in the Irish tongue', the 'poor bereaved mother' taking her turn last.[20] By the 1830s, however, John Donaldson noted that in eastern Ulster the custom was 'fast giving way to the singing of Latin psalms on these occasions particularly among the higher classes';[21] while in 1849 Crofton Croker printed a translation of a keen composed by a Mrs Hodder over the body of her husband, with the comment that her keening was 'singular, because the Hodder family hold a highly respectable rank among the gentry of the county and, at that time, the custom of keening had fallen into disrepute and was practised only by the peasantry'.[22] All levels of society were affected by widespread clerical disapproval of traditional funeral customs, beginning as early as the seventeenth century; certainly by the nineteenth the higher social orders were abandoning keening for other funeral practices more in keeping with Victorian sensibility.

Thus John O'Donovan, the historian and antiquarian, famous for his work with the Ordnance Survey project, remarked that:

> It would be very difficult to procure a genuine specimen [of a keen] now, as the people are beginning to feel ashamed of them and unwilling to respect them from fear of ridicule, of which they are very sensitive. All decent half-civilized people now laugh at these elegies and hence the better class of farmers have entirely given them up, except in very few instances, where some old female member of the family cannot be restrained from venting her grief in the real old strain of poetry, accompanying it with that howling which seems now to be almost peculiar to the old Irish.[23]

Meanwhile, in the absence of direct written or aural recordings, the attributes of the keen, or *caoineadh*, itself must be inferred from 're-creations' or performances of remembered *caointe*, as well as from manuscript sources, some of which are attested in oral tradition. Salient stylistic traits include use of direct address to the corpse; common thematic and poetic conventions; specific metrical types, along with a loose, usually non-strophic structure that usually includes a 'verse' and a chorus; and certain musical or quasi-musical forms to which the words are performed.

The direct address to the corpse, which can occur throughout the *caoineadh* but which is most common at the beginnings of 'verses', may take the form of the deceased person's name or descriptor, e.g. 'Muise, a Phádraig, a Phádraig' ('Oh, Patrick, Patrick'), 'Mo chara is mo stór tú, a Nóra Ní Dhomhnaill' ('My friend and my darling, Nóra Ní Dhomhnaill'), or 'Arú! agus a leanbh' ('Alas! Oh! Child');[24] or by formulaic terms of endearment, such as 'Mo grá thú agus mo thaisce' ('My love and my treasure') or 'Mo chara 's mo chumann!' ('My love and my darling!').[25] Exclamations of grief, such as 'Mo chreach is mo chás [trom]' ('My grief and my heavy case') or 'Mo chiach agus mo thuirse' ('My sorrow and my grief')[26] are also common at the start of a verse, although they can occur at any point in the lament, as illustrated in the following reconstructed keen:

Muise a Phádraig, a Phádraig,	Patrick, Patrick,
Agus a Phádraig bhoicht, tá tú sínte!	And poor Patrick, you are stretched!
Ó muise a Phádraig bhoicht,	Oh, poor Patrick,
Céard a dhéanfas mé?	What will I do?
Go deo na ndeor gan thú, gan thú!	For ever and ever without you, without you!
A Phádraig, ó hó, a Phádraig!	Pádraig, oh, Pádraig!
Ba fear sa ngleann thú,	You were a man in the valley;
Agus ba fear ar an ard thú,	You were a man on the hillock.
Ba fear ar an gcladach thú,	You were a man on the seashore,
Agus ba fear ar an gcnocán thú.	And you were a man on the hill.
Ara muise, céard a dhéanfas do Pheadairín bhocht?	And what will your poor little Peadar do?
Agus do mháithrín bhocht?	And your poor mother?
Och, och, ó;	Alas, alas, oh!
A, muise, ochón ó go deo!	Alas, alas, oh, forever![27]

Sometimes other participants in the wake or funeral are addressed, often when they are being censured for lack of respect or sincerity, or in disputes between relatives. Such outbursts allowed for the expression of otherwise literally unspeakable sentiments, giving, as Kevin Whelan comments, 'a direct voice to marital strife and conflicts between kin groups, precisely because the wake brought the two families together physically and because the shock of death exposed or released raw emotional states'.[28] Tomás Ó hAilín reproduces the following exchange between a mother keening her daughter and her daughter's sister-in-law:

Mo ghrádh is mo chiall tú	My love and my darling
Agus is mó fear maith d'iarr tú:	It is many's a good man sought you:
D'eitíos iad san	They I refused
Gur chuireas tú ar a gCliaraigh	And sent you to Cleary
De thalamh ná riantar	Whose land was not marked
Le capall ná le h-iarann	By horse or iron
Agus ná taithneann an ghrian air	And on which the sun never shone
Ach mar a dtaithnfeadh sé aniar air	Except from the west
Agus ní bhíodh t'ainm ar h-iarraidh	And he had no name for you
Ach a bhitch nó a striapach.	But 'bitch' or whore.

To this the dead woman's sister-in-law replied:

A mhná ná creididh í	Women, do not believe her,
Agus gurb é brí na hoibre	The gist of the matter is
Í bheith amuich deirionnach	That she'd be out late at night
Drúcht ar a heirball	With dew on her tail
Agus fear mná eile 'ce.	And another woman's man with her.[29]

The practice of direct address in both the *caoineadh* and in all communication surrounding the funeral proceedings reflects not only the relationship of the lamenter with the dead person but with all present and – by extension – with the entire community. It also lends immediacy to the lament, evoking the sense of disbelief that usually attends bereavement, while its use to either directly or indirectly address others reveals the extent to which funerals and wakes, like other liminal events, allows for the expression of strong, sometimes negative emotions.[30]

As will already be apparent, the use of second-person speech in the keen is also accompanied by a number of thematic and poetic conventions – some of which are so common as to constitute a kind of formula, including not only the epithets and exclamations of grief already detailed but also a range of conventional descriptions, themes and imagery. Praise of the dead person's positive traits, according to one respondent from Baile Mhic Íre, was compulsory, especially when paid keeners were involved: 'Pecu bhí sé go maith nú go holc do mholfí go hárd é agus ní bheadh ach an focal fónta ages na mná caointe [Whether he was good or bad he would be highly praised and the keening women would have only a good word].'[31] Physical description, often of a highly formulaic and conventional type, is also a common feature of keens, as the following example from West Kerry illustrates:

Bean na gruaige finne,	Woman of the fair hair,
Bean an éadain leithin,	Woman of the broad face,
Bean a' dá shúil ghlaise,	Woman of the two green eyes,
Bean a' tsróinín fhúinte,	Woman of the well-shaped little nose,
Bean a' bhéilín mhilis,	Woman of the sweet little mouth,
Bean na fiacla gile,	Woman of the bright teeth,
Bean an dá chíoch chruinne,	Woman of the two round breasts,
Máthair móirsheasar leinbh	Mother of seven children
In aos a bliain is fiche	In age, twenty-one
I nDún Úrlann curtha.[32]	In Dunurlin laid.

Such descriptions need not be taken literally. As Seán Ó Coileáin cautions, while there is certainly scope for 'the expression of real personal grief' in such passages, we should not always 'enquire too closely as to the accuracy of the epithets, since their faithfulness is not so much to the person being waked as to the tradition which requires that he be spoken of in the manner known to the performer and expected, even demanded, by the audience'.[33]

Where men were the subjects of a keen, virtues such as hospitality, generosity and competence as providers were especially praised. And in some cases – especially, perhaps, in better-off households (although the same practice has been noted in lesser families, as well)[34] – a modest genealogy was recited, sometimes accompanied by praise for a kind of opulent hospitality and heroism that echoes literary *marbhnaí*:[35]

Mo chara is mo ghrá croí!	My friend and my heart's love
A leinbh ón mBántír,	Child of Bantir,
Agus ón dá Ráithín,	And of Raheen,
Agus ó Chlaodach na Bláthaí,	And of Claodach of the Flowers,
Mar a mbíonn boird ar fhrámaíbh,	Whose tables are on trestles,
Soird ar phlátaíbh,	Every manner of things on platters,
Eachrach ar stáblaí,	Steeds in stables,
Fir óga cáfaois,	[?] young men,
Le mná na mbánchíoch,	With the white-breasted women,
Atá 'na lánluí.	Who are lying down.[36]

Many *caointe* contain the questions John Donaldson found 'absurd', such as 'Goidé a dhéanfaidh mé?' ('What will I do?'), as well as pleas that the dead arise and assist the living:

Éirigh suas id' sheasamh	Rise and stand up,
A's gaibh do sheisreach capall!	And tackle your ploughing-team!
Tóg fód chúig n-órdla ar treasnacht;	Plough a five-inch furrow;
Féach ormsa, a thaisce,	Look at me, my treasure,
'S gan tada 'gam mar thaca,	With nobody to help me
Ag dul ag baint ná ag gearradh!	When I go reaping or cutting![37]

Other keens contain words (sometimes ambiguous, sometimes explicit) of actual blame for the dead person. Angela Bourke has argued that one of the functions of keens, reflected in such texts, was the mode it offered women (the predominant keeners in traditional communities) to assert 'their identity as women in a way that contrasts sharply with the accepted norms of modesty and reticence in Irish society'.[38] Bourke has further argued that motifs of abnormal behaviour such as 'the loosening of hair and going naked or dressing in rags' – along with impossible athletic feats associated not only with laments like *Caoineadh Airt Uí Laoghaire* and related lament-songs like 'Caoineadh na dTrí Muire' but also with *geltacht*, compositions (like *Buile Suibhne*) dealing with madmen – reflect a phase in a 'transition rite' in which the figure in question – madman or keening woman – is seen as temporarily separated from society and its usual rules.[39] Hence the freedom of keening women at such 'liminal' times not only to alter their appearance but also to chastise friends, relatives, the clergy and even the dead.

The verse form most frequently utilized for keening is, as Seán Ó Coileáin puts it, 'of a most elementary kind', each line employing only two or three rhythmic feet, ending in a final, assonantally-rhyming foot of one to three syllables: a pattern that is generally maintained only throughout a given 'paragraph' of irregular length.[40] Sometimes, as in some of the examples cited above, the assonance is occasional or even absent altogether. The 'long, ragged rant'[41] thus produced has frequently been called *rosc*, a term that according to Proinsias Mac Cana was associated in Old Irish with non-syllabic 'pre-classical verse'. 'As used in the early tales,' he comments, 'the short-lined verse ... is distinguished by its very brevity, which imparts to it a litany-like and – one might almost say – rhythmical quality, by its lack of rhyme and, normally, by its use of linking alliteration.' He further notes that 'in later centuries ... the very appearance of the form, apart altogether from its content, was sufficient to evoke an impression of archaism and to convey an oblique reference to the remote reaches of native tradition.'[42] Indeed, as Virginia Blankenhorn points out, the 'types of poetry which employ these metres are, for the most part, thematically as well as metrically outside the mainstream of all native Irish verse traditions – those connected with death, religion, and gnomic wisdom.'[43] Breandán Ó Buachalla has martialled considerable evidence to argue that the term *rosc* denotes not a metre, but rather *uaim*, or alliteration; and he prefers to subsume these simpler forms under the category of *caoineadh*, a usage I will follow throughout this chapter.[44] But even if the term itself is inaccurate, the recognition of a distinct metrical category (or subcategory) is sound, since, as illustrated in the examples above, the majority of texts reported as having been performed in the context of wakes do reflect this pattern.

Many of the descriptions we have of keens – as well as of recordings of reconstructed keens – suggest or state that they were performed with a musical setting, although the written accounts sometimes leave the exact nature of that setting uncertain. For example, some simply speak of a 'cry' or a 'howl'. Others, however, suggest that the keen was performed in a clearly musical way, by talented professionals. As one commentator from the Iveragh Peninsula remarked: 'B'iad na daoine ab'fhearr chun olagón a chasadh daoine go mbíodh guth maith amhránaíochta acu. Bhíodh mná (agus fir leis) ann a bhíodh nótálta chun na mairbh a chaoineadh [The people who performed the best keen were those who had a good singing voice. There were women (and also men) who were noted for keening the dead].'[45] It is likely that regional variations obtained, as illustrated by the account an Englishman named John Geogh gave of a funeral procession between Dundalk and Newry in 1813:

> I had often heard the Irish cry at funerals in many parts of Munster and once even in the streets of Cork which was the most discordant howling of all the people together, but on passing these mountains I overtook a funeral at which I heard the real old cry made use of for many years by the original natives. It was not an indiscriminate shout like what I heard in Munster but a plaintive melancholy tune sung by about a dozen women only. The corpse was followed by an old woman with a petticoat about her shoulders who repeated a few words in Irish and when she ceased the other women who followed sung a verse of their song of lamentations. She then began again, the others followed and this they continued alternately the whole way. I felt a kind of soothing pleasingness in the sound though I did not understand the words and I continued two miles with the funeral.[46]

An earlier account, written by a Frenchman named de Latocnaye in 1796, reinforces this distinction, contrasting the keening in southern Ireland with the lamentation of mourners in County Louth, which de Latocnaye compared to 'Presbyterian psalm singing'.[47] This comparison holds true for other parts of the country, as well: performances of *caointe* by Labhrás Ó Cadhla of Rinn, County Waterford and Cití Ní Ghallachóir of Gaoth Dobhair, County Donegal, both feature a liberal use of *melisma* (several words or syllables set to one note), rhythmic freedom, and a simple, descending melodic line that is indeed remarkably reminiscent of Scottish psalm-singing and that accords well with the numerous descriptions of keens in terms of 'recitative', 'chant', or 'plainsong'.[48] These qualities can also be found in many of the musical transcriptions of keens from the time of J. C. Walker in the late eighteenth century to Liam de Noraidh in the twentieth. Ó Madagáin has observed that keens do not have individual tunes: in other words, one melody can serve for multiple laments.[49] There also seems to be a limited number of melodies associated with keens, suggesting their membership in what George Pullen Jackson and Bertrand Bronson termed a 'tune family': a pool of related tunes which, while varying in details, features a limited and closely related number of melodic possibilities and 'a general kinship in structure'.[50] Colette Moloney points out that one of Edward Bunting's transcriptions (probably from the singing of O'Neill 'the harper') represents the 'Goll', or solo verse part of the keen, as 'basically a four-bar phrase', which in performance 'could presumably be repeated ad lib until the keener had finished' – a practice obviously 'conducive to the chantlike method of delivery'.[51]

Yet the melody could apparently vary to some degree within the keen itself, as well as from verse to refrain, as illustrated by Eugene O'Curry's vivid and detailed description of a keen 'excellent in point of both music and words, improvised over the body of a man who had been killed by a fall from a horse, by a young man, the brother of the deceased':

> He first recounted his genealogy, eulogised the spotless honour of his family, described in the tones of a sweet lullaby his childhood and boyhood, then changing the air suddenly, he spoke of his wrestling and hurling, his skill at ploughing, his horsemanship, his prowess at a fight in a fair, his wooing and marriage, and ended by suddenly bursting into a loud piercing, but exquisitely beautiful wail, which was again and again taken up by the bystanders.[52]

Most descriptions and transcriptions of keens identify a call-and-response or verse and refrain structure, in which the keening woman (either throughout the proceedings or in alternation with others) performs the solo verse containing the address to the corpse, while others join in on the refrain; and in this respect it is again strikingly similar to the Gaelic psalm-singing tradition of the Hebrides. The refrain – referred to variously as the 'cry', *ologón, gol, gáir* or *caoinan* – consists of repeated exclamations of grief, such as 'ologón, ochón ó' ('alas, alas, oh'), or 'Dia linn go deo' ('God be with us forever'). The transcriptions we possess of such refrains reflect a close melodic relationship between refrain and verse, although many of the refrains seem to feature greater use of *melisma* appropriate to the use of few and repetitive asemantic phrases. There are exceptions, however. For example, the music of both verse and refrain noted by Bunting from keeners in County Armagh in 1840 is sparer than that found in other extant transcriptions.[53] While this may be simply a matter of scribal simplification, regional and individual variations should not be ruled out: even Labhrás Ó Cadhla's recorded performances, while using the same basic melody, vary in the amount of *melisma* they employ, and the two Árainn women who perform the 'cry' on Sidney Robertson Cowell's 1950s field recordings varied in their use of melodic ornamentation.[54]

Ó Madagáin has further speculated that there was a special kind of delivery (either sung or spoken) for the 'salutation', or opening line of each verse, a conjecture supported by accounts like Frank Keane's in 1814: 'The Mourner ... commences by some deep murmuring, repeating over and over the name of the deceased, such as "A Thomáis, a Thomáis, mo chumha is mo dhíth thú (Oh, Thomas, Thomas, my sorrow and my loss!)."'[55] – a method also used by one of Crofton Croker's informants (see below, p. 93). Given the paucity of our information, this remains an area of speculation, and it may well be that the practice was also subject to regional and individual variation. For example, judging from some accounts, this sort of murmuring could have been used throughout the entire keen.[56]

Figure 3.2: Edward Bunting (E. B.), *The Ancient Music of Ireland* (Dublin: Hodges and Smith, 1840), insert, p. 2. Reproduced from the original held by the Department of Special Collections of the University Libraries of Notre Dame.

There is also some ambiguity about the use of the word 'crooning' in this context, as the Irish word *crónán* can mean not only 'murmuring', 'crooning' or 'chanting', but also a 'drone' or 'bass' and, by extension, 'a song which is accompanied by a simple drone-type bass' or the refrain of a keen, to be sung by a group.[57] Patrick Dinneen recalled his mother 'crooning' Ó Rathaille's 'lays', although whether these were his elegies or other songs, he did not indicate. Dinneen defines *crónán* as 'any dull note long continued ... an indistinctly sung tune; a croon'.[58] Even the song 'It's Pretty to Be in Ballinderry' (see Figure 3.2), whose verse is set to a melodic song air, possesses what is designated in Bunting's manuscript as a *crónán*, a refrain of vocables set to a simple, descending melodic line. According to Bunting, the verse was 'sung by one person, while the rest of the party chant[ed] the *crónán* in consonance',[59] very much in the manner of the call-and-response described in so many accounts of keening. The *crónán* may also, in some areas, have come to mean keening in general.

It is clear, however, that the musical register of keens could vary anywhere from what one man described as 'díreach mar a bheadh amhrán brónach agus fonn leis [exactly like a sad song with a melody to it]'[60] to a form of elevated speech not unlike that used by traditional preachers in the American south.[61] An example of this kind of half-spoken, half-chanted or intoned verse is a performance of a keen re-enacted for collector Séamus Ennis by Seán Ó Conaola of Cois Fharraige, County Galway, in 1946, as Ennis lay on the floor before him with his hat upon his breast to impersonate a corpse.[62] Starting with a drone-like but spoken chant, Ó Conaola gradually begins to intone syllables, holding them on a single pitch, until the speech becomes heightened into a quasi-musical, then fully-sung wail, which in its more restrained moments sounds not unlike liturgical chanting. Perhaps this is the delivery Patrick Kennedy's godmother meant to convey in her description of the grieving mother who, after 'wringing her hands and rocking her body' – a prelude common to numerous accounts of keening – 'commenc[ed] her [caoineadh]. Slowly and plaintively it went on at first; but the tone and action became soon more wild and affecting, till it changed into a loud and vengeful wail.'[63] Pádraigín Ní Uallacháin uses the word 'recite' as one synonym for the south-eastern Ulster word *tuireamh* and notes that keeners were sometimes known in that region as 'rhymers'[64] – lexical suggestions that in keens the boundary between speech and song could be ambiguous. Ó Madagáin cites evidence of 'heightened speech' from a number of Scottish and Irish sources in relation to performances of prayer and litany, the recitation of Fenian lays, and at any time when a speaker is moved, surprised or excited. In *Father Allan's Island,* Amy Murray describes the performance of a Fenian lay in the Hebrides as: 'On the edge between speaking and singing ... as not only much of song amongst this people, but much of speech itself, so soon as there enters anything of passion into it.' Ó Madagáin cites similar reports from

Carna in County Galway and quotes Tomás de Bhaldraithe's description of an elderly woman from the same townland, whose voice,

> When she has a sad tale to tell – not necessarily one of death – ... rises into a recitative and returns again to ordinary speech when she turns to another topic. For instance, she fell and hurt her leg, so that she could not go to Mass: she was put out by that. In telling me that, complaining, she raised her voice and there was a kind of rhythm to the speech with a keen-like effect – something like recitative.[65]

Bunting, meanwhile, describes the Irish cry as 'being neither perfect recitative nor perfect melody, but a peculiar combination of both'.[66]

On the other hand, in some instances, the tradition could be a fully melodic one. We know, for example, that not only traditional religious songs like 'Caoineadh na dTrí Muire' ('The Song of the Three Virgins'), but also songs otherwise unconnected with the lament tradition, like Cathal Buí Mac Giolla Ghunna's song of repentance 'Aithreachas Chathail Bhuí' and a verse from the love song 'Má Théid Tú 'un Aonaigh' ('If You Go to the Market'), were employed in parts of Ulster in place of actual keens.[67] According to one source from Iorras in County Mayo, a song called 'Amhrán Iomartha' ('Rowing Song') was always sung at wakes, as the keening women clapped their hands and bent and lifted their heads 'mar bheadh fuireann bháid' ('like the crew of a boat').[68] It would thus appear that a variety of approaches to the musical or quasi-musical settings of keens existed.

Ó Madagáin, however, has posited a plausible connection between *caointe* and *marbhnaí* based on his comparisons of the few musically notated settings of both that we possess. The similarities are striking, for the melodies associated with *marbhnaí* are even more chant-like than those for *caointe*, with very free rhythm and refrains still simpler than those associated with keening.[69] Another similarity is the use of different melodies for elegies associated with different parts of the country (as in the two discrete tunes collected for *Marbhna Mhic Fínín Duibh* in Counties Cork and Kerry), suggesting that, as with keens, there may have been a limited regional repertoire of formal lament music rather than a specific melody for each *marbhna*.[70]

Lest this be thought simply a relatively recent process of musical-poetic assimilation, Ó Madagáin draws attention to the similarity between the music for these genres – especially *marbhnaí* – and that recorded for syllabic poetry of both Ireland and Scotland. He cites Francis Collinson's itemized description of the music for Scottish Fenian lays, which instances the recitation of a note 'on a monotone', 'the approach to this by one or more notes from above or below', 'the use of only part of scale' and a final 'descending cadence' – all of which, as Ó Madagáin observes, could be applied with equal accuracy to the extant settings for Irish *marbhnaí* (particularly the Kerry version of *Marbhna Mhic Fínín Duibh*) and, to a lesser degree, to melodies used for 'dirge' or verse sections of many keens.[71] Because of their scarcity, these connections are obviously tentative, yet they suggest a musical relationship not only between recorded performances of *marbhnaí* and the syllabic elegies of the classical tradition but also with the performance of syllabic poetry in general. This relationship becomes more plausible when viewed in the context of Eugene O'Curry's description of his father's performance of Ossianic poems:

> I do not remember having heard any other poem sung to the air of these Ossianic pieces but one, and that is a beautiful ancient hymn to the Blessed Virgin, some seven hundred or more years old. My father sang this hymn, and well too, almost every night, so that the words and the air have been impressed on my memory from the earliest dawn of life ... The air of this hymn is not popular; I have never heard it sung but by my own father. I know it myself very well, and I know several old poems that will sing to it.[72]

As Ó Madagáin points out, O'Curry's statement implies that a single air served for both Fenian lays and religious bardic poetry (in this case a thirteenth-century hymn called 'Sciathlúireach Mhuire', or 'Mary's Breastplate'). This, in combination with what we know about the airs for *marbhnaí*, suggests, if not homogeneity, at least a melodic relationship between both accentual and syllabic *marbhnaí*, syllabic heroic poetry (*laoithe*), and syllabic religious poetry – a relationship which in turn suggests that these forms have a long musical tradition in common. As the music of performers like Carolan illustrates, post-bardic *marbhnaí* and other post-syllabic forms were – at least for a time – judging from the melodic range of most of Carolan's compositions, chanted rather than sung outright, with 'something of the old recitation style' inherited from medieval and early modern bardic practice. Indeed, some of the participants of the 1792 Belfast Harpers' Festival were described as 'singing or reciting'.[73] Nor can this melodic tradition be separated entirely from the keening tradition; for despite Ó Madagáin's attempts to establish melodic traits for *marbhnaí* as distinct from keens, the small number for which we have melodies possess more musical commonalities than differences.

Indeed, if the musical settings of Seán na Ráithíneach's elegy and *Marbhna Mhic Fínín Duibh* are an accurate reflection of bardic practice and not simply a borrowing from the keening tradition, the link between elegy and keen may have been reasonably strong, especially when viewed in light of the non-musical parallels between the two genres. For example, the vocables 'í ú í ú í ú' in Phil Gleeson's performance of na Ráithíneach's *marbhna* seem comparable to representations of the 'Irish howl' in seventeenth-century British literature, noted variously as 'il-lil-lil-loo', 'aleleu' and 'pulilillew' (obvious counterparts to the Irish *aililiú* and *puililiú*) and to the refrains reported by later observers like de Latocnaye as belonging to funeral keens in Munster and south-eastern Ulster, e.g. 'pi lú lú', 'hú lú lú' and 'oh ah oh ah oh ah'.[74] The use in both keens and elegies of such motifs as genealogy, hospitality and physical prowess are other indications that some sort of generic connection may have existed. The ambiguous terminology of the two genres also seems to indicate an interrelationship between them: in the manuscript containing the laments for Mac Fínín Duibh, the terms *tuireamh*, *marbhna* and *caoine* are used interchangeably; and, as Pádraigín Ní Uallacháin's evidence suggests, in Oriel there was some variability in the use of the word *tuireamh*.[75] Thus, while Rachel Bromwich believes some of the themes found in *caointe* to be derived from literary *marbhnaí*,[76] it is also possible that they had co-existed in both the elegiac and keening traditions from an earlier period. James Carney prints a late seventeenth-century elegy (*tuireamh*) that employs a four-foot *caoineadh* metre in non-stanzaic, 'paragraph' form.[77] This poem is conventionally elegiac, with plentiful allusions to gods and heroes, but employs the vocative – although directed not to the subject of the lament but to the community. Using this elegy as an example, Carney speculates that the *caoineadh* metre represents a survival of an older, alliterative stress verse, predating syllabic poetry and re-emerging in post-bardic verse.[78]

If this is true, it is possible that both the *caoineadh* and the non-syllabic *marbhna* drew upon a shared and ancient verse tradition. This interconnection in turn may explain the confusion that Énrí Ó Muirgheasa experienced when he edited the texts of two *marbhnaí* in the early twentieth century. The first, which he printed in *Céad de Cheoltaibh Uladh*, is dated 1650 (although the manuscripts are of eighteenth- and nineteenth-century provenance) and composed in non-stanzaic four-foot, three-stress (x-x-y) *caoineadh*. Comments Ó Muirgheasa,

> I am not at all sure this poem is perfect. Such a poem is usually written in four-line stanzas, but the version in text has an uneven number of lines as if a portion of some stanza or stanzas were missing, and none of the copies I have seen had a perfect arrangement of stanzas. For this reason and partly on account of its great length I have printed the poem continuously though I have little doubt it is not the way the poet wrote it.[79]

On the versification of a *marbhna* which he prints in his second collection of Ulster songs and which is similarly composed in non-stanzaic four-foot *caoineadh*, however, he remains silent; perhaps his encounter with this second irregular example made him wonder whether the first was not as anomalous as he had originally believed.[80] This evidence is obviously too slender to lead to any conclusions, but it raises questions: Could there have been a range of elegy-types, drawing on various verse traditions, including that of keening? Were the forms once more closely linked than is now apparent? Indeed, if the observations of the Halls may be trusted, in the early nineteenth century *marbhnaí* as well as *caointe* were improvised:

> Besides *caoines*, extempore compositions over the dead, *thirrios* [*tuirrimh*], or written elegies, deserve mention. They are composed almost exclusively by men, as the *caoines* are by women. Many of them are of no mean pretensions as efforts of genius. Speci-

mens are to be found in manuscript in the house of every peasant who cultivates the language of his country. They differ from the keens in little more than that they are written with more regard to metre.[81]

A Middle-Irish lament-poem traditionally, though anachronistically, attributed to the tenth-century queen Gormlaith,[82] seems to underscore this ambiguous connection in its use of keen-like exclamations like 'Uchagán, mo ghalar féain' ('Alas, my own grief ') and a typical keening refrain ('Uchagán. uchagán' – 'Ologón, ologón') in an otherwise formal, first-person, syllabic composition:

> Uchagān, mo ghalar féain
>   uchagán, mo sccaradh réim sgéimh;
> anocht as dīleas mo shlad,
>   ō nach maireann mac í Néill.
>
> Alas! My own grief. Alas! My separation from my beauty. Tonight I am despoiled in earnest, since the son of Niall's descendant lives not.[83]

Whether this is a personal elegy or a stylized 'literary keen', in which the conventions of the keening tradition are employed for effect – as in the keens of sagas or in a number of extant bardic elegies – is uncertain.[84] Katharine Simms argues persuasively that the entire Gormlaith poem-cycle represents the work of a professional bard, who, in keeping with one of the stylistic strata of the *marbhna*, styled himself as 'chieftain's widow', taking on the feminine role of keener and the conventions associated with that role.[85]

The earliest evidence we have that keens were practised among the higher, as well as the lower, ranks of medieval Irish society includes a ninth-century penitential which enumerates penances for laments illicitly performed over the bodies of persons of varying social and religious rank, including lay men and women, 'a penitent nun', a 'cleric of the laity' and finally 'a bishop, or king or confessor or ruler of a chief town'.[86] Other early literary representations of keening, such as Deirdre's *Lament for the Sons of Uisneach* and Emer's lament for Cú Chulainn, reinforce the sense that the practice was widely known in early Irish society; while Blathmac's eighth-century poem to the Virgin clearly reflects familiarity with keening not merely as a literary convention but as an actual custom.[87] Later references in the bardic period provide still more support for the standard practice of keening in conjunction with, though separate from, the performance of poetic elegies. Drawing upon descriptions in the *Book of O'Conor Don*, Simms observes,

> After the burial of a chief it was customary for his kinsfolk and subjects in general to assemble on his grave and fill the air with lamentation, sometimes remaining all night, but there was a particularly prominent role allotted to the keening women and the poets ... Women are said to lie stretched on the grave all night, bathing it with their tears. They wring their hands and lament with music, or with sobs and howls. The poets take it for

granted this display of grief is largely conventional (indeed it was presumably in most cases the exercise of a professional art) so that to speak of the dead chieftain earning 'true tears' or 'true lamentation' from the women is the ultimate tribute. The bard, too, was expected to show visible symptoms of grief, whether sincere or not. Tadhg Óg Ó hUiginn protests: 'No feigned grief mine, my tears will flow while no one sees me.'[88]

Hence the use of the image of the grieving widow or lover in many bardic *marbhnaí*, as in the following passionate verses from *The Book of Magauran*:

> Anaibhind damh fo deachta
> a negmhais in fhir aenleaptha
> gairid li*m* lamh ri ho Cuind
> sa lamh fa*m* chind na cearchuill.
>
> Robadh gairid li*m*sa is les
> aenuir t*ara*m as taires
> t*r*uagh a Dhe os ga dul uai*m*
> gan mo chur is e a naenuaigh.

Misery it shall be for me henceforth to be without my couch-fellow; too short seemed my times with Conn's scion, his arm a pillow for my head.

Too swift in its coming did he and I feel the day when we should both be beneath the clay! Alas, O God, that he and I are not buried together so that he might not leave me![89]

This is obviously an artificial adoption of a feminine persona designed to convey sincerity, but the integrality of both the female keener and the male eulogizer to the ritualized mourning process is clear. A sixteenth-century elegy on two of the O'Haras laments the absence of either keening woman or poet at their deaths:

> (Ní fhagh)ann duine ar domhan,
> do mhnaoi ná dh'fhior ealadhan
> – dál as iongnadh don dá fhear –
> rádh na bhfionnbhan 's na bhfileadh.

No living being can hear a woman (keener) or poet reciting what fair women and poets say – a strange fate for those two heroes.[90]

Thus there is clearly a longstanding connection between the largely female keening tradition and the male, poetic one. This connection persisted in later centuries, eventually exemplified by the prominence of women themselves as composers of formal laments: several recognized seventeenth- and eighteenth-century Irish women poets, like their Scottish counterparts, were known primarily for their elegies.[91] We also know that some keening women – like Peig Nic Cuarta (descendant of seventeenth-century poet Séamus Dall Mac Cuarta) – were recognized poets in their own right.[92] One such woman, Siobhán Ní Liaghain from Sliabh gCua, County Waterford, was remembered for both her keens and her *marbhnaí foirmeálta* ('formal elegies').[93] According to John O'Daly, yet another Waterford 'poetess named Lucas ... was no less gifted than [elegist Máire Ní Dhonnagáin], but her muse was entirely devoted to keening at wakes, of which she made a regular profession and earned a sufficient livelihood by it'.[94] An Irish Folklore Commission report from County Cork, paraphrased by Gearóid Ó Crualaoich, states that the keeners 'who are especially good at crying and composing extempore verses in praise of the deceased ... are like poets in the wake house'.[95]

Taken together, the evidence suggests that the elegiac and keening traditions were at once distinct and interconnected, belonging not to specific social classes, but practised across the social spectrum, at least at some points in Ireland's cultural history. Perhaps keens were always common to all ranks, although elegies, like the songs of the recognized poets, may well have only become more common among the lower classes after the collapse of the bardic system and the greater proximity of poets to the broader community.

3. *The Death-Song*

A final category of lament-poetry complicates the picture yet again: the compositions that P. W. Joyce and Breandán Ó Madagáin, after him, have referred to as 'death-songs'. Ó Madagáin defines these as songs of lament that use *amhrán* metres, are set to common song-airs, and tend to be performed more frequently in local singing communities than either *caointe* or the more formal *marbhnaí*. They are, he says, 'In function ... not unlike English ballads, recalling, usually, some tragic happening, but having no part in the obsequies.'[96] Yet we have already seen evidence that even some non-laments, like 'Má Théid Tú 'un Aonaigh' and 'Aithreachas Chathail Bhuí', were occasionally substituted for *caointe* in the context of wakes; and apparently the opposite situation obtained, as well: that is, keens came to be performed as items of interest, apart from their original context. It seems clear, at any rate, that by the twentieth century, interchangeability of function between keens and death-songs existed in at least some communities, particularly after the practice of keening had become moribund. Nor are the poetic and musical distinctions as clear-cut as Ó Madagáin implies: there is, rather, a spectrum evident in what he classes as 'death-song', with the influence of keens at one end of the spectrum and that of formal elegies at the other, reflected to varying degrees in individual songs.

At one end of this spectrum are the songs most closely linked to the keening tradition, such 'An Bhean Chaointe' ('The Keening Woman'), 'one of the great songs of south-east Ulster'. Although composed in quatrains, it is metrically very free, employing the single final assonance of the simplest *caoineadh* forms and what Ní Uallacháin describes as a 'plaintive and chant-like' air, echoing 'the older tradition of extempore lamentation'.[97] Using many repeated lines and employing only second- and sometimes first-person references, as in wake-laments, it also features many of the motifs and turns of phrase associated with the *caoineadh os cionn coirp* – including a blessing on the dead, the reproof of a fellow-mourner for her want of respect, and the request to rise, in this case addressed not to the corpse but to the dead girl's friends and relations to assist in the burial:

> A chailín óg thall a rinn' an gáire,
> Nár fhágaidh tú an saol seo go bhfaighe tú croí cráite,
> Fá mise bheith 'g éagaoin fá mo níon na páirte,
> Bheas ag dul uaim amárach i gcórthaí clárthaí ...
>
> Éirigh, 'Eoghain, agus muscail Róise,
> 'S a Mháire na gcumann, bí tusa leofa,
> Dhéanfaidh Síle dheas an chomhra a chóiriú
> Agus cuirfi muinn Neillí bheag i ndeireadh a' tórraimh.
>
> Young girl over there who made the laughter
> May you not leave this world till your heart is tormented,
> At my lamenting my beloved daughter,
> Who will be leaving me tomorrow in a wooden coffin ...
>
> Rise up, Eoghan and wake up, Róise,
> And, dear Máire, you go with them,
> Fair Síle will prepare the coffin
> And we will bury little Nelly after the wake.[98]

'Eóin Búrcach' ('John Burke'), which dates back to at least the late eighteenth century, although rhythmically more regular and set to a straightforward song melody, is still extremely reminiscent of the *caoineadh*, with its repeated formulaic phrases, its single assonance per line and its continuous use of the vocative case. The song consists of a dialogue between a mother and daughter and contains many of the conventional themes and phrases of the keen, including the request of the other women present at the wake to 'druidigídh thart' ('draw near') and the injunction directed at an inattentive 'bean ud thall atá ag déanamh gáire' ('that woman laughing over there') to exhibit proper respect.[99]

Closer to *marbhnaí* are songs like 'Caoine ar Liam Ó Rinn', 'Sagart na Cúile Báine' and 'Caoineadh Uí Cheallaigh Chluain Leathan', which possess many of the hallmarks of the formal elegy. Some of these elegiac songs are also by known poets, such as Seán Ó Tuama, Antaine Raiftearaí and Máire Bhuí Ní Laoghaire, a fact that reinforces the status of these songs as a species of post-bardic *marbhna*. Some employ third-person narrative, either in part or in whole, and are more prone to rhythmic and assonantal regularity than the first group.

Some songs in this class, like 'Sagart na Cúile Báine' ('The Fair-Haired Priest') recall the common elegiac convention of grief reflected by disruption of the natural order:

Níorbh ionadh liom féin dá lasfadh an t-aer,
    Is na réaltaí chomh dubh le hairní,
An dealramh ón ngréin 's an ghealach í féin,
    Ó cailleadh ceann seasta na háite;
Paidir is cré an dá aspal déag,
    In onóir do Rí na Glóire,
Gan sinn a chur i gcré nó go mínítear an scéal
    Ar shagart na cúile báine.

I would not be surprised if the sky were on fire,
    And the stars turned as black as sloes,
The light gone from the sun and the moon itself,
    Since the head of the place has perished;
A prayer and the Apostle's Creed
    In honour of the King of Glory,
That we should not die until all is explained
    About the priest with the golden hair.[100]

'Caoine ar Liam Ó Rinn', in *caoineadh* metre, employs other equally conventional elegiac images, including the reference to keening women and to the martyred Rockite as noble 'rider':

Tá mná tí ag screadaigh i ngleanntaibh Uíbh Laoghaire,
Agus smúit go talamh ar mo Bharra bhreá naofa
I ndiaidh an mharcaigh seo do cailleadh go déannach
Is é Liam Ó Rinn, mo mhíle léan é!

Women are wailing in the glens of Iveleary,
And my beloved Gougane Barra is all covered with clouds.
All because of this hero lately departed,
For William Ring, my thousand-fold grief.[101]

Meanwhile, Raiftearaí's highly conventional 'Caoineadh Uí Cheallaigh Chluain Leathaní' ('Lament for O'Kelly of Cloonlahan') is, except for its use of a popular air, essentially a post-bardic *marbhna*, the dead patron's absence again reflected in the natural world:

Níl drúcht i gCluain Leathan ná féar
    Is ní ghaireann ann éan ná cuach,
Tá an duilliúir ag imeacht i léig
    Is na cranna ag éagaoin fuaicht;
Níl grian, níl gealach ar aer
    Is ní lasann aon réalta suas,
Ó síneadh Ó Ceallaigh in sa gcré,
    An fear soineanta séimh bhí suairc.

There's no dew nor grass on Cluan Leathan,
    And no bird or cuckoo calls there,
The leaves are all dying away,

> And the trees are complaining of cold;
> There is no sun, no moon up above,
> And not one star lights up the skies,
> Since O'Kelly was stretched in the clay,
> That gentle, gay, light-hearted man.[102]

Still other songs (some employing second-person – combined with third-person – speech), are more reminiscent of the personal elegy. Such a song is 'Donncha Bán', which recalls keening practices, but in a far more removed, stylized fashion than in our first examples, describing the disarray of the bereaved, keening woman who has travelled on foot to the site of her beloved's death:

> Tá mé ag teacht ar feadh na hoíche,
> mar bheadh uainín i measc seilbhe caorach,
> mo bhrollach oscailte is mo cheann liom scaoilte,
> is cá bhfaighinn mo dheartháirín romhan ach sínte …
>
> 'S a Dhonncha Bháin, nach é sin an buaireamh
> 's a fheabhas 's d'iomprófá spoir agus buatais;
> churfinn éadach faiseanta ort den éadach ba bhuaine
> is chuirfinn amach tú mar mhac duine uasail.
>
> All through the night I have made my way
> like a little lamb through droves of sheep,
> my bosom open and my hair let loose
> to find my brother stretched before me.
>
> And, Donncha Bán is it not a heartbreak
> – how well you wore the boots and spurs!
> I'd dress you in fashions of cloth enduring
> and send you out like a great man's son.[103]

Another striking example of a personal elegy that became absorbed into the greater song tradition is 'Úna Bhán', a seventeenth-century lament (possibly superimposed onto an older original) on the death of the daughter of a Cromwellian soldier. A twentieth-century version from oral tradition runs:

> A Úna Bhán a bhláth na ndlaoi ómra
> Thar éis do bháis de bharr droch-chomhairle
> Féach a ghrá cé acu ab fhearr den dá chomhairle
> A éin gcliabháin, is mé in Áth na Donóige.
>
> O Úna Bhán, my flower of the amber tresses,
> Gone to your death because of bad advice
> See my love which one were the better counsel,
> O bird in a cage and I in the Ford of Donogue.[104]

Although Ó Madagáin claims that the versions of this song that employ the chantlike lament music we have seen associated with elegies can be distinguished from the versions using a more common song-air – the first being a 'lament', the second a 'death-song' – both are (or have been) in the general repertoire and both are usually performed in the context of entertainment rather than that of either funeral or memorial. Furthermore, while many such popular elegies possess melodies that could be described as 'plaintive' or 'mournful', this is not invariably the case. As Ó Madagáin comments, 'As the bardic tradition faded, even in memory, the learned or semi-learned poets began to use ordinary song-tunes for the *marbhna*'. He notes that even a well-known poet like Seán Ó Tuama used the common air 'Ar Éirinn Ní Neosainn Cé hÍ' for his 1754 elegy on Seán Clárach Mac Domhnaill.[105] Thus, while the settings of these latter-day *marbhnaí* or elegiac 'death-songs' bear a greater melodic similarity to the ordinary airs of the traditional repertoire and may thus be placed in a general functional category as 'community entertainment', their poetic and thematic affinities reflect the older, professional lament tradition.

There are, certainly, many laments less stylistically related to either *marbhnaí* or *caointe*, such as songs memorializing boating disasters – like 'Bádaí na Scadán' ('The Herring Boats') or Raiftearaí's 'Anach Cuain', a lament on a drowning tragedy in Loch Corrib in 1828 – for which the term 'death-song' is perhaps the most apt. Yet others seem to fall more in the centre of the spectrum I have proposed. For example, 'Caoineadh na dTrí Muire' ('The Lament of the Three Marys'), a religious song of uncertain age, utilizes many of the conventions of the keen – including the motif of the 'three leaps' (also found in 'Donncha Bán' and *Caoineadh Airt Uí Laoghaire*) – as well as a depiction of the Virgin herself as a *bean chaointe*. Structurally, it employs a keen-like refrain ('Och ón ó agus och ón eile'), an extremely simple and chantlike melody and, despite its more regular rhythm, a simple single-assonance *caoineadh* metre.[106] Yet its formal, detached style distinguishes it from actual keening songs like 'Eóin Búrcach' or 'An Bhean Chaointe'. 'Fill a Rún', an eighteenth-century song well-attested in tradition is another case in point. It is the lament of a woman for her son, Doiminic Ó Dónaill, who 'turned' from a priest to a Protestant minister.[107] The song employs an *amhrán* metre, but takes the form of a *beochaoineadh*, or 'living keen', of the kind noted at leave-takings.[108] It is usually set to a close relative of the basic keening melody regularly employed by Labhrás Ó Cadhla of Waterford – a melody that in turn bears a strong resemblance to several other keening airs.[109] The use of a keening melody for a *beochaoineadh* – a form that has literary as well as popular precursors – in the context of a self-consciously composed lyric, gives the song the flavour of both a keen and of a quasi-literary composition.[110]

This indeterminacy of form reinforces the sense of a convergence or continuum of traditions, oral and literary, vernacular and elite, elegiac and ritualistic, that has existed in the realm of lament poetry since at least the eighteenth century; while the use of religious songs like 'Caoineadh na dTrí Muire', rowing songs like 'Amhrán Iomartha', and love songs like 'Má Théid Tú 'un Aonaigh' in the context of wakes blurs the already unclear distinctions between keens, elegies and 'death-songs' even further because of their functional interchangeability. Whether this reflects the historical interrelationship of musical lament traditions or their gradual assimilation into hybrid forms as the *caoineadh* and formal elegiac traditions waned is a question which may be impossible to answer within the bounds of our current knowledge.

II. *Caoineadh Airt Uí Laoghaire (The Lament for Art O'Leary)*

We have seen with all three categories so far discussed – the *marbhna*, the *caoineadh* and the more broadly defined 'death-song' – not only the parallels but the interaction between the elite, literary tradition and the vernacular, oral tradition. We have also seen that it is in the distinctions between the *caoineadh* and the *marbhna* that the greatest confusion can arise, and this is ultimately the area of dispute between the written and oral camps in the current debate about the origins of Irish laments.

Participants in the debate can be divided into roughly three groups: first, those who believe that most extant lament texts in the simpler *caoineadh* metres represent orally-performed or even orally-composed laments, generally categorizing only the most poetically sophisticated compositions in both syllabic or stress metres as *marbhnaí*; second, those who contend that all extant texts represent literary elegies; and third, those who believe that, while the texts of many keens are oral compositions, specific items – particularly *Caoineadh Airt Uí Laoghaire*, Eibhlín Dubh Ní Chonaill's famous lament on the death of her husband (murdered by Abraham Morris in 1773) – are a species of literary elegy, or *marbhna*. This section will discuss the arguments of the advocates of these three viewpoints, examining the relative strengths and weaknesses of their positions.

The most prominent proponents of the first perspective – that is, of viewing laments in the simpler *caoineadh* metres principally in the context of the oral tradition – are Angela Bourke and Seán Ó Coileáin; although many others, including Patricia Lysaght, Breandán Ó Madagáin, Tomás Ó hAilín and Rachel Bromwich, have expressed similar views. Such scholars, many of whom have wide experience of traditional Irish culture, call attention to external and internal evidence of both the oral performance of keens and of their impromptu composition.

The external evidence for oral composition, describing the act of keening as well as its content and form, comes from a 'mixed bag of historical, literary and folklore sources', both native and foreign, Irish and non-Irish-speaking, from the early nineteenth century to the present time.[111] The majority of these sources, however – including not only outside observers but also numerous informants for the Irish Folklore Commission – attest to the improvisational nature of keens. O'Curry, writing in 1873, describes the keen for the young man whose wake he witnessed as having been 'improvised' and goes on to state that, 'Sometimes the panegyric on the deceased was begun by one and continued by another, and so on, as many as three or four taking part in the improvisation.'[112] It is clear that John O'Donovan (who called them 'the real outpourings of untutored Nature')[113] also viewed keens as an improvised form – as did John Donaldson, Mr and Mrs Hall, J. M. Synge, P. W. Joyce and many other nineteenth-century commentators. Closer to our own time, scholars like Breandán Ó Madagáin, Tomás Ó hAilín, Seán Ó Súilleabháin and Patricia Lysaght have published descriptions of keening gleaned from ethnographic interviews, many of which contain examples of the 'texts' reportedly performed. Recorded re-enactments are much rarer for a number of reasons, including the belief that keening outside the context of a wake causes bad luck: at least one death has been attributed to this practice.[114] And although in the course of my own fieldwork I found few people who had witnessed keening and none who could remember any specific keens, John Ó Duibheannaigh, of Ranafast, County Donegal, was able to tell me that in his parents' time keens were still being performed and composed *ar an bhómaite* ('on the spot').[115] Noting the difficulties encountered in the attempt of twentieth-century folklorists to elicit keens from their informants, Breandán Ó Madagáin recounts a fortuitous meeting he had with a man who was reminded by Ó Madagáin's performance of a segment of *Caoineadh Airt Uí Laoghaire* of his own mother's keening. 'Oh!' he said, 'You reminded me of my mother and she keening my little brother who had died as a child, and later her keening my own father when he died long ago, and her own father and mother, my Grandfather and my Grandmother. That was exactly how she did it.'[116] This testimony strongly suggests that the performance and repertoire of *caointe* recorded by Joyce, Petrie, de Noraidh and Ó Cadhla (on whom Ó Madagáin has drawn for his own performances of *Caoineadh Airt Uí Laoghaire*) were not atypical, either in style or in content – although it does not provide any evidence about the compositional method involved.

As I have already observed, several prominent keening women were also recognized poets, and many descriptions of *mná caointe* testify to their skills as improvisatory composers. Such fluency was, as many have observed, a particular gift; yet even some non-professionals seemed to rise to the occasion in times of stress, judging from descriptions of some impromptu laments.[117] As noted above, however, sometimes set pieces rather than (or perhaps in addition to) improvised keens were performed at wakes; and although it is assumed that this practice reflects the decline of the keening tradition, lack of earlier evidence prevents us from making any definitive statement on the matter. P. W. Joyce, commenting on the tradition in County Limerick, observed that:

There are usually in a neighbourhood, two or three women, who are skilled beyond others in keening, and who make a practice of attending at wakes and funerals. These often pour forth over the dead person, a lament in Irish – partly extempore, partly prepared – delivered in a kind of plaintive recitative; and at the conclusion of each verse, they lead a choral cry in which the others who are present join, repeating throughout, 'Och-ochone!' or some such words.[118]

Of particular interest are Joyce's words 'partly extempore, partly prepared', a phrase that suggests several possibilities: a) that part of the keen was memorized in advance, the rest being improvised; b) that some keens were improvised and others memorized; or c) that set phrases were combined in keens with newly composed material. Crofton Croker seemed to believe that some keeners fully memorized their material while others employed a greater degree of improvisation. He describes a Mrs Harrington, a professional keener from south-west Cork whom he met in 1818, as having had an 'extraordinary' memory, and he clearly believed her to recite rather than to improvise her verse. According to Croker, she was 'dignified and solemn in her manner ... and the clearness, quickness and elegance with which she translated from Irish into English, though unable to read or write was almost incredible.' As in Francis Keane's account, he noted that she began by mumbling briefly before beginning her recitation,

> probably the beginning of each stanza, to assure herself of the arrangement, with her eyes closed, rocking her body backwards and forwards, as if keeping time to the measure of the verse. She then began in a kind of whining recitative, but as she proceeded and the composition required it, her voice assumed a variety of deep and fine tones, and the energy with which many passages were delivered proved her perfect comprehension and strong feeling of the subject.[119]

Croker contrasts Mrs Harrington's approach to that of Mrs Leary, another professional keening woman of the neighbourhood, who, while her 'memory was much less retentive', possessed a 'wonderfully rapid utterance'. Croker believed that Mrs Leary was at her best when she performed 'completely independent of memory', for 'her extemporaneous verses, which in cases of a break down she fluently supplied, always appeared to me to be far superior to those she had learned and attempted to repeat. She seldom succeeded in getting beyond three or four [memorized] verses, but if urged to proceed would improvise interminably.' Mrs Harrington, on the other hand, had, in Croker's view, 'adopted an artificial system for the arrangement of her thoughts and ... had studied the keen as a poetical composition'.[120]

Unfortunately, while all of this is tantalizing in its implications, it is also – like Joyce's phrase 'partly extempore, partly prepared' – ambiguous in its application. This is particularly true in relation to Mrs Harrington's performance, which may also have been at least partly improvised: the mumbling, for example, as Seán Ó Coileáin suggests, might have indicated a means of establishing 'the particular vowel assonance and final cadence to be observed in the remainder' of each passage.[121] Yet it is equally possible that she had indeed memorized all or part of her text. While Croker does not appear to have asked either woman for a description of her own performance, it is nonetheless clear that he had ascertained that some of Mrs Leary's 'text' was improvised. Whether her less successful recitation from memory represented an unusually bad performance or something she was only attempting at Croker's request, however, he fails to tell us.

As to how such improvisation could be achieved, the Halls may have been prescient in their observation that:

> The Irish language, bold, forcible, and comprehensive, full of the most striking epithets and idiomatic beauties, is peculiarly adapted for either praise or satire – its blessings are singularly touching and expressive, and its curses wonderfully strong, bitter, and biting. The rapidity and ease with which both are uttered, and the epigrammatic force of each concluding stanza of the keen, generally bring tears to the eyes of the most indifferent spectator, or produce a state of terrible excitement ... It is altogether extemporaneous; and it is sometimes astonishing to observe with what facility the keener will put the verses together and shape her poetical images to the case of the person before her.[122]

To those acquainted with the oral-formulaic theory, these descriptions are all highly suggestive. Ó Coileáin argues that we can detect the use of such a formulaic system in the composition of keens, deduced both from descriptive accounts of keens and from the surviving texts themselves. Certainly such depictions as Joyce's, Croker's and the Halls', with their emphasis on their subjects' 'wonderfully rapid utterance', the 'rapidity and ease' of their improvisations, with their 'epigrammatic force', are strikingly similar not only to descriptions of Lord's *guslars* but also to other instances of improvised verse in the Irish tradition.

Breandán Ó Buachalla has pointed out that the simpler forms of *caoineadh* metre lend themselves particularly well to genres such as the lullaby, prayer, satire and *agallamh beirte* – an improvised disputation in verse, especially popular in Munster. Noting its non-stanzaic form and its unornamented, simple rhyme and metric scheme, he finds 'gur oir sin cinnte don chaint ghearr, don aisfhreagra, don deisbhéalaí – agus don saothar a samhlaíodh a bheith a chumadh *ex tempore* [that it is certainly suited to short utterances, to retorts, to witticisms – and to work that would appear to be composed extemporaneously]'.[123] We also have evidence that work songs (for spinning, churning, ploughing, etc.) were often improvised, and many of these employ some version of the *caoineadh* metre.[124] An interesting connection between keens or elegies and some lullabies and occupational songs is the apparent interchangeability of certain refrains among these genres. For example, the refrain 'Seo-tho binn, binn, binn', commonly associated with lullabies, is found in one version of Diarmuid Ó Sé's *Marbhna Mhic Fínín Duibh*, while the *í ú í ú í ú* chorus used for Seán na Ráithíneach's elegy is also employed in milking songs like 'Crónán na Bó'.[125]

As far as the oral 'formula' itself is concerned, it is easy to identify not only frequently repeated epithets like 'mo ghrá is mo chumann tú' or 'céard a dhéanfas mé', but also more complicated formulaic patterns, including 'extended passages with parallel syntax'.[126] A complex example of such a pattern is evident in a keen published by John O'Donovan in the 1850s, composed for John O'Brien by the dead man's sister, featuring striking incremental repetition:

Tosóidh mé ag an talamh leat:	I will begin at the ground with you:
Bhí dhá chois dheasa agat,	You had two shapely legs,
Dhá cheathrú gheala agat,	Two white thighs,
Com seang cailce agat ...	A slender chalk-white waist ...
Súil chaoin ghlas agat,	A gentle grey eye,
Tré a dtug na mná taitneamh duit,	For which the women loved you,
A Sheáin! Ó!	Oh John! Oh![127]

The argument for this kind of formularity seems to be further strengthened by the appearance of whole lines from keens known to have existed previously, although some see this only as evidence that the lines have been plagiarized from 'fixed' originals. But in his analysis of this phenomenon in *Caoineadh Airt Uí Laoghaire* (*The Lament for Art O'Leary*), while Seán Ó Coileáin concedes the possibility that some lines from *Caoineadh Dhiarmada Mhic Eoghain na Toinne*, for example, could have been imported into Eibhlín Ní Chonaill's lament, he thinks it likelier, given the widespread nature of the conventions included in such lines, that such phrases belong not to a specific predecessor but – like the 'floating' lines and verses of lyric songs – to the tradition in general.[128] Certainly lines like 'A Eibhlín, éirigh id sheasamh' and 'Éirigh suas anois' have striking counterparts in laments collected in tradition, including ones I have noted above, such as, 'Éirigh, 'Eoghain, agus muscail Róise' or 'Éirigh suas id' sheasamh/A's gaibh do sheisreach capall!'[129] But Ó Coileáin displays his most convincing stylistic evidence for the oral-formulaic composition of *Caoineadh Airt Uí Laoghaire* in his comparison of discrete performances of the lament recorded possibly as many as fifty years apart from its principal source, a professional keener named Norry Singleton.[130] Although Cullen casts doubt on the transcription of two separate performances, suggesting that the variations could instead be scribal artefacts,[131] the possibility is still real enough to entertain Ó Coileáin's argument, especially in the light of similarities in the kinds of variation found in other keening texts. Ó Coileáin demonstrates the flexibility of the formulaic technique by pointing out what he calls 'internal and external variation' between the two versions. Instances of external variation feature the use or omission of extraneous material, as when, for example, Eibhlín's defence against accusations of her husband's parsimony is extended in one version, or when her meeting with Art at the market-house is missing in one version and present in the other. Internal variation includes the use of incremental formularity, as well as the interchangeability of lines or stanzas within the lament. It also includes the transposition of words within a phrase – for example, 'rumanna a *mbreacadh* domh' ('rooms painted for me') interchanged with 'seomraí a *nglanadh* domh'('rooms cleaned for me') – where both employ the same rhythmic and assonantal pattern and fulfill the same metric and conceptual functions. Ó Coileáin quotes the following passages to illustrate these variations:

Version 1:
Mo chara do daingean tu!
Lá dá bhfaca thu,
Ag ceann tí an mhargaidh,
Do thug mo shúil aire dhuit.
Is thug mo chroí taitneamh dhuit,
D'éalaíos óm charaid leat,
I bhfad ó bhaile leat.
Is domhsa nárbh atuirseach:
Do chuiris parlús dá ghealadh dhom,
Rúmanna dá mbreacadh dhom,
Bácús dá dheargadh dhom,
Bríc dá ceapadh dhom,
Róst ar bhearaibh dom, srl.

My steadfast friend!
On the day that I saw you
At the gable of the market-house
My eye heeded you,
And my heart loved you,
I eloped from my people with you,
Far from home with you.
I had no reason for regret:
You had a parlour brightened for me,
Rooms decorated for me,
An oven reddened for me,
Bread baked for me,
Roast on spits for me, etc.

Version 2:
Mo chara go daingean tu,
Do thug mo shúil aire dhuit
Do thug mo chroí taitneamh duit
Is d'éalaíos óm charaid leat.
Is domsa nárbh aithreach:
Do chuiris parlús dá ghealadh dhom
Seomraí dá nglanadh dhom,
Bácús dá dheargadh dhom,
Bríc dá ceapadh dhom,
Róst dá breacadh dhom, srl.

My steadfast friend!
My eye heeded you,
My heart loved you,
I eloped from my people with you,
I had no reason for regret:
You had a parlour brightened for me,
Rooms cleaned for me,
An oven reddened for me,
Bread baked for me,
Roast browned for me, etc.[132]

But do these variations, or, indeed formularity itself, necessarily signify improvisational composition? Or, in the manner of other traditional singers, might Norry Singleton simply have recomposed, consciously or otherwise, the lament during the intervening years, employing the conventional phraseology and structure of the genre? Or, indeed, like Scottish ballad-singer Anna Gordon, might she have provided two wholly discrete versions on separate occasions?[133] Certainly both lie within the realm of possibility, and it can also be argued that formulae can be found in any kind of traditional verse, as well as in much literary poetry, and do not necessarily reflect orality. Ruth Finnegan cites Anglo-Saxon scholar L. D. Benson as having shown that a highly formulaic style characterizes not only the "oral" epic of *Beowulf* but also ... some *written* compositions in Old English, including Old English translations from Latin originals'. Benson concludes that, 'To prove that an Old English poem is formulaic is only to prove that it is an Old English poem.'[134] But, as a number of scholars have noted, much of this argument depends upon the definition of 'formula'. For example, those scholars who sought to transform ballad commonplaces into Parry-Lord-style formulae not only broadly and simplistically defined the term 'formula', but ignored the recognition by previous ballad scholars of the use of recurrent phrases and epithets in the genre – as well as the use of words like 'oral', 'formula', 'form' and 'recreation' in their analyses of ballads as *memorized* texts.[135] They also ignored the remarkable stability of ballad texts, as opposed to the equally remarkable variability of the oral-formulaic texts identified by Lord and Rosenberg.

Breandán Ó Buachalla, the most vocal skeptic of the keen as oral poetry, argues that all lament poetry is a species of memorial or elegiac and essentially 'literary' poetry, whether orally or scribally transmitted. He also contests the application of the oral-formulaic theory to the genre, insisting that since the form does not answer to the 'strong version' of the theory it cannot be used at all. Ó Buachalla takes Parry and Lord at their word when they assert that formulas are not simply 'characteristic' of oral poetry but wholly 'pervasive'. He quotes Parry as placing the amount of formulaic material in orally improvised texts at ninety per cent, noting that the amount of formulaic phrases or lines in *Caoineadh Airt Uí Laoghaire* only comes to roughly twenty-five per cent of the total text, as edited by Seán Ó Tuama in 1961.[136] Parry's percentage, however, is based on Yugoslavian samples, which are both much longer and more numerous than the Irish ones; nor does Ó Tuama's text include all lines collected in oral tradition. Even more to the point is Rosenberg's observation that:

> The basis for understanding the composition of oral poetry ... is not the formula but the formulaic system, the verbal mold into which a variety of words are poured, but which remains relatively consistent through similarities of diction, syntax, accent, or alliteration ... Whether, therefore, two closely related groups of words are formulas by the strictest application of the Parry definition is secondary to the way in which the work of Parry and many psycholinguists has enabled us to understand the relationship of such word groups – originally in the mind of the speaker/singer/preacher.[137]

Given the close correspondence of sense, rhyme and the metrical function of the variant lines quoted above, 'keener' could arguably be added to this category. Pointing out that what constitutes an oral formula will necessarily vary from one genre to another, Rosenberg notes that 'each poetry that employs oral formulas must have its different kind of formulas and systems to meet the specific demands of the poetry'.[138] Furthermore, even if a given lament text contained – or consisted entirely – of memorized material, it would be fallacious to generalize about the genre on the basis of one example and thus to dismiss the oral-formulaic technique as a possible mode of composition within the keening tradition as a whole.

Ó Buachalla also dismisses variation – accepted universally by folklorists and by anthropologists and linguists as diverse as Albert Lord, Ruth Finnegan and John Miles Foley as a typical if not a defining feature of oral poetry[139] – in relation not only to *caointe* but all other poetry known from manuscript in the Irish tradition. He argues that since we find variation in both oral and manuscript versions of poems from the eighteenth and nineteenth centuries, distinctions between the two media are meaningless, as the 'fixed text' does not exist in either the oral or written tradition. We have already seen arguments in the context of medieval manuscripts that scribal variations may have represented not different 'recensions' of a given text, but – as Edgar Slotkin and others have maintained – fluid 'multiforms', demonstrating 'the betwixt and between' nature of medieval Irish literature, in which its practitioners (including scribes) were meant to be masters of both the oral and written idioms.[140] It is quite possible that this mentality also obtained in later centuries, as Alan Bruford has argued in relation to prose romances.[141] Yet while it is likely that some measure of flexibility always existed in scribal practice, it is still not established that more recent scribes enjoyed the same amount of latitude as did their medieval predecessors. The stability of many eighteenth- and nineteenth-century texts (including those of lyric songs) transcribed by individual scribes over time indicates greater consistency than variation; although in some cases, slight variations seem to be due to a scribe's attempt to correct deficiencies or omissions in his initial transcription.[142] The scribe may also have simply made mistakes in transcription, especially if he was depending on memory and/or oral performance. And since many nineteenth-century texts were transcribed from oral sources, it is probable that – the issue of composition technique aside – variation in oral performances accounts for a good number of the discrepancies found in manuscripts of eighteenth-century song texts.[143]

While Ó Buachalla describes the simpler *caoineadh* metres as particularly suited to oral, often extemporized verse forms like the *agallamh beirte*, the lullaby or (in Scotland) the waulking song, he ultimately dismisses any poetic distinctions between these forms and more intricate compositions in the metre. He emphasizes the fact that recognized poets in the seventeenth and eighteenth centuries utilized *caoineadh* in both complex and simple, even irregular forms, for laments as well as for other genres; and he cites examples of 'keens' reputedly performed in the context of wakes that reflect greater metrical complexity than is usually associated with the genre.[144] Specifically, he notes that some elegies by known poets, like Séamas Carthún's 1659 *Deorchaoineadh na hÉireann*, are even less regular than the non-stanzaic *marbnaí* in *caoineadh* metre we have already instanced above (in this case, maintaining only one final assonance from line to line); that some laments presented in the literature as oral *caointe* are formally complex, employing a consistent x-x-y – as opposed to the simpler-y – assonantal pattern, sometimes with di-syllabic assonances in the final foot; and that others, like the keen described by O'Donovan as having been performed by John O'Brien's sister over her brother's corpse, combine a short single-stress line, with no stanzaic breaks (the incremental description, quoted above, p. 95) with the following, more complex x-x-y quatrain:[145]

> Ba dheas é do chom i ngabhal an chéachta,
> Ba dheas í do shliasaid i ndiallaid chraorag,
> Ba bhreá é do sheasamh ar mhargadh's ar aonach
> Och a Sheáin, mo ghrá ná tréig sinn.
>
> Fine was your waist in the fork of the plough,
> Fine was your thigh in the crimson saddle,
> Splendid was your presence at the market or fair
> Och, John, my love, do not forsake us.[146]

Comparing the Irish and the Scottish situations, Ó Buachalla concludes that:

> An próiseas sin a tharla in Albain – meadaracht a samhlaíodh ó thús le haicme íseal shóisialta is le seánra míghradamúil ag teacht 'aníos' is á cur in ócáid ag filí aitheantúla – tharla a leithéid chéanna in Éirinn i gcás na meadarachta céanna. Mar cé gur le mná, mná anaithnid gan seasamh sóisialta go háirithe, agus lena gcuid caointe a samhlaíodh meadaracht 'Caoine Airt Uí Laoire' ó thús, ní i saothar na mban caointe ná i seánra an chaoine amháin a fhaightear an mheadaracht sin. Mar atá léirithe cheana, bhí an mheadaracht le fáil coitianta sa litríocht bhéil i dtús na haoise i gcúige Mumhan i seánraí difriúla, i bpaidreacha, i suantraithe, in agallaimh beirte, mar shampla ... Cé nach meadaracht lárnach an fhoirm áirithe sin i saothar aon duine de na filí aitheantúla a bhain earraíocht aisti, fós níor scorn leo í a úsáid, pé cúlra liteartha nó sóisialta a bhí aici nó a samhlaíodh léi.

> The same process that happened in Scotland – a metre associated from the beginning with a low social class and an undistinguished genre 'coming up from below' and occasionally being used by recognized poets – happened in Ireland in the case of the same metre. Yet although it is with women, anonymous women without particular social status and their keening, that the metre of *Caoine Airt Uí Laoire* was associated from the first, this metre is found not only in the works of keening women nor only in the genre of the keen. For as I have already explained, the metre was common in oral literature at the beginning of the century in Munster in different genres, in prayers, in lullabys, in *agallaimh beirte*, for example ... Although this particular form was not a central metre in the work of the recognized poets who made use of it, neither did they scorn to use it, whatever its literary or social background.[147]

This passage reveals an inconsistency – or at least an ambiguity – in Ó Buachalla's position. On the one hand, he posits the vernacular, oral and even improvisatory quality of the simpler forms of *caoineadh* metre in its pre-literary incarnation – largely on the basis of its inherent simplicity and flexibility – and describes the subsequent cultivation by literary poets of this originally 'lower' form. On the other hand, he seems to dismiss the presence of these arguably 'oral' qualities in the extant examples of *caointe*. Emphasizing that the existing texts constitute a 'speictream leathan ilghnéitheach [a broad, heterogeneous spectrum]'[148] and demonstrating the range of style and content within this spectrum – similar to my discussion of the stylistic continuum found in the *marbhna, caoine* and death-song – he himself discerns distinct subgenres and levels of artistic complexity. However, he ascribes them all to literary composers, without admitting the possibility that any of the known texts, simple or complex, could have originated in the oral tradition. This apparent contradiction can be resolved if we look at Ó Buachalla's argument as an effort to refute any connection between poetic style and oral composition, perhaps in the mistaken belief that his scholarly opponents view all 'oral poetry' as oral-formulaic poetry.

Furthermore, the existence of a compositional 'spectrum' does not mean that no stylistic distinctions or categories ever existed or that there was no consciousness of them in the poetic or scholarly community: as we have seen, tendencies, if not hard-and-fast distinctions, have been established clearly enough by scholars for at least the past two centuries (and less directly, since the bardic period) to cause the kind of confusion Ó Muirgheasa expresses in his encounter with non-standard *marbhna* texts. What is less clear is the significance of such ambiguous stylistic interrelationships and variations: whether they arise from differences in nomenclature, practice or from an eventual merging of genres – or indeed, from a combination of all of these factors.

In any case, this stylistic heterogeneity does not preclude oral performance or even composition during the funeral ritual; although whether O'Brien's sister's mixed-measure keen was an instance of the use of 'partly *extempore*, partly prepared' material, or of wholly prepared or memorized verse; or whether she could have improvised the more formal quatrain, as well – is impossible to establish. But metrically sophisticated improvisational verse has certainly been reported from the Irish tradition. Suggesting that much of the verse arising from poetic 'conventions' or courts of poetry held in taverns must have been improvised, Pádraig Breatnach cites a poem by Séamus Mac Coitir, preceded in the manuscript by the information that it was 'Composed ex tempore by Mr. James Cotter aforesaid at a conference in Buttevant about the year 1760'.[149] Breandán Ó Madagáin discusses instances of improvisation by eighteenth- and nineteenth-century poets like Tomás Rua Ó Súilleabháin, Diarmuid Ó Sé and Pádraig Ó Crualaoi, as well as by lesser-known local composers like Máire Chonnachtach Ní Dhomhnaill, of whom Séamus Mac Grianna remarked:

> Bhí buaidh ar leith aici. Thiocfadh rann cheoil léithe comh réidh is thiocfadh comhrádh le duine eile. Rud ar bith a n-abóraidhe léithe, thiocfadh léithe, dá mba mhian léithe é, freagar a thabhairt i gceól sa bhomaite air.

> She had a special gift. A verse of song would come to her as easily as ordinary speech to another person. Anything that was said to her, she would be able, if she wished, to reply to it in *ex tempore* song.[150]

Other, more recent, reports from both Ireland and Scotland exist of ordinary people also extemporizing songs;[151] and I myself, while not privy to specific texts, have heard stories of extemporized verse composed within living memory: both Neilí Ní Dhómhnaill and John Ó Duibheannaigh told me of hearing the Mac Grianna brothers of Ranafast, County Donegal, conversing in improvised poetry. Thus, while the co-existent, heterogeneous forms Ó Buachalla cites may in many cases represent literary compositions, his examples ultimately neither reinforce nor refute the possibility of either vernacular or oral composition in lament poetry as a whole.

Ultimately, without the kind of direct evidence provided by scholars like Lord and Rosenberg, who had the advantage of witnessing numerous performances of the poetry they studied and of interviewing the performers themselves, it cannot be proved retrospectively that oral-formulaic practice played a role in the composition of Irish laments. But neither can Ó Buachalla's claim that we are dealing solely with formally composed elegiac material, unrelated to the ritual keening tradition. In the absence of more convincing evidence, Ó Coileáin's theory is still tenable. For while, as Albert Friedman has warned, to argue strictly from style to function in traditional song 'is a tricky business',[152] the possibility of composing and recomposing in the manner Ó Coileáin suggests – especially in the presence of widespread testimony of keens *as* an improvised form – is at least plausible, and it offers a valuable insight into how such improvisation *might* have been achieved in the Irish lament tradition.

While Ó Buachalla eventually concedes that *caointe* were subject to oral as well as written delivery (although, at least in the texts we possess, not as part of the funeral ritual), he still places his greatest emphasis on their written rather than their oral nature – their status as *dánta* – viewing eighteenth-century verse primarily as poetry, to be read from the page in the context of a literary environment. In his discussion of *Caoineadh Airt Uí Laoghaire*, he comments:

> Dán é a bhfuil eiseadh fós aige, dar liomsa pé scéal é, sa tslí chéanna a bhfuil eiseadh ag 'Mac an Cheannaí', 'An Bonnán Buí', 'Im Aonar Seal', 'Dónall Óg', 'Gile mo Chroí' nó aon dán eile de chuid an ochtú haoise déag a thaitníonnn liom is a thugann sásamh dom – is iad á *léamh* agam arís is arís eile. Chomh fada linne agus ár dtadhallna le filíocht na haoise sin, is i bhfad i ndiaidh a cumtha thagaimidne uirthi, de ghnáth, agus is sa chomhthéacs céanna is túisce a thagaimidne uirthi trí chéile: i lámhscríbhinní.
>
> It is a poem which still exists, in my opinion at any rate, in the same way that 'Mac an Cheannaí', 'An Bonnán Buí', 'Im Aonar Seal', 'Dónall Óg', 'Gile mo Chroí' or any other eighteenth-century poem that pleases me and gives me satisfaction exists – *to be read* again and again. As for us and our contact with the poetry of that century, we have usually come upon it long after its composition, and it is in the same context that we come upon them all earliest: in manuscripts.[153]

This literary, written emphasis extends to the issue of the musical performance of laments. Claiming that it is impossible to prove that any given keen or elegy was originally intended for musical performance, Ó Buachalla argues that the known musical contexts for both forms could simply be a latter-day practice, not reflecting previous tradition. He maintains that since we do not possess any external evidence that, for example, *Caoineadh Airt Uí Laoghaire*, was performed or sung at the time of its composition, we can assume that the musical performances of it collected in the twentieth century are simply modern adaptations, analogous to Seán Ó Riada's arrangement of Peadar Ó Doirnín's 'Mná na hÉireann' or Seán Óg Ó Tuama's setting of the medieval hymn 'Deus Meus Adiuva Me' (to which could be added Peadar Ó Riada's recent setting of *Caoineadh Airt Uí Laoghaire*).[154] Obviously, except in cases when manuscripts indicate the use of a specific melody with a set of verses, it is impossible to prove that any given poem was originally sung (or was intended to be sung), let alone that it was sung to a specific air or in a given style. Yet lack of proof for one position does not constitute substantiation of its antithesis; and the existence of a long-standing musical tradition for specific genres like the keen or the elegy lends considerable credence to the likelihood that many if not most keens and elegies were performed musically, or quasi-musically, in one form or another throughout Irish history. Ó Buachalla's argument that since our earliest records of keens are in the form of non-musical manuscripts ignores the existence of musical notations of keens published as early as 1786.[155] Yet even without these, the existence of written sources for such texts does not preclude their musical performance – any more than does the lack of musical notation for other songs in the manuscript tradition, or indeed, in chapbook songsters of the period. Knowledge of melodies was generally assumed. This may explain why Dinneen, despite writing in his preface to *Filidhe na Máighe* (*The Poets of the Maigue*) that '[the poetry] was sung everywhere and to judge it fairly it should be considered in relation to the corresponding music', he failed to provide any musical notation. Ó Madagáin quotes a song collector, when asked whether he collected music as well as words, as having replied, 'Ní gá dom sin a dhéanamh ... tá an ceol ar eolas agam': 'I don't need to do that ... I know the music.'[156] Ultimately, despite his concession that the oral and literate modes are so closely intertwined as to be indistinguishable in the Irish poetic tradition[157] – a position with which both Bourke and Ó Coileáin would undoubtedly have a good deal of sympathy – Ó Buachalla's emphasis on the literary, non-performative aspects of *caoineadh* poetry and his rejection of any extant *caoineadh* texts as part of Irish funeral rites devalues the oral and vernacular traditions and undermines the concept of an interrelationship between the two cultural spheres.

* * * *

The most widespread position of the last fifty or so years on the keening tradition, lying between the oral and written poles, is undoubtedly that taken by Seán Ó Tuama, Louis Cullen and others, who, while granting the oral nature of the *caoineadh* in general, believe that certain compositions, particularly *Caoineadh Airt Uí Laoghaire*, represent not an improvised composition but rather an after-the-fact, literary piece – one, however, that interweaves traditional oral lament features with individualistic, literate 'poetic' expression. Ó Tuama, in particular, has emphasized the importance of reading *Caoineadh Airt Uí Laoghaire* with an awareness of the oral keening tradition; and he describes extempore, traditional keening in terms not unlike those found in oral-formulaic discussions – noting, for instance, that the keening woman would draw 'from the vast storehouse of themes and formulas used traditionally on such occasions and, of course improvise on them as she proceeded with her composition'.[158] Ó Tuama lists some of the conventions common to traditional *caointe* on which he believes Eibhlín's lament draws, including the direct address to the corpse, attempts to rouse the dead man, praise of his family and the generosity of his house, the drinking of the dead man's blood and the curse on those responsible for his death.[159] On the other hand, he takes the bitter exchange between Eibhlín and her sister-in-law for probable fact rather than generic convention, and he also apparently accepts the attribution of authorship to Eibhlín herself – an attribution on which scholars like Cullen and Ó Buachalla have cast doubt.[160]

Against these traditional features, however, Ó Tuama identifies certain traits as distinguishing this lament from many of those collected in oral tradition: specifically, its sheer length, its 'aristocratic' references to wealth and luxury, its widespread value as a poetic work within the oral tradition, its energy and its freshness. Ultimately, Ó Tuama sees *Caoineadh Airt Uí Laoghaire* as the transformation of 'a widespread and archaic folk-ritual' into 'a remarkable literary utterance', an utterance that transcends the genre, translating it into 'another dimension, the dimension of poetry'.[161] Ó Buachalla has reinforced this perspective in his analysis of the metrical aspects of the lament, pointing out the richness within simplicity exemplified by *Caoineadh Airt Uí Laoghaire* and other similar lament texts in their interchange of single- to triple-stressed lines, as well as in the transposition in the line-endings of dactyls, iambs, trochees and spondees – with the implication that such variety would be unimaginable in a spontaneous oral composition.[162] Louis Cullen has raised similar objections to the possibility of the oral and vernacular origins of the *Caoineadh*. Emphasizing its length (400 lines in the Ó Tuama edition), its 'ease of language', and its evident conversance with unspecified 'classical models', he concludes that the lament was part of a 'subliterary' tradition whose very conventionality signals not oral but literary origins: a view with which Ó Buachalla is in accord. He further notes its thematic and linguistic echoes of keens like those for Richard Cox and James Cotter, which he clearly takes as part of the same 'subliterary' tradition and as evidence that the lament 'was composed by one or more persons with some acquaintance with the old literature, conceivably even drawing on written texts'.[163]

There is a certain circularity about this argument, where the proponents rest their cases primarily on the excellence of the finished product, in the belief that Eibhlín's lament is simply too *good* to be oral – too individualistic, too aristocratic, too well-wrought. Angela Bourke argues that such a view devalues oral composition, vernacular culture and women by making the assumption that all that is truly 'poetic' (i.e. expressive, individual) must be literary and written – and, in the majority of cases, written by men. She points out that the enthusiastic note sounded by so many commentators from Frank O'Connor to Seán Ó Tuama about the beauty of the lament only highlights their marvel that a woman could achieve a work of such poetic distinction.[164] Much of the consensus about the literary nature of the lament, she asserts, comes from the influence of Ó Tuama's masterful edition, which, in spite of his own demurral on the matter, has led many readers to think of it as an *Ür*-text, a thing which we not only do not possess, but which – if the lament was indeed composed improvisationally – never existed in the first place. But, as Bourke points out, some segments of the lament (notably those dealing with charges of Art's maltreatment of his wife, a common enough theme in oral *caointe* generally) have been excised from Ó Tuama's edition, perhaps because they might serve to contradict the coherent artistic and personal image of Eibhlín he is trying to portray – at the expense, however, of presenting the tradition in all its variety. Bourke is at pains to show how such editing distorts the tradition itself, while attempting to validate it by making it conform to standards closer to our notion of what comprises elite poetry. Noting that this approach 'has given rise to a false polarization between "tradition" on the one hand and "inspiration" on the other', she finds Ó Tuama 'determined to regard such a fine poem as a product of individual, aristocratic genius, working in opposition to, rather than within, the people's tradition'.[165]

Both Bourke and Ó Coileáin have further argued that the 'clamour, the spaciousness, the haughtiness of the Gaelic big house' that Ó Tuama finds 'surprising ... in such a popular-type composition', are in fact typical of lament poetry; while, as Bourke observes, other popular forms like the waulking song, the international ballad, the Yugoslavian epic and the *Märchen* 'also abound in aristocratic details'.[166] As Sarah McKibben observes, while Eibhlín '*may* have enjoyed equivalent luxury in her actual life, similar lines about riches may be found in laments across the social stratum'.[167] Meanwhile, the metrical sophistication of some of the *Caoineadh*'s passages – and, indeed, of some of the other texts that Ó Buachalla cites – is not of a type that could preclude either vernacular or oral composition, especially if we think in terms of the kind of formulaic patterns discussed above, in which, for example, a stock of interchangeable end-phrases or end-phrase patterns could be drawn upon to vary the final foot from the dactylic to the trochaic. Recognition within tradition-bearing communities of the lament's extraordinary virtuosity is reflected not only by its long life in oral tradition but in such testimony as that reported in the 1790 *Journal of the Kerry Archaeological and Historical Society*, which stated that 'the song of Mme O'Leary on the death of her husband is praised above all others'.[168] Such recognition is taken by scholars who accept the lament's essentially oral nature as evidence not of its literary origins but of its status as 'the finest surviving realization of a tradition' that is fundamentally oral and vernacular.[169]

Along with arguments from such 'internal' evidence, however, Louis Cullen adds several from his reading of the historical record: for example, that the O'Connell family would have been too anglicized by the 1770s to make Eibhlín's mastery of an Irish poetic idiom credible. Yet John A. Murphy asserts that Irish was 'still used to a surprising extent' in the political arena several decades later during the heyday of Eibhlín's nephew, Daniel, and argues for the pervasive quality of the language even in the Liberator's *milieu*, despite the probable use of English in the family's everyday life, apart from interactions with 'inferiors'.[170] In Eibhlín's time, it is arguable that English would have been more the purview of the men of the family than of the women, who would naturally have had the greatest communication with Irish-speaking servants.[171] Cullen also questions the tradition of Eibhlín's reputation as a poet (although family papers tell us that she also keened her first husband),[172] as well as the family tradition that represents her mother, Máire Dubh, as a poet in her own right, having not only made a keen for her son, but also composed other kinds of improvisational poetry, including spinning songs and riddles.[173] He views the attribution of the keen to Ó Laoghaire's widow as simply part of the conventional trappings of the genre – at least partly on the basis of his mistrust of the authority of Mrs Morgan J. O'Connell, from whom Eibhlín's and her family's poetic reputation largely derives. Finally, he questions the date of the *Caoineadh*'s composition, given several references in the lament that, as Cullen puts it, 'makes sense only if the lines were composed after acquittal of [Abraham] Morris in September', four months after the murder.[174] Ó Tuama, by contrast, does attempt to 'make sense' of the several apparent time frames of the lament by assuming incremental composition at discrete junctures and by editing them accordingly. Whether this gives them a chronological order they do not in fact possess is, again, impossible to establish. Most scholars, on both sides of the argument, agree that we have no way of knowing which, if any, of the extant passages represents the 'original text' of the lament: given the malleability of the genre and the *Caoineadh*'s life in both oral and scribal tradition, the occurrence of editing and 'interpolation' is assumed – although ideas about the sources or the extent of this 'editing' process vary from scholar to scholar. Ó Tuama, for example, asserts that, 'This kind of literature above all is a collaborative event,' adding (a little ambiguously), 'I am personally confident that Norry Singleton has transmitted most of Eibhlín Dubh's lines to us (if she herself has added a little creatively to them, that, for me, is not a critical issue).'[175] The essence of such a view, however, is compatible with Angela Bourke's contention that:

> Any singer or lamenter may add to or edit a song or lament, sing more or less of it, or otherwise vary it, but always within the scope sanctioned by other singers and by the audience. Two singers in the same community may perform very different versions of the 'same' song, each maintaining allegiance to the tradition as she has received it.[176]

Given this circumstance, and in the absence of a manuscript 'original', Ó Tuama's edition remains hypothetical and the significance of the lament's chronology largely moot.

On the other hand, there is both textual and circumstantial evidence (some of which we have already seen) that indicates the perpetuation of the 'literary keen' into the eighteenth-century and beyond – a fact that offers us a possible *via media* through this epistemological wilderness. For instance, one of the extant laments for Silbhestar Ó Súilleabháin attributed to Diarmuid Ó Sé, *Tuireamh do Mhac Fínín Duibh*, possesses the epigram, 'Diarmuid na Bolgaighe do cheap ós cionn na cómhrann' ('composed by Diarmuid na Bolgaighe over the coffin'), despite the *tuireamh*'s having post-dated the actual funeral. Indeed, the lament seems to possess several attributes of the *caoineadh*, including direct address to the deceased, simple assonantal rhyme, formulaic phrases like 'Mo chara a's mo léir thu, a mharcaigh mhodhamhail, bhéasach' ('Alas, my friend, my gentle, mannerly rider') and 'Mo chroidhe thu agus mo chumann' ('My love and my darling'), as well as references to the hospitality and wealth of the dead man:

> Éirigh it' shuidhe, a chumainn, i bhfeighil an ghnó it' fhuirinn;
> Cuir iad súd chun suidhte id' phárlúr aoibhinn cluthmhair,
> Glaoidh ar fíon gan chustum, a's ar rósta ruadh o'n dteine.
>
> Rise up, my darling and attend to your company;
> Have them seated in your comfortable pleasant parlour,
> Call for wine without duty and for a roast red from the fire.[177]

Yet within the context of the *tuireamh* as a whole, these conventions seem far less integral than they would be to a typical keen, and they are further estranged from the standard *caoineadh* by the *tuireamh*'s overall formality and descriptive range. Its elegiac rather than ritualistic character is further revealed in its mention of the burial itself as a past event.

> Mo ghradh thu agus mo chumann! Do thuit an ceo ar do thighthibh;
> Níor fhan ceol ná seinnm ag smólaigh ná ag druide.
> Do thuit do chlú chun imill; d'imthigh do cháirde ar chnocaibh;
> Tá do phobal 'na [suidhe] ó bheith de shíor ag tuirseadh,

Ag gol go fuigheach a's ag sileadh i ndiaidh phlannda bhreágh na cruinne
A fhás ós cionn gach bile d'á aoirde a éirigh duille.
Agus mar bhárr ar thubaist, nuair a nochtais Leacht na Croise,
Do ghluaiseadar na triopaill le haghaidh tu a theacht 'na gcoinnibh,
Mar do chur Chríost ort goirm go tuamba glas na lice,
A laoch na ráidhte sultmhar a chuir na céadta ó thinne,
Cá bhfuil an fear, a bhile, a bheadh le faghail it' ionad?

My love and my darling! The mist fell upon you;
The song of the blackbird and starling did not remain.
Your fame fell to the brink; your friends left for the hills;
Your people are awake, constantly tiring themselves,
Weeping bitterly for the earth's fine flower
That grew above each tree from whose height sprang leaves.
And as a crown to the tragedy, when the Memorial Cross appeared,
The branches moved in order to take you into their keeping,
As Christ summoned you to the gray tombstone,
Oh, hero of the pleasant words, who cured hundreds of their sickness,
Where is the man, oh great one, to be found in your stead?[178]

Another lament for Ó Súilleabháin appears even closer to oral *caoineadh* models, with only three metric feet and one final assonance per line. Yet despite these keen-like traits and formulaic phrases at the beginning of each irregular stanza, it contains somewhat less formulary and more lexical variety than the typical keen, and it features an unusual amount of genealogical information, more reminiscent of the *marbhna* than the *caoineadh*:

Is mór an scléip le Gallaibh
Bás ár ngroíre flatha,
Gaol na triath sin Chaisil
Is Shúilleabháin an Bhealaigh,
Í Dhonnabháin ón gCala
Is Thaidhg an Dúna daingin
Is tiarnaí fionn an Charainn,
Do riaradh bia go fairseang
Gach bliain do bhíodh go dealamh
Ar Ghaoil is ar Ghallaibh.

Great is the revelry among the English
At the death of our stallion of princes,
Relation of those lords of Cashel,
And Sullivan of Bealach,
Donovan from Cala,
And Tadhg of Dún Daingean
And the fair lords of Carann
Who would lavishly dole out food
In time of shortage
To both Gael and Gall.[179]

These features, along with the sheer proliferation and variety of laments for Mac Fínín Duibh (many if not all of which were commissioned), in both self-evidently elegiac form and in this more keen-like style, cast doubt on the use of these texts as part of the funeral proceedings, let alone as improvised over the corpse. And this case is not exceptional: Louis Cullen makes a similar point about the multiple laments for Morty Oge O'Sullivan ('a figure related to both the O'Leary and O'Connell families').[180] Other, more isolated examples also exist, such as Máire Ní Reachtagáin's 1725 lament for her brother Seoirse, composed in quatrains, employing third- rather than second-person point-of-view and possessing a chorus that amounts to a highly stylized, literary cry, reminiscent of Gormlaith's lament:

Ochón ochón ochón mo ghéarghoin!	Mourn, mourn, my heart is breaking!
Ochón ochón ochón mo théagair!	Mourn, mourn, sorrow's wakening!
Ochón ochón ochón go n-éagad!	Mourn, mourn, till death takes me!
A Sheoirse Uí Reachtagáin, m'anacair ghéar thu.	Seoirse Ó Reachtagáin, I blame you.[181]

One version of the lament for John Burke possesses 'stage directions', indicating, for example, that one passage is spoken by Burke's wife and another by her mother – despite the fact that the lament is attributed not to Burke's wife but to Máire Bhuí Ní Laoghaire.[182] In other words, even some literary keens may be seen as a kind of redaction of a portion of the public ritual.[183]

This evidence once again lends support to the existence in the lament tradition of the 'spectrum' Ó Buachalla discusses and to the 'continuum' I have advanced. Unlike Ó Buachalla's spectrum, however, the continuum I propose encompasses not merely the literary, written and memorial, but the oral, vernacular and occasional, as well. It also accommodates the scribal tradition, which in some cases was undoubtedly involved in a 'complex relationship' between manuscript versions and 'oral diffusion',[184] not unlike that which existed in the *amhrán* tradition. Viewed in this context, the existence of the 'literary keen' does not nullify that of the improvised keen. For, as we have seen, both forms could draw on the shared traditions of the *marbhna* as well as on those of the *caoineadh os cionn coirp*. Compositions like *Caoineadh Airt Uí Laoghaire*, which are not as self-evidently 'literary' as the examples just discussed and which seem to inhabit some sort of middle territory along the continuum, will probably continue to cause controversy, particularly if scholars persist in dichotomizing the tradition.

Ó Coileáin's suggestion that different 'levels of oral tradition' may have co-existed in Irish culture is compelling,[185] especially when compared to similar arguments about the 'emergence' of the *amhrán* metres or to Hugh Shields's theories about the interaction of different cultural levels in relation to Irish heroic lays.[186] For while we may indeed be able to see the workings of orality in the Irish keening tradition, what finally matters is not the oral or written, vernacular or elite origins of that tradition. Of far greater importance is our recognition of distinct aesthetic conventions in the *caoineadh*, as well as our acknowledgement that the precise origins of the tradition do not determine the genre's compatibility with either oral or vernacular culture on the one hand or elite and written culture on the other. Ultimately what is of principal significance is the *caoineadh*'s perpetuation within traditional communities, not simply because of the oral features of the form, but because its aesthetic qualities appealed to and functioned as an artistic and emotional expression of the members of those communities. Indeed, even if the *caoineadh* were shown to have had its origins wholly in upper-class, 'literary' culture, its adoption and perpetuation by the 'illiterate peasantry' would merely reflect the reality that people within largely oral, traditional communities can possess a highly developed sense of aesthetics and can themselves participate in a sophisticated form of poetic composition.

Evidence from our earliest known sources onwards points to lament traditions in Irish society that were – at least by the eighteenth century – at once oral and literate, written and performed. How broadly these traditions were shared along the social spectrum is less clear, at least until the nineteenth century, when we begin to have records of keens and elegies performed by 'the lower orders' as well as by those of higher social rank. We have also seen that conventions of even the most formal professional lament poetry can be found in community song repertoires of the past two hundred years, whether in 'traditional' death-songs, in *caointe os cionn coirp*, *marbhnaí*, or in the compositions of illiterate but manifestly 'literary' songmakers like Máire Bhuí Ní Laoghaire or Antaine Raifteraí. And even if we cannot provide absolute proof of improvisatory oral composition through the evidence of textual cues like formularity, repetition, or dialogue, the fact remains (unless we choose to reject not only the literary evidence from medieval to modern times but every eyewitness account from Croker to Ó Madagáin as spurious) that the *caoineadh* is first and foremost an oral performance genre, both as part of the actual funeral ritual and in a broader context – a fact that its satisfactoriness as literature, whether read or recited, does nothing to contradict. In this regard I fully endorse Ó Buachalla's position that we cannot and should not construct an absolute dichotomy between oral and written composition;[187] for it seems clear that the oral tradition of performed keens and the literary tradition we know from manuscripts existed side-by-side.

Visualized thus, it is easier to see the tradition as culturally comprehensive rather than exclusive. John Miles Foley, in writing of 'primary oral culture' (that is, culture, as McLuhan and Ong would have it, uncontaminated by the written word), observes that:

> oral performance draws its meaning not only from the present event but equally from the diachronic and pan-geographic tradition of which it is only an instance, the process of generating meaning [proceeding] via metonymy, *pars pro toto*. One text recalls numerous others by synecdoche, just as one phrase or scene is always embedded conceptually in the word-hoard, in the experience of tradition.[188]

In the Irish example, this is just as true of post-literate culture, for as Gearóid Ó Crualaoich has pointed out, 'Notwithstanding that the majority of the Irish population could not, until relatively recently (*c.* 150 years ago), write or read in any language, Irish culture had, simultaneously, been a literate culture for at least 1500 years.' The traditional Irish storyteller, he argues, 'despite his never having been at school, participated in a culture that was literate to a degree. He was aware of and recognized that world of literacy.'[189] The *caoineadh*, with its interlocking phrases and its widespread formulaic conventions and imagery, capable of evoking a common history and worldview in a single line of verse, certainly constitutes the 'diachronic and pan-geographic tradition' Foley describes. Whether its 'word-hoard' is written or oral in origin or its mode of composition improvisatory or *post hoc* is of less importance than these artistic and cognitive interconnections, shared across the spectrum of time, place and social status. The Irish lament tradition teaches us that there is no need to make hard-and-fast distinctions between either learned and unlearned, literate and illiterate, in a society that has always inextricably linked the spoken and written word, and in which the consciousness of poetry as verbal art was never in question.

4 'FOR WANT OF EDUCATION': THE SONGS OF THE HEDGE SCHOOLMASTER

While the literary excellence of eighteenth-century Irish song in Gaelic has long been acknowledged in Irish scholarship, the English-language song tradition of the same period has received far less attention. This oversight may derive from an emphasis on Irish-language poetry that owes as much to politics as it does to letters – although it probably also reflects the more variable quality of songs in the English language. At least one genre of English-language song, however, is distinguished not only by at times comparable quality but also by stylistic and historical links to the older Irish tradition: the songs of the hedge schoolmaster.

This group of songs reflects influences in language and style that existed partly as a result of important social changes that occurred during the eighteenth century, including the disintegration of the Gaelic aristocracy and the compression of Catholic Irish society into a more condensed, less rigidly defined social order than the one that preceded it. On an artistic plane, as we have already seen, this resulted in the convergence of aristocratic and popular literature, especially in the realm of song-poetry. On an educational level, it contributed to the expansion of a system of instruction known as the 'hedge school'. Since many eighteenth-century Irish poets were at some time in their lives also hedge schoolmasters, these two developments were not unconnected; and both played a role in the generation of a new song-type which tradition itself attributes to the hedge schoolmaster.

A song called 'The Peregrinations of Fiachra McBrady', known in manuscript in Irish since the early eighteenth century but translated in 1793 for the *Anthologia Hibernica*, attests to the ubiquity of the hedge schoolmaster and his songs:

> If ye heard each disaster, of your poetaster,
> And Irish schoolmaster, since leaving Stradone;
> Thro' thick and thin splashing, the rain on him dashing,
> My friends in compassion, you'ld Brady bemoan.[1]

While the authors of many of these songs remain unknown, a significant number of later references either suggest or clearly identify schoolmasters as their composers. For instance, P. W. Joyce attributed a song called 'The Cottage Maid' to one 'Larry Dillon of Tipperary, a noted and successful classical teacher of the early part of the [nineteenth] century'.[2] Ulster song collector Sam Henry attributed a number of the songs in his large compilation to a variety of nineteenth-century schoolmasters, ascribing, for example, 'Mudion River', to Master Mullan, '"The Big Master" an itinerant schoolteacher'. Elsewhere, Henry credited 'The Flower of Gortade' to a man named Kane, who lived near a noted hedge school in County Derry and who, although not a schoolmaster himself, seems to have been profoundly affected 'by the proximity of so much learning'.[3] Less certain is the attribution of 'Under an Arbour of a Wide-Spreading Fagus' to a school-aged Eoghan Rua Ó Súilleabháin.[4] Many of the songs are of ballad sheet origin – judging by their uneven quality, often the work of penny-sheet hacks, or at least of writers whose skill in English was 'indifferent', at best; still others are the product of brilliant parodists. More importantly, however, all the songs included in this category exhibit one or more 'literary' features that reflect the influence of the classical and Gaelic traditions. And all share in the inheritance of learning left by the hedge school.

I. The Hedge Schools

As J. R. R. Adams notes:

> The origins of the hedge schools are obscure. In one sense they had always existed: before the days of universal state-funded education there would always have been people, themselves of humble station, who for a small fee would have taught some of the children of neighbours to the best of their ability. But documentation before the late eighteenth century is scanty.[5]

There is evidence of unofficial, local-initiative schools in Ireland as early as 1655, judging from the Commonwealth Records of that year, which state that '*severall popish schoolmasters doe reside in severall parts of the Counties* of Meath and Lowth and teach the Irish youth, trayning them up in superstition, idolatry and the evil customs of this Nacion'.[6] As evidence of the existence of such schools a little later in the same century, Adams cites the preface to a chapbook version in the Pepys Collection of *The Seven Wise Masters of Rome*, which states that 'of all histories of this nature, this exceeds, being held in such esteem in Ireland that it is of the chiefest use in all the English schools for introducing children to the understanding of good letters'.[7] Since inexpensive chapbooks were one of the principal sources of reading material in eighteenth-century hedge schools, it is fair to associate this statement with earlier unofficial schools for the non-elite.

According to Louis Cullen, education in Ireland, at least before the 1730s, was for the most part an upper-class, private phenomenon, with scribes often doubling as tutors for their wealthy patrons – like 'housebound scholar' Eoghan Ó Caoimh, who worked in 'no less than four households in Cork and Kerry in 1684'.[8]

Kevin Whelan has pointed out, however, that this situation also obtained in the households of dispossessed Catholic 'middlemen'. French traveller Coquebert de Montbret wrote of one such family, 'They have their children taught English, which they speak with great purity and they also speak Latin.'[9] Although such tutoring continued 'to a remarkably late date' (well into the eighteenth century), it was often from these private household positions that scribe-tutors launched full-fledged schools, in a shift from tutoring to schoolmastering that reflected 'increased demand from below'.[10] As the desire for literacy (primarily in English) among the middle and lower classes increased during the second half of the eighteenth century, so did the number of 'hedge schools'. As Niall Ó Ciosáin explains:

> By the second half of the eighteenth century, the greater frequency and regularity of market transactions within the Irish rural economy set a far higher premium on literacy than before ... Printed and hand-written commercial documents had become ubiquitous, and an ability to read was essential to the success of even small-scale farmers or weavers ... The increasing desirability of literacy, coupled with the rise in rural incomes consequent on commercialization, meant that parents were both more willing and more able than before to invest in education for their children. In the eighteenth and early nineteenth centuries, this meant an increasing tendency for rural communities in particular to hire schoolteachers.[11]

Lord Palmerston observed of his tenants in County Sligo in 1808:

> The thirst for education is so great that there are now three or four schools upon the estate. The people join in engaging some itinerant master: they run him up a miserable mud hut in the roadside, and the boys pay him half-a-crown, or some five shillings a quarter.[12]

By the 1830s, notes Ó Ciosáin, it seems that 'even the very poor in most areas had access to some sort of schooling, and that it was given priority within overall family strategies'. He quotes the report of parliamentary commissioners who spoke with town beggars in Corofin, County Clare in 1834:

> So anxious were these mendicants to show how attentive they were to the education of the younger class of the family, that frequently the commissioners were prevailed upon by their solicitation to sit down and hear the children read and inspect their copybooks, which evidenced a regular attendance at school and a laudable thirst for learning.[13]

The institution of the Penal Laws in the late seventeenth century, which among other things, denied education to those instructed by Catholic or Presbyterian teachers, is usually credited with hastening the rise of the hedge school. After the passage of the first of these measures in 1695, the remaining Catholic schools run by religious orders (not already suppressed under Cromwell) closed as many of the bishops and regular clergy were compelled to leave the country. Thus, as Patrick Dowling observes:

Figure 4.1: W. Carleton (W. C.), *Traits and Stories of the Irish Peasantry*, 6th edn (London: William Tegg, 1865), vol. 1, p. 283. Reproduced from the original held by the Department of Special Collections of the University Libraries of Notre Dame.

> The work of education was ... left mainly to the lay schoolmaster who was daring enough to risk his liberty in order to teach. Schools were set up in remote and mountainous districts where danger of detection was least likely to be incurred and where instruction might be carried on without serious or prolonged interruption.[14]

That some teachers were subject to real danger, at least during the earlier period of the Penal Laws, is clear from a number of contemporary accounts, including a declaration made by the Bishop of Derry in 1731 that 'popish schools' were all but non-existent: 'Sometimes a straggling schoolmaster sets up in some of ye mountainous parts of some parishes, but upon being threatened, as they constantly are, with a warrant or a presentment by ye churchwardens, they generally think proper to withdraw' – although, as Adams comments, 'Things were probably occurring in "ye mountainous parts" that the good bishop did not know about.'[15] Yet evidence of 'active persecution' of 'popish' schoolmasters exists throughout Ireland, especially in the early eighteenth century, in the form of warrants and assizement records.[16] Watty Cox, in an undated account of the school he attended in Longwood, County Meath, mentions that the scholars' studies 'were not unfrequently disturbed in Reading Made Easy, by the growl of the bull-dog and the menace of the priest-hunter'.[17] Over the course of the eighteenth century the Penal Laws were gradually relaxed, almost certainly due to the difficulty of enforcement. When the laws relating to education were 'liberalized' in 1782, one of the reasons given for their amendment was that they were deemed 'not to have answered the desired effect'.[18]

The hedge schools reputedly derived their name from the practice of conducting classes out of doors (to avoid implicating a local householder) in the shelter of a hedge or a bank which served to obscure the teacher and his pupils and thus protect them from discovery. While this may have been the motivation in some cases, especially in the early days of the Penal Laws, in other cases it probably had as much or more to do with either lack of shelter or the poor conditions of the ramshackle cabins frequently used as schoolhouses. One school in the parish of Killaloe was reported in the late eighteenth century to have been held in an 'open pasture field beside a furze hedge', where 'the children sat on the ground and did sums and writing on a slate laid on their knees';[19] and Watty Cox recalled having been 'taught in a large elm tree'.[20] In 1775 Richard Twiss noted a school near Dunleer, at which 'about a dozen bare-legged boys' were 'sitting by the side of the road, scrawling on scraps of paper placed on their knees; these boys, it seems, found the smoke in their school or cabin insufferable'.[21] According to Arthur Young, writing in 1776: 'Hedge Schools, as they were called (they might as well be termed ditch schools, for I have seen many a ditch full of scholars), are everywhere to be met with ... every child of the poorest family learning to read, write and cast accounts.'[22] Other schools, like those Henry Cooke and William Carleton attended, were little more than improvised affairs, 'a hovel under a hedge',[23] or a kind of dugout using banks or ditches as partial walling, the remainder being constructed of 'clay or green sods laid along in rows', which were roofed with thinly cut turf bound with wattles and thatched with rushes.[24] Along with such makeshift accommodations, however, barns, vestries and churches or chapels were sometimes used, although the term 'hedge school' was still routinely employed to describe them, even after the Penal Laws became obsolete with the passage of Catholic Emancipation in 1829. Even the urban counterparts of these rural academies were sometimes known as 'hedge schools', and Carleton observed in his autobiography that in the early nineteenth century 'there were nearly as many "hedge schools" in Dublin as there were of all other classes put together', crowded 'not merely by the poorer children, but by many of the better orders' – a circumstance he blamed on the dearth of 'schools of respectability' in the capital.[25]

School terms were seasonal, occurring mainly during the summer and early autumn, and were subject to interruption at times when the demands of farm work kept children at home or when inclement weather made the makeshift schoolhouses unendurable. Schoolmasters received their wages from the parents of each pupil; thus hedge schools were often known as 'pay schools', although this name also distinguished them from the free schools in existence, most notably the 'charter schools', instituted in the early eighteenth century as a means of at once educating and proselytizing their charges, while (in some cases) providing cheap labour for their Protestant directors.[26] By 1824 official reports put the number of Irish 'pay' schools – most of which were hedge schools – at 9,000, and the number of students at 400,000.[27] The size of the schools varied greatly, ranging, according to most early nineteenth-century reports, from five to 150, although the average number of pupils was about forty.[28] Fewer girls attended school, although this too varied: for example, in the parish of Killaloe, reports from the late eighteenth through the early nineteenth centuries reflect a ratio of about four boys to one girl, while Shaw Mason's *Statistical Account* from 1814–19 (which covered the entire country) indicates a ratio of only three to one.[29] Many schoolmasters received their training in the schools which they themselves had attended, but those with higher ambitions could become 'poor scholars', seeking the best instruction available. Joyce describes several poor scholars he knew in a school near Limerick, who 'were taught for nothing and freely entertained, with bed, supper and breakfast in the farmers' houses of the neighbourhood'.[30]

The hedge schools placed great emphasis on the 'three Rs', and in the majority of schools these were probably the only subjects taught.[31] Knowledge of arithmetic was held in such high regard that schoolmasters frequently followed their signatures with the epithet 'Philomath'.[32] Some schools, however, offered a much wider range of subjects, including bookkeeping, science, surveying, astronomy, history, religion, foreign languages – even dancing[33] – and attracted pupils with professional ambitions. Latin and Greek were crucial to both legal and clerical studies, and many schoolmasters advertised themselves as classical instructors. County Kerry had an especially good reputation for its classical schools, particularly the hedge school at Faha, which was seen as 'a sort of preparatory school for Salamanca'.[34] As Sir James Caldwell wrote in 1764, 'In order to qualify the Children for foreign Service, they are all taught *Latin* in Schools kept in poor Huts, in many Places in the Southern Part of the Kingdom.' Dowling cites an anonymous writer in 1776, relating that the poor, ragged boy in County Kerry who held his horse was 'well-acquainted with the best Latin poets'.[35] More ambivalently, Charles Smith, in his 1756 *History of Kerry*, wrote, 'It is well known that classical learning extends itself, even to a fault, among the lower and poorer kind in this county; many of whom, to the taking them off more useful works, have greater knowledge in this way, than some of the better sort, in other places.'[36] The Reverend William Hickey, though disapproving of classical education for the poor, describes having met a ragged goatherd, who spoke 'fluently' in Latin but had no English.[37]

Irish language and literature were also apparently taught in some hedge schools, and initially Irish was probably the usual medium of instruction, at least in Irish-speaking districts.[38] Louis Cullen notes the existence of 'people of little means who were literate in Irish ... even in the early eighteenth century'. By the latter part of the eighteenth century, however, most schools placed far greater emphasis upon the teaching of English, which by that time was indisputably the language of commerce and law.[39] Cullen associates 'the sharp increase of teaching' during this period with 'a decisive move towards English'.[40] Comments Sean Connolly, even schoolmasters who were 'students of Irish literature, preserving and transcribing manuscripts, and in some cases themselves composing poetry or other literary work', taught primarily in English.[41]

The hedge schoolmaster has acquired nearly as much traditionality as the songs with which he is credited. We know relatively little, in fact, about him, which is small wonder in view of the transient and semi-covert nature of his profession – and, indeed, in view of his ubiquity. We find him variously depicted as an erudite scholar, an inflated pedant and (particularly in the case of his female counterparts) a mere child-minder.[42] There is probably truth in all three views, for it is evident from the limited records and accounts available to us that the quality of instruction often varied greatly from one school to the next. At the lower end of the scale were those of doubtful character and even more dubious qualifications who, as J. R. R. Adams has noted, were 'probably very little better educated than the pupils whom [they were] attempting to teach'. Rev. Robert Trail reported that in early nineteenth-century Ballintoy, 'education of almost the entire parish extends only to the acquirement of reading English, writing a miserable scrawl, with perhaps a little arithmetic';[43] and the 1812 Commissioner's report described the instruction in many schools as extending 'no farther than reading, writing and the common rules of arithmetic ... but even this limited instruction the masters are very ill qualified to give.'[44] In the middle of the spectrum, perhaps, were masters like the 'elementary' teachers P. W. Joyce remembered from his youth: 'Many of them were rough and uncultivated in speech, but all had sufficient scholarship for their purpose and many indeed very much more'.[45] There were also, however, a number of schoolmasters whose qualifications were beyond reproach. Among these was John Condon, who ran an 'Intermediate' school in an upstairs room of a market house in Mitchelstown, County Cork, 'a large apartment fully and properly furnished, forming an admirable schoolroom'. The school was attended by both Catholic and Protestant students to whom Condon, 'a cultured and scholarly man', taught 'science, including mathematics, surveying and the use of the globes, and also geography and English grammar. He had an assistant who taught Greek and Latin.'[46] One factor which might account for the presence of at least some highly qualified hedge schoolmasters is the continuance of hereditary scholar families, some of whom turned to school-teaching to gain a livelihood.[47] Exactly how many of the major poets and scribes of the time had any connection with these hereditary families is unclear;[48] but those who worked as schoolmasters, like Peadar Ó Doirnín, Brian Merriman and Eoghan Rua Ó Súilleabháin, obviously had much to offer the communities in which they taught.[49]

Notwithstanding the presence of such genuine scholars in the ranks of these pedagogues, the popular image of the hedge schoolmaster remains less than flattering. He is frequently portrayed as a conceited pedant, inclined to drink and ludicrous in his use of the English language. There are numerous examples of the hedge schoolmaster's use of inflated verbiage in eighteenth- and nineteenth-century Irish literature, including that of Oliver Goldsmith's schoolmaster in 'The Deserted Village', who utters 'words of learned length and thundering sound' to amaze 'the gazing rustics ranged around'.[50] By the late eighteenth century, so well-established was the hedge schoolmaster as a figure of fun that he appears as one of the central characters in John O'Keeffe's 1781 ballad opera *The Agreeable Surprise*. Introduced as the 'new butler', his employer describes the erstwhile pedagogue as:

> a curst fellow, as ignorant as dirt. It seems he has been a schoolmaster here in the country, taught all the bumpkin fry what he calls Latin; and the damn' dog so patches his own bad English with his bits of bad Latin, and jumbles the Gods, Goddesses, Heroes, celestial and infernal together at such a rate; I took him to oblige a foolish old friend of mine, who intended him for Saint Omers; so I must keep him to draw good wine and brew balderdash Latin.[51]

Nor does 'Lingo', the schoolmaster turned butler, disappoint, uttering lines like 'O Caelum et terra! And have I studied Syntax, Cordery, Juvenal, and Tristram Shandy, to serve wine on my knee to a mighty cheesemonger!' Of an intended conquest, he sings:

> Oh how bella
> My puella!
> I'll kiss her seculorum:
> If I've luck, Sir,
> She's my uxor,
> O dies benedictorum![52]

The schoolmasters in William Carleton's fiction also have a tendency to spout Latin (or pseudo-Latin) words and phrases at every turn, or to quote whole lines from the classics, as happens when James McEvoy (a 'poor scholar' based loosely on Carleton himself as a boy) encounters a local schoolmaster at a farmer's house on his journey south to Munster. The schoolmaster, having been congratulated by the farmer on an amorous conquest, demurs, remarking, 'I can't say that the arrows of Cupid have as yet pinethrated the sintimintal side of *my* heart. It is not with me as it was wid Dido – hem – Non "hæret lateri lethalis arundo", as Virgil says.'[53] Carleton's Mat Kavanagh, on awakening from a hangover, declares, 'I'm all in a state of conflagration; and my head – by the sowl of Newton, the inventor of fluxions, but my head is a complete illucidation of the centrifugal motion, so it is.'[54]

While such ludicrous speech is obviously a caricature, there is, as Adams suggests, a basis for it in fact. The preface of an early nineteenth-century grammar entitled *A Practical Logical Essay on the Syntax of the English Language*, although more prolix than absurd, also indulges in casual Latin quotation.[55] The letters of commendation contributed by the author's schoolmaster friends to the 1822 Omagh edition reflect a style even closer to Carleton's portrayals. One letter reads, 'Who, possessing candour or discernment, that will not instantly confess, that the mutual dependence you take notice of between the subject and the attribute, bids defiance to any refutation?'[56] Carleton himself, in order to deflect any notion that the representation of Mat Kavanagh was 'by any means overdrawn', quotes an open letter from a Munster 'literary teacher', who, in defending himself from the attacks of a rival schoolmaster, wrote:

> With a due circumspection of the use of their synonymy, taking care that the import and acceptation of each phrase and word should not appear frequently synonymous ... I have done it, by an appropriate selection of catogoramatic and cencatogoramatic terms and words ... and although I own to you, that I have no pretentions to be an adept in poetry, as I have only moderately sipped of the Helicon Fountain; yet from my knowledge of Orthometry I can prove the correctness of it, by special and general metric analysis.[57]

II. Traits and Genres of the Hedge Schoolmaster Song

The Latinate tendencies of the hedge schoolmaster may in part reflect a practice also employed in Anglo-Norman grammar schools of an earlier date: the use of Latin as a medium for teaching English, or indeed any foreign language.

Latin had long been important in both the monastic and bardic schools and was, therefore, a logical tool for this end.[58] Some schoolmasters may well have learned – or even taught themselves – English in this manner. These factors, along with the schoolmaster's notion of his own erudition and his desire to impress his community and thus attract students, help to explain the highly Latinate flavour of his English vocabulary. It is, in any case, one of the most marked characteristics of his songs, as illustrated by this verse from 'The Colleen Rue':

> Kind sir, be easy and do not tease me
>   with your false praises most jestingly;
> Your dissimulation or invocation
>   are vaunting praises seducing me.
> I'm not Aurora or beautious Flora,
>   but a rural female to all men's view,
> That's here condoling my situation;
>   my appellation is the Colleen Rue.[59]

Such propensities are certainly parodied in O'Keeffe's *Agreeable Surprise*. Sings Lingo:

> SUCH beauties in view, I
>   Can never praise too high;
> Not Pallas's blue eye
>   Is brighter than thine.
> Not fount of Susannah,
>   Nor gold of fair Dana,
>   Nor moon of Dianna,
>   So clear can shine!
>   Not beard of Selinus,
>   Nor tresses of Venus,
> I swear by Quæ Genus!
>   With yours can compare;
> Not Hermes' Caduces,
>   Nor flower de luces.
> For all the Nine Muses,
>   To me is so fair.[60]

Since classical knowledge of any kind would have been highly respected by the schoolmaster's community, the use of learned allusion was one way in which he could display that knowledge.[61] Certainly, some must have felt a strong temptation to indulge excessively in this kind of rhetoric – with humorous results. Dowling quotes from a political speech in which Waterford schoolmaster James Nash delivered this fanciful challenge to Erin's enemies: 'Let them come on, let them come on; let them draw the sword; and then woe to the conquered! – every potato field shall be a Marathon and every boreen a Thermopylae.'[62]

Some writers have found the hedge schoolmaster's liberal use of allusion and luxuriant Latin vocabulary distasteful, or at best simply ludicrous. Frank O'Connor derisively describes the language of 'The Colleen Rue' as 'Babu English';[63] while P. W. Joyce, observing that the schoolmaster composers knew English 'only imperfectly', prefaces his transcription of 'The Cottage Maid' with the remark that although many of these 'effusions' are 'absurd' he feels compelled to include several as examples of 'this class of Anglo-Irish song'.[64] Dowling more tolerantly describes the hedge schoolmaster's language as a mixture of 'audacity, humour and pedantry':[65]

> In the flow'ry month of May, when lambkins sport and play,
>   As I roved to receive recreation,
> I espied a comely maid sequester'd in a shade,
>   On her beauty I gazed with admiration.
> Had Alcides seen her face before Dejanira's grace,
>   He would ne'er be consumed in the cedars:
> Nor would Helen prove the fall of the Grecian leaders all;
>   Nor would Ulysses be the Trojan invader.[66]

Even sporting events could be treated in this manner. Crofton Croker quotes a song on a hurling match played on the banks of the Owenboy River which contains the following verse:

> Were Homer the narrator and Virgil a spectator,
>   No praises could be greater, than were due this gallant corps;
> For never did the Grecians, nor the Romans called Patricians
>   Exceed the stout Milesians that defeated Barrymore.
> 'Twas in no combination, or field association,
>   But in rural relaxation, on the plains of Onnabuoy.[67]

Another song printed in 1792 makes, as Andrew Carpenter comments, 'playful use of the material of Homer's *Iliad*', and was perhaps composed by one of the 'more literate hedge schoolmasters' Adams thought likeliest to indulge in satire:

> I sing of a war set on foot for a toy,
> And of Paris and Helen and Hector and Troy,
> Where on women, kings, gen'rals and coblers you stumble,
> And of mortals and gods meet a very strange jumble ...
>
> Agamemnon and all the great chiefs of his house,
> Soon took up the cause of this hornified spouse;
> While Juno said this thing and Venus said that,
> And the Gods fell a wrangling they knew not for what.[68]

This penchant for classical allusion in Irish lyrics is not peculiar to the repertoire of the hedge schoolmaster, although he obviously took it to new extremes. Nor can it be dismissed as merely a borrowing from Neoclassical poetic convention. Its use undoubtedly reflected the schoolmaster's own training, as well as his desire to impress. Yet it is characteristic of, and probably partly indebted to, eighteenth-century Irish poetic forms – including the *aisling* – whose influence is apparent in a number of hedge schoolmaster songs. *Aisling* or 'vision' poetry, as we have seen, is a form with an ancient lineage, put to novel use by the Irish poets of the eighteenth century as a vehicle for expressing political disaffection and Jacobite sympathies. Political *aislingí* in the English language usually follow the allegorical *aisling* form fairly closely, with all the political significance intact – although usually without the Jacobite overtones. These songs we know mainly from later ballad sheet texts, e.g. 'Erin's Green Shore' and 'The Patriot Queen', both of which date from the first half of the nineteenth century and proclaim Daniel O'Connell rather than one of the Stuart pretenders as their saviour:

> One evening of late as I strayed
>   By the banks of yon clear silver stream,
> I sat on a bank of primroses,
>   Where quickly I fell into a dream,
> I dreamt that I met a young damsel,
>   Her equal I ne'er saw before,
> She sighed for the wrongs of her country,
>   As she strayed upon Erin's green shore.[69]
>
> I gently approached this fair female,
>   And courteously asked her her name,
> Or was she Minerva or Juno,
>   Who here from Elysium had came;
> This charmer did quickly make answer,
>   And said, in all nations I'm known,
> I am of Milesian extraction,
>   I am Ireland here claiming my own.[70]

As we have seen, the *aisling* had entered the popular song tradition some time in the eighteenth century, disseminated through the courts of poetry, manuscripts, oral tradition and – possibly – schools. But in the case of the political *aisling*, there is also a non-poetic factor linking the hedge schools to the genre: the well-known political activism of many hedge schoolmasters, chiefly in connection with organizations like the Defenders and United Irishmen of the 1790s. Many of the schoolmasters involved in the United Irishmen were among the best educated and most highly regarded teachers and scholars in the country, including County Mayo poet Ríocard Bairéad, Limerick mathematician James Baggott and Cork scribe Mícheál Óg Ó Longáin, who disguised himself as a poor scholar while acting as courier for the United Irishmen.[71] Commentators of the period were quick to identify the schoolmaster as a subversive figure, a 'petty demagogue, whose pride in his superior literature was the cause of his disaffection', and who 'became the officious minister of treason ... to an illiterate circle who looked up with wonder and implicit belief to the man who could read, and through this polluted channel received all their information and principles'.[72] In 1730 Sir Richard Cox inveighed against Irish Papists, who 'teach a little bad Latin, but much Superstition and more Treason'.[73] Many blamed the lowbrow literature taught in many hedge schools as 'seditious' (especially chapbooks relating the adventures of rapparees and highwaymen), finding 'the transition from theory to practice' to be 'but short'. Antonia McManus points out that since such chapbook tales had been common in hedge schools for more than twenty years before the '98 Rebellion, 'the popularity of the genre was merely a symptom rather than a cause of the lawlessness of the time'.[74] But insofar as the schools promoted literacy, these criticisms may have had some validity, for, as Kevin Whelan argues, the relatively higher literacy rates of late eighteenth-century Ireland 'and the consequent penetration of popular politicization in the 1790s are a direct tribute' to the educational success of the hedge school.[75] Ó Ciosáin, after observing that the involvement of schoolmasters 'in radical political activity' may have disrupted the operation of schools in some areas, comments, 'On balance, it is more likely that the widespread use of printed propaganda was a sign of a pre-existing literate public rather than a spur to further literacy'.[76]

Thus we find in the repertoire of the hedge schoolmaster not only political *aislingí*, but also songs like 'Blaris Moor', which dates from the 1797 execution of several United Irishmen at Blaris Camp, near Belfast:

> Assist now, you Muses and grant me no excuses,
> Concerning a few verses, it's treason I am sure,
> By the deed of colonel barber, we dare insist no farther;
> He's a perfidious villain who betrayed us, I am sure.[77]

'The Boys of Mullaghbawn', a song popularly associated with the United Irishmen, celebrates the virtues of the progressive South Armagh landlord Richard Jackson, who is described as a man 'unequalled for honour or for reason'/ [Who] never turned a traitor or betrayed the rights of man'.[78] Arguably, the allegorical 'bird' songs, from the Jacobite 'Royal Blackbird' (the Old Pretender) to 'The Green Linnet' (Napoleon) and 'The Blackbird of Avondale' (Daniel O'Connell) are also part of this tradition of erudite political song:

> Curiosity bore a young native of Erin
>   To view the gay banks of the Rhine,
> Where an Empress he saw and the robe she was wearing
>   All over with diamonds did shine;
> A goddess in splendour was never yet seen,
> To equal this fair one so mild and serene,
> In soft murmur she cried, my sweet Linnet so green,
>   Are you gone, will I ne'er see you more?[79]

More common than the political *aisling*, however, are songs in English in which the political and allegorical elements are conspicuously absent. Such songs also occur in the Irish-language tradition – particularly the *reverdie*, a song-type also attested in the Irish-language tradition, typified by encounters with a woman of otherworldly beauty amidst the glories of springtime. In the *reverdie*, as Gaston Paris observes, the woman is 'un personnage de rêve, qui se montre subitement dans le bois au milieu des fleurs et des oiseaux, une sorte de fée du printemps qui n'a pas de réalité corporelle'.[80] Although Ó Tuama admits to some commingling of the love *aisling* with both the Irish *reverdie* and the political *aisling*, he plainly believes the French form to have had the greater impact.[81] He also notes the influence on both the Irish *reverdie* and the *aisling* of the *pastourelle*, a genre in which a knight or nobleman tries to obtain the sexual favours of a low-born woman (usually a shepherdess), either through persuasion or force – a trope found in compositions by both Eoghan an Mhéirín and Eoghan Rua Ó Súilleabháin.[82]

Many of these non-allegorical songs share with the *aisling* two distinguishing features. First, the descriptive opening, in which the narrator – again in an outdoor setting but now wide awake, as in the *reverdie* – ventures forth in the early morning or evening and encounters a woman of supernatural beauty. The second feature is the narrator's interrogation of the woman, in which he imputes to her mythological status, following the formula which D. K. Wilgus has dubbed 'the goddess routine':[83]

> Are you Aurora, or the goddess Flora, Artemidora,
>   or Venus bright,
> Or Helen fair beyond compare, whom Paris stole
>   from the Grecian sight?[84]

Or, more outrageously,

> Are you any of these dames who agreed to strip,
> For Paris to view them on Ida's hill,
> Where Vulcan's fair bride obtained the golden prize,
> Which caused jealousy, spite and dire revenge?[85]

According to this formula, the woman denies divine origin; and afterwards, as Wilgus observes, 'the narrative can branch into almost any conceivable plot variation'.[86] Frequently, however, the action progresses no further and the song ends in a rhapsodic tribute to the maiden's beauty. Ó Tuama prefers to call such non-political songs in Gaelic *reverdies léannta* ('learned *reverdies*'), believing the 'goddess routine' to be not a hallmark of the *aisling*, but rather an independent poetic device applied first to the Irish *reverdie* and later to the political *aisling* but integral to neither form. According to Ó Tuama, this contrivance – which he traces to early medieval Latin poetry – emerged in the Irish poetic tradition in the late seventeenth century, and in the eighteenth century, he identifies Eoghan an Mhéirín and Seán Clárach Mac Domhnaill, both of whom were well-versed in classical literature, as two of the earliest purveyors of this fashion.[87] Indeed, the 'goddess routine' is conspicuously absent from the allegorical *aislingí* of Aogán Ó Rathaille, one of the first to employ the genre. Allusions to the classics, however, appear as early as the beginning of the seventeenth century in some love *aislingí*, in compositions by poets like Piaras Feiritéar and Pádraigín Haicéad, in praise poems to women composed as early as the mid-seventeenth century, and in non-political *reverdies*.[88]

I have dwelt upon the subject of the eighteenth-century *aisling* and its near relations because so many of the hedge schoolmaster songs clearly reflect their influence. We have already seen several examples of *aislingí* and '*reverdies léannta*'. Other songs in oral tradition, like 'Lough Erne's Shore', however, come closer to being straightforward *reverdies*:

> One morning as I went a fowling, bright Phoebus adorned the plain,
> It was down by the shores of Lough Erne I met with this wonderful dame.
> Her voice was so sweet and so pleasing, these beautiful notes she did sing,
> The innocent fowl of the forest their love unto her they did bring.[89]

Hedge schoolmaster *pastourelles* come in a variety of forms, but 'One Morning in May' runs fairly true to type:

> One morning in May, as I carelessly did stray,
> To view the green meadows and the lambs sport and play,
> In the clear morning dew, as I lay down to muse,
> A fair maiden of honour appeared in my view.
>
> Says I, 'Pretty maid, how happy we could be;
> For it is so ordained, love, that married we should be.
> Let me not see you frown, for this love is your own.'
> When these words they were spoken, sure, the tears trickled down.
>
> Come dry up your tears, there is nothing to fear,
> I would roam through the green fields for many's the long year,
> While the birds sang so sweet, this young man proved his deceit,
> Saying, 'Adieu, pretty fair maid, we will never more meet'.
>
> With my snuffbox and cane, the whole world I will range,
> Like Venus or Diana in search of her swain,
> While the moon does shine clear, I will mourn for my dear,
> Over mountains, clear fountains, where no one will hear.[90]

Other songs, however, like 'The Star of Sunday's Well' and 'The Flower of Gortade', are neither *aislingí* nor *reverdies léannta* or *pastourelles* but rather catalogues of deities quoted to extol the virtues of some female subject:

> Oh, were I as Homer that prince of the writers
> Who sang of Athenians and Spartans of old

> Could I paint with the skill of a Roman inditer
> The fame of this fair one can never be told
> Penelope, Venus, Diana and Flora,
> Whose beauty and chastity never can fade
> Fair Helen, Lucretia and famous Aurora
> Even these wouldn't equal the Flower of Gortade.[91]

Such songs also have antecedents in the Irish-language tradition (although somewhat more restrained than their English counterparts), and these may reflect another older strand of literary native poetry: eulogies for patrons and the women in their families. Some of the earlier bardic eulogies for women give special attention to the glories of their hair, as in the following, addressed to Gormlaidh, daughter of Brian Mág Shamhradháin, born in 1305:

> May the fair-skinned stately swan live long to feel proud of the waviness in that mass of hair with fair curling braids, a very diadem of even-branching twisted tresses ... In her white teeth, in the flowing of her hair, in her undisguised pleasure at story-telling; her comely hair stands with wavy curling surface over the delicate red-edged ruby of (her) mouth.[92]

This sort of rhetoric survived not only in the compositions of late seventeenth-century poets like Aogán Ó Rathaille ('Gile na Gile'), Pádraig Mac a Liondain ('Tá Dairtí ag Dul Tríom') and Turlough Carolan ('Bean Cól'), but well into the eighteenth century, as well as in subsequent oral tradition.[93] By the late seventeenth and early eighteenth centuries, as references to both classical and native goddesses become increasingly common, we find compositions like Séamus Dall Mac Cuarta's praise of Ailís Ní Chearbhaill, in which he likens his subject to both Helen and Deirdre;[94] and Carolan's 'Brighid Ní'c Fheorais', which includes the following lines:

> A Bhrighid bheag dheas, a bhéilin meala,
> Le'r baoruigheadh leat-sa fearaibh Chric' Fáil,
> A's gur éifeachtaighe gach stair dhá léightear dhúinn air dheise:
> Venus, Juno, Apollo, a's ná Deirdre an áigh.
>
> My lovely wee Bridget, oh, sweet honey-mouth,
> With which you tormented the men of Ireland,
> You surpass all accounts we may read of beauty:
> Venus, Juno, Apollo and valiant Deirdre.[95]

From the same period, the hedge schoolmaster song 'North Country Beauty' (1788) runs:

> You inspired Muses of sense and knowledge
> To me your mighty aid impart,
> To praise a Maiden who has inslaved me,
> And stole away my tender heart;

> Her majestic carriage is so enticing,
> Surpasses Hellen that Grecian queen,
> Or the bright Awrelia in all her splendor,
> Could never equal this comely Dame.[96]

Borrowings from medieval French song tradition which had by this time become widespread in popular song throughout Europe, intertwined with native Irish poetic conventions, also appear in the descriptions of female beauty of the period, in both Irish and English: rosy cheeks (often vying for supremacy with the lily), white skin, shining eyes and golden tresses, abound not only in eulogies, but also in Irish *aislingí*, in *reverdies* and in *pastourelles*. So, too, do the flowers, stars, pearls, lilies, diamonds and crystals – again, as Ó Tuama argues, probably derived from continental conventions:[97]

> Her hair linked like gold wavering over her shoulders
> Her cheeks red as roses in June,
> Her eyes bright as diamonds, her Lips the coral,
> Her skin white as lilies in bloom,
> Her teeth like the ivory well set in her head,
> Her Limbs they are straight and her waist slender made
> All art was employ'd in adorning this maid,
> Called beautiful Molly m'Koan.[98]

Not surprisingly, given this overindulgent verbiage, a number of parodies of hedge schoolmaster love songs found their way into print, as attested by 'Paddy in Love', printed in London in 1785:

> I have long been in love with a damsel hard by,
> She has a pig in the stable and a horse in the sty,
> Her cheeks are as red as the sun in the night,
> Her eyes shine as bright as the moon in day-light.
>   With my fal deral, &c.
>
> It would charm you to see her at church or at mill,
> Where she trips it so nimbly you'd swear she stood still,
> At milking her cow too the world must agree,
> She looks just like Vulcan ris'n out of the sea.
>   With my fal &c.[99]

Even Peadar Ó Doirnín could not resist parodying such excesses in a macaronic satire in which he mocks rival schoolmaster and scribe Muiris Ó Gormáin. Ó Doirnín satirizes both Ó Gormáin's English and his pretensions to learning, simultaneously burlesquing some of the well-worn conventions of both Irish and English-language songs of the era in his depiction of the scribe's ill-fated courtship with a girl he meets on the 'Turnpike Road'. After having introduced himself as 'Moresious Gormáin ... schoolmaster', the narrator relates,

> Ar ndul go tigh an óil dúinn shuíomar ar bord
> Mar Pharis ón Traí is mar Helen ón Ghréig,
> Bhí mise á pógadh is ise mar lóchrann
> Solais gan bhrón ag moladh mo léinn:
> 'You is very fine clothes, you is prettey vright prose,
> You is Latin vell spoke and fath me can name.
> Ach bhíomar ag ól gur thit mise 'mo cheo
> Is don deamhan sin orlach fuair Muiris dá feidhm.
>
> Going into an alehouse we sat down at the board,
> Like Paris of Troy and like Helen of Greece,
> I her a-kissing and she all afire,
> A flame without sorrow, a-praising my learning:
> 'You is very fine cloathes, you is prettey vright prose,
> You is Latin vell spoke and fath me can't name';
> But we were there drinking till I fell in a doze,
> And it's devil a bit did I get for my pain.[100]

Another class of hedge schoolmaster song that, like the *aisling* and *reverdie léannta*, reflects influence from more learned spheres than many are used to associating with folk tradition. This is the song of moral disputation, analogous to the *conflictus*, a poetic debate between allegorical figures of medieval Latin tradition. Derived from classical eclogues, the *conflictus* or *altercatio* was popular throughout Europe during the Middle Ages, commonly centering on such subjects as youth vs. age, summer vs. winter and body vs. soul.[101] One example of this genre in the Anglo-Irish song tradition, 'The Banks of Dunmore', contains elements of the *aisling/reverdie/pastourelle* pattern, i.e. an encounter with a woman of exceptional beauty, followed by an elaborate physical description.[102] Here, however, the resemblance ends, and the song becomes a dialogue between the maiden and the narrator in which she defends the Catholic faith and ultimately converts the erring poet. 'A Discussion between Church and Chapel' presents a more ponderous apology for Catholicism in the form of a debate between a Protestant Church and a Catholic chapel, although it again opens with a *reverdie*-like stanza:

> One morning early as day was breaking,
> Being in the charming month sweet of May,
> When flora's mantle had decorated,
> The fragrant pans all in rich array
> The lofty mountains I could survey them,
> The purling streams and the river clear,
> The crystal fountains and the billows roaring
> Where ships were sailing from far and near
>
> I being reconciled with the sweets of nature
> I was preparing take my way,
> Till over hearing a conversation,
> Which occasioned me to stay,

> Being a discussion in that place had taken,
> Between two neighbours in Cork town,
> About a chapel founded by Father Matthew
> But Shandon church it began to frown,
>
> This Church it broke out from its silence,
> And in great violence to the chapel said,
> What spark are you that stands behind me,
> My friends and neighbours you have betrayed,
> My predecessors you did inveigle
> To run away from their native home,
> Where my ancestors are clad on earth,
> And are still remaining until the day of doom,
>
> The prudent chapel then made answer,
> And was not angry nor yet confused,
> Madam sitting in your pomp and grandeur,
> I beg the favour to be excused,
> Though here I am standing both poor and naked,
> I don't inveigle or flatter none,
> I was erected by the true Milesian
> My ordination the Church of Rome.[103]

There are Irish-language models for these *conflictus*-like songs – including 'Ceithre Ráithe na Bliana', a debate between the four seasons of the year[104] – as well as at least one macaronic *pièce de résistance*, which has been attributed to the eighteenth-century Armagh poet Art Mac Cumhaigh, best known for his *aisling* 'Úr-chill an Chreagáin'. 'Tagra an Dá Theampall' ('The Disputation of the Two Churches') in fact opens as an *aisling*, the narrator awakening to overhear a vigourous debate between a newly-built Protestant church and a crumbling Catholic chapel. The Protestant church, responding to the Catholic chapel's comparison of the destruction of Pharaoh's army in the Red Sea to the coming victory of Irish Catholicism, replies bitingly:

> Your clergy maintains the Scripture contains
>   But mystical dreams and stories;
> False doctrine that leads your senses away
>   From heavenly grace and glory.
> Inventing such schemes for money to gain,
>   Of Limbo they treat laborious,
> Until Luther the great and Calvin of late,
>   Renounced their shameful chorus.

To which the Catholic church rejoins:

> 'Sé mo thuirse gur tréaghdadh maithe na nGael
>   In Eachroim 's ar thaoibh na Bóinne,
> 'S nach maireann i gcéim Eoghan an Chogaidh Ó Néill

>Chuirfeadh Cromail i bpéin 's a shlóite.
>Cha lasfadh King Harry, Beelsebub éitheach,
> Nó Liútar a bhuaradh Fódla,
>New Lights nó Seceders, Old Presbyterians,
> Swaddlers nó Quakers leofa.

>It's my sorrow that the Gaelic nobles were wounded at Aughrim and by Boyneside, and that Owen Roe of the Battles O'Neill does not live in power, for he would hurt Cromwell and his hosts. King Harry would not have ignited deceitful Beelzebub or Luther to trouble Ireland with New Lights or Seceders, Old Presbyterians, Swaddlers or Quakers.[105]

This subgenre, too, then, may owe much to the Irish-language tradition that preceded it, although some schoolmasters may also have been familiar enough with the medieval *conflictus* to imitate it in English. Since the *conflictus* had fallen out of fashion as a genre in English poetry by the time of the late Renaissance,[106] it is doubtful that it entered the Irish song tradition via British sources. And since the schoolmaster in collaboration with the local priest frequently provided the religious instruction for the community, it would hardly be surprising if he had used religion or morality as subjects for song.[107]

Yet another sort of hedge schoolmaster 'effusion', the local praise poem or geographic encomium, can be traced to the bardic practice of eulogizing the property of a noble patron. Hence the proliferation of such compositions as 'Castlehyde', a song that celebrates the splendours of the property of a certain Mr Hyde, which stood on the Blackwater, near Fermoy in County Cork. 'Castlehyde' also illustrates a continental medieval convention frequently associated with the *aisling* and with French genres like the *reverdie*: the image of the rose and the lily as rival hues; in *aislingí*, however, this image is used to describe the *spéirbhean*'s complexion rather than a landowner's garden:

>The richest groves throughout this nation and fine plantations you will see there;
>The rose, the tulip and sweet carnation, all vying with the lily fair.
>The buck, the doe, the fox, the eagle, they skip and play by the riverside;
>The trout and salmon are always sporting in the clear streams of sweet Castlehyde.[108]

Place-praise songs could also address a locality, rather than a demesne, a practice that may also owe something to *dinnseanchas*, or local place lore. A common feature of this sort of composition is the catalogue of the poet's many (and often exotic) ports of call, followed by a declaration that all are inferior to the subject of his song. Thus, in 'Old Arboe', a song in praise of a spot near Lough Neagh in County Tyrone, the narrator declares:

>I've travelled France and I've travelled Flanders
>And all the countries beyond the Rhine
>But in all my rakings and undertakings

Arboe your equal I ne'er could find
My course I've taken to Indian oceans
To the shores of Cana and Galilee
But in all my rakings and undertakings
Arboe, your equal I ne'er did see.[109]

More stiltedly, 'A New Song on the Beauties of Dunganstown' (composed, according to the chapbook songster in which it appears, by the author of 'Kingstown Harbour', and printed in Dublin in the 1820s) invites its audience to:

Then search all Asia, through proved Bavaria,
    Likewise Hungary and Italy,
Such groves and allies and fragrant vallies,
    In all your travels you ne'er can see.
With a church for service in the lovely arbour,
    No Snake nor Tiger to hiss or frown,
All garden dainties no goodness scanty,
    But peace and plenty in Dunganstown.[110]

Such songs were as ripe for parody as the hedge school *aisling* or *reverdie*, and gave rise to burlesques like 'Mudion River' (composed around 1825). On the surface a somewhat flowery, yet straightforward song of praise, 'the fun of … the old song is, that in the words of an old Agivey man, "Mudion's nae mair than a good sleugh"' – in other words, a ditch.[111] Better known is Richard Alfred Milliken's 1800 parody of 'Castlehyde', 'The Groves of Blarney'. According to Crofton Croker, Milliken, having heard a performance of 'Castlehyde' at a gentlemen's gathering, decided to compose a song 'at least equal in absurdity', in order 'to ridicule the songs which ignorant Irish village bards – with a vast fondness for rhyme, an imperfect knowledge of the English language, and a pedantic ambition to display the full extent of the classical knowledge – were and still are, in the habit of composing'.[112] Joyce regarded Milliken's song as a 'vile caricature', which 'working as a sort of microbe – gave origin to a number of imitations of the same general character' – not least, Milliken's own later 'De Groves of de Pool'.[113] Andrew Carpenter, however, suggests that the song, because of its praise of the 'radical' Arabella Jeffreys, also contains an 'anti-establishment message hidden in a seemingly nonsensical poem':

'Tis Lady Jeffreys that owns this station,
    Like Alexander, or Queen Helen fair;
There's no commander throughout the nation
    For emulation can with her compare.
She has castles round her, that no nine-pounder
    Could dare to plunder her place of strength;
But Oliver Cromwell he did her pummell,
    And made a breach in her battlement.[114]

One interesting class of hedge schoolmaster song is a heterogeneous category characterized by self-conscious references to the hedge school itself. For example, 'The Wild Sports of O'Sullivan' is almost a sung corollary to Eoghan Rua Ó Súilleabháin's much-quoted verse letter of 1784, in which the poet tried to enlist the assistance of Ned Fitzgerald of Gneeveguilla, County Kerry to advertise his qualifications as a schoolmaster:

> Reverend Sir–
> Please to publish from the altar of your holy Mass
> That I will open school at Knocknagree Cross
> Where, the tender babes will be well off,
> For it's there I'll teach them their Criss Cross;
> Reverend Sir, you will by experience find
> All my endeavours to please mankind,
> For it's there I will teach them how to read and write;
> The Catechism I will explain
> To each young nymph and noble swain,
> With all young ladies I'll engage
> To forward them with speed and care,
> With book-keeping and mensuration
> Euclid's Elements and Navigations,
> With Trigonometry and sound gauging,
> And English Grammar with rhyme and reason
> With the grown-up youths I'll first agree
> To instruct them well in the Rule of Three;
> Such of them as are well able,
> The cube root of me will learn
> Such as are of a tractable genius,
> With compass and rule I will teach them,
> Bill, bonds and informations,
> Summons, warrants, supersedes
> Judgement tickets, good
> Leases, receipts in full,
> And releases, short accounts,
> With rhyme and reason,
> And sweet love letters for the ladies.[115]

'The Wild Sports', from an early nineteenth-century ballad sheet, retails similar attainments, but adds details about the young poet's reputation that would surely have gone down less well with the parish priest:

> My name is O'Sullivan, the eminent teacher,
> My qualifications will ne'er be extinct,
> I read as good Latin as any in the nation,
> Without doubt I'm experienced in arithmetic.

My occupation is constantly teaching,
Indeed I have learned each capital rule;
Euclid's Optics and Moore's Navigation,
By deep penetration I have learn'd at school ...

Indeed I'm counted both in elocution,
By prosody rules I govern my tongue,
I governise book-keeping without confusion,
I'm a song to the Muses from Parnassus sprung.

I'm noted for dancing a jig in good order,
A minuet I'd march and foot a good reel,
In country dances I'm the leading partner,
I ne'er yet faltered from a crack in the heel.

I'd write a fine letter on paper or parchment,
Construe an author and give the due *senor* (?)
I'd court the fair maidens unknown to their parents,
And thrash in their barns without evidence.

I encounter the valiant of congregations,
I beat the courageous and humble the bold,
I'm the true son of an ancient Milesian,
In the annals of fame my name is enrolled.[116]

A charming song of seduction called 'The Turf and Reading-made-easy', printed in a 1788 Monaghan chapbook, relates the encounter of a poor scholar with an impressionable protegée on her way to school and contains multiple references to hedge school trappings. These include a conventional portrayal of the poor scholar and his ragged clothes and a reference to the piece of turf each pupil was expected to provide for fuel for the day, as well as to the popular primer *Reading Made Easy*. Although composed in a style more typical of contemporary street balladry than the more florid schoolmaster song, these lyrics convey a sense of the prevalence of the hedge school in late eighteenth-century Ireland:

You lads of the nation of high and low station,
Attend to my humorous ditty,
Believe me 'tis new, and is certainly true,
Perhaps you may say it is pretty;
It happen'd in spring when the small birds di[d] sing;
And fields were enambled with daisey's,
I met with my jewel a going to School,
With her Turf and her Reading made easy.

I rov'd up and down, thro' both country and town,
And was by my trade a poor scholar,
My earning I beg'd and likewise my bread,
My cloaths were not worth half a dollar;

> As I carelessly straid I did meet this fair maid,
> With a smile and a low courtsey said she,
> I'll give you my blessing and teach me a lesson,
> She opene'd her Reading Made Easy.[117]

Many hedge schoolmaster songs include the 'If I were a scholar' formula – also found in macaronic and Irish-language songs – often with added allusions to various paragons of classical learning:

> Were I like to Pliny or learned Socrates,
> Or Plato that poet of old,
> Could I write like Virgil, or indite like the Muses,
> By me her praises could not be told;
> Cupid shot the dart and well aimed it at me,
> I am bound and no mortals from death can me free,
> But you that's the model of fair chastity,
> By my charming young Molly m'Koan.[118]

A simpler variation on this theme appears in 'The Flower of Tyrone':

> If I was a scholar these words for to write,
> Or was I a headpiece these words to endite;
> But since I want learning these words for to pen,
> I must be admitted and so these words do end.[119]

Such lyrics are a powerful testament to the increasing prevalence of learning and literacy in late eighteenth-century Ireland, providing songs with new metaphors while reflecting the country's social realities.

III. Translations and Macaronics

Since a number of established poets were also hedge schoolmasters, it is tempting to ask whether they themselves could have contributed to the hedge schoolmaster repertoire – particularly since a number of the poets and poet-scribes of the period also dabbled in translation, with varying degrees of poetic success. For example, Clare poet Seón Lloyd attempted an English translation of his own *aisling* 'Cois Leasa dhom go hUaigneach ar Uair na Maidne im Aonar' ('By a Fort One Morning Lonely'), illustrating, as another Clareman and schoolmaster, Donncha Ó Mathúna, noted, a marked want of understanding of poetics and felicity of composition.[120] Diarmaid Ó Muirithe, in his examination of such translations, observes that their greatest fault lies in their false elegance and bombastic diction – faults often voiced about hedge schoolmaster songs.[121] In his 1773 manuscript, Lloyd took the liberty of replacing his references to largely native goddesses with classical ones, with the following results:

> To testify my ignorance of that blest one that favoured me,
> To alleviate my pains against the stream of woe,
> I freely asked with submission whether she was Helen or Juno
> Whom the Greek Deity received as a boast;
> Or Diana who delights in fields, or Venus who such beauty yields,
> Or Pallas who destroyed the Greeks and dispers'd thro' the shore,
> Or Dido who Pygmalion discharged for being a tyrant queen,
> Or the charmer who caused all our harbours to groan.[122]

The scribe-schoolmaster Peadar Ó Gealacáin used similar poetic license in his translation of Art Mac Cumhaigh's 'Úr-chill an Chreagáin':

> My dear, you vainly question me for uncertain is my night's repose.
> I am a wandering effigy, my residence is to and fro,
> My name is lovely Terpsichore, in Greece my sisters are well known,
> Had I been in Britain I'd be instantly in sweet Tyrone.

The original verse, as transcribed by Ó Gealacáin, runs:

> Créd é fáth do cheiste, óir ní chodlaim air an táobhsa 'Bhóinn.
> Is síogaidh beag leinibh me, do hoileadh le táobh Ghráineoig.
> I mbruighin cheart na n-ollamh bhíom go follas ag dúsgadh 'n chéoil.
> Innsa n-oídhche dá bhéinn ag Teamhar, bhéinn ar maidin i gclár Thír-Éoghain.
>
> Why do you question me, since I do not sleep on this side of the Bóinn.
> I am a child of the sídh, reared beside Grainneog.
> In the true homes of the learned I am known to awaken music.
> – at night in Teamhair, in the morning on the plain of Tír Eoghain.[123]

Ó Muirithe believes that the proliferation of translations and macaronic songs during this period sprang from the same linguistic braggadocio that inspired much of the macaronic verse of the medieval *scolares vagantes*: academic exuberance and pride in the knowledge of a foreign language.[124] Indeed, even in the late twentieth century I have been told by traditional singers that the insertion of an English word or phrase in an Irish song made it somehow more substantial, or 'firmer'.[125] While such comments may have reflected linguistic insecurity, Declan Kiberd observes that:

> The immense demand for macaronic ballads suggests a cheerfully bilingual community, whose members admired and enjoyed fluency in both languages. Far from indicating a loss of purity in Gaelic tradition, the very fact that the framing language in most of these ballads is Irish indicates a culture still confident of its ability to hold its own.[126]

As Ó Muirithe has also demonstrated, Irish macaronic song has a long history that can be traced at least as far back as the eleventh century in Gaelic and Latin hymns. According to Ó Muirithe, the macaronic songs in Irish and English that flourished in the eighteenth and nineteenth centuries are direct descendants of their medieval monastic and scholastic counterparts in both medieval Ireland and continental Europe, and he identifies at least six subgroups of the genre. (These, like many other genres and metres in the Irish poetic tradition, seem to have disappeared some time during the Middle Ages only to re-emerge in the eighteenth century.) Later Irish macaronic songs appear to represent a transitional form between wholly Irish songs and their English counterparts, combining French and Irish songs genres, Irish metrical forms and other paraphernalia of eighteenth-century Irish song, with English lines, phrases or verses inserted according to either generic models or apparent whim. The English components of these songs reflect a range of possible linguistic and stylistic influences, including British ballad sheet style, the Hiberno-English idiom and the more grandiloquent style associated with the hedge school, peppered with classical allusions and Latinate diction. I quote examples illustrating each category, respectively:

> And I wish I was in England
>   A merchantman to be,
> And my true love to be with me,
>   How happy we would be;
> She would pay the reckoning,
>   And I'd drink most merrily,
> And I'd swim the broad Atlantic
>   With my cailín fearúil fionn
>   [With my lively, fair-haired girl].

* * * * *

> Ar maidin inné is ea dhearcas an stuaire cailín;
> [It was yesterday morning I beheld the handsome young girl]
> Her limbs were complately and nately covered in green,
> A mala deas caol is a béal tais ba rómhilis binn,
> [Her fine, slender eyebrows and her soft, tender mouth]
> And I knew by her gazing she'd play the Hide and Go Seek.

* * * * *

> Where is Julius Caesar
>   And Hector and Milesius,
> Orthu seo níl trácht in aon chor [Of these there is no mention at all
>   Is ba mhór a nglóir fadó [And great was their glory long ago];
> The love of Naoise and Deirdre,
> Or Alexander's daring –
> Cheapadar siúd nár bhaol dóibh [They thought there was no danger],
>   Go leanfaidh an saol go deo [But that life would last forever].[127]

Some of these songs, with their cachet of higher learning originally associated with the cloister or university, may have served as a kind of bridge or apprenticeship for the hedge schoolmaster song; although, alternatively, they may have co-existed with them and with the translations that also proliferated at the time. A number of macaronic songs were composed by (or attributed to) known poets, several of whom were also schoolmasters: e.g. Eoghan Rua Ó Súilleabháin's 'Under an Arbour of a Wide-Spreading Fagus'; Uilliam English's 'Do Tharlaigh Inné Orm' ('I Met Yesterday'); Donncha Ó Súilleabháin's 'An Móta Glas' ('The Green Moat'); Andrias Mac Craith's 'Tá Céadar, Tá Caesar, Tá Treon' ('A Hero in Valour Most Brave'); Seán Clárach Mac Domhnaill's 'Comhracann mo Mhacaomh is Cannan chómh Binn' ('My Laddie Can Fight, and My Laddie Can Sing'); and Pádraig Mac a Liondain's 'The Angelical Maid'.[128] Of these, only 'Angelical Maid', 'Tá Céadar' and 'Fagus' are patently in the hedge schoolmaster mode – although scribe Pádraig Mac Gabhann's 'Angelical Maid for Whom I Rave' certainly belongs to that category. The others are in a pedestrian, even earthy, idiom, indicating a notable familiarity with current popular song in both Irish and English.

As we have already seen, however, poet and schoolmaster Peadar Ó Doirnín contributed to the hedge schoolmaster genre, exploiting it primarily for purposes of parody. It is worthwhile, however, in relation to hedge schoolmaster songs in English, to examine some of his wholly Irish compositions. For example, 'An Ghéag dá dTug Mé Grá Di' ('The Maiden to Whom I Gave My Love') contains lines worthy of a number of the female panegyrics we have already seen as part of the hedge schoolmaster repertoire:

> An ghéag dá dtug mé grá di is áille í ná Helen mhór
> is an triúr a nochtaigh a mbánchneas do Pharis fán úll óir,
> is gile a píob is a bráighe ná an bán-shneachta ar thaobh an róíd
> is tá an lile i ndeabhaidh 'e ghnáth ina dá ghruaidh is an dearg-rós.
>
> The maid I love is fairer than great Helen of old,
> and the three who showed their fair skin to Paris for the apple of gold,
> brighter is her throat than the white snow on the side of the road,
> and in her two cheeks the lily contends with the rose.[129]

If Ó Doirnín was not in fact imitating hedge schoolmaster style, northern Anglophone schoolmasters could well have imitated his. Meanwhile, although not a hedge schoolmaster as such, eighteenth-century Irish-language composer-harper Pádraig Mac a Liondain was reputed to have run a school of poetry at Killen Hill near Dundalk. Among his compositions is this curiosity:

> Now there lives a Dame that might save Queen Heccuba's harms
> And spare the sundry nations the pains they then took to Arms,
> Atrides still cou'd ease Iphigenia from her sad Alarms,
> If our Miss was there among the fair with her blooming Charms.
>
> On Ida's Mount there ne'er did a Creature contend for Love
> That should more justly gain Approbation from men and Jove,
> Than Miss Handlon, Kate, full as neat as the Nymphs above,
> When they descend their Grace to extend in each verdant Grove.[130]

These examples demonstrate that at least a few poets and scribes contributed to the class of compositions I have denominated 'hedge schoolmaster songs', especially within the macaronic and translation traditions, reflecting the traits I have identified as typical of the genre: Latinate diction, classical allusion, exploitation of native song genres and the conspicuous display of erudition. It is, at this stage, impossible to say how many known poets composed such songs; and without greater evidence, it is safer to assume – particularly given the sense that many poets had of themselves as custodians of native literary tradition – that it was chiefly less elevated schoolmasters, as well as some of the scribes or scribe/schoolmasters, who composed the majority of the wholly English-language songs. Yet it was very probably under the influence of such experiments in translation and macaronic song indulged in by poets, scribes and schoolmasters alike that the hedge schoolmaster songwriter proper appropriated not only forms like the Irish *aisling* and the *reverdie* for his new wholly English compositions, but also popular Gaelic metrical forms.

For example, Mac a Liondain's song employs the same *amhrán* metre used by Aogán Ó Rathaille for 'Is Fada Liom Oíche Fhírfhluich' ('The Drenching Night Drags On') or as that employed in the anonymous 'Tá Mé 'mo Shuí' ('I Am Sitting Up'), with lines of five feet and five assonantal stresses. These assonances rhyme both horizontally and vertically, as the following verse from 'Tá Mé 'mo Shuí' demonstrates:

> Tá mé 'i mo *shuí* ó d'*éi*righ an *ghea*lach ar*éir*,
> Ag *cur* tine *síos* gan *scíth*, s' á *fadú* go *géar*,
> Tá *bun*adh an *tí* 'na *luí* is tá *mi*se liom *féin*,
> Tá na *coi*ligh ag *glaoch* is tá n' *saol* 'na *gco*ladh ach *mé*.[131]

Compare this with the following verse from Mac a Liondain's song, paying special attention to italicized assonantal rhymes in both songs:

> Now *there* lives a *Dame* that might *save* Queen *Hec*cuba's *harms*
> And *spare* the sundry *Na*tions the *pains* they *then* took to *Arms*,
> Atrides still cou'd *ease* Iphig*e*nia from *her* sad A*larms*,
> If our Miss was *there* among the *fair* with *her* blooming *Charms*.

By far the most common native form found in hedge schoolmaster songs, however, is *ochtfhoclach*, a stress metre of considerable antiquity.[132] One of the most common forms of the metre is characterized by an eight-stress, 3A + B assonantal pattern, with monosyllabic cadences. The form enjoyed considerable popularity in Irish song-poetry after the seventeenth century, as illustrated by songs in Irish like 'Preab san Ól' and, in English, by those like 'The Colleen Rue':

> Kind sir, be *easy*/and do not *tease me*
> with your false *praises*/most jest*ingly*;
> Your dissimu*lation*/and invo*cation*
> are vaunting *praises*/alluring *me*.

I'm not Au*rora*/or the goddess *Flora*
    but a rural *female*/to all men's *view*,
That's here con*doling*/my situ*ation*
    my appel*lation*/the Colleen *Rue*.[133]

'The Boys of Mullaghbawn' (which, judging from historical allusions dates from the 1780s, but first appears on ballad sheets from the early nineteenth century) illustrates another, related pattern:

> Now to end my lamen*tation*,
> we are all in conster*nation*,
> for want of edu*cation*,
> I now must end my *song*,
> Since without hesi*tation*,
> we are charged with combi*nation*,
> and sent for transpor*tation*,
> from the hills of Mullagh*bawn*.[134]

As Hugh Shields observes of a similar song, while not always 'used regularly and tending to turn into consonantal rhyme ... the Gaelic pattern is reflected. Both melodic and poetic content make of this song a translation – except in mere verbal detail – from Irish lyric love song'.[135] Its obscure history makes it impossible to ascertain from what level, literary or popular, the form ultimately derives; however, it occurs so frequently in hedge schoolmaster songs that I am inclined to believe that it was they who first adapted it for use in English-language songs in imitation of the Gaelic poets with whom it was so popular.

IV. Neoclassicism and the Hedge Schoolmaster Song

The influence of the eighteenth-century British Neoclassical tradition on hedge schoolmaster songs is undeniably evident in these songs, but to what extent remains an open, and arguable, question. Certainly there are numerous examples of Neoclassical style, imagery and diction in the translations, macaronics and English-language songs of the period. The classical allusions and the invocation of the muses (though surprisingly rare in British ballads of this period), along with the 'feathered songsters', 'nymphs' and 'swains' that inhabit the groves, dales and 'verdant plains' of these songs obviously owe much to eighteenth-century English verse conventions, both popular and elite. Clare poet Ned Lysaght seems to have absorbed such influences – in this case in both Irish and English:

> Is binne a ceol ná lon 's ná smól,
> Is ná Philimeol ar chraobh na suile;
> Mar long faoi sheol
> Ar thoinn gan cheo
> Is ea chím mo stór i nGarrán a'Bhile.

> Philomel, I've listened oft
> To thy sweet lay night weeping willow;
> But oh, the strains more sweet, more soft,
> That flows from Kate of Garnavilla.[136]

Such songs obviously reflect, as Ó Muirithe remarks, an attempt to integrate Augustan poetic diction with the clever and exuberant language – and in many cases, the metric features – of Gaelic song, as Patrick O'Mahony's translation of 'Fáinne Geal an Lae' also illustrates:

> As I walked out one morning fair all in the summer time,
> Each bush and tree were clad in green and vallies in their prime,
> Returning homewards from a wake thro' fields I bent my way,
> There I espied a comely maid by the dawning of the day.[137]

That Augustan poetic conventions were widely disseminated in English-speaking Ireland is abundantly clear not only from the works of such well-known Anglophone writers as Goldsmith, Swift and Sheridan, but also of able contemporaries like Mary Barber, Constantia Grierson, Patrick Delaney, James Ward and Jonathan Smedley – as well as lesser lights like Nahum Tate and Matthew Pilkington. The works of Swift, Pope and Thompson were used as reading matter in some hedge schools, and a great deal of Neoclassical Irish verse also circulated anonymously on ballad sheets during the early eighteenth century, including the following excerpt from 'The Cavalcade: A Poem On the Riding the Franchises' (*c.* 1716):

> O thou, bright *Phoebus*, Ruler of the Day,
> Expel rough Winds and drive the Clouds away,
> Reserve ill Weather for the silent Night,
> Nor let rude Showers disturb the Glorious Sight:
> Then will each Heroe at the Nights approach,
> Come home with dry *Cockade* without a *Coach*,
> And own great *GEORGE* and *Jove* alternate sway,
> *Jove* rules the Night and *GEORGE* commands the Day.[138]

In the mid-eighteenth century, Sir Arthur Dawson composed a popular 'translation' of harper Turlough Carolan's 'Tomás Muiris Jones', rendered by Dawson as 'Bumper Squire Jones', and loaded with Neoclassical accoutrements totally absent from the original:

> Ye Lovers who pine
> For Lasses who oft prove as cruel as fair,
> Who whimper and whine for Lillies and Roses,
> With Eyes, Lips and Noses, or Tip of an Ear;
> Come hither, I'll shew you, how *Phillis* and *Chloe*,
> No more shall occasion such Sighs and such Groans;
> For what mortal so stupid as not to quit *Cupid*,
> When call'd by good Claret and Bumpers, 'Squire Jones.[139]

From perhaps a more unexpected quarter, come the following impeccable couplets by Irish-language poet Seán Ó Tuama:

> How entertaining Amaryllis finds
> A method to revive our drooping minds,
> And surveys sylvan groves in pleasing hours
> Amongst the stately trees and shady bowers.
> The feathered choir melodious notes do move
> With tunes attending to the heavens above.[140]

It is easy to see how set phrases from Neoclassical models could become horrifying clichés in the hands of schoolmaster songwriters, sometimes little removed from the kind of nonsensical speech John O'Keeffe gives his ex-schoolmaster, Lingo: 'Here [sic] this you azure woods, you purling plains, you verdant skies, you crystal swains, ye feathered fountains, trinkling groves, you cooing kids, ye capering doves!'[141]

Not surprisingly, a number of the British songs found in late eighteenth-century Irish-printed chapbooks also reflect the social and literary influences of the period. Classical allusions, for example, are common in many English and Scottish songs of the time, although such allusions tend to be more incidental and less integral to the forms they serve than those found in hedge schoolmaster songs – unless they occur in the context of drinking songs, hunting songs, or (and often to a lesser degree) pastoral songs. Pastoral songs of Irish origin appear to be relatively uncommon, the majority of those printed in Ireland during this period having been imported from England; but the popularity of Allan Ramsay's pastoral play 'The Gentle Shepherd' in hedge schools may have helped to familiarize many with the form's conventions. Many of these imported pastorals are of the type that met with success at Vauxhall Gardens, like 'The Cottage Boy', printed with music in Dublin in 1793 and in a Belfast chapbook in 1808:

> MORN shakes her locks, the budding rose
>   Smiles at the parting twilight grey,
>   In renovated beauty blows,
>   And sheds her perfume on the day
> When Lubin, Nature's rustic child,
>   Tries calm contentment to enjoy,
> And sweetly in his wood-notes wild,
>   Thus cheerful sings the Cottage Boy.[142]

One identifiably Irish pastoral is 'Molly Astore', written by Grattan parliamentarian and songwriter George Ogle. Essentially an English-style pastoral with an Irish veneer, the song's earliest known printing is on a London ballad sheet in 1775; and while it later appeared in a Limerick-printed chapbook, it was even more widely circulated in London, where it received several different printings, including ones that call for guitar or pianoforte accompaniment and another that mentions it as 'a favourite Irish air':

> As down on Banna's Banks I strayed one evening in May,
> The little Birds with blithest notes made vocal every spray,
> They sung their little tales of love, they sung them o'er and o'er,
> Ah, ghra-ma-chree, ma colleen ogue, my Molly Asthore.[143]

A few of the hedge schoolmaster songs surviving from late eighteenth- and early nineteenth-century chapbooks also have a heavy pastoral overlay; yet they ultimately reveal their Irish and schoolmasterish origins, as in 'The Flower of Nature'. This item comes closer than most Irish songs to the English style, partly because of the author's greater than usual mastery of English idiom and convention; yet it retains the internal rhymes of Gaelic song, the Hiberno-English identification of *ea* and *a* (as in *feature* and *nature*), as well as the set pieces and stylistic turns characteristic of hedge schoolmaster song, such as references to the contest on Mount Ida and to the ubiquitous rose and lily:

> Her person neat, her mein complete,
>   Her cheeks like two blown roses,
> Her skin outvies the lilies fair,
>   Fresh beauty it discloses;
> Her eyes appear like diamonds bright.
>   Or the orient stars of Morning;
> Her temples grac'd by auburn locks
>   So lovely her adorning.
>
> Had Paris seen this beauteous Queen,
>   Upon the mount of Ida,
> The golden apples as her prize,
>   He'd surely have resign'd her:
> For, from the other goddesses,
>   Tho' fair in ev'ry feature
> The golden prize would have been gain'd
>   By this Sweet flower of Nature.[144]

Conversely, I have discovered few English-printed ballads of the period at all reminiscent of the kind of highly florid, allusive sort we have seen in hedge schoolmaster songs – except, as I have mentioned, in some hunting and drinking songs, which often indulge in extensive classical allusion and appear to occupy a special category. Apart from these, an English-printed pastoral, 'The Cottager's Daughter' (with music by Vauxhall composer James Hook, printed in London, Alnwick, Morpeth and Dublin around 1800), suggests a related, hybrid style:

> Ah! Tell me, ye swains, have ye seen my Pastora,
>   O say, have you met the sweet nymph on your way,
> Transcendent as Venus and bright as Aurora,
>   From Neptune's bed rising, to hail the new day.
> Forlorn do I wander and long time have sought her,
>   The fairest, the rarest, for ever my theme;

> A goddess in form, tho' a cottager's daughter,
> That dwells on the borders of Aln's winding stream.[145]

But the majority of British pastorals printed on both sides of the Irish Sea contain far more shepherds than gods and owe less to the French *pastourelle* than to the Neoclassical pastoral:

> As Damon and Phillis were keeping of sheep,
> And free from all care, they retired to sleep,
> Soon Phillis arose, stept behind the green oak,
> To see how her Damon would look when he woke.[146]

If it is difficult to find pure pastorals of undisputed Irish origin, it is also highly unusual to find either the invocation of the muses or female praise songs of the hedge schoolmaster variety, with their 'Flowers', 'Stars', 'Diamonds', 'Phoenixes' and 'Pearls', in contemporary British printed ballads: so rare, in fact, that one is immediately led to suspect Irish influence. Crofton Croker believed that female praise songs exhibiting a 'fondness for local association', in which the honoured woman 'becomes the presiding goddess of the place', constituted, when found in England, 'a parasitical growth'; and he asserted that songs of this stamp, like 'The Lass of Richmond Hill', were 'known to be the productions of Irishmen'.[147] Indeed, this song, while displaying more Neoclassical than hedge school influence, was composed by Irish playwright and barrister Leonard MacNally and published in London in 1790 for the Vauxhall market, again with music by James Hook:

> This lass so neat, with smiles so sweet
> Has won my right good will,
> I'd crowns resign to call thee mine,
> Sweet lass of Richmond Hill ...
>
> How happy will the shepherd be,
> Who calls this nymph his own,
> O may her choice be fixed on me,
> Mine's fixed on her alone.[148]

It is therefore highly probable that other hybrid pastorals like 'The Cottager's Daughter' were either Irish-written or written in imitation of Irish songs.

Thus, while influence on Irish song composers from both British popular song and elite poetry must certainly be acknowledged, the overall effect of most hedge schoolmaster songs – with their convoluted Latinate vocabulary, assonantal rhymes, luxuriant literary allusions, and use of forms like the *aisling*, *reverdie* and *pastourelle* – is startlingly different from anything produced by British versifiers of the period, rendering the genre a thing apart from even its closest English and Scottish counterparts. Thus, although the diction may appear to be British, the use made of it in these songs is peculiarly Irish, even in such highly anglicized items as 'The Flower of Nature', or these lines from 'The Lovers' Meeting':

On a Summers Day, as late I wander'd,
Down by yon murmuring fountain's side,
Where resplendant Phoebus did cast his beams,
The pink and daisy display'd their pride.
I spy'd a damsel whose lovely features,
Might sure engage all the Knights in Troy,
And without her favour or hopes to gain her,
Sly Cupid's arrow would me destroy.[149]

Or, more conspicuously:

Ye balmy gales that erose the dales,
    And whisper through the grove,
Breathe on her lips and bosom fair,
    That I shall ever love,
And with thy odours feast each muse,
    And bid them all convene,
To aid the bard who sings the praise
    Of Tullymores fair queen.[150]

Figure 4.2: *A Compleat New Song Called Tullymore's Fair Queen, To which are Added THE CUCKOO'S NEST and MOLLY-O*
(Down, Graham & Lennin, 1809), Cleland Collection, Ulster Museum.
Reproduced courtesy the Trustees of National Museums, Northern Ireland.

Added to all of this is the possibility that at least part of the turgid style associated with much schoolmaster poetry may have pre-dated the Augustan Age. In 1583 Richard Stanyhurst (educated in Kilkenny and Oxford) published,[151] as an addendum to his translation of Virgil's *Aeneid*, 'An Epitaph, entitvled *Commune Defunctorum*, such as our vnlearned *Rithmours* accustomablye make vpon thee death of everie *Tom Tyler*, as yf yt were a *last* for euery one his *foote*, in which the quantitees of syllables are not too bee heeded':

> Coom to me, you muses and thow most chieflye Minerva,
> And ye that are dwellers in dens of darckened Averna;
> Help mye pen in wryting, a death moste soarye reciting,
> Of the good old Topas, soon too thee mightye syr Atlas.
> For gravitee the Cato; for wyt, Mars, Bacchus, Apollo;
> Scipio for warfare, for gentyl curtesye Cæsar.[152]

The fact that Stanyhurst's own verse scans with almost equal infelicity notwithstanding, the conventions he burlesques here are too close to the eighteenth-century schoolmaster's own style to dismiss as sheer coincidence. (Crofton Croker, certainly, took the addendum as 'an imitation of the Anglo-Irish style'.)[153] Rather, it is possible that the pretensions of earlier Anglo-Irish versifiers – along with the classically mediated educations of many hedge schoolmasters – had as much influence on their songs as did contemporary literary trends.

V. Social History and the Aesthetics of Popular Song

If we look at this sort of verse as a literary game, it is possible to view much of the schoolmaster-poet's output, both macaronic and wholly English, as a similar kind of diversion. There is indeed a whimsical genius in these 'effusions', deplored by collectors and scholars, but obviously enjoyed by singers – along with a strong element of play. Moreover, many of the songs possess an underlying tone of self-mockery that belies their apparent ponderousness.

In any case, they remained popular in both oral and printed tradition: the conventions of the hedge schoolmaster song, first evident from written sources in the last decades of the eighteenth century, endured without much change throughout much of the nineteenth century, affecting the repertoires of song communities well into the twentieth and twenty-first. Although Paddy Tunney is undoubtedly the most famous of recent traditional Irish singers to specialize in the genre (popularizing, for example, 'Moorlough Mary', 'Lough Erne's Shore' and 'Easter Snow', all learned from older family members), many other singers of the last fifty years have also included at least one or two specimens of the genre in their repertoires. Geordie Hanna of County Tyrone was well-known for his singing of 'Dobbin's Flowery Vale' and 'Old Arboe'; Len Graham traces his oral sources for 'The Flower of Gortade' back at least two generations;[154] and the late Tom Lenihan (1905–1990) was apparently the only source in recent oral tradition for 'Paddy's Panacea', although the song itself can be found in an 1899 collection called *The Emerald Isle Song Book*:

> Through my youthful progression to years of discretion
> My childhood's impression still clung to my mind.
> For at school or at college the bolus of knowledge
> I never could gulp till with whiskey combined;
> And as older I'm growing, time's ever bestowing
> On Erin's potation a flavour so fine.
> And how e'er they may lecture 'bout Jove and his nectar
> Itself is the only true liquor divine.[155]

Such conventions are still employed in contemporary Irish songs of a more traditional bent, especially for parodic or satiric purposes. Take, for example, Con 'Fada' Ó Drisceoil's 'The Miltown Fourteen', based on a macaronic song from County Cork and commemorating a frivolous court case in Miltown Malbay in 1991:

> Approach you Muses nine and preserve me from banality,
> As I sing in flawless rhyme of a routine illegality.
> You'll hear of Garda raids in a metre without blemishes
> And of our escapades in a West Clare licensed premises.
> Is é Annraoi an Poncánanch an chúis go rabhamar damanta.
> [It's Henry the Yank was the cause of our damnation.] [156]

The channels through which these conventions were transmitted existed partly as a result of a cultural transition that diminished social and intellectual distinctions within the native population, even as the social and economic base was shifting towards a broader, more commercial, more literate and more cosmopolitan model. The hedge schoolmaster himself emerges as an emblem of this transition. Highly respected for his learning, he was often at the centre of community life, frequently acting as general scribe, lawyer, religious instructor, political organizer and repository of tradition – a resource of 'Everything ... that the needs of a community would demand, and much that would add to its intellectual store'.[157] As Sean Connolly comments:

> The teacher, literate, bilingual, geographically mobile, was a key figure, permitting the transmission down the social scale of a variety of elements – fragments of the high culture of the vanished Gaelic order, snatches of classical erudition, borrowings form the oral and printed culture of Anglophone Ireland – in ways that are only now beginning to be unravelled.[158]

Kevin Whelan, observing that 'the Irish sense of gentility was much wider than that of the English or French', notes that 'the spectrum was broadened by the scale of the seventeenth-century upheavals, which created this underground gentry milieu, blurring the social categories so readily apparent in England or France'.[159] This process seems to have been reflected on a local community level, as well as on that of the more affluent middleman or the 'strong farmer', not only by the occasional presence of a scribe, poet or schoolmaster who could facilitate the cultural transmission Connolly describes, but also by the aspirations for the sort of knowledge embodied by the schoolmaster himself. In his description of community life in mid-nineteenth-century Donegal, Hugh Dorian describes men of any pretension to learning as 'local celebrities', and the schoolmaster as 'president' of any gatherings of these stars, without whose presence 'no meeting was complete'.[160] Hence, while on a material level distinguished from the rest of the community only by his learning in an age when schoolmasters and poets alike might also of necessity work as farm labourers or in other non-scholastic occupations, the schoolmaster occupied an honoured place in the community by virtue of his erudition and, especially if he was also a scribe or poet, by his literary activity. It is thus that in the Anglo-Irish song tradition from the eighteenth century to the present time one finds lyrics of not only ludicrous pedantry but also of distinction and genuine learning, with clear connections to the Gaelic song tradition of the same period. Obviously, not all hedge schoolmaster lyrics possess equal merit as poetry. Some are intentionally (or unintentionally) humorous; some are merely charming; but the best are highly expressive works of song-poetry. For example, although not published in book form until 1831, some of the songs of County Antrim schoolmaster Hugh McWilliams may have circulated in manuscript, in oral and in print form prior to this date, and several of his best have remained in oral tradition until the present day, including the popular 'A Man in Love':

> A man in love can feel no cold, for I not long ago,
> To see my girl like a hero bold set off through frost and snow;
> Fair Cynthia cheered me with her light along the tedious way,
> To that dear place though late at night, where all my treasure lay.[161]

One of the best hedge schoolmaster songs to have survived in print from late eighteenth-century chapbooks is 'The North Country Beauty', which, along with more typically pedantic but artful lines like:

> You inspired Muses of sense and knowledge
> To me your mighty aid impart,
> To praise a Maiden who has inslaved me,
> And stole away my tender heart

also contains verses like the following, more reminiscent of Elizabethan than Augustan lyrics:

> Come cruel death and quickly ease me,
> Of the pains which I endure,
> And pierce yon dart to my heart,
> That my sorrows may be no more;
> Since this lovely creature will shew no favour,
> To her poor and wounded swain,
> My endless sorrows are approaching,
> Come quickly death and ease my pain.[162]

Another song – which appears in versions of varying quality in early nineteenth-century chapbooks, but seems to have benefited from its sojourn in oral tradition – is 'Easter Snow' (or 'Estersnow'). The following version is from a Waterford chapbook dated approximately 1820:

> It being the twilight of the morning,
> As I roved out all on the dew,
> With my morning cloak wraped around me;
> Intending on my flocks to view,
> Where I beheld a charmer,
> Whose beauty oh it did shine bright,
> She far exceeds diana,
> Or the evening star that rules by night.[163]

To what extent such songs reflect the increasing literacy of the period is not entirely clear, although it is, practically speaking, impossible to separate such songs from their educational and literate context. While it is possible that schoolmasters may in some instances have sung them or taught them to local singers, it is doubtful that the songs themselves would have been used in the hedge schools as pedagogical tools. Yet they may have made their way into the homes of some of the pupils in printed form, as did *Robin Hood's Garland* and the ballads that the Halls excoriated in the mid-eighteenth century,[164] especially when they were published and sold locally, like those of the Laggan song-poets of the early nineteenth century.[165] But the fact that many were in print at a time when the market for cheap English-language material was expanding suggests that the genre was widespread and popular enough to be thought competitive with British songs of the period, which appeared either side-by-side in the same chapbooks or in ones of similar make and were designed for much the same market. Even given the limited quantity of Irish-printed items extant from the eighteenth century, there are a surprising number of hedge schoolmaster lyrics in small late eighteenth- and early nineteenth-century songbooks and, later, on ballad sheets and slips. Print alone does not prove popularity, as at least an initial printing could be paid for by the composers of the songs themselves. Yet, according to Charles Gavin Duffy, writing in the mid-nineteenth century about earlier tradition, 'The songs sung among the people were written originally by Hedge

Schoolmasters, and had a tendency to run into classic allusions, and abounded in sonorous "purple words" without much precise meaning, but which seemed to move the lively imagination of an Irish audience like music.'[166] Duffy's statement – and the popularity of the songs themselves – is reinforced by their currency in Patrick Kennedy's part of Wexford during the early part of the nineteenth century. Kennedy quotes or alludes to many hedge schoolmaster songs in his memoirs, including 'The Cottage Maid', 'Sheela na Guira', 'The Colleen Rua' and 'The Star of Slane'; and although he derides such songs, he is clearly amused by them, and depicts his fellow countrymen as relishing their 'beautiful hard words' and their 'gods and goddesses from east to west', and as possessing 'an instinctive respect for learning ... and no tendency to feel proud of their own ignorance'.[167] This in turn recalls the popularity among the Irish of the arcane diction of the Ossianic 'runs' and romances, often esteemed for their 'hard Irish'.[168] Hugh Shields cites the story of a monoglot Donegal man who once found himself in competition with the champion singer of the next – more anglicized – parish: a man who had been in America and tried to discomfit him by singing a song in English full of long words. Conall, not at all perturbed by his failure to understand these words, pronounced the song a 'very simple one' and retorted with a devastating verse of Irish which lavished abundance of rhyming and alliterative lexical riches on a girl's hair:

> Trom, trom, triopallach, lúbach, bachallach,
> Craobhach, cocánach, camógach, donn,
> Trillseach, torthannach, scuabach, drithlineach,
> Cluainteach, feamaineach, fada, righin, trom,
> Tá a dlaoi ór-folta ag fás go droithleanta,
> Ag soillsiú solais, fríd imeall a cinn
> Ar an pháiste mharánta, mhúinte, mhacánta,
> Mhordha, mhuscailteach, bháin-gheal, ghrinn.

> Heavy, heavy, clustering, mazy, ringleted,/branching, curling, twisting, dark,/plaited, plentiful (?), sweeping, shining,/seductive, twining, long, tensile, heavy./Her golden hair grows in tresses/diffusing light round the head/of the mild, well-mannered, modest child,/the noble, wakeful, fair, clear one.[169]

This and other examples of the reception of both 'hard' Irish and arcane English, suggests a cultural 'fascination with what's difficult' on all levels of Irish society. If monoglot Irish singers could delight in the classical allusions and assonantal metrics of the *aisling* and the *reverdie léannta*, they – and the increasing numbers of those with at least a smattering of English (and indeed growing numbers, especially in urban centers, of monoglot English speakers) – could certainly find entertainment and sometimes genuine artistry in the compositions of those who were participating in the creation of a modern English-speaking Ireland, while in their own fashion, perpetuating the legacy of their Gaelic literary past.

This was a shared, dynamic legacy; and we can surmise from Croker's and Duffy's testimony that the schoolmaster's songs were easily absorbed easily into a song tradition that already valued not only this legacy but also the novelty of a new (albeit largely hybrid) idiom: one whose scholarly trappings, far from deterring local singers, provided them with yet another medium through which they could express their linguistic and musical creativity, while linking them to known patterns of melody, metrics, narrative, and even to some extent, diction. They also reflected the new social realities exemplified by the existence of the hedge school, including the increasing role of the English language, of literacy, and of education itself in eighteenth-century Ireland. When such songs did receive their initial life in print, however, we can posit the same relationship between the songs and their singers as we have already seen operating with those originally written in manuscript form: that is, not only would the majority of singers still have learned them orally, but even those who learned them from print would have treated them primarily not as texts but as songs. Other influences, deriving either from print, from the growing dominance of English, and from the conventions of British balladry that came to bear upon the Irish song tradition, I will deal with in the following chapter.

5 THE EIGHTEENTH-CENTURY PRINTED BALLAD IN IRELAND

My sangs ... were made for singin', an no' for readin', but ye hae broken the charm noo, an' they'll never [be] sung mair.
— James Hogg's mother, to Walter Scott[1]

Many ballad scholars, including F. J. Child, Cecil Sharp, G. L. Kittredge, Gordon Gerould and David Buchan have vigourously agreed with Mrs Hogg's emphasis on the essential orality of the ballad form, and some have deplored the inimical effect of print upon the ballad tradition.[2] Child famously referred to printed ballads as 'veritable dunghills in which, only after a great deal of sickening grubbing, one finds a very moderate jewel',[3] and many twentieth-century scholars have made far-reaching claims about the dramatic changes wrought upon Western culture by the advent of print – some waxing elegiac about the oral or 'preliterate' 'lifeworld' and, in common with Albert Lord, viewing the realms of oral and print culture as fundamentally opposed. Yet, far from being antithetical to oral tradition, the printed ballad has played a central role in traditional and popular song, in Britain since at least the sixteenth century, and in Ireland since the eighteenth, having been approved by the lettered and the unlettered alike. Judging not only from the repertoire that has come down into recent oral tradition, but also from the records we possess of what people sang later in the period, eighteenth-century Irish traditional singers embraced the printed ballad; and, while it was long a truism in folksong scholarship that print stultifies the process of recreation and variation, the Irish example illustrates this has patently not been the case.[4]

The dichotomy between oral and printed ballads has been reinforced since the late eighteenth century by a long-standing scholarly distinction between two basic kinds of ballads in oral circulation. While both classes are primarily defined as 'narrative songs', the first consists of putatively older, 'traditional' ballads, many with continental counterparts; and the second, of 'broadside' ballads (also commonly referred to as 'street', 'stall', or 'come-all-ye' ballads). Until relatively recently, the majority of folklorists gave pride of place to the oral 'ballad of tradition' – characterized by a 'timeless', dramatic and impersonal narrative;

the 'ballad stanza' (abcb rhyme in alternating ⁴⁄₃ or ⁴⁄₄ stress quatrains); and such stylistic and structural traits as narrative compression, typed characters, incremental repetition and formulaic phrases known as 'commonplaces'. By contrast, the term 'broadside ballad' came to denote a more recent (primarily sixteenth–nineteenth-century) printed narrative song, composed by professionals of varying credentials and characterized by journalistic attention to detail; the use of quatrains employing up to eight or more stresses and (frequently) an aabb rhyme scheme; a subjective and moralistic narrative voice; realistic and contemporary settings and situations; and a narrative approach that is more reportorial than dramatic. By the time Thomas Percy and Joseph Ritson were working on ballads in the late eighteenth century, they were already making generic and aesthetic distinctions between the two varieties of song – although they claimed minstrel rather than 'folk' origins for many ballads in the first category. These distinctions were subsequently modified to reflect the view of nineteenth-century ballad scholars like Svend Grundtvig and F. J. Child that what they deemed the (mostly) older, traditional items were, as Child put it, the 'true popular ballads, the spontaneous products of nature', taken 'from the mouths of the people'; while the later broadsides, although 'sometimes not without grace', belonged to 'artificial literature'.[5] Since the late nineteenth century, when Child established an informal canon of the former genre with his *English and Scottish Popular Ballads*, this sort of ballad has continued to be defined, primarily in stylistic and aesthetic terms, as reflective of a long life in oral tradition.

In the late seventeenth and early eighteenth century, however, a 'ballad' was, as John Phillips's 1706 *New World of Words* put it, 'a common song sung up and down the streets' – a definition that was echoed almost verbatim in Bailey's *Universal Etymological Dictionary* of 1728.[6] This designation included not only narrative songs but lyric songs of all kinds, or their physical representation – a meaning it retains to this day in Ireland, when a singer may refer to a 'ballad', 'ballet', or 'ballat' to indicate the sheet on which the lyrics of a song are printed, or even handwritten.[7] Ballads were sold in a variety of formats: as broadsides (printed on a single side of a sheet of paper); broadsheets (printed on the front and back of a sheet); single-column slip ballads (cut from a sheet containing two or more songs printed in columns – a format that became increasingly common in the late eighteenth and early nineteenth centuries); in chapbooks; and in miscellanies. Chapbooks – which emerged in the sixteenth century, but were especially popular in the late eighteenth century – were sold either as ready-made booklets of eight to thirty-two pages of 4to, 8vo, 12mo, or 16mo size, or as unfolded sheets.[8] Eighteenth-century chapbooks encompassed everything from riddles and jests, fairy tales and prose romances, prophecies and literary abridgements, to eight-page songbooks and 'garlands' (a term applicable to, among other things, collections of songs and poems or to a long ballad in several parts). Songs printed in chapbooks or on ballad sheets often sported woodcuts, usually of a certain quaint crudity, and sometimes, as Friedman remarks, 'only the slenderest connection' with the ballads they were meant to illustrate.[9] Larger and better-bound miscellanies (which typically included a variety of verse and song) occupied the more expensive end of the ballad market: of these Henry Playford's and Thomas D'Urfey's *Wit and Mirth: Or Pills to Purge Melancholy* (1698–1720) and Allan Ramsay's *Tea-Table Miscellany* (1723–27) were two of the most popular.

By the early eighteenth century, British printed ballads encompassed a number of genres: 'old ballads' (historical and legendary favourites like 'Chevy Chase', 'The Blind Beggar of Bednal-Green' and 'The Children in the Wood' – whose aesthetic virtues Joseph Addison defended in *The Spectator*); 'Child' ballads (e.g. 'Barbara Allen' and 'Lord Bateman'); literary imitations, like David Mallet's 'William and Margaret' and John Gay's ''Twas When the Seas Were Roaring'; 'broadside' ballads, whose subjects ranged from tabloid crime and executions to the adventures of transvestite female warriors, accounts of sporting events, military and sexual exploits, etc.; Scottish and pseudo-Scottish ditties; topical and political songs; pastoral love songs; bawdy songs; drinking songs; theatre songs; and so on. Such were the balladic wares that English printers exported to Ireland during this period.

Adam Fox states the obvious when he comments that the implications of literacy 'vary between societies and over time and ... depend upon the particular circumstances of their dissemination and use'.[10] Thus, although printed balladry in Ireland initially depended almost entirely on imports from Britain, it increasingly displayed cultural, linguistic and literary qualities of its own – qualities that in turn came to exercise a strong influence on printed ballads in Britain. Moreover, despite the fact that Irish printed ballads embraced a broad linguistic and artistic spectrum, there is ample evidence to indicate that the audience for these songs became increasingly heterogeneous during the course of the century, reflecting not only growing literacy but also dynamic social interaction. This interchange belies the notion that the educated classes and the commonalty inhabited two wholly discrete cultural worlds, one literate and the other oral.

Unfortunately, as Hugh Shields notes, 'The [Irish] ballad press of the eighteenth century, so far as we know it, gives a patchy view of song repertory, for sheets and songbooks are unevenly preserved'.[11] Despite early allusions to ballads, few ballad sheets or chapbook songsters survive in Ireland from before 1700 – indeed, not in any numbers until the latter part of the eighteenth century.[12] This, however, seems not to be a result of the late arrival of print in Ireland; in fact, the first printing in Ireland took place in Dublin in 1550, and newspapers became increasingly widely available from their establishment during the second half of the seventeenth century until their 'dramatic increase' in the second half of the eighteenth century, both in quantity and in number of towns and cities publishing them.[13] The paucity of early ballad sheets raises the question of whether the Irish ballad trade before this period was particularly weak or whether a less lively antiquarian interest in broadsides and chapbooks meant the retention of far fewer items than in Britain during the same period.[14]

We know from several references, however, that ballads were reasonably widespread in Ireland from at least the late seventeenth century. Limerick-based Dáibhí Ó Bruadair disparaged *sráidéigse* ('street poetry') and, in a poem from 1675 or 1676, he took aim at 'aos órtha an fhuairsceidill' ('the chanters of the frigid sheets').[15] In 1692, a poet – possibly Cormac Ó Luinín – addressed Sir Richard Cox (Lord Chancellor of Ireland from 1703–07) thus:

> Ná raibh tú et cailleach an hata
> Ag crois margaidh lá geimhriota,
> Is caimbeul ort go suighe do chluais,
> A' bollsaireacht bailéd go chrithfhuar.
>
> May you not be with the hag that carries the hat
> In the market-place on a winter's day,
> With a scowl on your face from ear to ear,
> Bawling ballads and shivering with cold.[16]

This depiction accords with British accounts of some ballad-singers as husband-and-wife teams, in this case with the woman acting as 'bottler' or 'hat man'. While these early references are tantalizingly few, they do suggest the existence of a well-established ballad trade (at least in terms of distribution) in the last quarter of the seventeenth century. Other indirect evidence of the early Irish ballad trade exists in the form of newspaper reports and printers' advertisements. Of the former, perhaps the most interesting is a piece in the *Dublin Gazette* of 1712–13, which mentions the Dublin printing of two murder ballads, both in the Palatine, and while refuting their verity, relates their contents. The first title is especially designed to pique prurient interest:

> A true Discovery of this Barbarous and Bloody Murder on the Body of Sarah Walker, by a Palatine innkeeper in the County of Kildare, who is suspected to make it his common way of devouring and trappaning of several men and women that pass'd that way. Together with the manner of his Salting their Bodies in barrels and made use of the same for eating.[17]

Meanwhile, an advertisement by a ballad-singer named John Hicks of 'Smoke-Alley' (Smock Alley) appears in the Dublin *Flying Post* of 6 July 1708, recommending 'all sorts of the Newest Song Books and Ballads' to 'Country Chap-Men' and others. The Reindeer at Mountrath Street is mentioned several times: in *c.* 1722, as the publisher for 'The Weaver's Lamentation'; in the same year, for the 'Printing and Selling a Seditious Ballad'; in 1723, in relation to the piracy of a speech 'learnedly compil'd and Publish'd 3 Months ago by the Ingenious Society of Ballad-Singers of Mountrath Street; and in the 1740s, in connection with Goldsmith's putative youthful ballad-making.[18] It is thus clear that the Mountrath establishment was a site of ballad-printing for several decades, and the dearth of surviving sheets probably reflects the ephemerality of such 'low-grade publications' rather than a lack of trade.[19] Ballad sheets in the Gilbert Library in Dublin from the 1720s (albeit of the more upmarket variety) contribute a number of printers' names, including George Faulkner in Pembroke-Court Castle-street, Elizabeth Sadlier, on Blind-Key, S. Powell in Crane-lane, Tho. Fleming at the Salmon in High Street Dublin, and John Harding, in Molesworth Court. As Hugh Shields comments, 'Evidence is available ... that printers were numerous from the late seventeenth century ... [although] it is a measure of the domestic scale of the industry that the same person appears, at one time as a printer or seller, at another as a singer, of ballads.'[20]

Evidence of ballad writing and selling from the first half of the eighteenth century includes a mention by John Dunton in 1699 of a certain 'Dick', of Dick's Coffee House, who 'has a peculiar Knack of Bantering and will make Rhymes to any thing'; and a notice printed in 1722–3 of the wedding of 'Blind Paddy the Ballad Singer' to 'a young girl about fifteen Years of Age'.[21] In 1737 John Ray sent a letter from New York to one Peter Ennis, a pedlar in Coleraine who was apparently about to emigrate to America, advising him to buy in Dublin and bring with him:

> Sax Quire of Ballads, aw ald yens, as the Babs in the Wood, Chevy Chase ... The Blackmoor, Montross's Lines, Oft have I vow'd to Loove, nor dar Loove, Regard my Grief, Mineful Melpomeny, Young Filander, Macaferson and sindry other ald Songs ... Ballads at l6d a Quire, ald Loove Songs and others, as ye think fit.[22]

The earliest Irish-printed ballad we can date with any certainty is 'Mount Taragh's Triumph', which bears a 1626 Dublin imprint. Set to the tune of 'Mr. Basse, His Career' or 'Hunting the Hare', it describes a 'loyalty pageant' held in honour of Charles I at the Hill of Tara.[23] Like many of the ballads printed in and imported to Ireland from England through at least the first quarter of the eighteenth century, it is topical and aimed primarily at an educated, English-speaking audience. Many of the political ballads printed in Ireland during this period are no less 'loyal', and (when dealing with matters Jacobite) frankly anti-Catholic. Typical is *Labour Lost: Or, A New Ballad upon the Abdication of Three Blunderbus A--n, and Scurvy R---r; together with their Wives, who are gone to the Bath, to Improve their Tails, as their Husbands are gone to London, to Improve their Understandings*:

> God prosper long our Noble QUEEN,
> Our Lives and Safeties all;

A damn'd Rebellion once there did
In IRELAND *befall.*

To Vex the QUEEN and Check the State,
The *Whigs* have found a way,
The Child may rue that is unborn,
Their having so much Sway.[24]

By contrast, the London-printed but certainly Irish-composed 'Blackbird, or the Flower of England flown' is at once thoroughly Jacobite and Irish in tone. Although probably composed in the seventeenth century, its earliest known printing dates from *c.* 1718. The song employs the blackbird as a figure for James III, the Old Pretender (as it was later used in 'The Blackbird of Avondale' for Daniel O'Connell) and is composed in an elegant, Latinate style employing internal rhymes similar to those we have seen in hedge schoolmaster songs:

> Upon a fair morning for soft recreation,
>   I heard a fair lady making her moan,
> With sighing and sobbing and sad lamentation
>   Saying, my Black Bird most royal is flown;
>   My thoughts they deceive me,
>   Reflections do grieve me,
> And I am over-burthened with sad misery,
>   Yet if death it should blind me,
>   As true love inclines me,
> My Black Bird I'll seek out wherever he be.[25]

James Arbuckle, a Presbyterian minister (born in Ireland though educated in Glasgow) who was both a friend of Allan Ramsay and a satirist of Swift, provides us with revealing glimpses into the role of ballads in Irish society during the first quarter of the eighteenth century. Writing for *The Dublin Weekly Journal* on July 10 and 17 of 1725 under the pseudonym of 'Hibernicus', he confides his likes and dislikes in an entertaining fashion, giving us a view of middle-class Dublin taste into the bargain. He approves English ballads like 'the old Song of *Chevy-Chase*' and Lady Elizabeth Wardlaw's ballad 'forgery' 'Hardiknute', echoing and alluding to Addison in his idealized representation of their origins:

> Who the Men were, themselves have not thought fit to let Posterity know; but that they have been Men of Worth and Genius too, is evident from very many of those Half-sheet Performances, that serve for Furniture to the Walls of Country Ale houses and such like Places. These are for the most Part, little Heroick Poems, celebrating some worthy Action, performed either in the Cause of the Publick, or the Defence of distress'd Virtue. Several of them gained the Admiration of the first Writers in our Language.

ROYAL BLACKBIRD.

UPON a fair morning for soft recreation,
  I heard a fair lady was making her moan,
With sighing and sobbing and sad lamentation,
  Saying, "My Blackbird most royal is flown."
    My thoughts they deceive me,
    Reflections do grieve me,
And I am o'er burthened with sad misery.
    Yet if death should blind me,
    As true-love inclines me,
My Blackbird I'll seek out wherever he be.

Once in fair England my Blackbird did flourish,
  He was the chief Blackbird that in it did spring,
Prime ladies of honour his person did nourish,
  Because he was the true son of a king.
    But since that false fortune,
    Which still is uncertain,
Has caused this parting between him and me,
    His name I'll advance,
    In Spain and in France,
And I'll seek out my Blackbird wherever he be.

The birds of the forest all met together,
  The turtle has chosen to dwell with the dove,
And I am resolved in foul or fair weather,
  Once in the spring to seek out my true-love.
    He's all my heart's treasure,
    My joy, love, and pleasure,
And (justly my love) my heart follows thee,
    Who are constant and kind,
    And courageous of mind,
All bliss to my Blackbird wherever he be.

In England my Blackbird and I were together,
  Where he was still noble and generous of heart,
Ah, woe to the time that he first went thither,
  Alas! he was forced from thence to depart.
    In Scotland he's deemed,
    And highly esteemed,
In England he seemeth a stranger to be;
    Yet his fame shall remain,
    In France and in Spain,
All bliss to my Blackbird wherever he be.

What if the fowler my Blackbird has taken,
  Then sighing and sobbing will be all my tune,
But if he is safe, I will not be mistaken,
  And hope yet to see him in May or in June.
    For him through the fire,
    Through mud and through mire,
I will go, for I love him to such a degree,
    Who is constant and kind,
    And noble in mind,
Deserving all blessings wherever he be.

'Tis not the ocean can fright me with danger,
  No, tho' like a pilgrim I wander forlorn,
I may meet with friendship of one that's a stranger,
  Much more than of one that in Britain is born.
    I pray Heaven be spacious,
    To Britain be gracious,
As some there be odious to both him and me,
    Yet joy and renown,
    And laurel shall crown,
My blackbird with honour wherever he be.

Figure 5.1: 'The Royal Blackbird' (London: Such, H., [n.d.]). From the Leslie Shepard Collection; reproduced courtesy Irish Traditional Music Archive (2034-BS).

He also smiles on what he considers to have been love songs of 'about a Hundred, or a Hundred and Fifty Years ago', in which instead of 'forced Turns of Wit and laboured Allusions, we are entertained with the Language of undisguised Nature and true Affection'. As an example, he offers 'Phillis and Amyntas', a sentimental pastoral that would not have been out of place in *The Tea-Table Miscellany*.[26]

Both narrative and lyric English-printed ballads seem to have been widely available in the Dublin of 1725. Of the 'old ballads', popular in late seventeenth and early eighteenth-century England, a number are alluded to or survive in printed form in Ireland, some even appearing in commonplace books. These include 'Chevy-Chase', 'The Norfolk Gentleman's Last Will and Testament' (John Ray's 'Babs in the Wood'), 'The Wandering Jew's Chronicle', 'The Bishop of Canterbury', as well as David Mallet's ballad imitation 'William and Margaret', which was first published in London in 1724 and appeared in print in Dublin by at least 1725. Other popular imported narrative ballads appear to have included Martin Parker's 'Description of a Strange (and Miraculous) Fish', 'The Bloody Murder of Sir John Barley Corn' and 'Mournful Melpomene' (on the death of Charles I's daughter Elizabeth). Hibernicus' article, John Ray's list and a few surviving sheets also suggest the availability of ballads of the English and Scottish miscellany variety, e.g. 'Montrose's Lines' (printed in the 1733 edition of *Tea-Table*), Wilbye's madrigal 'Oft Have I Vow'd to Love', and 'Young Philander'. Much of the Neoclassically influenced rhymes circulating on ballad sheets seem not to have been songs at all but, instead, rather insipid verse. On the other hand, Dublin printer George Faulkner reprinted Henry Carey's satirical and singable 'Mocking Is Catching' in 1726, the same year it was first printed in London; and *The Tea-Table Miscellany* itself was first published in Dublin in 1729. This, of course, does not include ballad sheets and songbooks directly imported from Britain.

Noting that 'the Garrets of *Great Britain* and *Ireland*, are at present inhabited by a Set of People that have [not] the Good of the Rabble sincerely at Heart', Hibernicus deplores the Irish addiction to topical balladry, whereby:

> An important Debate in Parliament, or at the Council board cannot be heard of, but immediately the Arguments *pro* and *con* must be laid out in proper Stanza; and a falling Minister makes his Exit in a Ballad as naturally as if there were a standing Law for that purpose.[27]

During the 1720s, there was a flurry of topical balladry in Dublin associated with Jonathan Swift and his various causes, as well as with other polemicists, satirists and political commentators. There is some dispute over the attribution of a number of ballads to Swift, but items like 'Ireland's Warning ... an Excellent New Song, upon Woods's [sic] Base Half-pence' and 'An Excellent New Song Upon His Grace Our good Lord Archbishop of Dublin' (both attacking Wood's coinage) are commonly accepted as his own productions. More dubious is the 'Excellent New Song Upon the Late Grand-Jury' – which, if it is by Swift, is an example of his writing 'two degrees above Grub Street':[28]

> There's *Donevan*, *Hart* and *Archer* and *Blood*,
> And *Gibson* and *Gerard* all true Men and good,
> All Lovers of *Ireland* and Haters of *Wood*.
> *Which no body can deny.*[29]

Irish-language poets, too, dabbled in this kind of balladry – including Peadar Ó Doirnín, whose 'The Independent Man' seems to have had a very specific genesis. William Brownlow of Lurgan (who stood in a particularly ugly county bye-election against Francis Caulfield in 1753 for a seat in the Dublin Parliament) was also, apparently, a patron of Ó Doirnín,[30] yet the ballad expresses a desire to remain aloof from party politics and factions of all kinds rather than to declare any adherence to Brownlow. It also (ironically) employs the metrics and rhyme scheme – and presumably the melody – of 'Lilliburlero':

> In Heaven's great name, how can they blame
> The poor man, or shame him, in the long run?
> Ambition's their game, what else do they mean,
> But purchase high fame, great power and fun?
> They may swear a big oath that never they'll loath
> The poor dupe that votes for them, 'tis their plan;
> But I'll keep my own vote, I'll give it to none,
> Then what need I care for a Parliament man?[31]

Another schoolmaster-poet, best-known for that great anthem of *carpe diem*, 'Preab san Ól', and said to have composed lyrics in Irish to Carolan's melodies, as well as poems and songs in English, was Riocard Bairéad of Erris, County Mayo. While his few songs in English surviving from manuscript are rather slight, several are remarkable for a style even closer than 'The Independent Man' to that of the topical broadsides of the early part of the century:

> Here's a health to the generous, the brave and the good,
> To all those who think and act as they should,
> And in this all Freemason's health's understood –
>   Which nobody can deny.
>   Which nobody can deny.[32]

Like their counterparts in England, a number of satirical Irish ballads were set to the airs of popular 'old ballads' like 'The Bishop of Canterbury', 'Chevy-Chase' and 'Margaret's Ghost' (Mallet's 'William and Margaret').[33] One ballad set to the tune of 'Margaret's Ghost' appears as a nine-page 1747 production called 'Lovat's Ghost: or, the Courtier's Warning-Piece', which is at once a satire on

Hanoverian rule and a parody of Mallet's ballad.[34] Whether such ballads were ever sung is dubious, though some are clearly 'more singable than others'.[35] Yet even if they were sung in certain contexts, they clearly did not depend upon performance in the way the more popular ballads did. Hibernicus fires a volley at Swift (and probably the Scriblerians as a whole) when, having found fault with less pedigreed ballads – 'poor perishable Things, that are born and die in a Day' – he states that their quality is not to be wondered at, when 'immodest Images and indecent Expressions are adopted by Writers of Genius and Learning'. As Shields observes, 'This "municipal" tradition was anything but polite; it took invective and vituperation in its stride.'[36] Not surprisingly, this tradition could also run towards indelicacy. One entertaining (and singable) satirical ballad on Hugh Boulter, the then newly- minted Archbishop of Armagh, printed in 1725–26 and set to the tune of 'The Bishop of Canterbury', includes such verses as:

> One Day Importun'd by his L--day and --r,
>   To see *Tinny Park* and the great fall of Water.
> He begg'd their excuse but to please 'em he made,
>   By the help of their W-- r a Noble Cascade.[37]

Another 'excellent new ballad', this time on 'The *Wedding* of *Pritty Miss S--ally* to *Jolly* Old *J--o*', by 'Captain Gulliver', concludes:

> Oh now Crys the Mother! My Heart is at rest,
> My Daughter is Married and I'm therein blest,
>   Old *Jo*, has got hold of her *Fair Maiden-Head*,
> Which will hold him tugg, till We are both Dead,
>   When with Her He lies Down, down, dery down.[38]

While none of this would have raised the eyebrows of Playford and D'Urfey fans, Hibernicus obviously took exception. So did at least one influential Belfast Presbyterian: the *Records of the General Synod of Ulster* mention a complaint that 'several obscene ballads' had been printed in Belfast 'and dispers'd through the country'.[39] Such songs, however, began to dwindle by the late 1720s, probably as they were increasingly displaced by political pamphlets. However, the Biggar Collection in Belfast contains a number of early nineteenth-century ballads, election squibs and the like, which reflect much the same stylistic qualities as do their Dublin predecessors. The existence of similar collections in Cork from the same period seems to suggest that such sheets continued to be printed throughout the eighteenth century.[40] But that they did diminish in Dublin is reflected not only in the dearth of surviving sheets of this stamp but also in Hibernicus' relieved announcement that this 'Abuse of vulgar Metre ... seems to be pretty much laid aside at present'. Such ballads, at any rate, according to Hibernicus, were never 'so universal as your Half-sheet Histories of constant Lovers and cruel Parents', i.e. the more pedestrian, popular sort of ballad, which he found particularly noxious. Although none of the items to which he refers survive – perhaps because they were so universal – the types are familiar:

> If you catch a Gentleman's Servant, or a Tradesman's Apprentice with a printed Paper in his Hand, 'tis very great Odds but you will find it to contain a History of some young Lady, who fell in Love with one of their Station, and despairing of her Friends consent to make it a Marriage, makes off with her Lover in a disguised Habit, lists herself for a Soldier, or perhaps goes aboard a Man of War in Quality of a Cabbin-Boy … A wretched Jingler has it by this Means in his Power to debauch all the Apprentices and young serving Maids within the District of the Printing-house he works for.[41]

While this passage does not prove that racier British ballads like 'Mary Ambree' or 'The Seaman's Doleful Farewell' were widespread in Dublin during the time, it certainly hints at their availability.

Other sub-genres of the municipal tradition from the early part of the eighteenth century include both 'good-nights', like the 'Last Speech Confession and Dying Word of Francis Mc. Cabe, William Cunneen and Edward Fox, who are to be hang'd … 14th … May 1726, near St Stephen's Green', and elegies on such figures as 'The famous userer J–– S––will who died raving mad' and 'Madame Bently who Broak her neck Rideing towards Doney-Brook'. This last contains a passage commenting wryly not only on the commonness of elegies but also on their sometimes cynically premature appearance:

> Since it's grown a fashion so common
> That not a Whore, or Huckster Woman
> Or Bawd, or Butcher of the Town,
> Nor Thief, nor Rascal of Renown;
> But sometimes living, sometimes dead,
> Their Elegies are sung or said:
> And Ballad-makers for small fees,
> Do sing their Funeral Obleques.[42]

Many of the elegies printed in Dublin during this period are, like the political ballads, more poetic than balladic, obviously intended to be read rather than sung. A case in point is the 1720 elegy for James Cotter (also commemorated in multiple literary Irish-language laments) which appeared on a Cork-printed ballad sheet, perhaps for circulation at his execution. Its author seems to have been trying – vainly – to sound more like Shakespeare than Pope, but it served its purpose as topical commentary:

> And must he silent Dye and Pitiless fall,
> No muse to Sum up now his Virtues all,
> He who the Poor's Chiefest support was,
> Supply'd their Wants and Maintained their cause,

> Lo! tho' ingratitude's the basest Crime,
> That infects the most, in our Modern Times;
> His Manhood, I hope, no Man will deny,
> Nor dispute his Heroick Magnanimity?[43]

Other middle- to high-brow genres that appear in cheap (or relatively cheap) print in the early part of the century include hunting and drinking songs like 'The Drinking Match, A New Ballad in Imitation of *Chevy Chace*', written by 'a Person of Quality' and 'The Tipling Philosophers' by the prolific Ned Ward, printed in both London and Dublin in 1710. One verse of Ward's composition runs:

> PYTHAGORUS did silence enjoin,
>   On his pupils who wisdom would seek,
> Because he tippled good wine,
>   Till himself was unable to speak
> And when he was whimsical grown,
>   With sipping his plentiful bowls,
> By the strength of the juice in his crown,
>   He conceiv'd transmigration of souls.[44]

A version featuring a musical setting followed in 1720. This version, 'set by Mr [George] Leveridge and Sung at the Theatre in Dublin', apparently gave rise in 1721 to 'The Ancient Philosophers Vindicated against Tipling, Written by a Young Lady', a riposte with all the charms of a temperance tract:

> Now Tippling so common is grown and Drunkenness is no more a Vice,
> And Men must their Senses disown, if they would be thought to be wise,
> A Drunkard is then a Divine, Religion in Liquor consists,
> And Mankind may come in good Time, to be on the Leval with Beasts.[45]

The highly singable 'Kilruddery Hunt' (1744) first turns up on the flyleaf of a copy of Ramsay's *Tea-Table Miscellany*, with words by Dublin actor Thomas Mozeen and the air of 'Sheela Nee Guiry'. Commemorating a real hunt, the song is featured in a 1762 Dublin ballad opera called *Midas*, and occurs in at least one early nineteenth-century chapbook:[46]

> Hark, hark, jolly sportsmen, a while to my tale,
> To claim your attention I'm sure it can't fail;
> It's of lads and of horses and hounds that ne'er tire
> O'er stone walls or hedges, through dales, bogs or briar;
> A pack of such hounds or a set of such men –
> It's a shrewd chance if ever you meet such again;
> Had Nimrod the mightiest of hunters been there,
> 'Fore Gad, he'd have shook like an aspin for fear.[47]

The Dublin printing trade of the late 1720s also witnessed the ballad opera craze: most of the popular English ballad operas of the day were performed and reprinted in Ireland. John Gay's *The Beggar's Opera* was performed and published in Dublin in 1728, the year of its London debut. The new theatrical genre was already being imitated by Dublin playwrights when, in 1729, first the anonymous *Chuck, or The School-Boy's Opera*, then *The Beggar's Wedding*, by Charles Coffey, were performed in Dublin at Smock-Alley.[48] Coffey incorporated not only the air of the British 'Abbot of Canterbury' into his opera, but also Irish tunes like 'Ellen a Roon' and 'Lilliburlero'. Later Irish-composed ballad operas also featured songs set to Irish airs: the anonymous 1749 *Conspirators* employed the tune of 'The Rakes of Mallow'; John O'Keeffe's 1796 *Wicklow Mountains* used the air of 'Éamonn an Cnoic';[49] and Henry Brooke's 1749 *Jack the Giant Queller* included songs set to airs like 'Moll Roe', 'Bumper Squire Jones' and 'Grania Meuel'.[50]

Many British theatre and pleasure-garden songs also found their way into the more expensive Irish-printed miscellanies that began to appear in mid- to late-century, such as *The Merry Companion* (Dublin, 1752) and *The Chearful Companion* (Cork, 1770 and 1772) – which advertised itself as a collection of 'the most Favourite Songs and Airs Lately sung at the Theatres and Gardens'. Other anthologies, like *The Ulster Miscellany* (1753) and *The Muse's Choice* (Dublin, 1770), were more truly miscellaneous and, in the case of *The Ulster Miscellany*, more Irish in content. The *Miscellany* featured a wide array of material, from Manus O'Donnell's satirical *A Voyage to O'BRAZEEL*, to exemplary tales and philosophical dialogues, as well as pastorals, drinking songs, praises in verse of Swift and Sheridan, and one bawdy song – an oddity in this otherwise polite collection. The 1776 *Charms of Melody* called itself 'a select collection of the newest and most approved love and sentimental songs, lately sung at the Theatres, Public Gardens and in the politest private Companies ... particularly all the Songs and Airs in the favourite Opera of the Duenna' (Richard Brinsley Sheridan's highly successful ballad opera). Collections from the last years of the century contained songs of a more popular stamp than those of the earlier anthologies, reflecting broader, less purely patrician tastes. These included *The Billington: or, Vocal Enchantress; and Town and Country Songster* (Dublin, 1787) and *The Irish Nosegay: Or, Songster's Companion. Being a Select Collection of the Newest and Best Songs of Every Species and Adapted to Persons of Every Kind and Taste* (Dublin, 1789). The United Irishman anthology *Paddy's Resource* (printed in several editions in both Ireland and the United States, from 1795) is – because of its political focus – somewhat anomalous amongst these songsters, but it is clear that it aimed at roughly the same audience: its melodies are drawn primarily from the Vauxhall repertoire and Ramsay's *Tea-Table* (perhaps via *Johnson's Scots Musical Museum*), while its lyrics reflect influences from Burns, topical broadsides, theater songs and Neoclassical poetry.

It is clear from these publications that the middle- to upper-class ballad market in eighteenth-century Ireland followed roughly the same lines as it did in England, in quality if not in quantity, influenced by many of the same social trends and aesthetic fashions and reflecting as many points of convergence between the oral and the printed, the vernacular and the elite. For example, Oliver Goldsmith appears to have been well-acquainted with both orally circulated ballads and the ballad sheets of Mountrath Street. In fact, according to Forster, Goldsmith 'would write sheet ballads to save himself from actually starving; sell them at the Reindeer Repository in Mountrath Court for five shillings apiece, and steal out of college to hear them sung'.[51] The evidence indicates that his taste in ballads ranged from those of the dairy-maid Peggy Golden, 'who sung me into tears with Johnny Armstrong's "Last Good Night", or "The Cruelty of Barbara Allen'", to the literary ballads of Thomas Percy, who encouraged Goldsmith's work on 'Edwin and Angelina'.[52] In *She Stoops to Conquer*, the ditty-loving Tony Lumpkin sings songs and snatches of songs that reflect both Irish and British repertoire, including a fragment of 'The Knight and the Shepherd's Daughter', a British ballad that has not been reported in Ireland either in print or in the oral tradition,[53] and 'We are the boys that fears no noise where the thundering cannons roar' – lines similar to those that occur in a number of songs in oral tradition, primarily in Ireland and the United States.[54] Lumpkin's three-verse song on the Three Pigeons alehouse is a pastiche of drinking songs of the miscellany type, possibly parodying Ward's 'Tipling Philosophers', with a nod at the hedge schoolmaster tradition:

> Let school-masters puzzle their brain
>   With grammar and nonsense and learning;
> Good liquor, I stoutly maintain
>   Gives genius a better discerning.
> Let them brag of their heathenish gods,
>   Their Lethes, their Styxes and Stygians;
> Their Quis and their Quaes and their Quods,
>   They're all but a parcel of pigeons.[55]

In his biography of Goldsmith, Washington Irving presents the writer as being capable of singing a street ballad 'with a skill and pathos that drew universal applause',[56] an account contradicted by Joshua Reynolds, who wrote that 'His skill in singing those ballads ['Johnny Armstrong', 'Barbara Allen' and 'Death and the Lady'] was no ways superior to the professors of this art which are heard every day in the streets'.[57] Goldsmith seems to have worked on some of John Newberry's collections of nursery rhymes and, according to Johnson's report to Mrs Thrale, he tossed off 'An old Woman tossed in a Blanket', a 'favourite song', to display his indifference to the disastrous first-night reception of his *Good Natur'd Man*.[58] Taking all of these anecdotes into account, it is at least plausible that Goldsmith could have contributed to the Dublin ballad trade. Nor was he unique among the Irish middle class in his acquaintance with British ballads: Maria Edgeworth quotes a stanza of 'The Lass of Roch Royal' in the glossary to *Castle Rackrent*.[59]

From Goldsmith's description of Peggy Golden's – and his own – repertoire, it seems evident that 'old ballads', both from the more fashionable recent reprints and through oral tradition, had established themselves in the singing communities of Ireland by at least the 1730s. As we have seen, some recent printed versions of such ballads were available in Dublin in the 1720s. It also possible that only a few copies of a song may have been necessary to perpetuate it in oral tradition: oral versions of 'The Holland Handkerchief' (Child 272) have been collected throughout Ireland, while only one extant printed copy of the ballad is known.[60] An Irish version of 'The Lass of Roch Royal' (Child 76) appears in a Glasgow chapbook of 1799, having apparently circulated orally throughout Ireland and returned via a (now lost) ballad sheet to Britain in its hibernicized form.[61]

Theatre songs may also have circulated orally before becoming available in cheap print in the later part of the century. According to Sean Connolly, while the Dublin theatre of the seventeenth and eighteenth centuries depended 'heavily' on the upper classes, 'there was also, from an early stage, a significant popular audience for its productions'. In 1698 John Dunton remarked that the theatre was 'free to all classes and gives entertainment as well to the broom man as the genteel peer'. Another account describes four seating categories: the boxes, where the quality sat; the pit, which accommodated 'judges, wits, and censurers'; the middle gallery, where the 'cits' and their families congregated; and finally, the upper gallery, reserved for 'abigails, serving men, journeymen, and apprentices'. Seats ranged in price from 5s. 5d. for a box to two pence for the gallery. Despite comments like those of the playwright Charles Shadwell, who complained of the difficulty of finding 'Things that will do above and please below', Connolly notes that 'there was no simple opposition between genteel and plebeian taste'. Rather,

> Complaints in 1755 of 'the dreadful irregularities' that arose from 'young gentlemen' coming drunk into the theatre, as well as the high cost of admission to the notoriously rowdy pit, suggest that a preference for boisterous audience participation over silent appreciation of the finer points of dramatic performance was in many cases part of the shared experience of gentleman and commoner.[62]

During the same period, Thomas Arne's aria 'Water Parted from the Sea' was celebrated – along with an Italian castrato closely associated with it – in a Dublin street song set to the tune of 'Over the Hills and Far Away', itself recirculated by *The Beggar's Opera*:

> Tenducci was a Piper's son,
> And he was in love when he was young,
> And all the tunes that he could play
> Was 'Water parted from the *Say*'.[63]

As Shields observes, 'We need not underestimate the sharing of repertory between the ballad press and the music sheets'.[64] Indeed, a number of less expensive eight-page songbooks from the 1780s and 1790s also contain much that might appeal to middle-brow tastes, including theatre songs like David Garrick's 'The Soft-Flowing Avon' and 'Good-Morrow to Your Night-Cap' from O'Keeffe's 1785 *The Poor Soldier*; English pleasure-garden pieces, like Dibdin's 'Vauxhall Watch', Hook's 'To the Green Wood' and George Ogle's 'Shepherds I Have Lost My Love'; sentimental lyrics like 'Anna's Urn' (from William Jackson's *Lord of the Manor*); pastorals like 'The Wounded Swain' and 'Tom and Will'; Scottish and pseudo-Scottish ditties like 'Jocky and Moggy' and 'The Celebrated Scotch Air of Johnny and Mary'; and hunting and drinking songs, including Ward's ever-popular 'Tipling Philosophers'. They also include Dublin slang or dialect songs from the 1780s like 'Larry's Ghost' and 'De Night before Larry was stretch'd'. While Andrew Carpenter regards these as genuine lowlife street ballads, 'collected' and printed by parties unknown,[65] Hugh Shields classifies them as middle-class compositions, to be found not only in chapbooks but also in the manuscript of a contemporary Gaelic scribe who noted that they were 'quite the *Ton* with the elegant Inhabitants of Dublin in the year One Thousand Seven Hundred and Eighty Eight'.[66] I tend to agree with Shields that such language is too contrived for these songs to represent vernacular tradition – although this does not mean they did not have broad appeal.[67] A verse from 'Larry's Ghost' runs:

> May de Devil take Judges and all,
> And sweep all de Jury away,
> Dat left here poor Molly to bawl,
> And buried poor Larry in clay.
> *Bekaise why he hadn't de chink*.[68]

The majority of extant Irish-printed eight-page songbooks survive from the later part of the century. Although they may well have circulated in Ireland since the early 1700s, a mere three survive from the 1750s, and only thirty-five more from the 1760s. We know of a few small songbooks from the 1770s, although far more from the 1780s and 1790s, followed by a notable increase in production until slip ballads gradually displaced them from about 1825.[69] In appearance, these little books are comparable to those produced in Britain during the same period, often featuring songs as 'new', with woodcuts on their title pages, sometimes an indication of the melody to which the song is to be sung and, more rarely, an author's or performer's name. Remarks Moulden, judging from:

> the generally poor paper, the poor quality of the impressions, the type faces and decorations, the misprints, misspellings and omissions – it is obvious that, in the main, the section of the printing trade which generated them was at its cheap and limitedly skilled extreme.[70]

The trade seems to have been relatively conservative, at least partly for financial reasons, and whole printing forms were sometimes purchased or inherited.[71]

Because of their cheapness, it is easy to assume that these small songbooks were marketed solely to the less affluent; and while this is probably true to some degree, it is also possible that the widest possible public was intended. Some songbooks may indeed have been aimed at specific markets, including a middle-class one. For example, some featured only pastorals and sentimental songs; or, as in the case of one songbook printed in 1784 (probably in Dublin), mainly theatre songs, including Hook's 'To the Greenwood', 'The Western Dame', 'Jockey and Moggy', 'Vauxhall Watch' and 'Willy's Rare'. It also sports a classical-theatrical woodcut somewhat more refined than the cruder variety usually associated with small songbooks of the era. In other words, printers may have been identifying 'niche' markets. On the other hand, some members of the less prosperous classes may also have enjoyed such fare – perhaps those who frequented the upper galleries in Dublin – and thus have constituted potential buyers. By issuing such songs in both chapbook as well as the more expensive miscellany form, printers could embrace the broadest possible market. Some of the earlier topical single-sheet ballads of the period also reflect varying degrees of poetic and linguistic sophistication, suggesting that even in the early part of the century a range of registers rather than a dichotomy of elite and popular characterized the ballad trade.

As in Britain, some late eighteenth-century chapbooks were comprised of one or two songs, including 'old ballads' like 'Chevy-Chase', 'The Blind Beggar's Daughter of Bednal Green' (advertised as 'the rarest new ballad that ever was seen'),[72] 'Andrew Barton' and 'Johnny Armstrong's Last Good-Night'. Others featured such recent 'garlands' as a three-part version of Gay's 'Black-Eyed Susan' and tabloid ballads like 'The Oxfordshire Tragedy'. A few contained two or more songs on a similar theme, such as military or naval life, or Dublin slang songs. Some books contain primarily Scottish material, including the works of Burns. Yet others boasted greater diversity, advertising such varied contents as: *The Colleen Fuine to which are added The Shepherd's Boy, Susie's Wedding. The Answer to the Sailor Boy*; or *An Answer to Stauka an Vauraga. To which are added Johnny and Nelly. The Phoenix of Ulster[.] The Banks of the Dee*. One Limerick-printed collection contained songs ranging from 'The Bug-a-Boo' (a version of the seventeenth-century English ballad more commonly known as 'The Foggy Dew'), 'The Terrible Privateer' (also called 'Captain Death', about a British naval encounter during the Seven Years' War) and the Dublin underworld song 'Larry's Stiff'.

Given the paucity of small Irish-printed songbooks from the late eighteenth century, generalizations are difficult to make, but there is clearly a preponderance of British material in many of the surviving items. Of the Ulster-printed songbooks or garlands during this period, J. R. R. Adams comments, 'the prevailing atmosphere is English, with a scattering of Scottish and Irish songs'.[73] During the same period, we also begin to see more Irish-composed narrative ballads in imitation of British models.[74] For example, a garland entitled *The Dublin Tragedy, or the Unfortunate Merchant's Daughter* is just the kind of ballad Hibernicus would have scorned, treating as it does 'of a rich Merchant's Daughter in the town of Belfast, who was deluded by an Ensign in the army and for love him, dressed herself in man's apparel and sailed with him to England'. In style it could easily be taken for an early to mid-century British ballad, except for the slight awkwardness and artificiality of diction:

> Ye lovers far and near, unto me lend an ear,
>   Whilst I relate a doleful tragedy.
> 'Twill make your hearts to bleed
>   It's known full well to be no falsity.[75]

More sure-handed are songs like the good-night ballad 'The Dublin Baker' (also known as 'The Wild and Wicked Youth' or 'The Irish Robber's Adventure'):

> In Dublin sity I was bred and born,
> In Stephen's Green I died in scorn;
> I served my time to the baking trade
> And was always counted a roving blade.[76]

Of comparable quality is 'Sewball' (better known as 'Skewball'), which describes a horse race that took place in the Curragh in 1752:[77]

> Come gentlemen sportsmen, I pray listen all,
> And I'll sing you a song in praise of Sewball,
> And how he came over you shall understand,
> It was by Lord Melvin the peer of the land.[78]

In fact, by the second half of the century, the narrative broadside ballad or 'come-all-ye' form, with its long lines and typical aabb rhymes became so naturalized in Ireland that its adoption there amounted to 'something like a takeover'.[79] Some ballads of Irish composition are almost indistinguishable from their British counterparts, and in some cases represent mere localizations. The sharing of ballad airs can also make provenance difficult to determine. As John Moulden puts it, 'There is a case, in the evidence of influence from Britain upon the English-language song culture of Ireland, and in evidence of the reverse process, for considering the English-language song culture of Ireland and Britain as that of a unified area.'[80]

A number of Irish narrative ballads from the later part of the century, however, reflect native linguistic, metric, or thematic traits, constituting hybrid forms in which British 'come-all-ye' conventions coexist with varying degrees of Irish influence.[81] We have already seen, in hedge schoolmaster songs, Irish verse forms (including *ochtfhoclach* and five-stress *amhrán*), native song genres like the *aisling* and the place-praise song, and naturalized continental song-forms like the *pastourelle* and the *reverdie* transferred to both macaronic and English-language songs and even combined with the Neoclassical pastoral. A number of these conventions were also applied to narrative ballads. For example, a 1789 version of a well-known heiress abduction ballad called 'Willy Reilly and his Cooleen Bawn', while in most respects following both metric and narrative conventions of the British broadside ballad, begins with a classic *reverdie* opening:

> 'Twas on a pleasant morning all in the blooming spring
> When as the chearful songsters in consert did sing,
> The primrose and daisy bespangled every lawn,
> In arbour I espied my sweet Cooleen Bawn.[82]

Another ballad, 'Mc. Clure's Rambles', printed in Down around 1807, combines a five-stress *amhrán* metre with aabb broadside rhyme:

> Of late a strong notion of rambling entangl'd my mind,
> To seek out dame Fortune my strong resolution inclin'd,
> I set to the road like a rover with staff in my hand,
> And I never delay'd till I came to the town of Strabane.[83]

Indeed, during the last two decades of the century a number of extant eight-page songbooks, particularly from Limerick and Monaghan, include increasing amounts of Irish-composed material reflecting the influence of Irish language, poetry and culture. Hedge schoolmaster songs, for example, are plentiful; and drinking songs like the British 'Tipling Philosophers' and 'The Goblet of Wine' seem to have fit in well enough stylistically with the classically inflected schoolmaster songs for printers to find them good companion pieces in small songbooks containing such fare:

> My temples with clusters of grapes I'll entwine,
> And barter all joy for a goblet of wine;
> In search of a Venus no longer I'll run,
> But stop and forget her a[t] Bacchus's tun.[84]

Many hunting songs also fit in well stylistically with schoolmaster material, as did 'The Kilruddery Fox Chase', 'A New Hunting Song' and a song called 'The Bottle', which takes both hunting and drinking as its subjects:

> The sportsmen arous'd, when the horn harks away
> Shrill ech tantivy repeating,
> His warm wishing wife clings around him to stay,
> But shouts put to silence entreating.
> Yet what is his chace to the chace that we boast?
> So ho! here's a bumper, hark, hark, to the toast,
> Hit it off and be quick, lest the scent should be lost,
> And we're cast in the chace of a bottle.[85]

A few songs of the hedge schoolmaster type contain a line or two of Irish, spelled phonetically according to an orthography based on English – a practice reflecting the emphasis on literacy in that language. One such is 'Pearlha Nhe Kilthee Bawne' ('The Pearl of the Fair Hair', Monaghan, 1788):[86]

> One morning as I roved down by a shady grove,
> Where birds did sing harmonious,
> Within their downy throats they warbled pretty notes,
> In concert they sang melodious;
> Encompassed by a shade I saw a comely maid,
> Whose charms did soon trepan me,
> In cruel Cupid's chain, all for that blooming dame,
> Called Pearlha nhe kilthee bawne.[87]

The composer of 'Terry O'Brien's Adventure' had an earthier approach to romance:

> It was in Ennis Clare on an Easter Sunday morning,
> There I drank full plenty with Molly my darling
> Of punch and liquor of the best till we both grew hearty,
> Then to bed we did repair, I cared not for her party,
>   But sported till break of day
> Law an Ennish caur er mhading donough cauka
> Diolas f an ma youghante molly creenaf partee
> Da lin morshin er licbo veen, keanh clooher saustah,
> Eg ery dooh er mhadin da leg she gaureal
>   Agus dolemur flauna no gea.[88]

Shields, in evaluating these sometimes indecipherable macaronic texts, speculates that 'Prestige value must have dominated these Irish sheets, and it is to be wondered how some of them were deciphered at all. Perhaps the macaronic sheets, with alternating lines or verses in the respective languages, represent a compromise between intelligibility and cultural prestige.'[89] One song completely in Irish phonetics ('Eibhlín a Rún' or 'Ducatu no vanutu') also appears in the 1776 edition of *The Charms of Melody*, probably because of the popularity of the air after its inclusion in Coffey's *Beggar's Wedding* in 1729. 'Ileen Oge' or 'Savourneen Deelish', which appeared in a 1791 opera by George Colman and was later reprinted in both English and Irish slip ballads and chapbook collections, contains a one-line refrain in phonetic Irish. David Cooper notes that there was a 'craze for Irish folk music' in Britain during the 1780s, which may account for the greater number of Irish and pseudo-Irish songs that appear in British-printed eight-page songbooks of this period.[90] The 'craze' itself may have been at least partly due to the increasing popularity of Irish ballad operas, many of which drew upon exotic 'native' melodies.

Remarkably, a few singable translations of a number of Irish-Gaelic songs also appear in several surviving eight-page songbooks, including 'Byncheen Louahrea' ('An Binsín Luachra'), 'The Mayo Maid Deceived' ('Idir Caiseal agus Durlas'), 'Shawn a Glana' ('Seán Ó Duibhir a' Ghleanna') and a particularly elegant English version of 'Tá Daoine a' Rádh' ('People Are Saying') by one 'Mr Doyle', which was printed in Monaghan in 1789. The only known Irish version of the song was collected and published by Ó Muirgheasa in 1934. It begins:

> Tá daoine a' *rádh* go bhfuil *grádh* ag mo *mhui*rnín orm *fhéin*,
> Go *dei*mhin má *tá* chan *grádh* gan *cu*mann dó *é*;
> Ar *neamh*-chead mo *cháir*de agus a *lán* de mo *mhuin*ntir-se *fhéin*
> Mur *mai*ridh mé *ráith*e go *sásó*chaidh mé m'*in*tinn bheag *fhéin*.[91]

Doyle's translation runs:

> This country de*clare* sin*cere* that my sweet heart loves *me*,
> I'm very well *pleas'd* I *swear*, the truth it may *be*;
> In spight of re*la*tions that *tease* us to *ne*ver prove *kind*,
> If I live but one *quar*ter my *dar*ling will *plea*sure my *mind*.[92]

I have italicized assonantal rhymes in both the Irish version and the translation. Note that while Mr Doyle retained much of the internal rhyme patterns of the original's *amhrán* metre, he adopted the aabb perfect end-rhyme more typical of the English printed ballad.

Other signs of native influence in Irish printed ballads, both narrative and otherwise – apart from the use of Irish place and proper names – are reflected in such linguistic traits as the anachronistic English pronunciation of *ea* to rhyme with *say*, the rhyming of words like 'born' and 'harm', and the use of Hiberno-English expressions like 'a tall a tall'. P. W. Joyce, in *English As We Speak It in Ireland*, points to a number of examples of Hiberno-Irish in Irish song, including the use of 'be' to stand for the indicative of the verb, as in the phrase 'I'll seek out my Blackbird wherever he be' from 'The Royal Blackbird'; or the inversion of the auxiliary and the past participle,[93] as in the line 'This lovely charming maid, who has me betrayed', from 'Pearlha Nhe Kilthee Bawne'. Moulden further notes the presence of Ulster dialect in the orthography of a number of northern ballads he has examined, such as the spelling of 'they' as 'the'.[94] Dialect was also employed by the 'weaver poets' for whom, however, it was often a matter of choice: like Burns, James Orr could compose highly fluent Neoclassical verse.[95] The use of characteristically Irish assonantal rhyme instead of perfect rhyme is also common, especially in the schoolmaster songs. Obviously, these traits reflect not only Irish influence but Irish oral influence, in that they are features of colloquial speech.

Surviving late eighteenth- and early nineteenth-century chapbook songsters also contain a greater amount of, as Moulden puts it, 'vernacular' material, including a fair number of erotic songs, at least some of which were Irish-composed. Some, like 'Under the Rose; or, the Beagles Adventure' and 'Fight Your Cock in the Morning', employ the conventions of hunting songs and blood sports to describe sexual encounters; others, like 'The Musical Piper; or, Matthew Malone' use music as their metaphor. Oddly enough, such songs were often printed alongside 'politer' items like 'Shepherds I Have Lost My Love' or 'The answer to Shawn Ouge a Glanea'. One Limerick songbook contains a piece called 'The Gobbio', which uses martial imagery reminiscent of the finale of Jean de Muen's section of the *Roman de la Rose*:

> The Engineer resolved to [overcome],
> Having got two shells fixed to a bomb,
> The siege began and the match he did lay,
> And [soon?] he got on the cover'd way,
> He battered a breach, but missed his reach,
> His faggots being too small to fill the ditch,
> She off with disdain did fling him O.
> And bid him begone from her Gobbi-O.[96]

A few Irish-composed patriotic songs and even whole eight-page songbooks containing patriotic material also survive from the late eighteenth century and very early nineteenth century. These include 'Granua's Advice to her Children', 'The Rights of Man', 'The Establishment of Irish Freedom', 'The Vine-Cover'd Hills', 'The Irish Lamentation at Achrun' and an undated Dublin eight-page songbook called *The True Born Irishman, Containing an Excellent Collection of Patriotic Songs*. Overall, however, the proportion of such songs is slight in comparison with other genres; intriguing but exceptional are songs like 'A Friendly Caution' and 'The Peep-of Day Boys', both concerned with regional rather than national politics. My own examination of songs printed during this period leads me to concur with Shields, Moulden and Zimmermann that patriotic songs 'make up a fairly small proportion of the chapbook texts of the early nineteenth century'.[97] By contrast, as William Allingham was later to note, 'Nearly one-half of the whole number [of available ballads] owe their inspiration to Cupid.'[98]

Just as fewer sheets and chapbooks survive from eighteenth-century Ireland than from England, so also do fewer accounts of the ballad trade and ballad-singers – and even fewer of chapmen and hawkers. Thus, except for the few early references I have already cited, we must turn to later sources, like the memoir of Aynsworth Pilson, which includes the following description of the ballad trade in late eighteenth-century Downpatrick:

> Ballads were in much request and were purchased and read by the younger people. They were ... put into circulation by professional ballad singers, who traversed the street with thick folds of them over their left arm, whilst the right hand extended to the purchaser the literary condiments, receiving at the same time the half-penny, which was dropped into a capacious purse, placed in front of the performer. The proper tune

appended to the ballad was sung by the professor and thus the public were immediately in possession of the matter and the air at the same time. These ballads were sometimes of a plaintive character, but more frequently exhibited humour, wit and sarcasm.[99]

Depictions of the ballad- and chapbook-seller as a public nuisance are reminiscent of British accounts of the same period: in May 1816 *The Belfast News-letter* reported that 'the town has been sadly annoyed by itinerant ballad-singers, who collect crowds of people, especially at each end of Bridge Street, so that passengers cannot get forward'. Several months later, a man who styled himself 'Observer' wrote to the *News-letter* to complain sarcastically of 'the delightful harmony and exquisite compositions, that day and night resounds about our corners, emanating from the musical and poetical talents of our regular ballad-singers'.[100] Mid-nineteenth-century census figures and records from Dublin Castle indicate that many ballad-singers were itinerant, sometimes travelling in twos or threes, including husband-and-wife teams.

Maura Murphy estimates potential earnings for ballad-singers during this period at an average of three shillings per day or a pound a week, substantially more than a labourer's wage – although there are accounts of female ballad-singers with children in east Galway 'so poor and miserable that the authorities had not the heart to interfere'.[101]

In eighteenth-century Ireland, however, ballad-singers may not have been as important in the sale and distribution of ballads as non-performing chapmen, hawkers and 'flying stationers'. Typical advertisements of the period are those supplied by John Brown of Monaghan, 'where Chapmen and Dealers can be *well assorted* with Books, Pamphlets, Ballads, Black and Coloured Pictures, Hardware, &, on moderate Terms'; or by W. Goggin of Limerick, 'where Country Chapmen may be supplied with Histories, Manuals, Penny-books, Spelling-books, Primmers, large and small Pictures, plain or painted, a large assortment of Ballads, and every other Article in the Bookselling and Stationery Business on cheaper Terms than at any other Shop'.[102] We know very little about these pedlars and chapmen, whose operations were, as Adams puts it, 'particularly shadowy', but it would have been left for them to serve the large rural areas where there were few booksellers.[103]

Some ballad-singers – and perhaps chapmen – composed their own ballads, as, apparently, did several printers.[104] Many ballads were reprinted from memory, dictation, or from stock purchased or inherited by the printer.[105] Other ballads were commissioned or sold to printers by local poets, as appears to have been the case with the songwriters J. R. R. Adams dubbed the Laggan 'poet-laureates'. Adams's study of several song-poets in eastern Donegal during the first decade of the nineteenth century emphasizes the ease with which such poetasters could get their poems published, using printers like John and Robert Buchanan of Londonderry, who sold garlands 'primarily to the chapmen', supplying them 'on the lowest terms'.

IRISH STREET BALLADS.

Figure 5.2: J. Hand (J. H.), 'Irish Street Ballads',
in J. Denvir, *Monthly Irish Library*, vol. 19 (1903), p. 22.

While, as Adams comments, 'Most of the garlands consisted of standard fare, pirated from many sources ... a proportion were severely local, plainly intended for circulation in the Laggan'.[106] Several of these indicate authorship, and some of the songs, if not actually written by hedge schoolmasters or poor scholars, certainly reflect 'hedge school education in all its glory'.[107] John Moulden lists a number of similar-sounding 'effusions', at least some of which he ascribes to a 'very local' Drogheda song-poet, 'probably John Sheil'.[108]

One fascinating late eighteenth-century poem, attributed to Aeneas Lamont, describes the route from 'commission', composition and performance, to distribution and finally to oral transmission:

> ... forced, for bread, to tune a song;
> A ballad singer up and down
> He wander'd long from town to town
> 'Till thinking on his rhyming friend
> To whom he neither gives nor lends;
> He seeks him out and finds him blest;
> Of health, peace, plenty, all possest.–
> With pity mov'd, he took him in,
> And questioned why he looked so thin;
> The wretch disclo's his hist'ry plain,
> And happily seem'd free from pain.
> With servile cringing in his face,
> Not knowing how to feel disgrace,
> He begged a favour from the art
> He slighted once with all his heart:–
> He begged his friend would write a song,
> To claim the attention of the throng
> That might repay his toil with gains,
> And yield a shilling for his pains.
> With willing pen he wrote the verse
> Which village songsters yet rehearse
> And oft the simple honest strains
> Delighted much the list'ning swains;
> They bought the ballad and retir'd ...[109]

The change from ballad sheet to chapbook form 'meant more songs could be sold more cheaply and, it may indicate that the printers believed that the potential existed for an extension of the market'.[110] This presumes not only greater literacy but also sufficient income to afford such books. In the early nineteenth-century chapbooks were sold for threepence or sixpence each. This figure has led Niall Ó Ciosáin, after weighing both the average wages and expenditures of unskilled labourers at the time against the price of chapbooks, to conclude that such a book, 'while perhaps a luxury, was not an impossible one'.[111] Chapbook culture may have at once reflected and sped the increase of literacy among the general populace.

Along with Hibernicus' account, reports of ballads or other ephemera being pasted on walls are few but telling, as in the 1736 comment of a Dublin printer, who explained the poor quality of a religious leaflet which was merely designed 'for pasting up in the several apartments in houses, being worthy of the perusal of old and young, who have a desire to live and die well'. Even as early as 1716, a Dublin bishop requested that one of his tracts be reprinted as a broadside and sold for 1d, since 'such papers as are designed for every body's reading ought as near as may be to be accommodated to every body's purse as well as capacity'.[112]

Reading aloud was certainly practised in Ireland – although obviously performance would have spread a song far more efficiently and with the necessity for even fewer copies of the text.[113] As for local song-poets, we can reasonably assume that the songs they had printed in songbook form or disseminated in manuscript (or simply orally) would have had at least a hearing in their own communities. On the other hand, in districts where songbooks contained unfamiliar material, children who were taught English in the schools – or the schoolmasters themselves – could have acted as mediators for illiterate and/or Irish-speaking adults. While we have no specific reports of chapmen or hawkers singing songs from the books they sold, they too might have disseminated songs and their melodies. Ultimately, however, even if a songbook failed to indicate its songs' melodies, as one twentieth-century farmer is supposed to have commented after purchasing a ballad, 'I've got the words now. I can go to the mountains for the air.'[114]

We have little to go on when it comes to knowing precisely which printed ballads entered the song tradition during the eighteenth and early nineteenth centuries. However, some of the earlier song transcriptions in the Bunting Collection afford us some glimpses into what was popular at the turn of the eighteenth century. The collection includes either melodies or texts for a wide variety of songs associated with previously or currently printed ballads, including 'Shule Aroon', 'Molly Bawn', Gay's ''Twas When the Seas Were Roaring', the Scottish Jacobite ballad 'My Laddie Can Fight and My Laddie Can Sing' and such 'raking' songs as 'Staca an Mhargaidh' and 'Whist the Cat from under the Table'. There are also texts for several songs in British narrative broadside style which I have been unable to trace in either British or Irish eighteenth- or early nineteenth-century print sources. These include 'The County Tyrone' (popular in the twentieth-century travelling community), 'The Ploughmen' and 'The Squire's Daughter and Her Love Billy' (the last two belonging to the female transvestite ballad subgenre). Patrick Kennedy's memoirs *The Banks of the Boro* and *Evenings in the Duffrey*, recalling events from the author's youth in County Wexford around 1819–21,[115] also gives us some insight into song repertoire of the period, since many of the songs mentioned in them can be found in print in England or Ireland twenty years or more before this time. Among those Kennedy quotes are variants of an unexpectedly high number of Child ballads, including 'Lord Bateman', 'Sir Hugh' and 'Young Hunting'; versions of British 'broadside' ballads like 'Pretty Polly Oliver', 'The Faithless Sea Captain' and 'The Golden Glove'; hedge schoolmaster songs, like 'Castle Hyde', 'The Colleen Rue', 'Sheela na Guira' and 'The Buncheen of Lucharoe'; as well as other Irish-composed ballads like 'The Bantry Girls' Lament for Johnny', 'The Royal Blackbird' and 'The Banks of Clody'. In addition there are texts that belong to two sub-genres already attested in print by at least the 1820s: comic songs, such as 'The Connaught Man at the Review', 'The Widow's Pig' and 'Billy O'Rourke', apparently of proto-music hall or song and supper club origin; and songs of sensibility with an Irish patina, like 'Gra Gal Machree' and 'Bouchal na Gruaga dhowna', in the sentimental tradition of late eighteenth-century Vauxhall songs. Kennedy also includes songs by local poets, like the 'Banks of the Urrin' by John Rogers; 'The Beauty of Brie' (schoolmaster verse at its most turgid, 'made by Tom Blanche, the little tailor'); and 'A New Song in Praise of the Great Mr Breen', a more down-to-earth composition by Mickey Connors, a weaver.[116]

While not all of these songs were necessarily learned from print (in fact Kennedy sometimes informs us that they were learned from servants or were, in fact, 'never seen in print'), all either had a life in printed form or were influenced by eighteenth-century genres that did.[117] It is difficult to assess the extent to which print functioned in the dissemination of ballads during this period, but Kennedy makes it clear that both manuscript and print were sometimes employed. In *Evenings in the Duffrey*, he describes how Mickey Connors, who had 'made a book full of songs', having been entertained by:

> a poor honest goose-plucker ... at Molly Finn's *public* ... composed an ode in his honour on the spot; and so pleased was the poor, simple, vain creature, that he took the manuscript to Wexford town, got some quires printed and employed himself singing it at fair and market till he became a thorough tinker.[118]

Kennedy also relates a number of stories about Denis O'Brien, a pedlar and moneylender of the 1770s, who often scribbled ballads (and frequently composed the music) 'by the side of the road', and later published a pamphlet apparently so incendiary that O'Brien was only narrowly saved from the gallows by George Ogle, whom O'Brien afterward styled 'the Apollo of Wexford'.[119] One singer in *The Banks of the Boro* is even described as musically literate: on one occasion she is coaxed into singing partly because 'she was *learned* to sing by note when Tench, the dancing-master made his last round through the country'.[120] Wexford may not have been typical of Ireland generally, since it was more heavily anglicized than many areas – and it is clear that some of the singers were modestly middle class – but it supplies at least a partial portrait of the song tradition during the period. It also allows us to see the overlap in repertoire between Wexford and other parts of the country: Gerald Griffin's 1827 *Suil Dhuv, the Coiner* mentions both 'The Colleen Rue' and 'Sheela-na-Guira'.[121] Since Griffin is primarily associated with Limerick and Cork, we can infer that at least two of the hedge schoolmaster songs popular in Wexford had currency elsewhere in the southern counties of Ireland during the beginning of the nineteenth century.

Despite the small number of these sources, they cite such a large proportion of songs found in cheap songbooks of the late eighteenth century that – in combination with other evidence – they confirm the impression that print had made an appreciable impact on Irish culture in general and the song repertoire in particular in at least the more anglicized parts of the country by the turn of the century. That these songs appeared in the context of an extensive oral tradition which absorbed and interacted with songs in print, is hardly surprising. As in Britain, 'The contents of [cheap print] did not destroy circulation by word of mouth. Sometimes it enshrined material from the oral realm; certainly it fed back into it. The written word helped instruct people in what to sing, what to retell and how to express themselves in ways which greatly enhanced and enriched their cultural world.'[122]

Admittedly, examples of the interaction between vernacular and elite culture in Ireland during this period in relation to ballads are relatively few: besides the presumed marketing of both 'high-faluting' and 'low-faluting' songs to both the middle classes and the commonalty,[123] we possess the evidence I have outlined above: scattered accounts of the widespread popularity of theatre songs, stories of Goldsmith's balladeering, descriptions of the apparently ubiquitous ballad trade, the currency of hedge schoolmaster songs, the increasing but still patchy literacy of the country as a whole, and Patrick Kennedy's invaluable depiction of a singing community at the turn of the eighteenth century. Taken together, however, they are highly suggestive of a less stratified, more democratic song culture than most associate with 'folk tradition', similar to that which Thomas Crawford has ascribed to Scotland; a tradition in which, at least in certain areas, 'practically everybody took part', and in which literary and elite influences intermingled with popular ones to produce a unique repertoire in the context of (in at least some cases) a more or less heterogeneous social and cultural milieu.[124] Social historian Sean Connolly has distinguished between 'an élite culture defined by transmission through the printed word, its access to the worlds of law and high politics, and its observance of a particular code of politeness and behaviour' and a 'culture of the common people: not necessarily illiterate, but primarily dependent on the spoken word, governed by custom and ritual, localistic, community-minded and conservative'.[125] Yet he has also pointed out numerous nexuses of cultural interchange in eighteenth-century Ireland, ranging from festivals, sporting events, dress and diet, to music, noting complaints about dairymaids wearing hoops and harpers performing Charles Dibdin melodies. 'Linked by the bridges of shared interest, patronage and emulation of social superiors', the various strata of Irish culture have never existed wholly in isolation from each other.[126]

Certainly, by the late eighteenth century, the Irish had made an indelible mark upon the printed balladry of the English-speaking world, contributing much that was distinctive and singular to the genre. This contribution was reflected in the many new song-forms that emerged not only from the integration of English and Irish influences in both narrative and lyric ballads but also in the emergence of genres like the Irish macaronic song, translations of Gaelic song, Dublin slang songs, and the many sub-types of the ever-popular hedge schoolmaster genre that flourished in both print and oral tradition. Throughout the eighteenth century, cultural and social interaction had led to the widespread ownership and perpetuation of a number of cultural forms, forms that included the printed ballad. While this was true to some extent in England, the phenomenon was much more pronounced in the Irish and Scottish traditions, where general respect for knowledge and education of a sort that embraces both oral and written forms helped to ensure the continuing vitality of the verbal arts, read, spoken, or sung. It is no coincidence that both Scotland and Ireland retained a thriving and rich oral tradition – along with their written ones – long after that of England had waned.

6 THE EIGHTEENTH-CENTURY IRISH BALLAD AND MODERN ORAL TRADITION

> The written text, for all its permanence, means nothing, is not even a text, except in relationship to the spoken word. For a text to be intelligible, to deliver its message, it must be reconverted into sound, directly or indirectly, either really in the external world or in the auditory imagination.
>
> – Walter Ong[1]

Hugh Shields has emphasized the degree to which oral rather than printed transmission has dominated the Irish song tradition, instancing the lack of printed sources for many of the older British ballads that have been found in Irish oral tradition, a fact which he believes reflects a cultural 'tendency to place less reliance on alphabetic aids'. In support of this observation, however, he cites 'Sir James the Ross' (Child 213), a ballad that seems to have been introduced into Ireland initially via an 1826 Omagh songbook. The song was subsequently recovered from oral tradition in 1975 in the same location in a form so close to the 1826 text that, says Shields, the two 'must be linked by an initial act of straightforward literal memorization'.[2] Whether an older, orally transmitted song or an eighteenth-century printed one, it uses all the devices of the classic 'ballad of tradition'. The ballad of 'Sir Hugh' (Child 155) appeared in the polite 1776 Irish-printed anthology *Charms of Melody*, as did a polished version, 'with little traditional character', of 'The Grey Cock' (Child 248), which nonetheless 'can be recognized as the main influence on an oral version from North Antrim sung in 1975'.[3] These songs took their place alongside songs that may never have been recorded, demonstrating, despite the predominance of oral transmission in the Irish song tradition, the strong reciprocity of oral and print media within that tradition. This reciprocity, as we shall see, has persisted to this day.

While there is not sufficient space to discuss nineteenth-century printed song in any detail, it is worth noting that all of the genres – and many individual songs – from the eighteenth-century ballad tradition are attested in print in the nineteenth century, with the addition of new songs written in these genres or in those that developed or were imported during this period. These latter song-types include sentimental parlour ballads (like Marion Crawford's 'Kathleen Mavourneen'); music hall songs from both sides of the Atlantic (to be followed eventually by vaudeville and pantomime); American minstrel songs (including Stephen Foster compositions), a great many of which were printed as broadsides or sheet music; and newer historical, political and 'national' ballads written in various styles, including Napoleonic and O'Connellite songs, as well as (later in the century) songs connected with Fenianism and the Land League, and more localized ballads like 'Dunlavin Green' and 'The Lamentation of Hugh Reynolds'.[4]

There were also updated forms of older genres like the *pastourelle*, such as 'Down by the Canal' or 'The Factory Girl', which feature industrial settings, or 'The Cavan Road', in which both local references and the theme of emigration feature prominently. The ever-increasing number of emigration songs employed a variety of idioms, their forms, diction and content reflecting the times in which they were composed: sometimes narrative, sometimes lyric, but increasingly sentimental. Even a few songs in Irish, like 'Caoineadh na dTrí Mhuire' ('The Lament of the Three Marys') were available in print during the century, as were English translations of songs like 'An Droighneán Donn' ('The Blackthorn Stick'), 'Bean an Fhir Rua' ('The Red-Haired Man's Wife') and Raiftearaí's 'Anach Cuain'.[5] Horse-racing and other sporting songs, hunting and drinking songs and comic *cantes-fables* (frequently reflecting stage influence) also continued to appear in print. Scottish imports remained popular, especially in Ulster; and many English ballads were reprinted in Ireland, including the ubiquitous 'All around My Hat'. These genres have persisted, to varying degrees, in local singing communities, although their collective repertoires have shrunk noticeably in recent years.

Of all these genres, however, Hugh Shields maintained that the narrative ballad, first widely disseminated in the eighteenth century, has dominated the traditional repertoire. Writing in 1993, he commented:

> Present-day ballad singing greatly favours new ballads [i.e. 'broadside ballads' or narrative ballads of the reportorial, 'come-all-ye' type] … Listeners expect an explicit story: a sequence not just chronological but complete, accompanied by dates, places, names of persons if recent facts are claimed: everything that implies a reasonable attitude to the causes and effects of things.[6]

Sam Henry's Ulster-based collection, Colm Ó Lochlainn's *Irish Street Ballads* and other twentieth-century anthologies and recordings seem on the whole to confirm this assessment, not only in terms of survivals from previous tradition but also of much recent composition. Stock openings like 'Come all ye loyal lovers', 'Ye feeling-hearted Christians', 'My name it is', etc.; and the use of formulaic ballad phrases, journalistic details and chronological sequence – all legacies of the eighteenth-century narrative 'broadside' ballad – abound in songs still circulated in recent oral tradition. Not all of these conventions were necessarily learned directly from printed sources – and, in fact, we know that in many cases they were not; although, just as in Kennedy's day, many latter-day song composers have had their songs printed on ballad sheets, or even in books.[7]

It is notoriously difficult to generalize about repertoire based purely upon what has been collected from oral sources (or indeed from written ones) since 1800, since fieldwork has often been implemented haphazardly and incompletely, sometimes impeded by the collector's aesthetic biases, as well as by temporal and geographical gaps. In attempting to assess the degree of influence of the printed ballad on more recent tradition, John Moulden compared several tune anthologies – abstracting 'a list of the names of items in each collection whose introduction into (or reinforcement within) the oral tradition was probably affected by popular print' – and found widely varying results between different kinds of collections. 'It is interesting', he notes,

> that it is the very local collections, tending to be made by local people or from the repertory of a single player, that show the highest proportion [of titles known from printed balladry] ... It implies that those who seek to use data derived from this kind of comparison need to proceed with considerable caution.[8]

There is also the question of ephemerality, especially of local songs. While certain items may remain in a singing community's repertoire indefinitely, others may cease to be sung, either from lack of continued relevance or because those who sang the songs have died. A statement by Patrick Kennedy illustrates this point. Writing of Mickey Conners' verse, he remarks, 'Scores of Mick's songs were popular between Bunclody and Enniscorthy during his life and for some years later. I have only one entire one in my memory'.[9]

Few singers' repertoires consist solely of narrative ballads, however – but it is fair to say that most genres now represented in the English-language tradition owe something to the various forms of the eighteenth-century *printed* ballad and its successors. Repertoire, however, varies from community to community and singer to singer, reflecting a variety of tastes. For example, the Tunney family of West Fermanagh (Paddy Tunney, in particular) have shown a special affection for hedge schoolmaster songs – although their collective repertoire also includes comic songs, narrative ballads, nineteenth-century emigration songs and political items. The combined repertoire of East Galway singers Sarah and Rita Keane reflects a preference for lyric songs, including sentimental parlour ballads, although they also sang 'Child' ballads as well as songs in Irish. Others singers, like Tom Lenihan of Miltown Malbay and Elizabeth Cronin of Cúl Aodha, had capacious repertoires that seem to embrace every conceivable genre.

Few would disagree, however, that – despite the high proportion of solely orally circulated songs in the modern Irish repertoire – the printed ballad (in the broadest sense of the word), whether narrative or lyric, has made an indelible mark on the Irish song tradition.[10] This influence extends to matters of language as well as form. As Shields observes:

> What has become poetic diction today may have originally been commonplace language ... And the new ballad was so much marked by the eighteenth-century contribution that some of the diction remained and the traditionality of newly composed songs has been measurable in proportion to the author's use or neglect of it.[11]

Thus many compositions of the past hundred years or so retain not only the structure of the older print genres – especially in the case of narrative ballads – but also much of their diction and style, as 'The Trial of John Twiss' (*c*. 1895) illustrates:

> John Twiss from Castleisland, it's true it is my name:
> I never did commit a crime, why I should deny the same,
> I own I was a sportsman with spirit light and gay:
> Both paid spies and informers, my life they swore away.[12]

John Maguire's 'The Molly Maguires' (probably composed in the 1920s or 1930s) is also a good example of the ability of later song-poets to exploit older idioms:

> I stood amazed, I on them gazed[,] I wandered with surprise,
> For the clothing that they wore it was dazzling to my eyes.
> There was every lad, a handsome lass, with heart and hand did go.
> You would think that they came from Cornacreeve or Follum down here below.[13]

Other more recent songs, however, combine common 'broadside ballad' conventions with modern vocabulary and usage, as in 'The New Tractor', composed by County Derry singer Eddie Butcher around 1940:

> For this young man he ploughs with a tractor machine,
> There are no lie about it for him I have seen;
> For corn or hay sure he needs none at all,
> Just get him a gallon of paraffin oil.[14]

Some Dublin street ballads even blend older parlance with twentieth-century urban slang, as in 'The Cruise of the Calabar':

> The Captain cried: "Tis a pirate's brig, and on us she does gain!
> When next I sail for Clondalkin, boys, be japers I'll go by train!'[15]

'The Tailor Bawn' unites the long line and aabb rhyme scheme of the 'come-all-ye' with internal vertical assonances and the distinctive Hiberno-Irish of County Cork to create yet another hybrid ballad form:

> There was not a tramp in the nation, ugly, fair or fine,
> And people of very low station were pulling out airy times.
> We drank with journeymen bakers and every queer *spréachán*.
> You'd think, when you'd look at their features, they were cousins of Tailor Bawn![16]

Still other songs employ the stylistic conventions and diction of the hedge schoolmaster genre, sometimes seriously and sometimes for the purpose of satire, as in 'The Shannon Scheme':

> If I were Homer, the ancient roamer,
> I'd write a poem on a noble theme,
> And I'd sing the story and praise the glory
> Of that wondrous project, the Shannon Scheme.[17]

A somewhat more sober example is 'Misses Limerick, Kerry and Clare', a *conflictus*, or song of disputation (a number of which survive from nineteenth-century ballad sheets), in which three allegorical maidens debate the provenance of Daniel O'Connell's statue:

> You noble heroes of Paddy's nation,
> Draw near a while until I relate
> Of a conversation between three girls
> The other night had a great debate.
> They rose no rows nor no noisy voices.
> They spoke quite civil as I could see.
> They drew down heroes from their three counties
> To know who'd boast of their history.[18]

Jimmy Crowley's 'A Sorrowful Lamentation' – published as a ballad sheet by the Cork Songmaker's Club – combines the form and stylistic conventions of the street ballad with the Latinate verbiage of the hedge school and the chorus (as well as the melody) of an Irish drinking song in order to satirize the taxes imposed in the 1970s by Finance Minister Richie Ryan:

> So come all ye lads that live out by and are adept at distillation,
> Your trade I'm sure will much improve with all this talk about inflation;
> So fill for me a flowing bowl of sweet poteen, the grand potation,
> And we'll drink a health to Richie Ryan, the cause of all our deprivation.
>   Chorus: Ólaim puins is ólaim tae [I drink punch and I drink tea], etc.[19]

Newer genres and songs have continued to coexist with old, making for interesting contrasts in diction and style, as well as form, in the present traditional repertoire: ballads including words like 'trepan', with the archaic meaning of 'beguile' or 'ensnare', the use of 'discourse' as a verb, and set phrases like 'wounded swain' and 'straight took my way' can be found side-by-side with songs featuring 'sweet colleens', 'cabin homes' and the 'thees' and 'thys' of Victorian and Edward-ian verse. 'The Banks of the Lee' is typical of these sentimental but popular songs, drawing not only on (literally) flowery imagery but on the preoccupation with mourning that has haunted balladry since the days of David Mallet:

> I will pluck my love some roses, some blooming Irish roses:
> I will pluck my love some roses, the finest every grew,
> And I'll place them on the grave of my own dear darling Mary,
> In that cold and silent graveyard where she sleeps 'neath the dew.[20]

A number of songs combine Victorian diction and imagery with Latinate verbiage – and in the following example – with a loose variety of *ochtfhoclach*:

> Sweet boyhood recollections that ever fondly bind me
> To the friends I left behind me far o'er the raging sea;
> And then dear Kilnamartyra, where one time I resided,
> And now I am divided by the ocean wide from thee.
> Age is overtaking me and youth has long forsaken me,
> The friends that once delighted me perhaps I'll see no more
> But until my days are over and death has come and taken me,
> I fondly will remember thee, dear land that I adore.[21]

The extent to which print determined or disseminated the songs we know from more recent oral tradition is an open question, but the situation is certain to have varied regionally. William Barry's 1871 account, however, while possibly somewhat overstated, suggests fairly widespread diffusion of ballads in the country as a whole:

> At the racecourses, fairs and regattas, the ballad minstrel is certain of bringing about him or her, a large audience, and may be seen disposing of the wares in thick sheaves at the close of each ditty. The peasantry when coming to the market town for small purchases, invariably bring back in a basket or wallet the newest ballad; and in the cabins and even farmhouses, a few of the broadsheets will be found pasted on the walls under the coloured effigy of a saint performing a miracle, or of Napoleon prancing over the peaks of the Alps on a steed.[22]

Ballad-selling also figures prominently in the recollections of singers who were children during the first half of the twentieth century. For example Fermanagh singer John Maguire recalled:

> I remember a long time ago I went to Clones with my father in a pony and cart, and at that time when they had their marketing done there was always ballad singers on the Diamond. They sung lots of songs and they told you before it what the song was. And there was a wee boy would go about with a great lot of them in his hand and he would sell to the people round about. They were priced from about twopence to threepence apiece and I remember they used to get them all sold every one of them. Nearly everyone bought a *ballad* ... [Another ballad seller] was singing this song about people sailing away to America and my father bought the ballad. So I got it in my pocket and was very fond of it and kept it. I have the song yet.[23]

Mikeen McCarthy (see Figure 6.1) describes such a transaction from his own perspective as a teenage ballad-seller in County Kerry during the 1940s – although instead of fairs or markets, his 'pitches' were mostly public houses:

> You'd go into a pub, only you'd have the ballads in your hand; you'd just walk over and you'd say, 'would you like to buy some songs, some ballads'? They'd start looking at them then. Well, they'd take them all away like, they'd start reading them all then and picking them out. They'd ask you then, 'could you sing that one for us, could we know the air of it'? 'Yeah', I'd say; I'd sing it then. They'd buy me a bottle of lemonade or something and I'd sit down and I'd sing it, and then often had to sing it maybe two or three times. There'd be some girl maybe or some boy interested in it ... And then I'd sell that ballad – I might sell a dozen of them then in a pub; and when I [got] paid for my ballads then, over singing it, a feller['d] go round with a hat ... then and make a collection for me and, bejakers, the money was greater than that.[24]

Figure 6.1: Mikeen McCarthy. Photo by Pat Mackenzie. Used by permission.

Ballad-selling in country areas seems to have remained relatively common until the 1950s, with some local circulation of ballad sheets at sporting events and even sales at fairs and in shops through the 1970s. Although Tom Munnelly did not remember ballads having been sold at fairs in County Clare during this period, he did recall an incident that occurred at a *fleadh cheoil* in Scariff in 1966, when a man who had a review copy of Colm Ó Lochlainn's newly-published *More Irish Street Ballads* was 'showing it around':

So, we got talking later, and he went looking for the book and it was gone. About an hour later, we went out into the street and there were some traveller kids outside, selling individual pages of it. So the tradition [was still alive] with the traveller kids, even if they weren't getting the broadsheets to sell.[25]

Whether they learn their songs from oral or written sources, however, modern traditional singers do not typically draw a distinction between the two media: all the singers I have spoken to on the subject have asserted that it was the song rather than the source that mattered. 'The song can be just as good if it was written with a gold pen', Packie Manus Byrne (see Figure 6.2) declared to me: 'It's all the same'.[26]

Figure 6.2: Packie Manus Byrne. Photo by author.

Vincie Boyle of Mullagh, County Clare, informed me that Healy's song collections (first published in the 1960s) had been invaluable to him as a source for song lyrics;[27] and other singers I know have related similar stories of learning from print, radio, or sound recordings. Éamonn Mac Ruairí of Tory Island told Lillis Ó Laoire of getting a song that he had already heard and taken 'a fancy to' from a songbook; he had learned another song from a written transcription given him by his aunt.[28] Tom Munnelly's fieldwork confirms this catholic openness to song sources. Commenting on the fact that Tom Lenihan (a singer with one of the largest repertoires in West Clare) had learned a song from the pages of *Ireland's Own*, he wrote, 'In a society that is mostly literate nowadays one has to come to terms with informants who will find material in print and add it to their oral repertoire'. In fact, in the course of his fieldwork, he discovered that if singers made any distinction between sources at all, they tended to feel that learning from either print or recordings was somehow 'superior' to learning by ear.[29] Admitting that he had had to come to terms with his own bias that 'purely oral' material somehow had 'an "edge" on material which can be shown to be influenced by print', Munnelly acknowledged that:

> In many respects this weekly magazine [*Ireland's Own*] fulfils the same needs as the ballad seller, for it has carried at least one page of songs in every issue since its foundation in the early years of this century. Aimed at a mainly rural and emigrant audience it has reflected the prevailing tastes of a high percentage of Irish singers throughout this period. The song page acts as an Exchange and Mart wherein requested songs are printed and others are sought for. Over the years sentimental and patriotic doggerel, vaudeville, pop songs and quite a large number of traditional songs have appeared, all being grist to the *Ireland's Own* mill.[30]

Although there are exceptions (for example, Donegal singer Packie Byrne, whose years of singing in English folk clubs made him much more conscious about matters of repertoire), singers tend not to differentiate between genres any more than they do between the sources of their songs. As Tom Munnelly remarked, 'It's far more important to the singer that the song engages them and that it's a 'good' [song]'. Although 'they still have a pecking order ... it's a very much personalized pecking order':

> And I have never met any of the older singers who would not be quite happy to sing a pop song if it meant something to them – it was about something that they appreciated. All the time that they were growing up, they didn't differentiate between locally made songs, between broadsheet songs, if it was popular in the area and you were singing to people.[31]

Packie Manus Byrne went so far as to say that if a song 'wasn't from your own area in the old days, people didn't reckon much to it ... They didn't want to know, because it didn't relate to anything that they related to'.[32] Similarly, Kitty Hayes, of Coore, West Clare, told me that a 'good' song 'would be something to do with the surroundings and the countryside'.[33] Certainly local songs (or *localized* songs), especially concerning emigration, have remained extremely popular throughout Ireland to the present day. Yet one singer from the Bloody Foreland, in West Donegal, who had learned many of the Irish-language songs popular in her home area, fell in love with ballads in English which she heard while in service in East Donegal – and during the brief time I spent with her it was obvious which she preferred.[34]

According to Mikeen McCarthy, the ballads that sold best when he was hawking sheets in County Kerry in the 1940s were either newly composed or new to the area. This would seem to confirm the effectiveness of the claim of novelty that typified ballad titles and advertisements throughout their existence. "'Tis like the hit records today now,' commented Mikeen, 'When the hit record 'd come out it'd make plenty of money. Well in my way of life, in my occupation, when a new ballad would come out I'd make plenty of money'. Of course, 'new' in Mikeen's community often simply meant newly printed onto ballad sheets from 78 recordings – or even newly printed from his parents' repertoire. When travelling in his father's home area, he was frequently asked whether he had copies of his father's songs, including 'old ballads' like 'The Blind Beggar [of Bednall Green]', to sell:

> 'Why don't you get those printed', they'd say, 'Those are the songs you'd sell, and if you get them printed I'll buy about a dozen of them off you next time I meet you'. So that's how I got them in print then myself. My father [would] write them out for me and I'd go in to the printing office then, then I'd get them printed. Well, they were the songs that did [sell], and many a time after I went into the pubs after selling ballads like and ... I'd hear all the lads inside on a fair day now, we'll say markets and meetings; well, when they'd have a few pints on them, 'tis then you'd hear my songs sung back again out of my ballads.[35]

The facility – already noted – with which songs can move between printed and oral media is amply illustrated by this story. Yet it also reflects an ongoing tension between the old and new; for, as John Moulden observes, the singing community has always 'expected continuity and ... sought novelty'.[36] In a humourous illustration of how the repackaging of texts as 'ballets' could actually trick singers into thinking old songs were recent compositions, Packie Manus Byrne told me,

> I learned some songs off the penny sheets, all right, because I had an opportunity; I was at fairs and I used to throw a couple o' pennies to a street singer and they'd hand me a sheet or two. Aye. I [had] a good enough opportunity of learnin' them, but I never bothered where they came from or anything. But I had an advantage, then, on the other hand, because I'll bring home this song and I'll say to me mother, 'God, I've got a lovely song – great words and all'. And, 'Well, how does it go?' She would stop whatever she was doing, of course, to hear this song and, she would listen for a wee while and – *she* would start and sing it![37]

Writing – by all measurements a more advanced tool of literacy – has also long played a prominent role in the perpetuation of the singing tradition. Two manuscript songbooks, one from the 1850s and another from a slightly later date, reveal the practice of making 'ballet' books, although the later 'Higgins' manuscript, judging by 'the laboured fashion evident in the formation of the letters and their combination', was maintained only 'with the expenditure of considerable effort'.[38] The number of singers who kept ballet books or collections of songs in manuscript in the past century is prodigious – in Tom Munnelly's experience, 'more than I can possibly enumerate'. 'In the early days', he added, 'I used to ask everywhere I'd go, because most houses would either – they'd have their copy books filled out, or they'd have things from *Ireland's Own* and ballads – broadsheets – bunged into them'.[39] Jimmy Callaghan of Roslea, County Fermanagh, told me that he had learned all of his father's songs at the age of fourteen, when, at his father's insistence, he wrote down his entire repertoire – although he says that he never looked at the written texts afterwards.[40] Hugh Shields reports that in the 1930s, Donegal singer Joe McCafferty, who was (unusually for his generation and place) literate in both Irish and English, took down a ballad from his father over several sittings. He also made lists of his repertoire which he sent to Shields.[41] Packie Byrne told me that he would sometimes write songs down as they were being sung (on one occasion from a tinker girl in a caravan) – or as much as he could keep up with, at any rate: 'I wouldn't write down the song, but I would write down a couple o' lines in every verse, and then I would make up the remainder if I couldn't remember them. But, oh, God, yes! I won't deny it: I used the pen on songs'.[42] Packie, however, would have been among the first in his area to learn to write; his parents' generation was, by and large, illiterate: hence, the dearth of ballet books in his locality. Even a generation later, as Mikeen McCarthy, whose mother was illiterate, remarked, "'Twas very few travelling people had any bit of education that time. What I had wasn't worth talking about either, but I could read and write and I could learn a bit of a song anyway.' As I have observed, his father wrote out the lyrics of his songs for his son to have printed, while Mikeen himself seems to have recorded the words of his mother's songs for the same purpose.[43] Lillis Ó Laoire reports that several singers on Tory Island – an area with a reputation for possessing both a strong oral and written culture – have noted down the words of songs, including Éamonn Mac Ruairí, who possesses a 'neatly kept folder with the songs written out and stored carefully for safekeeping', and his cousin Kitty Nic Ruairí, who 'kept many, many copybooks with songs written out in Irish and in English'.[44] Other Tory Island singers reported learning songs from manuscripts, but took pride in their never having written down a song – an attitude which Ó Laoire suspects 'can be directly linked' (since the 1930s) to the presence of folklore collectors, who could easily have communicated their bias in favour of oral sources to their informants.[45] Blissfully ignorant of such preconceptions, a Connemara singer I know used to write out the lyrics of songs she was learning and tape them to her kitchen window so that she could work on them while she was washing the dishes.[46]

It might be argued that at least some of these instances (e.g. the scribe of the 'Higgins' manuscript and Mikeen McCarthy and his father) are merely examples of what Walter Ong calls 'residual' or 'transitional' orality, in which writing is a tool of only marginal importance, while the community in question preserve 'much of the mind-set of primary orality'.[47] Indeed, Shields comments that 'ballots', whether printed or handwritten, serve merely as 'memory aids to singing', and as such 'are treated with only such respect as aids deserve. Magilligan people,' he continues, 'have often given me tatty manuscripts of song texts and sometimes recent newspaper cuttings, etc., of published texts, but the old broadsides have perished without trace.'[48]

While Ong posits an intermediate stage between primarily oral and primarily literate societies, he also claims that writing itself 'alters thought', arguing that the technology of writing itself – rather than other aspects of a culture in which writing is pervasive – affects cognitive and attitudinal differences between literate and non-, or even semi-literate, individuals, replacing cultures that are intuitive and subjective with ones that foster abstract, analytic reasoning and that move in 'interlocked, sequential, linear patterns'. 'Writing', he continues, 'separates the knower from the known', distances objects of knowledge, sets them in 'perspective' and makes for 'objectivity'. Describing the difficulties encountered by one of his students from a 'residually oral' culture in learning to write, Ong concludes, 'Writing swamps a whole universe of orally based thought and discourse'. And, echoing Buchan's lament for the loss of the 'oral ballad' during the increasingly literate nineteenth century, he declares:

> The mind that has become literate can no longer produce an *Iliad*, a *Mwindo Epic*, or the beautiful and intricate thought patterns in the oral interchanges of Chinua Achebe's Ibo villagers. With literacy, certain things die. But you have to die in order to continue with life ... The desire for literacy can justifiably be salted with fear, for learning to read and write represents a passage from one 'mentality', one state of consciousness, to another.[49]

Even without the evidence of numerous studies confirming that the qualities supposedly determined by literacy enumerated above are actually tied to social and educational systems rather to literacy *per se*, it seems clear that Ong cannot insist so strongly on the cognitive effects of literacy on the one hand and the concept of 'residual orality' on the other without seriously contradicting his thesis that it is writing itself rather than either social or educational factors that determine the traits he defines as 'literate'. Ong asserts that the process of becoming literate effects cognitive changes in the individual, or, as he puts it, 'restructures consciousness'. If this is true, can degrees of literacy be represented in psychological or cognitive terms? Shouldn't such changes be measurable? If only in terms of the social and psychological differences that Ong, Goody, McLuhan and others have described between primarily oral and primarily literate societies, we are left with nothing but a tautology based on an *a priori* causal link between literacy and these differences. If, for example, a person in a 'residually oral' culture displays certain traits that have been denominated as 'oral' and others as 'literate', that person becomes a piece of evidence in a self-fulfilling proposition, to the exclusion of more complex explanations for these traits and other differences between oral and literate persons or cultures. Furthermore, Ong's examples of 'residual orality' – such as Thomas Aquinas' organization of his manuscripts in 'quasi-oral' fashion – are not convincing: the use of rhetorical strategies in Aquinas' writing could as easily reflect the centrality of rhetoric in medieval pedagogy and scholarship as a 'consciousness' that was mid-way between the oral and the written.[50] By defining the literate mind as an essentially modern, Western, educated one, such an argument also has the effect of simply creating a new way of differentiating 'primitive' or 'marginal' cultures from our own, changing the terminology but not the conceptual superiority that goes with it – a superiority that Ong unwittingly embraces even as he writes nostalgically of the communal and integrative nature of the oral 'lifeworld'.

Even if the 'orality' argument could not be dismissed as unsound in itself, there is also much evidence from socio-linguistics, anthropology and neurology to support the position that formal schooling has much more to do with the supposed traits of literacy than does literacy itself. For example, on the basis of their comparison of three different kinds of literacy in the Vai community of Liberia, Scribner and Cole have concluded that 'literacy is nothing more than a type of structural coupling between organism and world mediated through the technology of a script' – a coupling that 'leads to changes in the state of both organism and world' – but only to changes that are local rather than global in nature.[51] Shirley Brice Heath's study of literacy in three American communities revealed that each community combined oral and literate skills in different ways, depending on such societal factors as class and ethnic background.[52] Hildyard's and Hidi's study of elementary school children found that until the age of twelve there were no differences between their oral and written texts, greater complexity only appearing after the children were taught how to revise their written work.[53] Studies of aphasia in literates and illiterates reveal similar findings, i.e. that there are few neurological differences between the two groups and that those that do exist are products of education rather than of literacy itself.[54] All of this supports Keith Thomas's sensible observation that 'literates and illiterates need not necessarily have different mental habits'.[55]

These findings also help to explain the ease with which traditional singers – whether 'residually' oral or fully literate – move between the oral and literate spheres in their dealings with songs and song texts. Of Tory Island singers, Ó Laoire observes:

> Like everywhere else, differences exist among individuals regarding literacy standards, and although many became accomplished in reading and writing, others fell shorter of this mark to varying degrees. Neither does literacy seem to have affected oral transmission to any great extent, and from out testimony, it seems that Éamonn [Mac Ruairí] and Jimí [Ó Dúgáin] had no difficulty in being literate while still maintaining their ability to absorb songs orally.[56]

Joe McCafferty was completely literate in English and Irish, comfortable with writing and translating texts of songs, as well as with the act of making lists – a supposed hallmark of literacy (despite the fact that oral genealogical lists have also existed in many cultures, including that of medieval Ireland).[57] As Shields comments, 'Joe is a singer who combines oral art with a degree of literacy and with a respect for literacy which is not unusual in Irish folk tradition.'[58] Aodh Ó Duibheannaigh (d. 1984) of Ranafast, County Donegal, who grew up in an area known for its oral artistry, was completely literate in Irish and English, worked for the civil service in Dublin, and later collected songs for the Irish Folklore Commission. He was also especially proud of having caused local song-poet Seán Bán Mac Grianna to marvel when, as a boy, he learned three of his songs by ear in a single night.[59] The Mac Grianna brothers, two of whom were published novelists, were also reportedly adept at orally improvising verse. This permeability of the line between 'vernacular' and 'literary' as well as 'oral' and 'literate' is also evident in the Irish-language repertoire, perhaps most obviously in the case of blind song-poets like Máire Bhuí Ní Laoghaire and Antaine Raifteraí, whose songs exhibit a number of 'literary' traits. Thus, not only can 'literary' songs enter the vernacular song tradition; they can be composed by the illiterate and by those outside the circles of the educated elite. Alternately, literary figures like Dominic Behan could compose songs in convincing broadside idiom.[60] Current-day singers of traditional songs, whether born into a singing community or not, also tend to learn both words and melodies primarily by ear: while they, too, may copy the words or use books to refresh their memories, their principal reference tends to be aural. Notes Moulden:

> It is very unusual to find that a song has been taken from print or manuscript and sung, without first having been heard. It seems almost as if the singer is unable to accept the 'songness' of the song; unable to imagine the song, without hearing it; unable to 'audialise' the song. It might be conjectured that the art of the song, in this oral situation, is so far a matter of hearing – that so much is lacking in the absence of a performance – that the impulse to sing a song is dependent on having first heard how it might go.[61]

Similarly, Hugh Shields, observing that many university-educated singers prefer to learn by ear, writes, 'A disposition to orally transmitted singing, like *le bon sens* at least potentially, is well distributed through mankind.'[62]

None of this proves that traditional singers are 'residually' oral; only that they participate in a particular kind of performance practice. Eric Montenyohl points out that the traits Ong selects to represent 'primary orality' – including the use of formulae – are 'examples of oral *performance*', identified chiefly through his analysis of Homeric and other epic verse: in other words, Ong has taken the salient traits of verbal performance and applied them not only to entire cultures but to the psyches of individuals within them.[63]

Performance, clearly, is essential to the Irish singing tradition; in a way it *is* the tradition: hence the importance of ballad-sellers as singers. Indeed, catching the ear was deemed crucial to selling a ballad: as the Victorian London journalist Henry Mayhew was told 'on all hands … it was not the words that ever "made a ballad, but the subject; and, more than the subject, – the chorus; and, far more than either – the *tune*!"'[64] A catchy melody and a compelling subject are certainly crucial to the appeal of songs, although other factors – such as social and emotional context, singing style, and all the other 'paralinguistic' features of performance – are often equally important. Those familiar with the whole complex of community performance conventions can, of course, learn a text independently (as with the farmer who 'went to the mountains for the air' of his song), but they will still almost certainly introduce it into their own communities through the medium of performance. The role of song as a form of interpersonal communication undoubtedly contributes to this dynamic. John Ó Duibheannaigh has described the manner in which conversation used to be interspersed with song at an *airneál*, or house visit, quite naturally, as though song were simply a heightened form of speech. He also spoke of the profound effect a song might have upon the listeners present, eliciting everything from laughter to tears.[65] The importance of communication in relation to song also offers greater insight into why singers often characterize songs as 'good' when they speak to their personal or collective experience, implying an aesthetic that is as much social as it is artistic.

Yet is there such a thing as an 'oral' or 'vernacular' song aesthetic? Citing Basil Bernstein's distinction between the 'restricted linguistic code' ('public language') associated with lower-class English dialects and 'the elaborated linguistic code' ('private language') characteristic of upper- and middle-class dialects, John Moulden argues that the songs of Thomas Davis and *The Nation* did not 'take' among 'the ordinary people' because they were in 'the wrong language' – that is, language that was 'text-based' as opposed to 'oral-based':

> Instead of the people's oral linguistic mode they used the elite literary mode of the magistrates and gentry. It was not until literacy and education had created a group of people in Ireland who aspired to be middle class that the poems of Thomas Davis and his fellows began to look like ballads.[66]

While it is true that few of the political songs from sources like *Paddy's Resource* and, later, *The Nation*, seem to have entered the popular repertoire in Ireland, how much of this has to do with literary language *per se* is a moot point: as we have already seen in both the Irish- and English-language traditions, the literariness of a text has not necessarily been an obstacle to its absorption into tradition, even before the mid- to late nineteenth century when the educational changes Moulden describes would have occurred. Yet, as Shields points out, many of these songs are 'difficult to accept as oral poetry', concerned as they are 'with moral abstractions' rather than with human situations or local political events and figures.[67] And, notes Moulden, 'Even though [the writers of such songs] sought to politicise 'the crowd', the cultural values that underpinned their attempt were still essentially those of the elite'.[68] Only a relatively small number of songs from patriotic newspapers like *The Northern Star* and the chief political song anthology of the day, *Paddy's Resource*, appeared in chapbook songsters – and the anthology itself would have been unaffordable for most chapbook-buyers. Linguistically, some of its songs convey the register of earlier topical broadsides (set to such tunes as 'Derry Down'); others seem to reflect the influence of Burns's political verse, an impression the preponderance of Scottish melodies used for such songs reinforces; a minority are even in French. Many – like much topical verse – simply make for painful singing, like 'The Dictates of Reason', set to the tune of 'Logie of Buchan':

> Brave Irish no longer inactive remain,
> Attend to the dictates of Reason and *Paine*;
> 'Tis to freedom they call you, no longer delay
> Your rights are at stake – and are lost if you stay.
> Shall men as the heads of a nation preside,
> Who cannot the test of inquiry abide,
> Let them boast of their virtues and plead for the state,
> So felons remonstrate in view of their fate.[69]

Shields notes that northern song collector John Hume listed twenty-nine patriotic songs out of 102 items as being 'in use' in County Down in the mid-nineteenth century. 'By "use" he must have meant to indicate singing', comments Shields, but 'by what singers and how far detached from the support of print it is difficult to say'.[70] According to David Wilson, many songs from the *Nation* and *Paddy's Resource* were performed among United Irishmen in exile; but while this information is interesting in itself, it tells us little about how popular the songs of the earlier anthology were in the general population at home, especially in the late eighteenth and early nineteenth centuries.[71]

In assessing the role of linguistic codes in the acceptance of songs into singing communities, one could argue that hedge schoolmaster songs possessed the advantage of stylistic congruity with native Irish repertoire. Yet many of the late eighteenth-century Vauxhall pastorals, like 'The Banks of the Banna' and the flowery Victorian pieces – both employing the 'elaborated' linguistic code – also found their way into the song tradition by the early and mid-nineteenth century.[72] In support of Moulden's class distinctions, however, Tom Munnelly found that in Miltown Malbay there was a difference between what was popular in the town and what was popular in the country: the town (with its middle-class aspirations) favouring songs by poets like Thomas Moore, Robert Burns and light opera – a selection reflected in the similar drawing-room tastes of many of Joyce's *Dubliners*; the country preferring narrative ballads, *pastourelles*, music hall numbers, sentimental emigration songs and other more 'popular' fare.[73] Yet there are exceptions: some of Moore's songs have turned up in recent oral tradition, and literary productions like Joseph Campbell's 'My Lagan Love' and Padraic Colum's 'She Moved through the Fair' have long been popular in many rural singing communities. There are also regional differences: Robert Burns has historically enjoyed greater popularity among traditional singers in the north; he was the one song-composer in English whom John Ó Duibheannaigh said was highly regarded in northwest Donegal when he was young.[74] Remarks Bronson, 'Always there seems to have been this borrowing back and forth, this *va-et-vien* between the country and the town, between the upper and lower levels of society'.[75] Such interchange, leading to heterogeneity of repertoire, is reflected as much in latter-day tradition as it is in late eighteenth-century chapbooks and in Patrick Kennedy's Wexford: Mikeen McCarthy's best-sellers included songs as diverse as 'The Green Mossy Banks of the Lee' (a nineteenth-century *pastourelle*), 'Kathleen Mavourneen' (a sentimental 1830s song in the style of Moore), 'Eileen McMahan' (a latter-day *aisling* of the broadside variety), 'The Old Bog Road' (a sentimental emigration song), 'Patrick Sheehan' (a nineteenth-century political slip ballad composed by Charles Kickham) and the venerable 'Blind Beggar [of Bednall Green]'.

In attempting to characterize what constitutes a 'traditional' or 'vernacular' aesthetic, it might be more useful to examine the criteria used by traditional singers themselves. For example, local interest is often a factor in the acceptability or popularity of a song. So, too, is the frequent demand that songs that 'make sense', a term Shields relates to the Irish concept of *brí* – 'significance', 'sense', or 'meaning'. He offers, as an example, Tom Lenihan's reaction to an American music hall song called 'The Bicycle', in which a newly initiated cyclist runs into an elderly woman and a child, who subsequently destroy his machine – a process the song describes in some detail. 'I never sung it no place because I didn't ever get much sense, you know, in the bloody thing'.[76] Shields also quotes a friend of Eddie Butcher, who described his audience in Magilligan as liking 'a good song … something that had a bit of a meaning with it, a story till it, you know'.[77] Packie Manus Byrne told me that he disliked 'She Moved through the Fair' because, as he put it,

> In my opinion, it doesn't really make proper sense. Like, 'My young love said to me, my mother won't mind/My father won't slight you for your lack of kine' – well, that part of it, you could get away with *that*. Well, then she just walked away from him – which was a bit of a rude thing to do! And she moved through the fair, and then he had to watch her move here and move there. Well, of course she was movin' here and there: if she was in the same spot all the time, she wouldn't be movin'! I think it's a wee bit, you know – some amateur composed this at the very start and then it was 'improved on' and spoiled.[78]

On further enquiry, I discovered, that 'sense' to Packie could mean one of several things. On the one hand, it could mean that a song consisted of a complete narrative: 'I was led to believe that songs should be long, sensible ones, with a story', he told me.[79] Even small gaps in the story line struck him as flaws, as I learned when I sang him a fairly (but not perfectly) 'complete' version of the narrative ballad 'The Holland Handkerchief'. Yet in his view, even a lyric song could 'make sense' and have a 'good story', if it hewed to his own idea of poetic and artistic order. Shields has observed that, 'For Irish singers the term "story" seems more often to refer to real-life meaning to be found in one or more circumstances, narrative or merely objective, mentioned within the song or, outside it, providing a context in the reality of the past: circumstances any of which a singer of Irish might describe the term *údar*'.[80] Such a definition obviously obtains in the case of emigration songs and songs of local interest. Yet there is also the question of whether a song speaks to a singer on a personal level; or, as I think true in Packie's case, conforms to an individual singer's conception of aesthetic excellence. For all the talk in folklore circles of 'passive' and 'active' tradition-bearers, traditional singers do, by and large, possess their own standards of taste.

These standards can be seen at work in the amount and kind of variation or re-creation of songs that is permitted or practised within a community or by a particular singer. My own fieldwork has convinced me that the ideal of textual stability – if not the reality – is the norm for non-improvisational genres, a belief shared by Hugh Shields, who quotes Robert Butcher of Magilligan as having praised his father's singing by saying, 'He neither put till nor tuk from'. As Shields comments, such praise, while 'unverifiable', is also 'plausible ... Some singers sound as if their songs never vary and successive renditions, when recorded, may indeed show detailed memorial reproduction of both words and music'.[81] Of the Omagh version of 'Sir James the Ross' which agreed so closely with the 1826 printed text, he comments that it was 'evidently transmitted orally for a century and a half without alphabetic interference'.[82]

In practice, of course, verbatim repetition cannot be depended upon and variation in oral tradition is accepted as inevitable. The extent to which variation is tolerated, however, may vary from community to community and even from household to household: Packie told me that his parents would argue in bed about the 'right words' to a song, calling him in during the wee hours as an arbiter.[83] I have even heard of cases in which people came to blows over the right way to sing a song, dissenting parties hurling a boot, pieces of turf – or, in one case, a dog – at the offending singer.[84] Stephen Gwynn, taking down the words of an Ossianic lay from an illiterate Donegal man, commented on the precision with which his informant insisted that he 'must write [it] down, syllable for syllable, that the song might be got "the right way"'.[85] Seán Corcoran notes that in the Fermanagh area he documented, each song is followed by a discussion, which includes such matters as whether the singer has the '*right words*' and whether the story is '*true*'.[86] Lillis Ó Laoire found that singers on Tory Island have similar –

and very definite – ideas of correct (*ceart*) and incorrect (*ciotach*) renditions of songs. This evidence runs counter to the theory that the concept of the 'fixed' or 'original' text is non-existent in oral tradition, which is so often represented as essentially characterized by variation, fluidity and improvisation. Yet Ireland is not alone in possessing an oral tradition that emphasizes exact reproduction of texts: Somali poetry, too, can be subject to 'heated disputes between a reciter and his audience concerning the purity of his version';[87] the Vedic tradition possesses texts which are fixed 'by means of elaborate mnemonic schemes that keep them as invariant as writing';[88] and in Britain remarkable textual stability of ballads has been reported.[89] Buchan's notion that the fixed text becomes part of the traditional aesthetic only after the introduction of writing when people, 'with an awed respect for the authority of the printed word, come to believe that the printed text is *the* text' is simply not supported by the ethnographic evidence.[90]

When variation does occur, however, there are still standards by which the text is judged. Ó Laoire found that singers on Tory tended to be tolerant of certain small variations (such as the replacement of one pronoun with another), provided that they either did not materially change the meaning of the lyrics or that they supplied an acceptable variant 'reading'. They were less tolerant, however, of such alterations as the omission of verses, the transposition of verses, or the replacement of a line or phrase of a song with one from another verse or song – one which may have accommodated the metrics of the line but which made for an incomplete or slightly distorted realization of the lyrics as a whole.[91] This kind of attention to verse order is significant in a non-narrative tradition that is noted for 'floating verses' and even the conflation of different songs. During his brief career as a ballad-seller, Mikeen McCarthy experienced a more tangible form of textual criticism. He recalls that when his father would hear young Mikeen singing one of the songs he had taught him, "'Tisn't the singing at all he'd be listening to, 'tis the song, and if I made a mistake in the song I'd have a belt on the ear that night off of him. He'd say, "You made a mistake here in this verse and that verse. D'you know, he always put me right." This became more confusing, however, when some of the 'old timers' corrected his father's versions,

> and then my father'd be contradicting me that he was wrong again, so you'd never know which one of them was right like. But I sang them the way that my father wrote them out anyway, and I imagine myself that that was near enough anyway.[92]

Apart from the story of his parents' late-night debates, Packie Manus Byrne made his south Donegal community sound fairly tolerant of minor divergences:

> As far as possible, they would try to stick to the way they first heard it. Or the way they learned. Which probably would be changed by that time. It would maybe be fourteenth- or fifteenth-hand. Instead of secondhand. And … probably they wouldn't do it deliberately, but sooner than get stuck in the middle of a verse, they *would* improvise a little bit, of course, aye. We all do it – and I still do it – aye.[93]

One kind of variation that seems to be widely accepted – even applauded – is the replacement, whether learned or deliberately interpolated in performance, of proper names, locations, occupations, or other narrative details. Sometimes this technique is used in order to localize a song (as in the case of the transposition in County Clare of 'Lovely Old Miltown' for 'Lovely Old Fintown'); at other times – as when a singer substitutes a ballad character's name with that of a member of the company – it is employed for comic effect.

In reality, then, there is a constant tension within the tradition between variability and stability, creation and recreation. In Chapter 2, I discussed Eleanor Long's categories of traditional singers: 'perseverating' (conservative singers who may retain even the most garbled phrases in their attempts to faithfully reproduce a song); 'confabulating' (stylistic improvisers who feel free to revise a song to their liking); 'rationalizing' (singers who also feel free to manipulate their material, but are possessed of more abstract motivations); and 'integrative' (those who, with 'the value-system of a poet', not only remake received material but also create new songs).[94] All of these categories exist in the Irish singing tradition. Despite the ideals of the fixed text, *ceart*, or the right words, changes do occur, either through faulty memories or through conscious or unconscious alterations of melodies and/or texts of songs.

While some of these alterations can lead to confusing or garbled texts, as when unfamiliar words are rationalized or mispronounced, verses interchanged, and so on,[95] others can lead to neutral changes – or even to improvements. Probably the most common change that ballad scholars view as an 'improvement' is the sloughing off of non-essential details, a process noted in variations of broadside ballads as well as in oral 'texts'. In some cases this process can lead to lyricization, in which the narrative elements of a song are whittled away, leaving only its 'emotional core'. Shields believes the Irish tradition to be particularly prone to this kind of recomposition because of the native Irish predilection for the lyric idiom.[96] Such a process is evident not only in older ballads like 'The Lass of Aughrim' but in songs of broadside origin as well, such as 'The Strands of Magilligan', a haunting song of little narrative content that derives from three different British songs, two primarily lyric but one strongly narrative.[97]

Many Irish singers clearly fall into Long's last three categories, feeling free (to varying degrees) to alter their material. Shields comments:

> Some singers like ... to leave their mark on inherited verses by partial changes. A youth departing to America alone, by the addition of eight lines, is allowed to marry and take the girl along with him: about half a century separates the two versions. Another singer adds flowery embellishment or elucidates the action; he is ready to identify his interpolations if anyone bothers to ask. Another ... improvises forgotten words so that successive renditions sound quite different.[98]

Like Packie Manus Byrne, Fermanagh singer John Maguire (who also learned songs from written sources) felt free to supplement forgotten lyrics, especially when he had only heard a song once or twice: 'I'd remember the story and if I remembered the story you see it wasn't too hard to put in a word if you wanted, into it'.[99] This kind of 'confabulating' or 'integrative' recomposition requires an intimate knowledge of the poetic idiom in question. Hugh Shields instances Eddie Butcher's amendments of Dublin librarian Alf Mac Lochlainn's comic song, 'My Son in America', which Shields had printed for Butcher with the usual ballad sheet instruction, 'To the tune of'. Butcher made a number of changes to the song (all of which the song's author himself termed 'improvements'), replacing standard English with dialect and colloquial language and localizing the references. He then proceeded to sing the song in his community and even to record it, adhering closely to his own 'fixed text' ever afterward. To Shields this is an example of song 'folklorisation', an adaptation of a song with more 'educated' or 'text-based' diction to the 'oral-based' idiom Butcher knew and preferred.

But – again – does quotidian diction define the 'oral' or 'vernacular' aesthetic? In his discussion of Padraic Colum's 'She Moved through the Fair' and the Irish song tradition, Shields describes Butcher's lack of interest in Colum's song (though he sang a related traditional song called 'Our Wedding Day') and Butcher himself as a singer and song poet 'so strongly possessed of his own traditional style and experience as to be immune to the modern influences which have made Colum's poem popular as a song'.[100] He also examines what seems to be a redaction of the song recorded in 1966 from the late Antrim singer Robert Cinnamond, whose version apparently combines elements of Colum's poem with those of related traditional songs.[101] He applauds Cinnamond's version as a '"folklorisation" – and a very beautiful one – of Colum's poem', but still sees too much in it that is literary to accept that it has done more than progress 'some way ... towards becoming a popular poem'[102] – undoubtedly because, while eschewing the most artificial lines of Colum's poem ('And then she went homeward with one star awake,/As the swan in the evening moves over the lake'), it still retains something of Colum's own composition:

> My young love stepped from me and she went through the fair
> How fondly I watched her move here and move there;
> And then she went homewards with her geese and her gear,
> Ah, that was the last that I saw of my dear.[103]

By way of explaining Cinnamond's incomplete adaptation of Colum's song to a fully 'ethnic' idiom, Shields comments that complete or true popularization ('folklorisation')

> is inhibited by the decline of the *old* folk tradition along with the kind of society that produced it. On the other hand, progress towards a new kind of popularisation is

encouraged by the rise of a tradition too greatly detached from the old one by such factors as the displacement of populations, the increasing influence of a literate conception of art, the thorough commercialisation of its dissemination.[104]

While I agree with Shields about the artificially rapid changes imposed on the tradition through increasing commercialization and cultural disengagement, I am less convinced that the 'literate conception of art' is a new force – or the most influential one – in this process, since many different kinds of 'literary' influences, both Irish and British, have long been evident in the Irish song tradition.

Packie Manus Byrne, too, dislikes Colum's poem. Yet he sings, composes and recomposes songs in a variety of idioms, particularly that of the parlour song – a genre which was at one time disdained by some collectors as less 'authentic' than older song forms. Defining the 'ethnic', 'folk', or 'oral' aesthetic too narrowly runs the risk of diminishing the role of the individual and of individual taste and creativity in tradition and of rejecting 'the contaminating intrusion of non-folk products' as though they were 'noxious weeds'.[105] Contemporary folklorists are fully aware of this danger, however, and recognize the breadth – and significance – of popular tastes. Shields himself blithely notes that a traditional singer from Wicklow liked 'the recently composed '*Whistling Gypsy*' better than its source the old '*Dark-eyed Gipsy*' (Child 200), which he also sang'.[106] Tom Munnelly, observing that Tom Lenihan preferred the sentimental 'Christmas Letter' to anything else in his repertoire, added that:

> the song that without a doubt meant more to John [Reilly–a traveller from whom Munnelly had recorded a unique version of the Child ballad 'The Maid and the Palmer'] than any other song was ... the sentimental music hall, Victorian song 'There Are Two Little Orphans'. And in fact it meant so much to him that – I've three recordings of John singing that – but he never got through it without breaking down crying: it moved him that much.[107]

Examples like these could be enumerated endlessly, even in the Gaeltacht, which is (inaccurately) less associated with recent popular song. Lillis Ó Laoire instances Tory singer Teresa McClafferty's affection for the New York parlour ballad 'There's a Dear Spot in Ireland';[108] Connemara singer Joe Heaney's repertoire included the Vernon Dalhart tearjerker 'The Prisoner's Song' (or 'I Wish I Had Someone to Love Me'); and sentimental songs like 'Noreen Bawn' and 'Far Away in Australia' were popular in Arranmore, County Donegal, in the early twentieth century.[109] The homemade recordings of Bairbre Quinn (née Ní Chonghaile), which date from the late 1950s to the 1970s, contain everything from traditional songs to hits from the radio, reflecting – as her niece, Deirdre Ní Chonghaile, has put it – a 'multi-faceted musical landscape'.[110] Clearly, a song's emotional or aesthetic appeal for a community or for an individual singer is what lends it 'authenticity' – not received notions of what constitutes traditionality. A number of ballad scholars, including Gerould and Buchan, believed that the printed ballad had contaminated the oral ballad tradition; and early-twentieth-century British collectors frequently excluded many songs of parlour or music hall origin in their search for authenticity.[111] Defining the tradition solely in terms of orality, Ozark collector Max Hunter erased a ballad he had recorded from Arkansas singer Almeda Riddle in the 1960s after discovering that she had supplemented her song with verses learned from a book. The days of such dogmatic distinctions are over, but students of traditional culture must still be cautious.

David Atkinson has noted a resistance to variation in 'literary' or, as he calls it, 'centripetal' song (a category roughly congruent with Bernstein's 'elaborated linguistic code'), while viewing 'vernacular' (or 'centrifugal') song as possessing an 'outward' frame of reference that allows for 'endless recapitulation and re-creation across time and space in print, writing and sound'. He makes the salient point that 'The textualization of folk songs into cheap print does not impose the aura of permanence and stability that might be expected from a condition of potentially exact reproducibility over time and space'.[112] But is it the 'centrifugality' of a song or the conventions of the tradition in which it is sung that determine the possibility of variation? For example, in opera (in current performance practice) – and in much 'pop' music – the lyrics of a song are generally repeated exactly as they were composed. However, it is, I suggest, the context that determines this process; and – although songs possessing qualities like formularity and repetition undoubtedly lend themselves to variation more easily than those that do not – any song, once in the domain of the traditional singer, *may* be altered.[113]

Many songs with such qualities, both narrative and lyric, come to us from the sixteenth century on and reflect a range of stylistic and structural genres; but as I have demonstrated, many of these genres were 'literary' (or at least written) in genesis. Treating the Child ballad as a distinct poetic or song genre rather than the passive product of oral tradition, Thomas Pettitt argues that its supposedly 'oral' features (formularity, repetition, use of dialogue and so on) are at least as much generic and formal as they are attributable to the processes of oral tradition: 'The balladic mode represents a distinct aesthetic', he writes, adding that '"ballad" characteristics are not merely oral characteristics, but the combined result of both the pressures to which a text is subjected in tradition and the text's inherent qualities, including the metrical vehicle'.[114] Whether the 'improvements' often discerned in songs after a life in oral tradition represent something inherent in orality itself is still an open question; however, the presence of similar changes in broadside texts suggests that they may, again, have been guided as much by the aesthetic of a particular song idiom or even era than by the more abstract forces of variability or orality – or even an 'ethnic' aesthetic. Certainly, stylistic features of songs in the Irish traditional repertoire have not remained constant, but have reflected both new song-forms and the poetic language of the time in which they originated. Thus when Packie Manus Byrne does a restoration job on an early twentieth-century parlour ballad, he works within the stylistic and linguistic constraints of that genre. Adaptations can also occur: Eddie Butcher took a text and trimmed it to his favoured linguistic idiom; and if Robert Cinnamond did in fact rewrite Padraic Colum's poem, he did so, like Eddie, drawing on his knowledge of a variety of song-genres and styles and relying on his own aesthetic preferences. As with other poets, the 'selectivity' of these singers 'was controlled by the artistic tradition in which [they] had decided to work'.[115]

While many traditional singers may share the aesthetic preferences the majority of folksong scholars have often expressed for the simplicity of diction and structure and immediacy of expression associated with both older genres and 'folk' or 'oral' forms, we must be wary of expecting the 'folk' to adhere to any imposed aesthetic instead of recognizing the validity of what singers have always done: absorb, create and re-create, incorporating new fashions and poetic idioms and genres into their repertoires as they retain the old. De Sola Pinto has remarked that the 'directness, simplicity and honest earthy realism' of eighteenth-century popular repertoire increasingly incorporated songs combining sentimentality with 'stock poetic diction'.[116] Clearly Ireland has not been immune to this process, either in the eighteenth century or the present time. Historically, in both cases, traditional song has at once reflected and influenced the literary fashions of the middle and upper classes. Nor are song communities or individual singers identical in their aesthetic tastes. As Robin Morton observes, 'A song alone is a fairly isolated thing. Some may be minor works of art, but decisions about what is, and what is not, art is a very personal matter. What one person sees as "good" might very well be called "bad" by his neighbour'.[117]

Phillips Barry was one of the first folksong scholars to identify the importance of the individual singer within the tradition, as well as the forces that lead to 'the re-creation of a traditional ballad – the breaking away from tradition with the individual consciousness of the singer in revolt'.[118] Edward Ives goes so far as to say that 'communities *qua* communities can do nothing; it is individuals within communities that do everything'.[119] A text may be preserved almost exactly as it was printed, or it may be altered, consciously or unconsciously, according to the aesthetic preferences of the individual singer. Yet, as we have also seen, the individual is often constrained by community standards, so that the individual talent is in constant interaction with the tradition – and, potentially, as songwriters begin to claim intellectual property rights for their songs, with copyright law. They are not, however, necessarily ruled by either.[120] The licence to alter according to personal taste is one of the most remarkable features of a tradition, which – despite the stabilizing forces of community custom and aesthetics and, often enough, of print – allows for and even encourages innovation and re-creation within the bounds of the poetic idiom in question, whether narrative broadside ballad, parlour song or music hall ditty. Yet, as several scholars have demonstrated, the same kinds of variations associated with oral tradition are often found in different printings of broadside ballads and are sometimes clearly the work of broadside redactors rather than merely examples of orally collected variants.[121] Thus variation or 'multiformularity' – as some have argued in relation to medieval texts – cannot even be claimed as unique to oral tradition.[122]

How then do we define the Irish song tradition? Ultimately, we are left not with a dichotomy of oral and written, vernacular and elite, or even individual and communal, but rather with a dynamic tradition that encompasses all of these in a continuum of aesthetic and creative endeavor. This continuum includes repertoire from at least the late eighteenth century to the present. Although there are obviously fads in traditional song, as in everything else, two centuries of song-collecting have revealed not a progressive casting-off of one song-type for another, but rather a retention of song-types and styles from different eras, so that – using the analogy of a staggered geological display – none is wholly buried under another but all are at least partially visible. Thus, while a number of oral, as well as printed, songs have undoubtedly been lost in the process, the nature of the tradition is such that changing fashions and influences do not signal its death-knell but take their place in a reciprocal relationship between the old and the new: a process of absorption, creation and recreation of which the eighteenth-century printed ballad is only one historical element. As Leslie Shepard reminds us: 'The broadside was not a new phase of human activity but rather a convenient chapter in an ageless story. The act of printing was, so to speak, merely superimposed on an oral tradition that had already found new directions'.[123]

But the tradition cannot be defined solely in terms of its repertoire or even aesthetics. As I noted earlier, it also encompasses a wide range of extra-textual qualities, including performance style and social context. In fact, in many respects it may be more fruitful to discuss the song tradition primarily in terms of performance – that is, in terms of the conventions of groups of people within individual singing communities, with their own aesthetics, performance practices, rules of etiquette and even (as we have seen) critical apparatuses: For it will by now be apparent that traditional singing is a highly social, as well as an intensely personal, activity. Such a discussion would, however, exceed the scope of this study. Moreover, most singers would agree that no amount of contextual analysis is adequate to describe the essence of the tradition or to convey the experience of aesthetic fulfillment, self-expression, fellowship and deeply felt emotion that lie at its core. Finally, in any real appreciation of a singing tradition, 'literacy', 'orality', and all the rest of the abstractions must fall away – until all that remains is the human voice.

NOTES

Introduction

1. L. Ní Mhunghaile, 'The Intersection between Oral Tradition, Manuscript, and Print Cultures in Charlotte Brooke's *Reliques of Irish Poetry* (1789)' in M. Caball and A. Carpenter (eds), *Oral and Print Cultures in Ireland, 1600–1900* (Dublin: Four Courts Press, 2010), p. 20.
2. I take the term from Seán Ó Tuama's and Thomas Kinsella's *An Duanaire 1600–1900: Poems of the Dispossessed*, repr. (1981; Mountrath: The Dolmen Press, 1985).
3. R. Finnegan, *Literacy and Orality: Studies in the Technology of Communication* (Oxford: Blackwell, 1988), p. 175.
4. N. Hudson, '"Oral Tradition": The Evolution of an Eighteenth-Century Concept', in A. Ribeiro and J. G. Basker (eds), *Tradition in Transition: Women Writers, Marginal Texts, and the Eighteenth-Century Canon* (Oxford: Clarendon Press, 1996), pp. 162.
5. Ní Mhunghaile, 'Intersection', p. 15.
6. J. M. Foley, *The Theory of Oral Composition: History and Methodology* (Bloomington, IN: University of Indiana Press, 1988), pp. 2–3; and A. Friedman, *The Ballad Revival: Studies in the Influence of Popular on Sophisticated Poetry* (Chicago, IL: University of Chicago Press, 1961), p. 170.
7. Friedman, *The Ballad Revival*, pp. 168–71; Foley, *The Theory of Oral Composition*, p. 3.
8. N. Hudson, 'Constructing Oral Tradition: The Origins of the Concept in Enlightenment Intellectual Culture', in A. Fox and D. Woolf (eds), *The Spoken Word: Oral Culture in Britain, 1500–1850* (Manchester: Manchester University Press, 2002), p. 251.
9. R. Wood, *An Essay on the Origianl Genius and Writings of Homer* (London: H. Hughs, 1775), p. 284.
10. L. I. Davies, 'Orality, Literacy, Popular Culture: An Eighteenth-Century Case Study', *Oral Tradition*, 25:2 (2010), p. 316.
11. Foley, *The Theory of Oral Composition*, pp. 3–4.
12. Hudson, 'Constructing Oral Tradition', pp. 242–4.
13. See Hudson, 'Constructing Oral Tradition', pp. 240–7; and N. Hudson, *Writing and European Thought 1600–1830* (Cambridge and New York: Cambridge University Press, 1995), pp. 72–3.
14. Friedman, *The Ballad Revival*, p. 172.
15. Hudson, 'Constructing Oral Tradition', pp. 245–6.
16. Hudson, *Writing and European Thought*, pp. 108–9.
17. Hudson, 'Constructing Oral Tradition', p. 247.

18. See S. Lerer, *Inventing English* (New York: Columbia University Press, 2007), pp. 172–80.
19. J. Addison, *Spectator Papers* Nos. 70, 74 and 85, in J. Addison, R. Steele and others, ed. G. Smith, 4 vols, repr. (1907, London; J. M. Dent, 1950), vol. 1, pp. 215–19, 228–32 and 264–6.
20. Friedman, *The Ballad Revival*, p. 172.
21. J. Pinkerton, 'A Dissertation on the Oral Tradition of Poetry', *Select Scottish Ballads*, 2 vols (London: J. Nichols, 1783), vol. 1, p. xvi.
22. A. Lord, *The Singer of Tales* (Cambridge, MA: Harvard University Press, 1960; New York: Atheneum, 1974), pp. 4 and 30.
23. Lord, *The Singer of Tales*, pp. 35 and 31.
24. B. Rosenberg, *Can These Bone Live? The Art of the American Folk Preacher*, rev. edn (1970; Urbana and Chicago, IL: University of Illinois Press, 1988), p. 4.
25. Lord, *The Singer of Tales*, p. 37.
26. Finnegan, *Oral Poetry: Its Nature, Significance and Social Context* (Cambridge: Cambridge University Press, 1977), p. 65.
27. Lord, *The Singer of Tales*, p. 6.
28. Lord, *The Singer of Tales*, pp. 137–8.
29. Lord, *The Singer of Tales*, p. 129.
30. See J. M. Foley, *Traditional Oral Epic: The 'Odyssey', 'Beowulf', and the Serbo-Croatian Return Song* (Berkeley and Los Angeles, CA: University of California Press, 1990).
31. E. A. Havelock, 'Orality and Literacy, an Overview', *Language and Communication*, 9:2–3 (1989), p. 97.
32. E. A. Havelock, *The Literate Revolution in Greece and its Cultural Consequences* (Princeton, NJ: Princeton University Press, 1982), p. 82.
33. R. Katz and E. Katz, 'McLuhan: Where Did He Come From, Where Did He Disappear?', *Canadian Journal of Communication*, 23:3 (1998), at http://www.cjc-online.ca/index.php/journal/article/view/1046 [accessed 15 July 2008].
34. Katz and Katz, 'McLuhan'.
35. W. J. Ong, *Orality and Literacy: The Technologizing of the Word* (New York, 1982; repr. London and New York: Routledge: 2000), pp. 8–9.
36. W. J. Ong, 'Writing Is a Humanizing Technology', *ADE Bulletin*, 74 (Spring, 1983), p.14.
37. E. Oring, 'On the Concepts of Folklore', in E. Oring (ed.), *Folk Groups and Folklore Genres: An Introduction* (Logan: Utah State University Press, 1986), p. 7.
38. Ní Mhunghaile, 'Intersection', p. 16. For the many elaborations of this theory, also known as 'stadial theory', see (among others) J. L. Meek, *Social Science and the Ignoble Savage* (Cambridge: Cambridge University Press, 1976) and J. G. A. Pocock, *Barbarism and Religion*, 5 vols (Cambridge: Cambridge University Press, 1999–2011), vol. 4, throughout.
39. Ong, *Orality and Literacy*, pp. 14–15.
40. J. Goody and I. Watt, 'The Consequences of Literacy', in J. Goody (ed.), *Literacy in Traditional Societies* (Cambridge: Cambridge University Press, 1968), p. 68.
41. B. Rosenberg, 'The Complexity of Oral Tradition', *Oral Tradition*, 2:1 (1987), p. 77.
42. R. Finnegan, 'What Is Oral Literature, Anyway? Comments in the Light of Some African and Other Comparative Material', in Foley (ed.), *Oral-Formulaic Theory: A Folklore Casebook* (New York: Garland, 1990), pp. 262–4.
43. R. Finnegan, 'What Is Oral Literature, Anyway?', p. 254.

44. W. Chafe and D. Tannen, 'The Relation between Written and Spoken Language', *Annual Review of Anthropology*, 16 (1987), p. 398.
45. Rosenberg, 'The Complexity of Oral Tradition', p. 80.
46. R. Finnegan, *Oral Poetry*, pp. 23 and 48.
47. D. R. Olson, 'Literacy as Metalinguistic Activity', in D. R. Olson and N. Torrance (eds), *Literacy and Orality* (Cambridge: Cambridge University Press, 1991), pp. 257–8.
48. W. A. Foley, 'Literacy', in *Anthropological Linguistics: An Introduction* (Malden, MA: Blackwell Publishers, 1997), p. 419. See also G. E. R. Lloyd, *Demystifying Mentalities* (Cambridge: Cambridge University Press, 1990).
49. See, for example, R. Narasimhan, 'Literacy: Its Characterization and Implications', in D. R. Olson and N. Torrance (eds), *Literacy and Orality* (Cambridge: Cambridge University Press, 1991), pp. 177–97.
50. W. Foley, 'Literacy', pp. 428–9.
51. D. P. Pattanayak, 'Literacy: An Instrument of Oppression', in D. R. Olson and N. Torrance (eds), *Literacy and Orality* (Cambridge: Cambridge University Press, 1991), p. 105.
52. See W. Foley, 'Literacy', pp. 429–31.
53. W. Foley, 'Literacy', p. 433.
54. For example, see F. G. Andersen and T. Pettitt, 'Mrs. Brown of Falkland: A Singer of Tales?', *Journal of American Folklore*, 92:363 (January–March, 1979), pp. 1–24.
55. Quoted in Finnegan, *Oral Poetry*, p. 72.
56. Finnegan, 'What Is Oral Literature, Anyway?', p. 255.
57. Finnegan, 'What Is Oral Literature, Anyway?' pp. 263–72.
58. Rosenberg, 'The Complexity of Oral Tradition', p. 81.
59. Narasimhan, 'Literacy', p. 178.
60. Finnegan, 'What Is Oral Literature, Anyway?', p. 254.
61. Rosenberg, 'The Complexity of Oral Tradition', p. 88.
62. N. Hudson, 'Challenging Eisenstein: Recent Studies in Print Culture', *Eighteenth-Century Life*, 26:2 (Spring 2002), p. 84.
63. Hudson, 'Challenging Eisenstein', p. 95.
64. D. Raven, 'How Not to Explain the Great Divide', *Social Science Information*, 40:3 (2001), pp. 377 and 382; and Lloyd, *Demystifying Mentalities*, p. 112.
65. See R. Chartier, *The Cultural Uses of Print in Early Modern France*, trans. L. D. Cochrane (Princeton, NJ: Princeton University Press, 1987).
66. A. Fox, *Oral and Literate Culture in England 1500–1700*, Oxford Studies in Social History (Oxford: Oxford University Press, 2000), p. 5.
67. B. Reay, *Popular Cultures in England 1550–1750*, Themes in British Social History (New York: Longman, 1988), p. 198.
68. D. Donoghue, 'Orality, Literacy, and Their Discontents', in *New Literary History*, 27:1 (1996), pp. 145–59.
69. See C. Lindahl, 'The Oral Undertones of Late Medieval Romance', in W. F. H. Nicolaisen (ed.), *Oral Tradition in the Middle Ages*, Medieval & Renaissance Texts & Studies, 112 (Binghamton, NY: Medieval & Renaissance Texts & Studies, 1995), pp. 59–75.
70. W. W. Newell, 'The Study of Folklore', *Transactions of the New York Academy of Sciences*, 9 (1890), pp. 134.
71. J. Brunvand, *The Study of American Folklore: An Introduction*, 2nd edn (New York: W. W. Norton, 1978), p. 7.

72. D. Ben-Amos, 'Toward a Definition of Folklore in Context', *Journal of American Folklore*, 84 (1971), pp. 13.
73. Finnegan, *Oral Poetry*, p. 134.
74. D. Buchan, 'Oral Tradition and Literary Tradition', in D. Dugaw (ed.), *The Anglo-American Ballad: A Folklore Casebook* (New York and London: Garland, 1995), p. 221.
75. E. J. Lawless, 'Oral "Character" and "Literary" Art: A Call for a New Reciprocity between Oral Literature and Folklore', *Western Folklore*, 44:2 (1985), pp. 81 and 87.
76. J. Q. Wolf, 'Folksingers and the Re-Creation of Folksong', *Western Folklore*, 26:2 (April 1967), at http://web.lyon.edu/wolfcollection/re-creation.htm [accessed 15 August 2011].
77. H. Shields, 'Impossibles in Ballad Style', in J. Porter (ed.), *The Ballad Image: Essays Presented to Bertrand Harris Bronson* (Los Angeles: Center for the Study of Comparative Folklore and Mythology, University of California, 1983), p. 192.

1 The Medieval Background

1. S. Ó Coileáin, 'Oral or Literary? Some Strands of the Argument', *Studia Hibernica*, 17–18 (1978), p. 7.
2. R. Ó hUiginn, 'The Background and Development of Táin Bó Cúailnge', in J. P. Mallory (ed.), *Aspects of the Táin* (Belfast: Universities Press, 1992), p. 33.
3. Kim McCone resurrects this charge in his own argument for the literary and monastic character of medieval Irish literature in *Pagan Past and Christian Present in Early Irish Literature*, Maynooth Monographs, 3 (Maynooth: An Sagart, 1990).
4. J. Carney, *Studies in Irish Literature and History* (Dublin: Dublin Institute for Advanced Studies, 1955), p. 79.
5. Carney, *Studies in Irish Literature*, p. 277.
6. J. F. Nagy, 'Orality in Medieval Irish Narrative', *Oral Tradition*, 1–2 (1986), p. 280.
7. K. H. Jackson, *The Oldest Irish Tradition: A Window on the Iron Age* (Cambridge: Cambridge University Press, 1964), p. 53.
8. G. Murphy, 'Saga and Myth in Early Ireland', in E. Knott and G. Murphy (eds), *Early Irish Literature* (London: Routledge and Kegan Paul, 1966), p. 97.
9. J. Carney, 'Introduction', in E. Knott and G. Murphy (eds), *Early Irish Literature*, (London: Routledge and Kegan Paul, 1966), p. 2.
10. Ó Coileáin, 'Oral or Literary?', pp. 19 and 23.
11. Nagy, 'Orality in Medieval Irish Narrative', pp. 282–3.
12. E. Slotkin, 'Medieval Irish Scribes and Fixed Texts', *Éigse*, 17:4 (Winter 1978–9), pp. 446–7.
13. G. D. Zimmermann, *The Irish Storyteller* (Dublin: Four Courts Press, 2001), p. 37.
14. Ó Coileáin, 'Oral or Literary?', p. 12.
15. Nagy, 'Orality in Medieval Irish Narrative', pp. 280 and 290. For evidence of or claims for exact retention in traditional communities, see also Ó Coileáin, 'Oral or Literary?', pp. 17–21; Finnegan, *Oral Poetry*, pp. 73–87; and A. Bruford, *Gaelic Folk-Tales and Medieval Romances: A Study of the Early Modern Irish Romantic Tales and their Oral Derivatives* (Dublin: The Folklore of Ireland Society, 1969), pp. 59–60.
16. See D. A. Binchy, 'The Background of Early Irish Literature', *Studia Hibernica*, 1 (1961), p. 12; and also Ó Coileáin, 'Oral or Literary?', pp. 18–19.

17. G. Mac Eoin, review of D. A. Binchey (ed.), *Scéla Cano Meic Gartnáin* (Dublin: Dublin Institute for Advanced Studies, 1963) and C. O'Rahilly (ed.), *Cath Finntrágha* (Dublin: Dublin Institute for Advanced Studies, 1962), in *Studia Hibernica*, 4 (1964), p. 245.
18. G. Mac Eoin, review of E. Knott and G. Murphy, *Early Irish Literature* (London, 1966), in *Studia Hibernica*, 7 (1967), p. 247.
19. Ó Coileáin, 'Oral or Literary?', p. 30.
20. Bruford, *Gaelic Folk-Tales*, pp. 45–6.
21. Nagy, 'Orality in Medieval Irish Literature', p. 288.
22. Slotkin, *Medieval Irish Scribes*, pp. 449–50.
23. Slotkin, *Medieval Irish Scribes*, pp. 441 and 450.
24. P. Mac Cana, '*Fianaigecht* in the Pre-Norman Period', in B. Almqvist, S. Ó Catháin and P. Ó Héalaí (eds.), *Fiannaíocht: Essays on the Fenian Tradition of Ireland and Scotland* (Dublin: Folklore of Ireland Society, 1987), p. 75.
25. Bruford, *Gaelic Folk-Tales*, p. 48.
26. A. Bruford, 'Oral and Literary Fenian Tales', in B. Almqvist, S. Ó Catháin and P. Ó Héalaí, *The Heroic Process: Form, Function, and Fantasy in Folk Epic: The Proceedings of the International Folk Epic Conference, University College Dublin, 2–6 September 1985* (Dunleary: Glendale Press, 1987), p. 26.
27. Quoted in Nagy, 'Orality in Medieval Irish Narrative', p. 276.
28. J. F. Nagy, *The Wisdom of the Outlaw: The Boyhood Deeds of Finn in Gaelic Narrative Tradition* (Berkeley, CA: University of California Press, 1985), p. 6.
29. Nagy, 'Orality in Medieval Irish Narrative', p. 273.
30. J. F. Nagy, 'Oral Tradition in the *Acallam na Senórach*, in W. F. H. Nicolaisen (ed.), *Oral Tradition in the Middle Ages*, Medieval and Renaissance Texts and Studies, 112 (Binghamton, NY: Center for Medieval and Renaissance Texts and Studies, 1995), p. 80.
31. Nagy, 'Oral Tradition in the *Acallam na Senórach*', p. 84.
32. Nagy, 'Oral Tradition in the *Acallam na Senórach*', pp. 85–6.
33. Nagy, 'Oral Tradition in the *Acallam na Senórach*', p. 94.
34. J. F. Nagy, *Conversing with Angels and Ancients: Literary Myths of Medieval Ireland* (Ithaca and London: Cornell University Press, 1997), p. 7.
35. K. Simms, 'Literacy and the Irish Bards', in H. Price (ed.), *Literacy in Medieval Celtic Societies* (Cambrige: Cambridge Univeristy Press, 1998), p. 253.
36. Bruford, *Gaelic Folk-Tales* 45–6 and 55. See also Nagy, *Conversing with Angels*, p. 20; and Lindahl, 'Oral Undertones', p. 75.
37. Bruford, *Gaelic Folk-Tales*, p. 46.
38. Bruford, *Gaelic Folk-Tales*, p. 55.
39. Nagy, 'Oral Tradition in the *Acallam na Senórach*', p. 85.
40. Bruford, *Gaelic Folk-Tales*, p. 45.
41. Bruford, *Gaelic Folk-Tales*, pp. 58–9.
42. Ní Mhunghaile, 'Intersection', p. 21.
43. Bruford, *Gaelic Folk-Tales*, p. 56, and Murphy, 'Saga and Myth', p. 192.
44. Bruford, *Gaelic Folk-Tales*, pp. 37 and 33.
45. A. Bruford, 'The Singing of Fenian and Similar Lays in Scotland', in H. Shields, *Ballad Research* (Dublin: Folk Music Society of Ireland, 1986), p. 55.
46. See T. McCaughey, 'Performance of *Dán*', *Ériú*, 35 (1984), pp. 39–57.
47. H. Shields, *Narrative Singing in Ireland: Lays, Ballads, Come-All-Yes and Other Songs* (Dublin: Irish Academic Press, 1993), p. 13.
48. Mac Cana, *Fianaigecht*, pp. 82 and 93–4.

49. Bruford, *Gaelic Folk-Tales*, p. 2.
50. Murphy, 'Saga and Myth', pp. 192 and 178.
51. Bruford, *Gaelic Folk-Tales*, p. 2.
52. Bruford, *Gaelic Folk-Tales*, pp. 59.
53. Nagy, 'Orality in Medieval Irish Narrative', p. 280.
54. Bruford, *Gaelic Folk-Tales*, pp. 248–9.
55. See D. Dumville, review of K. McCone, *Pagan Past and Christian Present in Early Irish Literature* (Maynooth, 1990), in *Peritia*, 10 (1996), pp. 389–98.
56. Bruford, 'Oral and Literary Fenian Tales', p. 56.

2 Songs of the Dispossessed: Eighteenth-Century Irish Song-Poetry

1. C. Ó Háinle, 'An Ceol san Fhilíocht Chlasaiceach', in P. Ó Fiannachta (ed.), *An Ceol i Litríocht na Gaeilge*, Léachtaí Cholm Cille, VII (Maynooth: An Sagart, 1976), p. 50.
2. Quoted in Knott, 'Irish Classical Poetry', in E. Knott and G. Murphy (eds), *Early Irish Literature* (London: Routledge and Kegan Paul, 1966), p. 64. Knott also quotes a translation of an Irish poem describing an audience listening 'to verses and poetic lays eloquently uttered by declaimers and royal bards' (p. 64).
3. Quoted in Ó Háinle, 'An Ceol', pp. 50–2 and 49–50.
4. Quoted in Ó Háinle, 'An Ceol', p. 50.
5. Simms, 'Literacy and the Irish Bards', pp. 238–41. The highest rank of poet was the *ollamh* or 'master-poet', whose honour price was equal to that of a petty king.
6. Bruford, *Gaelic Folk-Tales*, p. 55.
7. Nagy, 'Orality in Medieval Irish Narrative', pp. 274 and 290.
8. Niamh Whitfield cites Ann Buckley as noting that the term *cruit* originally indicated a kind of lyre that 'in Ireland ... was superseded some time during the later tenth or eleventh century by the trilateral harp, to which the name was transferred'. See N. Whitfield, 'Lyres Decorated with Snakes, Birds and Hounds in *Táin Bó Fraích*', in P. Harbison and V. Hall, *A Carnival of Learning: Essays to Honour George Cunningham* (Roscrea: Cistercian Press, 2012), p. 219. See also A. Buckley, 'Musical Instruments in Ireland from the 9th to the 14th centuries: A Review of the Organological Evidence', in G. Gillen and H. White (eds), *Irish Musical Studies*, 1, (Blackrock: Irish Academic Press 1990), pp. 13–57.
9. Ó Háinle, 'An Ceol', pp. 34 and 44.
10. G. Yeats, 'The Rediscovery of Carolan', in B. Harris and G. Freyer (eds), *Integrating Tradition: The Achievement of Seán Ó Riada* (Ballina/Chester Springs, PA: Irish Humanities Center; Dufour, 1981), pp. 90–1; and P. Ní Uallacháin, *A Hidden Ulster: People, Songs and Traditions of Oriel* (Dublin: Four Courts Press, 2003), pp. 343–6.
11. Simms, 'Literacy and the Irish Bards', p. 251.
12. Simms, 'Literacy and the Irish Bards', p. 249.
13. Quoted in P. A. Breatnach, 'The Aesthetics of Irish Bardic Composition: An Analysis of *Fuaras Iongnadh, a Fhir Chumainn* by Fearghal Óg Mac an Bhaird', *Cambrian Medieval Celtic Studies*, 42 (Winter, 2001), p. 52.
14. P. Breatnach, 'The Aesthetics of Irish Bardic Composition', p. 52.
15. Simms, 'Literacy and the Irish Bards', p. 250.
16. Quoted in Simms, 'Literacy and the Irish Bards', p. 249.
17. Simms, 'Literacy and the Irish Bards', p. 251.
18. Bruford, *Gaelic Folk-Tales*, p. 55.
19. P. Breatnach, 'The Aesthetics of Irish Bardic Composition', p. 52.

20. P. A. Breatnach, 'Form and Continuity in Later Irish Verse Tradition', *Ériu*, 44 (1993), p. 127.
21. Quoted in Ní Uallacháin, p. 344.
22. P. A. Breatnach, 'Oral and Written Transmission of Poetry', *Eighteenth-Century Ireland*, 2 (1987), pp. 61–2.
23. P. Breatnach, 'Oral and Written Transmission of Poetry', pp. 62–3.
24. The use of the term *amhrán* to denote accentual (as opposed to syllabic) metres is of long standing. Although some scholars tend to reserve the term primarily for four-six stress quatrain forms, these metres can include a wide range of verse-types. For a discussion of some of the confusion surrounding the term, see V. Blankenhorn, *Irish Song-Craft and Metrical Practice Since 1600* (Lewiston, NY and Lampeter: Edwin Mellen, 2003), pp. 28–9.
25. Blankenhorn, *Irish Song-Craft*, p. 360.
26. For example, Eoghan Rua Ó Súilleabháin's 'Cois na Siúire' is set to the tune of 'An Clár Bog Déil', while one is directed to sing his 'Cois Abhann i nDé' to 'An Síoda atá id Bhaillet?' See *Amhráin Eoghan Ruaidh Ó Súilleabháin*, ed. P. Ua Duinnín (Dublin, 1901), pp. 16 and 18.
27. *An Duanaire*, p. 127.
28. R. A. Breatnach, 'A Musical Link between *Dán* and *Amhrán*', *Ceol*, 4:2 (1981), pp. 106–9. For a clearer idea of how syllabic poetry might have been performed, see V. Blankenhorn, 'Observations on the Performance of Irish Syllabic Verse', *Studia Celtica*, 44 (2010), pp. 135–54; and W. Gillies, 'Music and Gaelic Strict-Metre Poetry', *Studia Celtica*, 44 (2010), pp. 111–34.
29. B. Ó Madagáin, 'Coibhneas na Filíochta leis an gCeol, 1700–1900', in P. Riggs, B. Ó Conchúir and S. Ó Coileáin (eds), *Saoi na hÉigse: Aistí in Ómós do Sheán Ó Tuama* (Dublin, 2000), p. 95.
30. G. Yeats, 'The Rediscovery of Carolan', p. 91; and G. Yeats, *The Harp of Ireland: The Belfast Harpers' Festival, 1792 and the Saving of Ireland's Harp Music by Edward Bunting* (Dalkey: Belfast Harpers' Bicentenary, 1992), p. 14.
31. *Amhráin Eoghain Ruaidh Ó Shúilleabháin*, p. 86.
32. D. Corkery, *The Hidden Ireland: A Study of Gaelic Munster in the Eighteenth Century* (1924; Dublin: Gill and Macmillan, 1996), p. 105.
33. P. A. Breatnach, 'Múnlaí Véarsaíocht Rithimiúil na Nua-Ghaeilge', in P. de Brún, S. Ó Coileáin and P. Ó Riain, *Folia Gadelica* (Cork: Cork University Press, 1983), p. 55; and G. Murphy, *Early Irish Metrics* (1961; repr., Dublin: Royal Irish Academy, 1973), pp. 23–5. For a discussion of the process of metrical 'flattening out' of syllabic *laoithe*, see T. McCaughey, 'Performance of *Dán*', pp. 39–57.
34. A. Bruford, 'Song and Recitation in Early Ireland', *Celtica*, 21 (1990), p. 68.
35. Carney believes classical Old Irish forms like *draignech* and *deibhidhe* to be derived from a previous accentual form and 'the popular songs and poems of the last four centuries' to be descended 'directly from the old and natural tradition', owing 'little if anything to the intervening artificiality'. See J. Carney, 'Three Old Irish Accentual Poems', *Ériu*, 22 (1971), p.53; G. Murphy, 'Notes on Aisling Poetry', *Éigse*, 1 (1939), pp. 47–9; and J. Travis, *Early Irish Versecraft: Origin, Development and Diffusion* (Ithaca: Cornell University Press, 1973), pp. 39–40. Murphy follows Thurneysen's lead in his leanings towards Latin origins (Murphy, *Early Irish Metrics*, p. 25), while Travis points to native origins, in the belief that 'Celtic verse forms derives from speech stress' (Travis, *Early Irish Versecraft*, p. 38).

36. Quoted in R. Breatnach, 'A Musical Link', p. 105.
37. D. Thomson, *An Introduction to Gaelic Poetry* (New York: St. Martin's Press, 1974), p. 129.
38. Ó Tuama, 'Introduction', *An Duanaire*, pp. xix.
39. *The Irish Liber Hymnorum I*, ed. J. H. Bernard and R. Atkinson, Henry Bradshaw Society Series, vol. 13–14 (London: Henry Bradshaw Society, 1898), vol. 13, p. 167.
40. P. Breatnach, 'Múnlaí Véarsaíocht Rithimiúil', pp. 60 and 69, note 26.
41. P. Breatnach, 'Múnlaí Véarsaíocht Rithimiúil', pp. 66–8. Osborn Bergin made a similar connection in a 1937 paper on 'The Origin of Modern Irish Rhythmical Verse' (quoted in Murphy, 'Notes on Aisling Poetry', p. 48), in which he compares lines from the eleventh-century macaronic hymn 'Deus meus, Adiuva Me', like *tuc dam do sheirc, a meic mo Dé* to post-seventeenth-century songs with lines that could be scanned identically. Good examples of the latter might be Aogán Ó Ráithaille's 'Aisling Ghéar do Dhearcas Féin', or even such a recent composition in English as 'A Stór mo Chroí, When You're Far Away'.
42. P. Breatnach, 'Múnlaí Vearsaíocht', pp. 67–8.
43. Thomson, *An Introduction to Gaelic Poetry*, p. 129.
44. Ó Tuama, 'Gaelic Culture in Crisis: The Literary Response 1600–1850', in T. Bartlett, C. Curtin and others (eds), *Irish Studies: A General Introduction* (Dublin: Gill and MacMillan, 1988), p. 36.
45. Brian Ó Cuív, commenting on Keating's 'Óm Sceól ar Árdmagh Fáil Ní Chollaim Uíche', says, 'Such a poem, though in accentual metre, is in its own way as literary a production as any *dán*. It is a by-product of the bardic schools and in a sense vindicates their existence for five centuries. Though they were to disappear within a half-century, their effect was to endure'. See B. Ó Cuív, 'An Era of Upheaval', *Seven Centuries of Irish Learning 1000–1700* (Cork: Mercier, 1971), p. 125.
46. P. Mac Cana, 'Irish Literary Tradition', in B. Ó Cuív (ed.), *A View of the Irish Language* (Dublin: Stationer's Office, 1969), p. 45.
47. P. Breatnach, 'Aesthetics', p. 61.
48. *The Book of Magauran: Leabhar Mhéig Shamhradháin*, ed. L. McKenna (Dublin, 1947), pp. 237 and 379.
49. Simms, 'Literacy and the Irish Bards', p. 252.
50. Ó Tuama, *An Grá*, p. 315. Dáithí Ó hOgáin notes a reference in a 'warrant' by poet Seán Ó Tuama to less cultivated poets who are 'iarmhar na n-athach tuaithe ... ag rith le rannaibh agus ag iomlat le hamhránaibh' ('the progeny of the rural churls ... bustling with quatrains and bandying with songs'). See Ó hÓgáin, 'Folklore and Literature: 1700–1850', in M. Daly and D. Dickson (eds), *The Origins of Popular Literacy in Ireland* (Dublin: Department of Modern History, Trinity College and Department of Modern Irish History, University College Dublin, 1990), pp. 1 and 10, note 5.
51. *An Duanaire*, pp. 116–17.
52. *An Duanaire*, pp. 114–15.
53. 'Ós Follas don Chléir' contains alternating stanzas of stressed and syllabic verse. See *Amhráin Eoghan Ruaidh Ó Súilleabháin*, p. 65.
54. Knott, 'Irish Classical Poetry', pp. 65–6.
55. Travis, *Early Irish Versecraft*, pp. 38–9.
56. L. Cullen, *The Hidden Ireland: Reassessment of a Concept* (1969, Cork; Mullingar: Lilliput Press, 1988), p. 47.
57. Simms, 'Literacy and the Irish Bards', p. 252.
58. D. Kiberd, *Irish Classics*, (Cambridge, MA: Harvard University Press, 2001), p. 38.

59. Simms, 'Literacy and the Irish Bards', pp. 251–2.
60. Louis Cullen points to the importance of scribal activity as a means of employment and the dominance of English rather than Irish in urban areas, where printing thrived: see L. Cullen, 'Patrons, Teachers and Literacy in Irish', in M. Daly and D. Dickson (eds), *The Origins of Popular Literacy in Ireland* (Dublin: Dept. of Modern History, Trinity College, 1990), pp. 38–40. Indeed, even in Dublin, poetry in Irish was circulated via manuscript (R. A. Breatnach, 'The End of a Tradition: A Survey of Eighteenth Century Gaelic Literature', *Studia Hibernica*, 1 (1961), pp. 138–40).
61. Kiberd, *Irish Classics*, p. 10.
62. Kibered, *Irish Classics*, p. 5.
63. Ó Cuív, 'An Era of Upheaval', pp. 121–2.
64. Kiberd, *Irish Classics*, p. 5–6.
65. Kiberd, *Irish Classics*, pp. 36–7.
66. Kiberd, *Irish Classics*, p, 14.
67. P. Breatnach, 'Oral and Written Transmission of Poetry', pp. 63–5. See also Cullen, 'Patrons', pp. 18–20. Kiberd points out that even the numerous religious writers of the time, wrote, like Flaithrí Ó Maolchonaire, 'chum leasa na ndaoine simplidhe' ('for the benefit of the simple people') – bearing in mind that these 'simple people' would have had either to be literate or to have heard the texts read (Kiberd, *Irish Classics*, p. 23).
68. P. Ó Ceallaigh, 'The Tunes of the Munster Poets (II)', *Ceol*, 1:2 (1963), p. 23.
69. Ó Cuív, 'An Era of Upheaval', p. 120.
70. Corkery, *The Hidden Ireland*, p. 145. See Cullen, *The Hidden Ireland*, in which he asserts that 'Not only is the case that the mass of Irishmen lived in abysmal poverty and oppression doubtful but the case that the poets themselves did so is unimpressive' (p. 19). Most recent social historians agree, however, that enormous poverty existed in Ireland – as in many other countries – during the late seventeenth and eighteenth centuries, although the black-and-white picture Corkery presents has been largely discredited. What is clear, however, is that while many poets undoubtedly lived in virtual poverty, even as late a poet as Eoghan Rua viewed himself as culturally distinct from the peasantry: in one poem he pronounces, 'Is gur scagadh mo thréad as caise d'fhuil Ghaedheal/I gCaiseal na réacsa cúigidh!' which Corkery renders as, 'I come of the stock of the Gaels of Cashel of the provincial kings!' (Corkery, *The Hidden Ireland*, p. 196). See also Ó Tuama, 'Gaelic Culture in Crisis', p. 37.
71. Cullen, 'Patrons', p. 20.
72. S. Connolly '"*Ag Déanamh* Commanding"': Élite Response to Popular Culture, 1660–1850', in J. S. Donnelly, Sr, and K. A. Miller (eds), *Irish Popular Culture* (Dublin: Irish Academic Press, 1998), p. 16.
73. S. Connolly, '"*Ag Déanamh* Commanding"', p. 11.
74. Connolly, '"*Ag Déanamh* Commanding"', pp. 14–15. See also H. Brennan, *The Story of Irish Dance* (1991; Lanham, MD: Roberts Rinehart, 2001), pp. 45–61.
75. Brennan, *The Story of Irish Dance*, pp. 23 and 51–2.
76. Connolly, '"*Ag Déanamh* Commanding"', p. 16.
77. Thomas Dineley, quoted in Brennan, *The Story of Irish Dance*, p. 18.
78. R. Breatnach, 'The End of a Tradition', pp. 133–40. Of course, in a number of cases, these categories overlapped. See also P. Ní Uallachain's discussion of the dissemination of manuscripts in southeastern Ulster in *A Hidden Ulster* (especially pages 21–2 and 435–67).
79. M. Ní Úrdail, *The Scribe in Eighteenth- and Nineteenth-Century Ireland: Motivations and Milieu* (Münster: Nodus, 2000), p. 235.

80. Quoted in P. Breatnach, 'Oral and Written Transmission of Poetry', p. 65.
81. P. Breatnach, 'Oral and Written Transmission of Poetry', pp. 58–9.
82. See P. Breatnach, 'Form and Continuity', pp. 125–38; and P. Ó Ceallaigh, 'The Tunes of the Munster Poets' (I), *Ceol* 1:1 (1963), pp. 11–13. Although we have no way of knowing exactly how many songs of literary poets entered the oral tradition, they include Tomás Ó Caiside's 'An Casaideach Bán', Peadar Ó Doirnín's 'Úr-Chnoc Chéin Mhic Cáinte', Aindrias Mag Craith's 'Slán le Máith', Eoghan Rua Ó Súilleabháin's 'Slán chun Carraig an Éide', Tomás Rua Ó Súilleabháin's 'Amhrán na Leabhar' and the mock-elegy 'Eoghan Cóir' by Riocard Bairéad.
83. Ní Úrdail, *The Scribe*, pp. 174–5.
84. Ó Madagáin, 'Coibhneas na Filiochta leis an gCeol', p. 83.
85. P. Breatnach, 'Oral and Written Transmission of Poetry', p. 59. My translation.
86. Ó Madagáin, 'Coibhneas na Filiochta leis an gCeol', p. 84.
87. Blankenhorn, *Irish Song-Craft*, p. 346.
88. Cullen, *The Hidden Ireland*, p. 17.
89. Ó Tuama, 'Gaelic Culture in Crisis', p. 39.
90. Corkery, *The Hidden Ireland*, p. 135.
91. Quoted in B. Ó Madagáin, 'Functions of Irish Music', *Béaloideas*, 53 (1985), p. 188.
92. Murphy, 'Notes on Aisling Poetry', p. 40.
93. B. Ó Buachalla, An Aisling do Rinneas ar Mhóirín', in *Aisling Ghéar: Na Stíobhartaigh agus an tAos Léinn 1603–1788* (Dublin: An Clóchomhar, 1996), pp. 528–95.
94. Murphy, 'Notes on Aisling Poetry', p. 45.
95. D. K. Wilgus, 'Irish Traditional Narrative Songs in English: 1800–1916', in D. J. Casey and R. E. Rhodes (eds), *Views of the Irish Peasantry* (Hamden, CT: Archon Books, 1977), p. 118.
96. Ó Tuama, *An Grá*, p. 184.
97. D. O'Sullivan (ed. and trans.), *Songs of the Irish: An Anthology of Irish Folk Music and Poetry with English Verse Translations* (New York, 1960; Dublin and Cork: Mercier Press, 1981), pp. 135–8.
98. Murphy, 'Notes on Aisling Poetry', pp. 48–50.
99. S. Ó Tuama, *An Grá in Amhráin na nDaoine* (Dublin: An Clóchomhar, 1960), pp. 184–202.
100. Ó Tuama points to several Irish love songs written in the beginning of the seventeenth century, particularly a love *aisling* in which the poet does not interrogate the *spéirbhean* but speculates about her identity as 'Iuno thréin, Bhenus no Minerbha' ('Powerful Juno, Venus or Minerva'). He notes that about a century later Eoghan an Mhéirín and Seán Clárach Mac Domhnaill employed classical references freely, being themselves 'great people for Latin', and asserts that this 'learned manner' was what gave rise to the pattern Eoghan Rua and othere were to follow (Ó Tuama, *An Grá*, pp. 189–90). Ó Tuama leaves unexplained how and why this trait appears in Irish song at this juncture, omitting any discussion of, for example, possible contemporary European influences from academic or literary spheres.
101. Ó Buachalla, *Aisling Ghéar*, p. 541. Ó Buachalla also points to the use of the outdoor encounter with a woman and questioning of her identity in Irish Fenian romance (*Aisling Ghéar*, pp. 538–9).
102. Writes Shields, 'In the case of songs in literary style, it is as if their style was made more acceptable to orally conditioned singers by their patriotic tone' (*Narrative Singing*, p. 107).

103. Cullen, *The Hidden Ireland*, p. 16.
104. Cullen, *The Hidden Ireland*, p. 11.
105. As is Máire Bhuí Ní Laoghaire's later 'Seó Leó, a Thoil'. See B. Brennan, *Máire Bhuí Ní Laoire: A Poet of Her People* (Cork: Collins Press, 2000), p. 72.
106. Ó Buachalla, *Aisling Ghéar*, Chapter 12.
107. Ó Madagáin, 'Coibhneas na Filiochta leis an gCeol', p. 89, and 'Functions of Irish Music', p. 188.
108. C. Moloney (ed.), *The Irish Music Manuscripts of Edward Bunting (1773–1843): An Introduction and Catalogue* (Dublin: Irish Traditional Music Archive, 2000), p. 148.
109. Mac Cana, 'Irish Literary Tradition', p. 45.
110. Shields, *Narrative Singing*, p. 24.
111. Mac Cana, 'Irish Literary Tradition', p. 45.
112. Cullen, *The Hidden Ireland*, p. 17.
113. *Cathal Buí: Amhráin*, ed. B. Ó Buachalla (Dublin: An Clóchomhar, 1975), p. 75. My translation, after Thomas Kinsella.
114. O'Sullivan, *Songs of the Irish*, p. 118. My translation.
115. P. Breatnach, 'A Musical Link', p. 103.
116. Ní Uallachain, *A Hidden Ulster*, pp. 280–4.
117. Ó hÓgáin, 'Folklore and Literature', pp. 2–3.
118. Ní Uallacháin, *A Hidden Ulster*, pp. 337 and 348–50.
119. J. Doan, 'The Folksong Tradition of Cearbhall Ó Dálaigh', *Folklore*, 96:1 (1985), pp. 67–86.
120. There has also been debate as to whether they entered the Irish bardic tradition via French or English models. See M. Mac Craith, *Lorg na hIasachta ar na Dánta Grá* (Dublin: An Clóchomhar, 1989), pp. 26–41.
121. Ó Tuama, *An Grá*, p. 184.
122. S. Ó Tuama, 'Love in Irish Folksong', in *Repossessions* (Cork: Cork University Press, 1995), pp. 142–3.
123. See P. Zumthor, *Histoire Littéraire de la France Médiévale* (1954; Génève: Slatkine Reprints, 1973); and R. Boase, *The Origin and Meaning of Courtly Love: A Critical Study of European Scholarship* (Manchester: University of Manchester Press, 1977).
124. Quoted in Doan, 'The Folksong Tradition of Cearbhall Ó Dálaigh', pp. 73–4. My translation.
125. Quoted in Doan, 'The Folksong Tradition of Cearbhall Ó Dálaigh', p. 72. My translation.
126. *Folksongs of Britain and Ireland*, ed. P. Kennedy (London Cassell, 1975; London and New York: Oak, 1984), p.111. My translation. I have used poetic licence in translating 'iasc na Finne'. The Finn is a river that flows through Counties Donegal and Tyrone and is known for its salmon fishing.
127. A. Carpenter (ed.), *Verse in English from Eighteenth-Century Ireland* (Cork: Cork University Press), p. 327. My translation.
128. *Peadar Ó Dornín: Amhráin*, ed. B. Ó Buachalla (Dublin: An Clóchomhar, 1970), p. 61.
129. Ó Tuama, 'Love in Irish Folksong', pp. 157–8. Elsewhere Ó Tuama writes: 'nach amhráin tuaithe sa chiall choitianta iad in aon chor, ach amhráin saothraithe ealaíonta idir cheol agus fhocail' ['they are not rural folksongs in the received sense at all, but rather songs artistically crafted in both music and words'], Ó Tuama, *An Grá*, p. 264.
130. S. Ó Súilleabháin, 'Irish Oral Tradition', in B. Ó Cuív, *A View of the Irish Language* (Dublin: The Stationery Office, Rialtas na hÉireann, 1969), p. 49.
131. Ó Súilleabháin, 'Irish Oral Tradition', 47.
132. Flower, p. *The Irish Tradition* (Oxford, 1947; Dublin, The Lilliput Press, 1994), p. 142.

133. Corkery, *The Hidden Ireland*, p. 147.
134. Mac Cana, 'Irish Literary Tradition', p. 41.
135. Kiberd, *Irish Classics*, p. 319.
136. Ó Súilleabháin, 'Irish Oral Tradition', pp. 47–9.
137. Ó Tuama, *An Grá*, p. 281.
138. Ó Tuama, *An Grá*, p. 278.
139. O'Sullivan, *Songs of the Irish*, p. 49. My translation.
140. *Folksongs of Britain and Ireland*, p. 112. My translation. For another version, see L. Ó Muirí, *Amhráin Chúige Uladh* (1927, Dundalk; Dublin: Gilbert Dalton, 1977), p. 85.
141. Corkery, *The Hidden Ireland*, p. 147.
142. *The English and Scottish Popular Ballads*, F. J. Child (ed.), 5 vols (1882, Boston; New York: Dover, 1965), vol. 1, pp. 159–61.
143. J. Heaney, *Joe Heaney: The Road from Connemara* (Inverin: Cló Iar-Chonnachta Teo, 2000) [2-vol. CD set and booklet], notes, p. 30; and *Ceolta Gael 2*, ed. M. Ó Baoill (Cork and Dublin: Mercier Press, 1986), pp. 29–30.
144. J. Henigan, '*Sean-Nós* in America: A Study of Two Singers' (MA thesis, University of North Carolina at Chapel Hill, 1989), p. 19.
145. Shields, *Narrative Singing*, p. 74.
146. *Údar*: 'author', 'originator', 'source', 'origin'. See N. Ó Dónaill, ed., *Foclóir Gaeilge-Béarla* (Dublin: Oifig an tSoláthair, Rialtas na hÉireann, 1977, p. 1296.
147. Henigan, '*Sean-Nós* in America', p. 26.
148. Pádraig Ó Crualaoi related 160 pages' worth of 'Seanachas Filíochta' to the Irish Folklore Commission, which included 'an account of most of the important poetic families and poets from the area going back to the close of the seventeenth century' (P. Breatnach, 'Oral and Written Transmission of Poetry', p. 57).
149. Henigan, '*Sean-Nós* in America', pp. 18–19.
150. S. Bán Mac Grianna, *Ceoltaí agus Seanchas*, ed. I. Ó Searcaigh (Ranafast: Coiste Choláiste Bhríde, 1976), pp. 18–19.
151. Quoted in Ní Úallachain, *A Hidden Ulster*, pp. 348–9.
152. Shields, 'A History of "The Lass of Aughrim"', in G. Gillen and H. White (eds), *Musicology in Ireland*, Irish Musical Studies, 1 (Dublin: Irish Academic Press, 1990), p. 70; and T. Coffin, 'Mary Hamilton and The Anglo-American Ballad as an Art Form', in M. Leach and T. P. Coffin (eds), *The Critics and the Ballad* (1961; Carbondale, IL; London and Amsterdam: Feffer and Simons, 1973), pp. 245–56.
153. The *údaraí* – or background narratives to songs – can vary as much as the songs themselves.
154. Quoted in Blankenhorn, *Irish Song-Craft*, p. 362.
155. Blankenhorn, *Irish Song-Craft*, p. 362.
156. P. Breatnach, 'Oral and Written Transmission of Poetry', p. 65. Breatnach bases this assertion on the comparison of items in Ó Crualaoi's repertoire to early manuscript versions of the same songs.
157. Mac Grianna, *Ceoltaí agus Seanchas*, p. 24; and Shields, *Narrative Singing*, p. 148.
158. É. Ó Muirgheasa, *Céad de Cheoltaibh Uladh* (1915, Dublin; Newry: Comhaltas Uladh, 1983), p. iii.
159. Shields, *Narrative Singing*, p. 27.
160. Ó Muirí, *Amhráin Chúige Uladh*, p. 120.
161. The seven-verse variant was collected from Neilidh Ní Annluain, County Armagh; see Ó Muirí, *Amhráin Chúige Uladh*, pp. 144–5. Róise Bean Mhic Grianna's verses were

collected by Pádraig Ua Cnáimsí; see *Róise na nAmhrán: Songs of a Donegal Woman* (Dublin: RTÉ 178, 1994) [CD and notes], notes, p. 43.
162. *Cathal Buí*, pp. 138–45.
163. Ó Muirgheasa, *Céad de Cheoltaibh Uladh*, p. 251. The sixth line is the only one with a corresponding line in the other manuscript. My translation.
164. Ó Muirgheasa, *Céad de Cheoltaibh Uladh*, p. 251. My translation.
165. Ó Muirí, *Amhráin Chúige Uladh*, p. 145. My translation.
166. T. Ó Concheanainn, 'Moll Dubh an Ghleanna', *Éigse*, 11:4 (Autumn 1966), p. 276; taken from Royal Irish Academy manuscript 23 A 1, transcribed by Daniel Malone in 1830. Malone wrote down the song in two other manuscripts, as well, in 1827–8. The earliest manuscript source we have for the song is in Edward Bunting's manuscripts (1802).
167. Ó Concheanainn, 'Moll Dubh an Ghleanna', p. 284.
168. RIA 3 B 38, MS Dublin, Royal Irish Academy (hereafter RIA), p. 101. My translation.
169. See Ó Muirí, *Amhráin Chúige Uladh*, pp. 68–70.
170. Ó Muirí, *Amhráin Chúige Uladh*, p. 137. My translation.
171. Contrasts of length and style exist even between these two variants, although they were collected in the same townland during roughly the same period.
172. *Amhráin Mhuighe Seóla*, ed. E. Bean Mhic Choisdealbha (1923; Bealadangan: Cló Iar-Chonnachta, 1990), p. 141–2.
173. *Abhráin Grádh Chúige Connacht: Being the Fourth Chapter of the Love Songs of Connacht*, ed. D. Hyde (London, 1893, 3rd edn; repr., Dublin; New York: Barnes and Noble, 1969), pp. 112–13, 115–17 and 109–11.
174. J. Ritson, *Scottish Songs*, 2 vols (London, 1794), vol 1, p. lxxxi.
175. Quoted in Ní Mhunghaile, 'Intersection', p. 17.
176. Coffin, 'Mary Hamilton', pp. 250.
177. Bruford, *Gaelic Folk-Tales*, p. 249.
178. J. Ross, 'The Sub-Literary Tradition in Scottish-Gaelic Song Poetry', part 2, *Éigse*, 8:1 (1955), pp. 6–7.
179. E. D. Ives, '"How Got the Apples In?" Individual Creativity and Ballad Tradition', *Journal of the Folklore and History Section of the American Folklore Society*, 14 (1997), p. 50.
180. E. Long, 'Ballad Singers, Ballad Makers and Ballad Etiology', in D. Dugaw (ed.), *The Anglo-American Ballad, A Folklore Casebook* (New York: Garland, 1995), p. 237.
181. Long, 'Ballad Singers', pp. 240–3.
182. H. Shields, '"The Proper Words": A Discussion on Folk Song and Literary Poetry', *Irish University Review*, 5 (1975), pp. 274–91; and Mac Grianna, *Ceoltaí agus Seanchas*, pp. 35–7.
183. P. M. Byrne, personal interview, Ardara, 20 August 2004. Paddy Tunney is known to have contributed new verses to songs like 'The Green Fields of Canada', 'The Song of Temptation' and 'Out of the Window'. See Shields, '"The Proper Words"', p. 288; and T. Munnelly, review of P. Tunney, *The Stone Fiddle* (Dublin: Gilbert Dalton, 1979), in *Ceol*, 5:1 (1981), pp. 27–8.
184. J. Q. Wolf, 'Folksingers and the Re-Creation of Folksong'.
185. Flower, *The Irish Tradition*, p. 159.
186. C. Lindahl, 'The Oral Aesthetic and the Bicameral Mind', *Oral Tradition*, 6:1 (1991), pp. 131–2.
187. Shields, *Narrative Singing*, pp. 77–8.
188. See Mac Grianna, *Ceoltaí agus Seanchas*, pp. 18–25.

189. S. O'Boyle, *The Irish Song Tradition*, *The Irish Song Tradition* (Dublin: Gilbert Dalton, 1976), p. 10.
190. Ó Súilleabháin, 'Irish Oral Tradition', 45.
191. From 'Gleann Domhain', by Peadar Breathnach, who lived in Glefinn, Donegal, and who died in 1870 (Ó Muirgheasa, *Dhá Chéad de Cheoltaibh Uladh* repr., 3rd edn (1934; Dublin: Office of Government Publications, 1974), p. 315). My translation.
192. Mac Grianna, *Ceoltaí agus Seanchas*, p. 46. My translation. Note the use of the phrase 'ceann dubh dilis', from the opening line of a well-known song dating from perhaps as early as 1724 (this, judging by the inclusion of its air in John and William Neal's *Collection of Celebrated Irish Airs*, published in this year).
193. *Croch Suas É*, ed. M. Ó Conghaile (Bealdangan: Cló Iar-Chonnachta, 1986), p. 50. From 'Cailín Álainn', undoubtedly the best-known song composed by Tomás Mac Eoin (b. 1937) of Carraroe, County Galway. My translation.
194. Ó Tuama, 'Love in Irish Folksong', p. 154.
195. Lord, *The Singer of Tales*, p. 130.
196. Shields, *Narrative* Singing, p. 77.
197. Buchan also suggests that it was impossible, after 1810 (after 'general literacy destroyed the oral mode') for persons like Mrs Brown of Falkland, who seemed to have a foot in both the literate and oral worlds, to have composed oral ballads (D. Buchan, *The Ballad and the Folk* (London and Boston, MA: Routledge and Kegan Paul), p. 75).
198. T. Crawford, 'Lowland Song and Popular Tradition in the Eighteenth Century', in A. Hood (ed.), *The History of Scottish Literature, II: 1660–1800* (Aberdeen: Aberdeen University Press (1987), pp. 123–39.

3 'Éirigh i do Sheasamh': Oral and Literary Aspects of the Irish Lament Tradition

1. K. Simms, 'The Poet as Chieftain's Widow: Bardic Elegies', in D. Ó Corráin, L. Breatnach and K. McCone (eds), *Sages, Saints and Storytellers: Celtic Studies in Honour of Professor James Carney*, Maynooth Monographs, 2 (Maynooth: An Sagart, 1989), pp. 400–1.
2. Simms, 'The Poet as Chieftain's Widow', p. 401.
3. This term (which has also often been applied to both keening and the performance of Fenian lays) is, in some ways, unsatisfactory because of its association with opera and oratorio, whence it derives. However, it is the only word that conveys the concept of verse 'sung in the rhythm of ordinary speech with many words on the same note', and therefore has utility in the present context. See *The New Oxford American Dictionary*, ed. E. J. Jewell and F. Abate (Oxford: Oxford University Press, 2001), p. 1422.
4. P. A. Breatnach, 'Marbhna Aodha Ruaidh Uí Dhomhnaill', *Éigse*, 15:1 (Summer 1973), pp. 31–50.
5. *Irish Bardic Poetry: Texts and Translations*, ed. O. Bergin, D. Greene and F. Kelly (Dublin: Dublin Insitute for Advanced Studies, 1970), p. 101.
6. *Dánta Aoghagáin Uí Rathaille: The Poems of Egan O'Rahilly*, ed. and trans. P. S. Dinneen, The Irish Texts Society, 3 (London: D. Nutt, 1900), pp. 116–25.
7. B. Ó Buachalla, *An Caoine agus an Chaointeoireacht* (Dublin, Ireland: Cois Life, 1998), p. 65. See also Blankenhorn, *Irish Song-Craft*, pp. 9–10 and 246–7.
8. P. Breatnach 'A Musical Link', p. 107; and O'Sullivan, *Songs of the Irish*, p. 80.
9. O'Sullivan, *Songs of the Irish*, p. 79.
10. P. Breatnach, 'A Musical Link', p. 108. See also *Diarmuid na Bolgaighe agus a Chómhursain*, ed. S. Ó Súilleabháin (Dublin: Oifig Díolta Foillseacháin Rialtais, 1937), p. 73.

11. B. Ó Madagáin, 'Irish Vocal Music', in R. O'Driscoll (ed.), *The Celtic Consciousness*, (Portlaoise, 1981; New York: Braziller, 1982), pp. 321–2.
12. P. Breatnach, 'A Musical Link', p. 108. It is interesting in this context that while the majority of Seán Clarach's elegy for Séamus Ó Domhnaill is set to an *amhrán* air, the concluding *feartlaoi* (epitaph) could not have been sung to the same air. The use of the freer kind of melody employed for lays and keens for this portion of the elegy would obviate the difficulties otherwise raised by this distinction.
13. Ó Madagáin, 'Irish Vocal Music', p. 311.
14. Ní Uallacháin, *A Hidden Ulster*, p. 142. See also T. Ó hAilín, 'Caointe agus Caointeoirí', i, *Feasta* 23:10 (Eanáir 1971), p. 9.
15. Quoted in Ní Uallacháin, *A Hidden Ulster*, pp. 142–3.
16. P. Lysaght, '*Caoineadh os Cionn Coirp*: The Lament for the Dead in Ireland', *Folklore*, 108 (1997), p. 75.
17. G. Ó Crualaoich, 'The "Merry Wake"', in J. S. Donnelly and K. A. Miller (eds), *Irish Popular Culture* (Dublin: Irish Academic Press, 1998), pp. 182–3. The report from County Galway gives a similar picture, adding, 'There is twice as much keening when it is a young woman or a young man who has died and in such cases especially (though it is the common practice anyway), the keen is kept up on the day of the funeral all the way to the graveyard' ('The "Merry Wake"', p. 183).
18. Mr and Mrs Samuel Hall observe as much in their description of the wake of a member of the McCarthy family. After stating that a professional keening woman was usually hired for such occasions, they note, 'It often happens, however, that the family has some friend or relation, rich in the gift of poetry; and who will for love of her kind give the unbought eulogy to the memory of the deceased' (S. C. Hall, *Ireland: Its Scenery and Character*, 3 vols (London, 1841–3), vol. 1, p. 225).
19. Mrs J. M. O'Connell, *The Last Colonel of the Irish Brigade: Count O'Connell and Old Irish Life at Home and Abroad 1745–1833*, 2 vols (London: Kegan Paul, Trench, Trübner & Co., 1892), vol. 1, p. 24.
20. P. Kennedy, *Evenings in the Duffrey* (Dublin: M'Glashan and Gill, 1869), p. 129.
21. Ní Uallacháin, *A Hidden Ulster*, p. 143.
22. C. Croker (ed.), *The Keen of the South of Ireland*, Early English Poetry, Ballads and Popular Literature of the Middle Ages, vol. 30 (London, 1844; repr. New York: Johnson Reprint, 1965), pp. 90–1.
23. J. O'Donovan, *The Journal of the Kilkenny and South-East of Ireland Archeological Society*, New Series, 2 (Dublin: The University Press, McGlashan and Gill, 1859; Dublin: Royal Society of Antiquaries of Ireland, 1997), p. 27, note *k*.
24. Lysaght '*Caoineadh os Cionn Coirp*', p.78; Ó hAilín, 'Caointe agus Caointeoirí', ii, *Feasta*, 23:11 (Feabhra 1971), p. 8; and *World Library of Folk and Primitive Music, v. 2: Ireland*, track 28 (Rounder 1742, 1998) [CD and notes].
25. Ó hAilín, 'Caointe agus Caointeoirí', i, p. 10; and Ó hAilín, 'Caointe agus Caointeoirí', ii, p. 5.
26. Ó hAilín 'Caointe agus Caointeoirí', i, p. 10; and A. Partridge, '"Is Beo Duine Tar Éis a Bhuailte": Caoineadh Magaidh as Béara', *Sinsear*, 3 (1981), p. 70.
27. Lysaght, '*Caoineadh os Cionn Coirp*', p.78. There is an interesting similarity in the repetitious references to 'hill' and 'valley' in one of the translations of keening texts offered by the Halls in their description of the lament tradition: 'Swift and sure was his foot ... on hill and valley ... his people were man, both on hill and valley' (Hall, *Ireland*, vol. 1, p. 227).

28. K. Whelan 'The Cultural Effects of the Famine', in J. Cleary and C. Connolly (eds), *The Cambridge Companion to Modern Irish Culture* (Cambridge: Cambridge University Press, 2005), p. 141.
29. Ó hAilín, ii, p. 7. My translation.
30. See A. Bourke, 'More in Anger Than in Sorrow: Irish Women's Lament Poetry', in J. N. Radner, *Feminist Messages: Coding in Women's Folk Culture* (Urbana and Chicago, IL: University Press of Illinois, 1993), pp. 160–81.
31. Ó hAilín, 'Caointe agus Caointeoirí', i, p. 8. My translation.
32. Ó hAilín, 'Caointe agus Caointeoirí', ii, p. 7. My translation.
33. S. Ó Coileáin, 'The Irish Lament: An Oral Genre', *Studia Hibernica*, 24 (1988), p. 103.
34. For example, see Ní Uallacháin, *A Hidden Ulster*, p. 145.
35. For a detailed description of this kind of lament, see Eugene O'Curry, *On the Manners and Customs of the Ancient Irish*, 3 vols (Dublin: Kelly, 1873), vol. 1, p. cccxxiv.
36. Quoted in Ó Buachalla, *An Caoine*, p. 72. My translation.
37. S. Ó Súilleabháin, 'The Keening of the Dead', in *Irish Wake Amusements*, 4th repr. (1961; Dublin: Mercier Press, 1979), p. 132.
38. Bourke, 'More in Anger', p. 166.
39. A. Partridge, 'Wild Men and Wailing Women', *Éigse*, 18:1 (1980), p. 36.
40. Ó Coileáin, 'The Irish Lament', p. 102; Blankenhorn, *Irish Song-Craft*, p. 8.
41. A. Bourke, 'Performing, Not Writing: The Reception of an Irish Woman's Lament', in Y. Prins and M. Schreiber (eds), *Dwelling in Possibility: Women Poets and Critics on Poetry* (Ithaca, NY: Cornell University Press, 1997), p. 135.
42. Blankenhorn, *Irish Song-Craft*, pp. 90–1.
43. Blankenhorn, *Irish Song-Craft*, p. 91.
44. Ó Buachalla, *An Caoine*, pp. 54–60.
45. Ó hAilín, 'Caointe agus Caointeoirí', i, p. 8.
46. Ní Uallacháin, *A Hidden Ulster*, pp. 143–4.
47. Ní Uallacháin, *A Hidden Ulster*, p. 144.
48. Ó Madagáin, 'Irish Vocal Music', p. 314.
49. Ó Madagáin, 'Irish Vocal Music', p. 317.
50. B. Bronson, *The Ballad as Song* (Berkeley and Los Angeles: University of California Press, 1969), pp. 142 and 111.
51. Moloney, *The Irish Music Manuscripts of Edward Bunting*, p. 132.
52. Quoted in Ó Madagáin 'Irish Vocal Music', pp. 317–18.
53. Ó Madagáin 'Irish Vocal Music', pp. 317–19.
54. See *Songs of Aran*, coll. Sydney Robertson Cowell (Folkways Records, FW 04002,1957) [CD and notes].
55. Quoted in Ó Madagáin 'Irish Vocal Music', p. 312.
56. Ó hAilín 'Caointe agus Caointeoirí', i, p. 8. There is ambiguity in this account, however.
57. Moloney, *The Irish Music Manuscripts of Edward Bunting*, p. 141.
58. Ó Madagáin, 'Coibhneas na Filiochta leis an gCeol', p. 95.
59. Quoted in Moloney, *The Irish Music Manuscripts of Edward Bunting*, p. 141.
60. Ó hAilín, 'Caointe agus Caointeoirí', i, p. 7.
61. See B. Rosenberg, *Can These Bones Live?*.
62. Lysaght, '*Caoineadh os Cionn Coirp*', p. 70.
63. Kennedy, *Evenings in the Duffrey*, p. 129. For a similar description, see Ó hAilín, 'Caointe agus Caointeoirí', i, p.8.
64. Ní Uallacháin, *A Hidden Ulster*, pp. 142 and 46.

65. Quoted in Ó Madagáin, 'Song for Emotional Release in the Gaelic Tradition', in P. E. Devine and H. White (eds), *Irish Musical Studies*, 4 (Dublin: Four Courts Press, 1996), pp. 264–5.
66. Quoted in Moloney, *The Irish Music Manuscripts of Edward Bunting*, p. 132.
67. See Ó hAilín, 'Caointe agus Caointeoirí', i, p. 8; Ní Uallacháin, *A Hidden Ulster*, p. 141; and Mac Grianna, *Ceoltaí agus Seanchas*, p. 16.
68. Ó hAilín, 'Caointe agus Caointeoirí', i, p. 8.
69. Ó Madagáin, 'Irish Vocal Music', pp. 325–6.
70. This concept is supported by Labhrás Ó Cadhla's use of a single basic melody for the keens he performed, including *Caoineadh Airt Uí Laoghaire*. The melody provided by the Halls in their description of the keening tradition of County Kerry, 'to which [the keen] is usually chanted', is remarkably similar to Ó Cadhla's. See Hall, *Ireland*, vol. 1, p. 225, and L. Ó Cadhla, *Amhráin ó Shliabh gCua* (Dublin: RTÉ, 2000) [CD and notes], tracks 2, 12, 18 and 32.
71. Ó Madagáin, 'Irish Vocal Music', pp. 325–6.
72. Quoted in Ó Madagáin, 'Irish Vocal Music', p. 326.
73. Yeats, 'The Rediscovery of Carolan', p. 91; and *The Harp of Ireland*, p. 14.
74. Ní Uallacháin, *A Hidden Ulster*, p. 144.
75. Ní Uallacháin, *A Hidden Ulster*, 141–2.
76. R. Bromwich, 'The Keen for Art O'Leary', *Béaloideas*, 5:4 (Winter 1947), p. 242.
77. *Poems on the O'Reillys*, ed. James Carney (Dublin: The Dublin Institute for Advanced Studies, 1950), pp. 139–46.
78. J. Carney, 'Three Old Irish Accentual Poems', p. 54.
79. Ó Muirgheasa, *Céad de Cheoltaibh Uladh*, p. 191.
80. Ó Muirgheasa, *Dhá Chéad de Cheolta Uladh*, pp. 218–20.
81. Hall, *Ireland*, vol. 1, p. 229. Perhaps this was not exclusively – or always – the case; that is, if the translation of the lament Kennedy's godmother ascribes to the bereaved mother of her story is in any way an accurate reflection of the original. It is entirely possible that the lament was composed after the fact and attached to the story; yet the association of such elegiac verse with the act of keening lends credence to the Halls' observations. See Kennedy, *Evenings in the Duffrey*, pp. 129–30.
82. Simms, 'The Poet as Chieftain's Widow', p. 405.
83. *Irish Bardic Poetry*, pp. 208 and 310.
84. *Irish Bardic Poetry*, pp. 202.
85. Simms, 'The Poet as Chieftain's Widow', p. 406.
86. E. J. Gwynn, 'An Irish Penitential', *Eiriú*, 7 (1914), pp. 170–1.
87. Lysaght, 'Caoineadh os Cionn Coirp', p. 66. For recent popular associations of the practice of keening with the Virgin's lament, see Partridge, 'Caoineadh na dTrí Muire agus an Chaointeoireacht', in B. Ó Madagáin (ed.), *Gnéithe den Chaointeoireacht* (Dublin: An Clóchomhar, 1978), pp. 67–81.
88. Simms, 'The Poet as Chieftain's Widow', pp. 401–2.
89. *The Book of Magauran*, pp. 34–6 and 303.
90. *The Book of O'Hara: Leabhar Í Eadhra*, ed. L. McKenna (1951; Dublin: Institute for Advanced Studies, 1980), pp. 290–1.
91. Examples include Máire Nic a Liondain (fl. 1771), of County Louth; Máire Ní Reachtagáin, (d. 1733), of Dublin City; Caitlín Dubh, of County Clare, and Máire Ní Dhonnagáin, of County Waterford. See *The Field Day Anthology of Irish Writing. Irish Women's Writing and Traditions*, ed. A. Bourke and others, 5 vols (Cork: Cork Univer-

sity Press, in association with Field Day; New York: New York University Press, 2002), vol. 5. Well-known Scottish women elegists of the period include Sìleas na Ceapaich, Màire Nighean Alasdair Ruaidh and Mairearad Nighean Lachlainn.
92. Ní Uallacháin, *A Hidden Ulster*, pp. 147–8.
93. Ó hAilín, 'Caointe agus Caointeoirí', i, p. 9.
94. J. O'Daly, *The Poets and Poetry of Munster* (Dublin: John O'Daly, 1860), pp. 211–12.
95. Ó Crualaoich, 'The "Merry Wake"', p. 182.
96. Ó Madagáin also quotes P. W. Joyce as having made the somewhat ambiguous comment on 'a tune of this kind' in one his manuscripts that 'Caoines' are 'still sung by the people – sung only, however, as things of memory, but never as far as I know applied to their original and proper use', i.e. as laments performed in the presence of the dead (Ó Madagáin 'Irish Vocal Music', p. 327).
97. Ní Uallacháin, *A Hidden Ulster*, p. 140.
98. Ní Uallacháin, *A Hidden Ulster*, pp. 137–9.
99. Ó Muirí, *Amhráin Chúige Uladh*, p. 73.
100. *Croch Suas É*, p. 183. My translation.
101. Brennan, *Máire Bhuí Ní Laoire*, pp. 90–1.
102. *Raifteari: Amhráin agus Dánta*, ed. C. Ó Coighligh (Dublin: An Clóchomhar, 1987), p. 129. My translation.
103. *An Duanaire*, pp. 336–9.
104. B. Ó Madagáin, *Caointe agus Seancheolta Eile: Keening and Other Old Irish Musics* (Inverin: Cló Iar-Chonnachta, 2005), pp. 54 and 124.
105. Ó Madagáin, 'Irish Vocal Music', p. 327. The choice of air may have had something to do with the fact that one of Seán Clárach's own *aislingí* was set to it. Seán Ó Tuama and his contemporaries also set elegies to airs like 'Éamonn an Chnoic' and 'Ceo Draíochta'. It is interesting that Raiftearaí's 'Caoineadh Uí Cheallaigh Chluain Leathaní' also appears to be set to the air of 'Ar Éirinn Ní Neosainn Cé hÍ'.
106. See Partridge, 'Caoineadh na dTrí Muire', pp. 67–81.
107. Local tradition has it that the song was in fact composed by Ó Dónaill's brother, who was also a priest. See Ó Muirgheasa, *Céad de Cheoltaibh Uladh*, pp. 187–90.
108. B. Ó Madagáin, 'Ceol an Chaointe', in B. Ó Madagáin (ed.), *Gnéithe den Chaointearacht* (Dublin: An Clóchomhar, 1978), p. 38. See also Ó Madagáin, *Caointe agus Seancheolta Eile*, pp. 16–18 and 86–8.
109. Including that given by the Halls, *Ireland*, vol. 1, p. 225. Listen to tracks 12, 18 and 32 on Ó Cadhla, *Amhráin ó Shliabh gCua* and to 1–6 on the CD accompanying Ó Madagáin's *Caointe agus Seancheolta Eile*. Ó Madagáin draws on airs transcribed by P. W Joyce, George Petrie and Liam de Noraidh (one of whose sources was Ó Cadhla).
110. See, for example, the seventeenth-century elegy, in non-stanzaic form, on the exile of Philip Mac Aodha Uí Raghallaigh (*Poems on the O'Reillys*, pp. 139–46).
111. Lysaght, '*Caoineadh os Cionn Coirp*', p. 70.
112. Ó Madagáin, 'Irish Vocal Music', pp. 317–18. O'Curry describes another wake at which more than one keener presided (quoted in Ó Súillebháin, 'The Keening of the Dead', p.136), and Patricia Lysaght cites other descriptions of keeners chanting alternate verses or taking turns at leading the lament (Lysaght, '*Caoineadh os Cionn Coirp*', p. 71).
113. O'Donovan, *Journal*, p. 27 note *k*.
114. Ó Madagáin, 'Irish Vocal Music', p. 328, note 4.
115. J. Ó Duibheannaigh, personal interview, 6 October 2004. John was 82 years old at the time of this conversation.

116. Ó Madagáin, 'Song for Emotional Release', pp. 256–7.
117. See, for example, the description of an unpremeditated keen made by a Scottish woman at the graveside of her husband. See Ó Madagáin, 'Functions of Irish Music', p. 146.
118. Quoted in Ó Madagáin, 'Irish Vocal Music', p. 312.
119. Croker, *The Keen of the South of Ireland*, pp. xxiv–xxv.
120. Croker, *The Keen of the South of Ireland*, p. xxvi.
121. Ó Coileáin, 'The Irish Lament', p. 101.
122. Hall, *Ireland*, vol. 1, pp. 225–6. If he was representing himself accurately, Hall had some knowledge of Irish Gaelic. Hall calls the Irish language 'very rational and beautiful in its philosophy and far less difficult to learn than is generally imagined'. See S. C. Hall, *Hall's Ireland*, M. Scott, ed., cond. ed., 2 vols (London and Sydney: Sphere Books, 1984), vol. 2, p. 460.
123. Ó Buachalla, *An Caoine*, p. 70.
124. Ó Madagáin, 'Functions of Irish Music', pp. 158–9 and 205. See also O'Sullivan, *Songs of the Irish*, pp. 14–21 and 32–40.
125. Ó Madagáin, 'Irish Vocal Music', pp. 322–3, and O'Sullivan, *Songs of the Irish*, p. 33.
126. Rosenberg, *Can These Bones Live?* p. 12.
127. O'Donovan, *Journal*, p. 27 note *k*.
128. Ó Coileáin, 'The Irish Lament', p. 113.
129. Ní Uallacháin, *A Hidden Ulster*, p. 138; and Ó Súilleabháin, 'The Keening of the Dead', p. 132.
130. Ó Coileáin, 'The Irish Lament', pp. 109–12. There is some uncertainty about the date of the first transcription: although the year 1800 is mentioned, there is ambiguity as to whether this refers to the *flourit* of Norry Singleton or the date of the manuscript itself – and the actual transcription may have been made some years later. Singleton's second performance is said to have been transcribed close to her death in 1873 (see 'The Irish Lament', p. 109; S. Ó Tuama, 'The Lament for Art O'Leary', in *Repossessions* (Cork: Cork University Press, 1995), pp. 86–7; and Cullen, 'Contemporary and Later Politics', 34–5).
131. L. Cullen, 'The Contemporary and Later Politics of Caoineadh Airt Uí Laoire', *Eighteenth-Century Ireland*, 8 (1993), pp. 34–5.
132. Quoted in Ó Coileáin, 'The Irish Lament', p. 110.
133. See H. O. Nygard, 'Mrs. Brown's Recollected Ballads', in P. Conroy (ed.), *Ballads and Ballad Research* (Seattle: University of Washington Press, 1978), pp. 68–87.
134. Finnegan, *Oral Poetry*, pp. 69–70.
135. A. Friedman, 'The Oral-Formulaic Theory of Balladry A Re-Rebuttal', in J. Porter (ed.), *The Ballad Image: Essay Presented to Bertrand Harris Bronson* (Los Angeles, CA: Center for the Study of Comparative Folklore and Mythology, University of California, 1983), pp. 225–6.
136. Ó Buachalla, *An Caoine*, p. 38.
137. Rosenberg, *Can These Bones Live?* pp. 76–8.
138. Rosenberg, *Can These Bones Live?* p. 77.
139. For example, Ruth Finnegan notes that, 'apart perhaps from the *Rgveda*, instances of identical transmission without the aid of writing over a long period are not easy to find, and it is the variability rather than the verbal identity of orally transmitted pieces that is most commonly noted' (Finnegan, *Oral Poetry*, p. 140).
140. Slotkin, *Medieval Irish Scribes*, pp. 446–7. See also Simms, 'Literacy and the Irish Bards', pp. 238–57.

141. Comments Bruford, 'Seventeenth- and eighteenth-century scribes show no compunction about improving on their exemplars: the differences are far greater than can be explained by textual misreadings or mishearings' (Bruford, *Gaelic Folk-Tales*, p. 48).
142. See P. de Brún, 'Caoine ar Mhac Fínín Duibh', *Éigse*, 13:3 (1970), p. 221.
143. For an interesting discussion of this subject, see P. Breatnach, 'Oral and Written Transmission of Poetry'.
144. Ó Buachalla, *An Caoine*, pp. 68–70 and 85.
145. Ó Buachalla, *An Caoine*, pp. 67 and 70–81.
146. O'Donovan, *Journal*, p. 27, note *k*.
147. Ó Buachalla, *An Caoine*, pp. 86–7.
148. Ó Buachalla, *An Caoine*, p. 81.
149. P. Breatnach, 'Oral and Written Transmission of Poetry', p. 63.
150. Ó Madagáin, 'Functions of Irish Music', p. 145. Ó Madagáin cites other instances, both Irish and Scottish, of this phenomenon, including a story about Tomás Rua Ó Súilleabháin having improvised a song in *ochtfhoclach* for a shepherd to remind Daniel O'Connell of his promise of a new suit (Ó Madagáin, 'Functions of Irish Music', p. 163).
151. Ó Madagáin, 'Functions of Irish Music', pp. 145–6.
152. Friedman, 'The Oral-Formulaic Theory of Balladry', p. 230.
153. Ó Buachalla, *An Caoine*, p. 46.
154. Ó Buachalla, *An Caoine*, p. 31. Interestingly, Ó Buachalla has chosen examples of trained modern composers artfully setting poetry to music, perhaps to emphasize his belief that *caointe* are works of literature rather than part of vernacular tradition. It is probable, however, that 'Deus Meus', as a hymn, was intended to be sung – and possible that Ó Doirnín's poem was also intended for performance, since others of his compositions have had a long life as songs in oral tradition.
155. See Ó Madagáin, 'Irish Vocal Music', p. 317, for a discussion of melodies printed by J. C. Walker in 1786 and Bunting in 1840. See also Ó Madagáin, 'Ceol an Chaointe', pp. 47–52, for a reproduction of a 'Caoinan, Or Irish Funeral Song', a melody with words, printed by William Beauford in 1791.
156. Ó Madagáin, 'Coibhneas na Filiochta leis an gCeol', p. 100.
157. Ó Buachalla, *An Caoine*, pp. 50–3.
158. S. Ó Tuama, 'The Lament for Art O'Leary', p. 83.
159. S. Ó Tuama (ed.), *Caoineadh Airt Uí Laoghaire* (1961; Dublin: An Clóchomhar, 1993), pp. 22–3.
160. Cullen, 'The Contemporary and Later Politics of *Caoineadh Airt Uí Laoire*', p. 29; Ó Buachalla, *An Caoine*, p. 89.
161. Ó Tuama, 'The Lament for Art O'Leary', pp. 78 and 99.
162. Ó Buachalla, *An Caoine*, pp. 70–5.
163. Cullen, 'The Contemporary and Later Politics of *Caoineadh Airt Uí Laoire*', p. 19.
164. Bourke, 'Performing, Not Writing', pp. 137 and 140–5.
165. Bourke, 'Performing, Not Writing', pp. 141–2.
166. Bourke, 'Performing, Not Writing', p. 142.
167. S. E. McKibben, 'Angry Laments and Grieving Postcoloniality', in P. J. Mathews (ed.) *New Voices in Irish Criticism* (Dublin: Four Courts Press, 2000), p. 221.
168. Quoted in Ó Coileáin, 'The Irish Lament', p. 107.
169. Bourke, 'Performing, Not Writing', p. 141.

Notes to pages 105–13   227

170. J. A. Murphy, 'O'Connell and the Gaelic World', in K. B. Nowland and M. R. O'Connell (eds), *Daniel O'Connell: Portrait of a Radical* (New York: Fordham University Press, 1985), pp. 32–3.
171. McKibben, 'Angry Laments', p. 223.
172. Ó Tuama, *Caoineadh Airt Uí Laoghaire*, p. 72.
173. Cullen, 'The Contemporary and Later Politics of *Caoineadh Airt Uí Laoire*', pp. 30–1. See also Tuama, *Caoineadh Airt Uí Laoghaire*, pp 24 and. 72; and Mrs J. O'Connell, *The Last Colonel*, vol. 1, pp. 11 and 24 and vol. 2, pp. 202–3.
174. Cullen, 'The Contemporary and Later Politics of *Caoineadh Airt Uí Laoire*', p. 10.
175. Ó Tuama, 'The Lament for Art O'Leary', p. 87.
176. Bourke, 'Performing, Not Writing', p. 145.
177. *Diarmuid na Bolgaighe*, pp. 66–7. My translation.
178. *Diarmuid na Bolgaighe*, p. 67. My translation.
179. De Brún, '*Caoine ar Mhac Fínín Duibh*', p. 224. My translation.
180. Cullen, 'The Contemporary and Later Politics of *Caoineadh Airt Uí Laoire*', p. 10.
181. *The Field Day Anthology of Irish Writing*, vol. 5, pp. 424–7.
182. Brennan, *Máire Bhuí Ní Laoire*, pp. 86–9.
183. M. Ní Dhonnchadha, 'Caoineadh ón Ochtú hAois Déag, Téacs agus Comhthéacs', in M. Ó Briain and P. Ó Héalaí (eds), *Téada Dúchais Aistí in Ómós don Ollamh Breandán Ó Madagáin* (Inverin, Conamara: Cló Iar-Chonnachta, 2002), pp. 193–6.
184. Cullen, 'The Contemporary and Later Politics of *Caoineadh Airt Uí Laoire*', p. 19.
185. Ó Coileáin, 'The Irish Lament', p. 114.
186. Shields, *Narrative Singing*, pp. 10–33.
187. Ó Buachalla, *An Caoine*, p. 35.
188. J. M. Foley (ed.), 'Introduction', *Oral Tradition in Literature: Interpretation in Context* (Columbia, MO: University of Missouri Press, 1986), p. 17.
189. G. Ó Crualaoich, *The Book of the Cailleach: Stories of the Wise Woman Healer* (Cork: Cork University Press, 2003), p. 17.

4 'For Want of Education': The Songs of the Hedge Schoolmaster

1. Carpenter, *Verse in English*, p. 498.
2. P. W. Joyce (ed.), *Old Irish Folk Music and Songs* (London and New York: Longmans, Green and Co., 1909), p. 201.
3. J. Moulden (ed.), *Songs of the People: Selections from the Sam Henry Collection, Part One* (Belfast: Blackstaff Press, 1979), pp. 107 and 58.
4. D. Ó Muirithe, *An t-Amhrán Macarónach* (Dublin: An Clóchomhar, 1980), p. 204, note 44.
5. J. R. R. Adams, '"Swine-Tax and Eat-Him-All Magee": The Hedge Schools and Popular Education in Ireland', in J. S. Donnelly and K. A. Miller (eds), *Irish Popular Culture*, (Dublin: Irish Academic Press, 1998), p. 98.
6. Quoted in A. McManus, *The Irish Hedge School and Its Books, 1695–1831* (Dublin: Four Courts Press, 2002), p. 15.
7. Adams, '"Swine-Tax"', p. 98.
8. Cullen, 'Patrons', p. 16.
9. K. Whelan, *The Tree of Liberty: Radicalism, Catholicism and the Construction of Irish Identity 1760–1830* (Notre Dame, IN: University of Notre Dame Press, 1996), pp. 10–11.

10. Cullen, 'Patrons', p. 28.
11. N. Ó Ciosáin, *Print and Popular Culture in Ireland, 1750–1850* (Basingstoke: Macmillan; New York: St. Martin's Press, 1997), pp. 27–8.
12. Quoted in McManus, *The Irish Hedge School*, p. 73.
13. Quoted in Ó Ciosáin, *Print and Popular Culture*, p. 48.
14. P. J. Dowling, *The Hedge Schools of Ireland* (London and New York: Longmans, Green and Co., 1935), pp. 1–19 and 20.
15. Adams, '"Swine-Tax"', pp. 99–100.
16. See W. P. Burke, *The Irish Priests in the Penal Times, 1660–1760* (Waterford: Irish University Press, 1968), pp. 394–6.
17. P. Connell, *Parson, Priest and Master: National Education in Co. Meath, 1824–41* (Dublin: Irish Academic Press, 1995), p. 16.
18. Adams, '"Swine-Tax"', p. 99.
19. S. Kierse, *Education in the Parish of Killaloe* (Killaloe: Boru Book, 1987), p. 36. Hugh Dorian, describing schools in the Fanad Peninsula of Donegal in the mid-eighteenth century, commented, 'From the miserable looking habitation of which he was man, master and owner', the teachers of 'olden times' would more appropriately be called 'cave schoolmasters'. See H. Dorian, *The Outer Edge of Ulster: A Memoir of Social Life in Nineteenth-Century Donegal*, ed. B. Mac Suibhne and D. Dickson (Dublin: The Lilliput Press, 2000), p. 99.
20. Connell, *Parson, Priest and Master*, p. 16.
21. Quoted in Adams, '"Swine-Tax"', p. 113.
22. Quoted in E. Cahill, 'The Native Schools of Ireland in the Penal Era', *The Irish EcclesiasticalRecord*, 55 (1940), pp. 22–3.
23. H. Cooke, *Henry Cooke's Centenary*, ed. R. Crawford and E. Dunlop, (Draperstown, 1888; repr. Ballymena: Braid Books, 1993), p. 19. See also Adams, '"Swine-Tax"', p. 113.
24. W. Carleton, 'The Hedge School', in *Traits and Stories of the Irish Peasantry*, 2 vols (London: William Tegg, n.d.), vol. 1, p. 294.
25. W. Carleton *The Autobiography of William Carleton*, rev. edn (Downey, 1896; London: MacGibbon & Kee, 1968), pp. 167–8.
26. Dowling, *The Hedge Schools of Ireland*, pp. 35–8 and 52; and Adams, *The Printed Word and the Common Man: Popular Culture in Ulster, 1700–1900* (Belfast: Institute of Irish Studies, Queen's University of Belfast, 1987), pp. 11–12.
27. McManus, *The Irish Hedge School*, p. 31.
28. In his *Statistical Survey of County Clare, 1808*, Hely Dutton put the number of pupils between 20 and 100 scholars, 'boys and girls mixed together' (Kierse, *Education in the Parish of Killaloe*, p. 31).
29. Kierse, *Education in the Parish of Killaloe*, throughout; Adams, '"Swine-Tax"', p. 115.
30. P. W. Joyce, *English As We Speak It in Ireland* (London: Longmans, Green, & Co.; Dublin: M. H. Gill & Son, 1910), p. 157.
31. P. J. Dowling, *A History of Irish Education, A Study in Conflicts of Loyalty* (Cork: The Mercier Press, 1971), p. 88. See also D. H. Akenson, *The Irish Education Experiment: The National System of Education in the Nineteenth Century* (London: Routledge and Kegan Paul, 1970), p. 50.
32. Akenson, *The Irish Education Experiment*, pp. 49–52; and Dowling, *The Hedge Schools of Ireland*, pp. 74–6.
33. McManus, *The Irish Hedge School*, p. 118.
34. Quoted in McManus, *The Irish Hedge School*, p. 88.

35. Dowling, *The Hedge Schools of Ireland*, p. 50.
36. Quoted in Dowling, *A History of Irish Education*, p. 87.
37. It is impossible to enumerate the classical schools in Ireland during this period with any precision; the best indication probably comes from Brenan's study of the parochial returns for Kildare and Leighlin in 1824, in which he found that 'sixteen of the 262 teachers upon whom he had information were conducting schools with enough Latin taught to be classified by him as "classical schools"' (Akenson, *The Irish Education Experiment*, p. 52).
38. Dowling, *The Hedge Schools of Ireland*, pp. 53 and 72.
39. Dowling, *The Hedge Schools of Ireland*, p. 53; and Dowling, *A History of Irish Education*, pp. 92–4. See also Cullen, 'Patrons', p. 31.
40. Cullen, 'Patrons', p. 32.
41. S. Connolly, 'Translating History: Brian Friel and the Irish Past', in A. J. Peacock (ed.), *The Achievement of Brian Friel*, Ulster Editions and Monographs, 4 (Gerrard's Cross: Colin Smythe, 1993), p. 151.
42. Akenson, *The Irish Education Experiment*, p. 54; and Dowling, *The Hedge Schools of Ireland*, p. 107. While far fewer numbers of women than men engaged in schoolteaching, they were by no means absent from the profession: the parochial records of Kildare and Leighlin list 275 male teachers and 96 female, over half of whom taught more than the 3 R's, 'including occasionally Music, Drawing and French'. See M. Brenan, *Schools of Kildare and Leighlin A.D. 1775–1835* (Dublin: M. H. Gill and Son, 1935), pp. 79 and 86–7.
43. Adams, '"Swine-Tax"', p. 109; and Adams, *The Printed Word*, p. 13.
44. Adams, *The Printed Word*, pp. 111.
45. Joyce, *English as We Speak It in Ireland*, p. 162.
46. Joyce, *English as We Speak It in Ireland*, 155–6.
47. D. Kennedy, 'Education and the People', in R. B. McDowell (ed.), *Social Life in Ireland 1800–45* (Cork: The Mercier Press, 1957), p. 63; and Dowling, *The Hedge Schools of Ireland*, pp. 21 and 118–33.
48. Ó Tuama, 'Introduction', *An Duanaire*, p. xxi; and Ó Tuama, 'Gaelic Culture in Crisis', pp. 37–9.
49. Dowling, *The Hedge Schools of Ireland*, pp. 118–33; and Kennedy, 'Education and the People', p. 63.
50. *Eighteenth-Century Verse*, ed. R. Lonsdale (1984; Oxford: Oxford University Press, 1987, p. 528.
51. J. O'Keeffe, *The Agreeable Surprise: A Comic Opera, in Two Acts*, 4th edn (London: 1795), p. 6.
52. O'Keeffe, *The Agreeable Surprise*, p. 16.
53. W. Carleton, 'The Poor Scholar', *Traits and Stories of the Irish Peasantry*, 2 vols (London: William Tegg), vol. 2, p. 281.
54. Carleton, 'The Hedge School', p. 292.
55. S. Alexander, *A Practical Logical Essay on the Syntax of the English Language* 2nd edn (Liverpool: C. Bentham & Co., 1830), p. ix.
56. Adams, *The Printed Word*, p. 113.
57. Carleton, 'The Hedge School', p. 300. In 1808 Eugene O'Sullivan, a classical schoolmaster, who was conducting his own defence in a court case in 'pure Ciceronian Latin', was reported by The *Cork Advertiser* as having refused 'to descend to that humble vernacular expression common to the profanum vulgus. No, his glowing mind, stored with the

riches of Rome and Athens, was wafted, swift as with the Daedalean wing, to the highest summit of Mount Parnassus' (quoted in McManus, *The Irish Hedge School*, p. 128).
58. Dowling, *The Hedge Schools of Ireland*, pp. 5 and 13–15.
59. Carpenter, *Verse in English*, p. 507.
60. O'Keeffe, *The Agreeable Surprise*, p. 10.
61. Akenson, *The Irish Education Experiment*, p. 52; and Carleton, 'The Hedge School', p. 276.
62. Dowling, *The Hedge Schools of Ireland*, p. 113.
63. F. O'Connor, *A Short History of Irish Literature* (New York: G. P. Putnam's Songs, 1967), p. 139.
64. Joyce, *Old Irish Folk Music*, pp. 200–1.
65. Dowling, *The Hedge Schools of Ireland*, p. 113.
66. Joyce, *Old Irish Folk Music*, pp. 201–2.
67. C. Croker, *Popular Songs of Ireland* (London: Henry Colburn, 1839), p. 158.
68. Carpenter, *Verse in English*, p. 510.
69. Georges-Denis Zimmermann, *Songs of Irish Rebellion: Political Street Ballads and Rebel Songs 1780–1900* (Hatboro, PA: Folklore Associates, 1967), pp. 178–9 and 176–9.
70. Zimmermann, *Songs of Irish Rebellion*, pp. 176–7.
71. McManus, *The Irish Hedge School*, pp. 35–6.
72. Whelan, *The Tree of Liberty*, p. 83. Some may have indeed participated in secret societies. According to Roy Foster, 'the classic picture of hedge schoolmasters as conduits of subversion' can be substantiated by court records (quoted in McManus, *The Irish Hedge School*, p. 81).
73. Dowling, *A History of Irish Education*, p. 78.
74. McManus, *The Irish Hedge School*, p. 35.
75. Whelan, *The Tree of Liberty*, p. 83. See also McManus, *The Irish Hedge School*, p. 37.
76. Ó Ciosáin, *Print and Popular Culture*, p. 28.
77. Zimmermann, *Songs of Irish Rebellion*, pp. 131–2.
78. S. O'Boyle, *The Irish Song Tradition*, p. 53.
79. Zimmermann, *Songs of Irish Rebellion*, p. 184.
80. Quoted in Ó Tuama, *An Grá*, p. 174. Translation: 'She is the figure of a dream, who reveals herself suddenly in the woods amidst flowers and birds, a sort of spring fairy with no corporeal reality.'
81. Ó Tuama, *An Grá*, pp. 187–9.
82. S. O Tuama, *An Grá*, pp. 184–94.
83. Wilgus, 'Irish Traditional Narrative Songs in English', p. 118.
84. Joyce, *Old Irish Folk Music*, p. 202.
85. 'The Lovely Maid of Erin's Isle', quoted in Zimmermann, *Songs of Irish Rebellion*, p. 91.
86. Wilgus, 'Irish Traditional Narrative Songs in English', p. 119.
87. Ó Tuama, *An Grá*, p. 188.
88. Ó Tuama, *An Grá*, pp. 188–93. A number of early eighteenth-century elegies, like Séamas Dall Mac Cuarta's 'Tuireamh Mhurcha Crúis', Fearghas Mac Bheatha's 'Tuireamh Phádraig Mhic a Liondain' and Pádraig Mac a Liondain's 'Tuireamh Shéamais Mhic Cuarta' also employ a good number of learned references. See S. Mac Cuarta, *Dánta*, ed. Seán Ó Gallchóir (Dublin: An Clóchomhar, 1979), pp. 32–7, and P. Mac a Liondain, *Dánta*, ed. Seosamh Mag Uidhir (Dublin: An Clóchomhar, 1977), pp. 1–3 and 37–9.
89. P. Tunney, *The Stone Fiddle* (Dublin: Gilbert Dalton, 1979), pp. 115–16.
90. From the singing of Len Graham and Eithne Ní Uallacháin.

Notes to pages 126–32   231

91. Tunney, *The Stone Fiddle*, pp. 120–1.
92. *The Book of Magauran*, pp. 313–14 and 61–70.
93. See, for example, Uilliam English's 'Tá Óigbhean sa Tír', in Ú. Nic Éinrí (ed.), *Canfar an Dán: Uilliam English agus a Chairde* (Dingle: An Sagart, 2003), p. 92.
94. Mac Cuarta, *Dánta*, pp. 30–1.
95. *Amhráin Chearbhalláin, The Poems of Carolan*, ed. T. Ó Máille (London: Irish Texts Society, 1916), p. 119. My translation.
96. © British Library Board (and all subsequent citations from the British Library, hereafter, BL) BL 11622.df.34.(2), Monaghan, 1788.
97. Ó Tuama, *An Grá*, pp. 126–30.
98. 'Reilly's Praise of His Lovely Molly', BL11622.df.34.(38), Monaghan, 1789.
99. In *The Lady's Evening Companion. Being a choice collection of songs, sung this season at Vauxhall, and other public places of entertainment*, BL RB.23.a.21766.(31), London, 1985.
100. *Peadar Ó Dornín: Amhráin*, p. 52. My translation. Ó Gormáin was in fact a well-regarded Irish scholar and even assisted Charlotte Brooke with her work. See S. de Rís, *Peadar Ó Doirnín: a Bheatha agus a Shaothar* (Dublin: Oifig an tSoláthair, 1969), p. 124.
101. F. J. E. Raby, *A History of Secular Latin Poetry in the Middle Ages*, 2 vols (1934; Oxford: The Clarendon Press, 1957). vol. 2, pp. 282–308.
102. Tunney, *The Stone Fiddle*, pp. 43–4.
103. Zimmermann, *Songs of Irish Rebellion*, pp. 198–9. I have regularized the spelling. A medieval French poem called 'Le Débat de Synagogue et d'Église' is cited in Zumthor, *Histoire Littéraire de la France Médiévale*, p. 273.
104. See Ó Muirgheasa, *Céad de Cheoltaibh Uladh*, pp. 1–2.
105. Carpenter, *Verse in English*, pp. 325.
106. S. Marx, *Youth Against Age: Generational Strife in Renaissance Poetry* (New York: Peter Lang, 1985), p. 155.
107. Dowling, *The Hedge Schools of Ireland*, pp. 114–17. See also Dowling, *A History of Irish Education*, p. 98; McManus, *The Irish Hedge School*, p. 125; and Brenan, *Schools of Kildare and Leighlin*, pp. 65–9.
108. Joyce, *Old Irish Folk Music*, pp. 203–4.
109. O'Boyle, *The Irish Song Tradition*, pp. 80–1. Compare the following verse from Pádraig Mac a Liondain's 'Tá Dairtí ag Dul Tríom': 'Shiúlfainn thart an Éigipt, Arménia is an Spáinn de ruaig,/Agus tiortha treabhra, tréadacha na Gréige, cé álainn snua;/D'fuillfinn thart ina dhiaidh sin go hÉirinn gan spás ar luas,/Is ghlacfainn dom mar fhéirín géis chaomh na scáiní dual'. (See Mac a Liondain, *Dánta*, pp. 44–5). Translation: 'I would hasten through Egypt, Armenia and Spain/And the tilled lands and pastures of Greece,/ But no matter how beautiful I'd leave them all behind me, for Ireland without delay/And as a reward would take the gentle swan of the lovely tresses'.
110. BL1078.k.12.(5), Dublin, *c*.1830. Worse still are songs like 'A New Song in Praise of the Catholic Church of Kanturk' and 'Lines Written on St. Mary's Chapel Ship Street, Drogheda', by Micheal M'Cabe.
111. The usual word in Ulster is 'sheugh', meaning a ditch (a dyke or bank). See Moulden, *Songs of the People*, p. 107.
112. Croker, *Popular Songs of Ireland*, pp. 141–2.
113. Joyce, *Old Irish Folk Music*, p. 203.
114. Carpenter, *Verse in English*, pp. 523–4.
115. Carpenter, *Verse in English*, p. 385–6.

116. Ó Muirithe, *An t-Amhrán Macarónach*, pp. 156–7.
117. BL 11622.df.34.(2), Monaghan, 1788.
118. BL 11622.df.34.(38), Monaghan, 1788. See also *Dánta Phiarais Feiritéir*, ed. P. Muldowney (Aubane, Cork: Aubane Historical Society, 1999), p. 75.
119. BL 11622.df.34(20), Monaghan, 1788. This trope also appears in Irish-language verse from the seventeenth to the nineteenth centuries: see, for example, 'Freagra ar Phiaras le Filidh Eile, in *Dánta Phiarais Feiritéir*, p. 75; and Tomás Rua Ó Súilleabháin's epithalamium 'A Eoghain Mhaith Uí Shúilleabháin', in T. Ó Súilleabháin, *Amhráin*, ed. M. Ní Shúilleabháin (Maigh Nuad: An Sagart, 1985), p. 25.
120. D. Ó Muirithe (ed.), '"Of English Fayre I Am Scarce Indeed": Amhráin Ghaeilge agus a nAistritheoirí ca. 1700–1800', *Leachtai Cholm Cille*, 29 (1999), p. 145.
121. Ó Muirithe, '"Of English Fayre"', p. 158; and D. Ó Muirithe, '"Tho' Not in Full Stile Compleat": Jacobite Songs from Gaelic Manuscript Sources', *Eighteenth-Century Ireland*, 6 (1991), p. 93.
122. Ó Muirithe, '"Of English Fayre"', pp. 146–9.
123. RIA 3 B 38, pp. 242–3.
124. Ó Muirithe, '"Of English Fayre"', p. 145.
125. N. Ní Dhomhnaill, tape recorded interview, 27 June, 1979, Ranafast, County Donegal, and Conal Ó Domhnaill, quoted in *Folksongs of Britain and Ireland*, p. 117, note 34.
126. Kiberd, *Irish Classics*, p. 63.
127. Ó Muirithe, *An t-Amhrán Macarónach*, pp. 79, 70 and 134.
128. See Ó Muirithe, *An t-Amhrán Macarónach*, pp. 95, 65, 110–11, 128–30 and 98; and *Amhráin Sheagháin Chláraigh Mhic Dhomhnaill*, ed. P. Ua Duinnín (Dublin: Connradh na Gaedhilge, 1902), pp. 14–16 and 98–100.
129. De Rís, *Peadar Ó Doinín*, pp. 16. My translation.
130. Mac a Liondain, *Dánta*, p. 52.
131. O'Boyle, *The Irish Song Tradition*, p. 88, slightly amended.
132. For a comprehensive discussion of this complex metre, see Blankenhorn, *Irish Song-Craft*, pp. 203–30. See also Carney, 'Three Old Irish Accentual Poems', pp. 59–96; and P. Breatnach, 'Múnlaí Véarsaíocht Rithimiúil', pp. 54–71.
133. Joyce, *Old Irish Folk Music*, p. 202.
134. O'Boyle, *The Irish Song Tradition*, p. 52, slightly amended. An analogous song in Irish is 'Seán Ó Duibhir an Ghleanna'.
135. H. Shields, 'Singing Traditions of a Bilingual Parish in North-West Ireland', *Yearbook of the International Folk Music Council*, 3 (1971), pp. 117.
136. Ó Muirithe, '"Of English Fayre"', pp. 155–6.
137. Ó Muirithe, '"Of English Fayre"', p. 143.
138. Carpenter, *Verse in English*, p. 103.
139. Carpenter, *Verse in English*, pp. 299–301.
140. Quoted in Corkery, *The Hidden Ireland*, p. 284.
141. O'Keeffe, *The Agreeable Surprise*, p. 20.
142. BL P.P.6154.k, Dublin, 1793; and BPB 1808: 25, Item 1031[T], Belfast, 1808, Linen Hall Library, Belfast. A London-printed copy indicates James Hook and Mr (Robert) Anderson as the composers.
143. Croker, *Popular Songs of Ireland*, p. 138–9.
144. 'Arise, My Love', pp. 7–8, Derry, 1812. Courtesy of Queen's University Belfast, Gibson Collection MS 37.
145. BL 11606.aa.24.(73), Alnwick, *c.* 1800.

146. *Damon and Phillis's Garland, containing five excellent new songs, etc.*, BL 11621.c 5.(49), Newcastle, *c.* 1780.
147. Croker, *Popular Songs of Ireland*, p. 124.
148. See L. P. Wenham, *Frances l'Anson, The Lass of Richmond Hill* (Richmond, North Yorkshire: L. P. Wenham, 1986).
149. BL 11622.df.34.(16), Limerick (Goggin), late eighteenth century.
150. From 'Tullymore's Fair Queen', BELUM.X183.1980, Ulster Museum, Downpatrick, 1800.
151. In Kilkenny, his teacher was Peter White, who founded one of the few Catholic schools in sixteenth-century Ireland (1565).
152. R. Stanyhurst, *Translation of the First Four Books of the Aeneis of P. Vergilius Maro: With Other Poetical Devices Thereto Annexed*, ed. Edward Arber (Westminster: Archibald Constable and Co., 1895), pp. 154–5.
153. Croker, *Popular Songs of Ireland*, p. 143. In turn, Thomas Nashe took Stanyhurst to task for lines like: 'Then did he make heavens vault to rebounde, with rounce robble hobble/ Of ruffe raffe roaring, with thwick, thwack, thurley bouncing'. Quoted in *The Oxford Handbook of Tudor Literature: 1485–1603*, ed. M. Pincombe and C. Shrank (Oxford: Oxford University Press, 2009), p. 216.
154. J. Holmes and L. Graham, *Chaste Muses, Bards and Sages*, Free Reed, FRR007 [LP and notes], notes, 1971.
155. T. Munnelly (coll. and ed.), *The Mount Callan Garland: Songs from the Repertoire of Tom Lenihan* (Dublin: Comhairle Bhéaloideas Éireann, 1994), pp. 10–13.
156. C. Ó Drisceoil, *The Spoons Murder and Other Mysteries* (Dublin: Craft Recordings, 2006), pp. 66–70.
157. Dowling, *The Hedge Schools of Ireland*, pp. 108–17 and 150.
158. S. Connolly, '"*Ag Déanamh* Commanding"', p. 16.
159. Whelan, *The Tree of Liberty*, pp. 10–11.
160. Dorian, *The Outer Edge of Ulster*, p. 121. Antonia McManus presents additional evidence about the social status of hedge schoolmasters, noting, 'The people displayed their appreciation by conferring honorary titles on their finest poets and scholars, titles such as "The bright star in mathematical learning", "The star of Ennistymon", "The great O'Baggot" and "The great O'Brien par excellence"' (McManus, *The Irish Hedge School*, p. 94).
161. J. Moulden, *Songs of Hugh McWilliams, Schoolmaster, 1831* (Portrush: Ulstersongs, 1993), p. 2.
162. BL11622df.34.(2), Monaghan, 1788.
163. BL 11622.de.21(9), Waterford, *c.* 1820. This song appears in a number of different chapbooks and ballad sheet versions from the 1820s on.
164. *Hall's Ireland*, vol. 2, p. 426.
165. See J. R. R. Adams, 'The Poets Laureate of Donegal: Rural Rhymers of the Laggan in the First Decade of the Nineteenth Century', *Ulster Folklife*, 34 (1988), pp. 68–75. We also know that *Watt's Hymns* circulated in hedge schools throughout Ireland (see McManus, *The Irish Hedge School*, p. 136).
166. Quoted in *The Petrie Collection of the Ancient Music of Ireland*, ed. D. Cooper and L. Ó Laoire (Cork: Cork University Press, 2002), p. 9.
167. Kennedy, *Evenings in the Duffrey*, pp. 43 and 115.

168. J. H. Delargy, 'The Gaelic Storyteller', *Proceedings of the British Academy*, 31 (1945), pp. 206–7.
169. H. Shields, 'Singing Traditions', p. 110.

5 The Eighteenth-Century Printed Ballad in Ireland

1. J. Hogg, *Domestic Manners of Sir Walter Scott* (Stirling, 1909; repr. Folcroft, PA: Folcroft Library Editions, 1970), p. 53. Ironically, Mrs. Hogg went on to complain, 'And the warst thing o' a', they're nouther right spell'd, nor right setten down'.
2. Gerould, for example, comments, 'The wonder is that the power of musical and poetical expression among common folk was not altogether destroyed by [the circulation of broadsides]'. See G. Gerould, *The Ballad of Tradition* (Oxford: Clarendon Press, 1932), p. 243.
3. Quoted in S. B. Hustvedt, *Ballad Books and Ballad Men* (Cambridge, MA: Harvard University Press, 1930), p. 254.
4. See Gerould, *The Ballad of Tradition*, p. 243; and A. Friedman (ed.), *The Viking Book of Folk Ballads of the English-Speaking World* (New York: The Viking Press, 1956), p. xxxiv.
5. F. J. Child (ed.), *English and Scottish Ballads*, 8 vols (Boston, MA: Little, Brown and Company, 1860;), vol 1, p. vii.
6. J. Phillips, *The New World of Words; or Universal English Dictionary*, 6th edn (London, 1706). Nathan Bailey's dictionary defined ballad as 'a song, commonly sung up and down the streets'. See N. Bailey, *An Universal Etymological Dictionary* (J. Darby, etc.: London, 1928).
7. See H. Glassie, *Passing the Time in Ballymenone: Culture and History of an Ulster Community* (Philadelphia, PA: University of Pennsylvania Press, 1982), pp. 57–8.
8. L. Shepard, *The History of Street Literature* (Newton Abbot: David and Charles, 1973), p. 26.
9. Friedman, *The Ballad Revival*, p. 47.
10. Fox, *Oral and Literate Culture in England*, p. 11.
11. H. Shields, 'Ballads, Ballad-Singing and Ballad-Selling', in *Popular Music in 18th-Century Dublin* (Dublin: Folk Music Society of Ireland and Na Píobairí Uilleann, 1985), p. 26.
12. J. Moulden, 'The Printed Ballad in Ireland: A Guide to the Popular Printing of Songs in Ireland, 1760–1920' (PhD dissertation, National University of Ireland, Galway, 2006), pp. 182–6.
13. P. K. Fallon, *Printing, Literacy, and Education in 18th-Century Ireland: Why the Irish Speak English* (Lewiston, NY: Edwin Mellen Press, 2005), pp. 101–2.
14. This does not mean the complete absence of such interest, but from my inspection of the existing Irish collections from the early eighteenth century, printed ballads of this period tend to appear in commonplace books rather than in large compendia of ballad sheets like the Pepys or Evans collections.
15. Hugh Shields, *Narrative Singing*, p. 43.
16. Quoted in Shields, *Narrative Singing*, p. 44. See also D. O'Sullivan, 'A Courtly Poem for Sir Richard Cox', *Éigse*, 4 (1943–4), pp. 284–7. Shields notes that the word *fuar* could also imply 'valueless'.
17. Shields, *Narrative Singing*, p. 97.
18. Moulden, 'The Printed Ballad', p. 182; Shields, 'Ballads', pp. 27–8; and Shields, *Narrative Singing*, p. 99.

19. Shields, 'Ballads', p. 28. We have records of printers operating at the premises from 1724 to at least 1764 (Moulden, 'The Printed Ballad', p. 969).
20. Shields, *Narrative Singing*, pp. 44–5.
21. H. Shields, 'Ballads', p. 28.
22. Quoted in Shields, *Narrative Singing*, p. 168. (There is evidence of prose chapbook trade from at least the late seventeenth century, when the names of Dublin chapbook publishers appear in the Chester port books. See Ó Ciosáin, *Print and Popular Culture*, p. 53.)
23. Moulden, 'The Printed Ballad', p. 176; and Shields, *Narrative Singing*, p. 43.
24. BL 1890.e.5.(120), Dublin, *c.* 1713.
25. BL 1876.f.1.(86), London, 1718.
26. 'Hibernicus', *The Dublin Weekly Journal*, 10 July 1725 (Dublin, 1725), p. 58.
27. 'Hibernicus', *The Dublin Weekly Journal*, 10 July 1725 (Dublin, 1725), p. 57; and 'Hibernicus', *The Dublin Weekly Journal* 17 July 1725 (Dublin, 1725), p. 61.
28. Swift, quoted in Friedman, *The Ballad Revival*, p. 157.
29. BL C.121.g.8.(37), Dublin, 1723.
30. K. Clendinning, 'The Armagh Bye-Election of 1753', *Review: Journal of the Craigavon Historical Society*, 2:1, at http://www.geocities.com/craigavonhs/rev/clendinningarmaghelection.html [accessed 21 January 2007].
31. De Rís, *Peadar Ó Doirnín*, p. 47.
32. 'A Masonic Song', in N. Williams (ed.), *Riocard Bairéad: Amhráin* (Dublin: An Clóchomhar, 1978), p. 94.
33. The air originally given for 'William and Margaret' is that of 'Fair Rosamund'.
34. BL, General Reference Collection 1608/5493.
35. Shields, 'Ballads', p. 26.
36. Shields, 'Ballads', p. 26.
37. 'An Excellent New Ballad', BL 1890.e.5.(32); or BL C.121.g.8.(40.), Dublin, 1725–6.
38. Press A.7.5, no. 214, Dublin, 1730, Trinity College Dublin, Early Printed Books.
39. Quoted in Adams, *The Printed Word*, p. 74.
40. See Moulden, 'The Printed Ballad', pp. 52–3, for a breakdown of collections throughout Ireland by date.
41. 'Hibernicus', *The Dublin Weekly Journal*, 17 July 1725, pp. 61–2.
42. Quoted in Moulden, 'The Printed Ballad', p. 179.
43. 'On the Unfortunate, tho' much Lamented Death of James Cotter Esq., who was Executed at Cork on the 7th of May 1720 for Ravishing Elizabeth Squib a Quaker', quoted in B. Ó Buachalla, 'The Making of a Cork Jacobite', in P. O'Flanagan and C. G. Buttimer (eds), *Cork History and Society* (Cork, 1993), p. 490.
44. E. Ward, *Wine and Wisdom: or, the Tipling Philosophers. A Lyrick Poem* (London: J. Woodward in Scalding-Ally over-against Stocks-Market, 1710), pp. 2–3.
45. 'The Ancient Philosophers Vindicated against Tipling, Written by a Young Lady' (Dublin, 1721).
46. Shields, *Narrative Singing*, p. 99; and Moulden, 'The Printed Ballad', p. 593.
47. H. Shields (ed.), *Old Dublin Songs* (Dublin: Folk Music Society of Ireland, 1988), pp. 12–14 and 68.
48. *Chuck* was later attributed to Colley Cibber, but Edmund Gagey believed it to be an Irish play, possibly based on Cibber's 1702 afterpiece *The School Boy*. See E. M. Gagey, *Ballad Opera* (New York and London: Benjamin Blom, 1937), pp. 90 and 105. See also H. Koon, *Colley Cibber: A Biography* (University Press of Kentucky, 1986), p. 45.
49. Shields, 'Ballads', p. 29.

50. W. H. Rubsamen (ed.), *Irish Ballad Operas and Burlesques II*, facs. (1749; New York and London: Garland, 1974), pp. 5, 19 and 11.
51. Quoted in L. Shepard, *The Broadside Ballad: A Study in Origins and Meaning* (1962, London; Hatboro, PA: Legacy Books, 1978), p. 87. Colm Ó Lochlainn attributes 'The March of Intellect' to Oliver Goldsmith, an attribution which, while interesting, remains unsubstantiated. See Ó Lochlainn, *More Irish Street Ballads* (Dublin, 1965; London and Sydney: Pan Books, 1978), pp. 104–5, 111 and 211–13.
52. H. Shields, *Oliver Goldsmith and Popular Song in 18th-Century Dublin* (Dublin: Folk Music Society of Ireland, 1985), pp. 4–6.
53. Shields, *Oliver Goldsmith*, p. 4.
54. O. Goldsmith, *She Stoops to Conquer, or The Mistakes of a Night*, 3rd edn (London: F. Newbery, 1773), p. 46. Moulden cites an Orange song by Colonel William Blacker about the Siege of Derry called 'The Crimson Banner', whose 'unofficial and unprinted' chorus runs: 'We are the boys who fear no noise and never will surrender' (Moulden, 'The Printed Ballad', p. 1014).
55. Goldsmith, *She Stoops*, p. 10. Both Goldsmith's song and 'The Tipling Philosophers' can be sung handily to slip-jig melodies.
56. W. Irving, *Oliver Goldsmith: A Biography* (London: John Murray, 1849), pp. 298–9. The song itself can be found in an eight-page songbook printed by Magee in Belfast in 1763.
57. Quoted in Shields, *Oliver Goldsmith*, p. 8.
58. I. and P. Opie (eds), *The Oxford Dictionary of Nursery Rhymes* (1951; Oxford: Oxford University Press, 1997), pp. 33–4.
59. M. Edgeworth, *Castle Rackrent*, ed. G. Watson (1964; Oxford and New York: Oxford University Press, 1999), p. 113.
60. H. Shields, 'Printed Aids to Folk Singing, 1700–1900', in M. Daly and D. Dickson (eds), *The Origins of Popular Literacy in Ireland* (Dublin,1990)', p. 150.
61. See H. Shields, 'A History of "The Lass of Aughrim"', pp. 60–1.
62. Connolly, '"*Ag Déanamh* Commanding"', pp. 11–12.
63. Shields, 'Ballads', p. 29.
64. Shields, 'Ballads', p. 30.
65. Carpenter, *Verse in English*, p. 430.
66. Quoted in Shields, 'Ballads', p. 30.
67. Shields, *Narrative Singing*, pp. 90–1.
68. BL 11622.df.34.(37), W. Goggin, Limerick, 1788.
69. Moulden, 'The Printed Ballad', pp. 182–6. There is general agreement that these songbooks disappeared around 1840.
70. Moulden, 'The Printed Ballad', p. 108.
71. Moulden, 'The Printed Ballad', pp. 122 and 197.
72. Quoted in Moulden, 'The Printed Ballad', p. 571.
73. Adams, *The Printed Word*, p. 76.
74. At least one notable Irish poet contributed to eighteenth-century popular balladry: Eoghan Rua Ó Súilleabháin composed 'Rodney's Glory' to celebrate an English naval victory in 1782, in which he had participated as 'an ordinary seaman' (Shields, *Narrative Singing*, p. 165). His style reflects sufficient acquaintance with sea-battle ballads not only to imitate them in subject and style but also in diction and scansion – although he employs an unusual hornpipe metre and matching rhyme scheme. The earliest surviving printed text appears in a Limerick-printed eight-page songbook from 1782.
75. Shields, *Old Dublin Songs*, p. 26.

76. Shields, *Old Dublin Songs*, p. 24.
77. Shields, *Narrative Singing*, p. 97. Shields tells us that this song is 'precisely datable', but doesn't provide his source for this information.
78. BL 11606.aa.24, Glasgow, 1801. For a different text, see Shields, *Narrative Singing*, p. 97.
79. Shields, *Narrative Singing*, p. 86.
80. Moulden, 'The Printed Ballad', p. 358. The same is also true of dance tunes throughout the eighteenth century, with much exchange between Ireland, Scotland and England in evidence.
81. A few songs in Irish actually employ ballad metrics and narrativity, including 'Cuach mo Londubh Buí' and 'Máire Ní Mhaoileoin', but their stylistic and linguistic conventions are unmistakably from the Irish-language tradition (see Shields, *Narrative Singing*, pp. 35 and 93).
82. BL 11622.df.34.(13), Monaghan, 1789.
83. BPB 1807:4, Graham and Lennin, Downpatrick, c.1807, Linen Hall Library.
84. 'The Goblet of Wine', BL 11622.df.34.(29), Monaghan, 1787.
85. 'The Bottle', BL 11622.df.51(14), Limerick, W. Goggin, c. 1810.
86. For comments on the dearth of Irish type during this period, see Ó Ciosáin, *Print and Popular Culture*, pp. 159–60.
87. BL 11622.df34.(2), Monaghan, 1788.
88. BL 11622.df.51.(9), Limerick, c. 1810. The Irish is a translation of the English. I give the orthography as found in the chapbook.
89. Shields, 'Printed Aids', p. 147.
90. D. Cooper, 'Lámh Dearg: Celtic Minstrels and Orange Songsters', *Celtic Cultural Studies, An Interdisciplinary Online Journal* (1999), at http://www.celtic-cultural-studies.com/papers/01/cooper-01.html [accessed 1 March 2007].
91. E. Ó Muirgheasa (ed.), *Dhá Chéad de Cheoltaibh Uladh*, pp. 83–4.
92. BL 11622.df.34.(13) Monaghan, 1789.
93. P. W. Joyce, *English as We Speak It in Ireland*, pp. 86–7.
94. Moulden, 'The Printed Ballad', pp. 85–6.
95. J. R. R. Adams has noted that Burns's *Poems, Chiefly in the Scottish Dialect* was immensely popular in late eighteenth-century Ulster, going through a number of editions in Belfast from 1787 through 1800 (Adams, *The Printed Word*, pp. 73–4).
96. BL 1622.df.34.(21), Limerick, late eighteenth century.
97. See Shields, *Narrative Singing*, p. 107; and Moulden, 'The Printed Ballad', pp. 278. Zimmermann estimates the proportion to have been 'between one and two-fifths' (Zimmermann, *Songs of Irish Rebellion*, p. 22).
98. W. Allingham 'Irish Ballad Singers and Irish Street Ballads' *Ceol*, 3:1 (1967), p. 5.
99. Quoted in Adams, *The Printed Word*, p. 34. The mention of ballads as opposed to songbooks raises the question of whether ballad sheets existed throughout the period of the chapbook songster – unless the singer in this case was selling uncut books, as occasionally happened.
100. Quoted in Adams, *The Printed Word*, p. 121.
101. M. Murphy, 'The Ballad Singer and the Role of the Seditious Ballad in Nineteenth-Century Ireland: Dublin Castle's View', *Ulster Folklife*, 25 (1975), pp. 90 and 87.
102. See BL 11622.df34.(26) and BL 11622.df34.(12).
103. Adams, *The Printed Word*, pp. 120 and 29.
104. Moulden, 'The Printed Ballad', pp. 96–7 and 958.
105. Moulden, 'The Printed Ballad', pp. 103, 116 and 197.

106. Adams, 'Poets Laureate', p. 69.
107. Adams, 'Poets Laureate', p. 74.
108. Moulden, 'The Printed Ballad', p. 614.
109. I am indebted to Hugh Shields and John Moulden for uncovering this gem. See Moulden, 'The Printed Ballad', pp. 263–4.
110. Moulden, 'The Printed Ballad', p. 185.
111. Ó Ciosáin, *Print and Popular Culture*, pp. 22–3. We have little even in the way of anecdotal information on sales until Gavin Duffy's comments on printers in the 1840s issuing 'millions of yards annually of street ballads' and John Hand's claim that some O'Connellite ballads sold up to a million copies. See Moulden, 'The Printed Ballad', p. 255; and J. Hand, *Irish Street Ballads* (facs., Dublin: Carraig Books, 1976), p. 23.
112. T. Barnard, 'Learning, the Learned and Literacy in Ireland, c. 1660–1760', in T. Barnard, D. Ó Cróinín and K. Simms (eds), *A Miracle of Learning: Studies in Manuscripts and Irish Learning: Essays in Honour of William O'Sullivan* (Aldershot: Ashgate, 1998), p. 220.
113. For examples of such events, see R. Gillespie, 'Reading the Bible in Seventeenth-Century Ireland', in B. Cunningham and M. Kennedy (eds), *The Experience of Reading: Irish Historical Perspectives* (Dublin: Rare Books Group of the Library Association of Ireland, 1999), pp. 10–38.
114. S. O'Boyle, *The Irish Song Tradition*, p. 28.
115. M. E. Cohane and K. S. Goldstein, 'Folksongs and the Ethnography of Singing in Patrick Kennedy's *The Banks of the Boro*', *The Journal of American Folkore*, 109:434 (Autumn 1996), pp. 425–36.
116. Kennedy, *The Banks of the Boro*, p. 117; *Evenings in the Duffrey*, pp. 43 and 200.
117. For example, Kennedy cites 'The Lady and the Farmer' as 'one of those English ballads that he never saw in print, but that had been naturalized here a long time' (*The Banks of the Boro*, p. 116).
118. Kennedy, *Evenings in the Duffrey*, p. 199. It is interesting to see even at this date the connection made between ballad-selling and travellers.
119. Kennedy, *Evenings in the Duffrey*, pp. 183–7.
120. Kennedy, *The Banks of the Boro*, p. 60.
121. Moulden, 'The Printed Ballad', p. 259.
122. Fox, *Oral and Literate Culture in England*, p. 9.
123. See V. de Sola Pinto, 'Introduction', *The Common Muse*, ed. de Sola Pinto and A. E. Rodway (London: Chatto and Windus, 1957), p. 8.
124. Crawford, 'Lowland Song', p. 123.
125. Connolly, "'*Ag Déanamh* Commanding'", p. 10.
126. Connolly, "'*Ag Déanamh* Commanding'", pp. 15 and 11.

6 The Eighteenth-Century Irish Ballad and Modern Oral Tradition

1. W. Ong, 'Writing Is a Technology that Restructures Thought', in G. Baumann (ed.), *The Written Word: Literacy in Transition* (Oxford: Clarendon Press; New York: Oxford University Press, 1986), p. 31.
2. H. Shields, 'Literacy and the Ballad Genre in Ireland', *Aspecten von het Europese Marktlied: Twelfth International Folk Ballad Conference 1981* (Brussels, Centrum voor Vlaamse Volkscultuur,. 1982), p. 154. The ballad was also printed in small songbooks in Belfast in 1808, 1823 and 1825.

3. H. Shields and T. Munnelly, 'Scots Ballad Influences in Ireland', *Ceol Tíre*, 15 (October 1979), pp. 8–9.
4. For a discussion of the impact (or the lack thereof) of the songs published by the Young Irelanders in *The Nation* and *The Spirit of the Nation* (1843), see Moulden, 'The Printed Ballad', pp. 280–5. Moulden tells us that only sixteen out of the 109 songs printed in *The Spirit* were issued as ballad sheets.
5. N. Williams, 'Gaelic Texts and English Script', in M. Caball and A. Carpenter (eds), *Oral and Print Cultures in Ireland, 1600–1900* (Dublin: Four Courts Press, 2010), p. 95. Lady Gregory also recalled a report of Raifteari's 'Song of Repentance' sold as a ballad, 'with the English on one side and the Irish on the other'. See Lady Gregory, *Poets and Dreamers: Studies and Translations from the Irish* (1903, Dublin; New York: Oxford University Press, 1974), p. 128.
6. Shields, *Narrative Singing*, p. 91.
7. For example, Charlie McCoy of Glendalough had his ballad, 'Spider Kelly', printed in 1960. See H. Shields, 'Collecting Songs "by Hand"', 1954–1966', *Irish Folk Music Studies: Éigse Cheol Tíre*, 5–6 (1986–2001), p. 74.
8. Moulden, 'The Printed Ballad', p. 269–71.
9. Kennedy, *Evenings in the Duffrey*, p. 199.
10. Few attempts have been made to quantify the number of songs in the oral tradition which can be traced back to printed sources, although both Colin Neilands and John Moulden have made estimates of printed songs that were retained in oral tradition. Their figures seem to accord roughly with Thompson's for Britain: that is, at least 10–15 per cent (Moulden, 'The Printed Ballad', pp. 268–71). Looking at the matter from another angle, Steve Gardham has estimated that 'ninety-five of the standard English folk-song repertoire, or ninety-eight per cent of the English and Irish folk-song repertoire ... as noted from singers' has, as David Atkinson remarks, 'also circulated in cheap printed form'. See D. Atkinson, 'Folk Songs in Print: Text and Tradition ', *Folk Music Journal*, 8:4 (2004), pp. 457 and 475, note 7.
11. Shields, *Narrative Singing*, p. 90.
12. T. Ó Canainn, *Down Erin's Lovely Lee: Songs of Cork* (Skerries: Gilbert Dalton, 1978), p. 44.
13. J. Maguire and R. Morton, *Come Day, Go Day, God Send Sunday: The Songs and Life Story, Told in His Own Words, of Traditional Singer and Farmer, John Maguire from Co. Fermanagh* (London: Routledge and Kegan Paul, 1973), p. 21.
14. H. Shields, *Shamrock, Rose and Thistle: Folk Singing in North Derry* (Belfast: Blackstaff Press, 1981), p. 128.
15. Ó Lochlainn, *More Irish Street Ballads*, pp. 34–5.
16. D. Ó Cróinín (ed.), *The Songs of Elizabeth Cronin, Traditional Singer* (Dublin: Four Courts, 2000), pp. 269–70.
17. J. Carroll and P. McKenzie, *Around the Hills of Clare*, Musical Traditions Records MTCD331–2 (2004) [CD and notes], notes, p. 11. The song was written in 1927 by Sylvester Boland.
18. Tom Munnelly, *The Mount Callan Garland*, pp. 70–1.
19. Ó Canainn, *Down Erin's Lovely Lee*, pp. 40–1.
20. Ó Canainn, *Down Erin's Lovely Lee*, p. 56.
21. 'The Kilnamartyra Exile', in Ó Canainn, *Down Erin's Lovely Lee*, pp. 74–5.
22. Quoted in Moulden, 'The Printed Ballad', p. 254.
23. Maguire and Morton, *Come Day, Go Day*, pp. 37–8.

24. M. McCarthy, recorded interviews, with D. Turner and J. Carroll, no date, and 28 November 1975, London, England.
25. T. Munnelly, recorded interview, 15 July 2004, Miltown Malbay, County Clare, Ireland.
26. P. M. Byrne, recorded interview, 20 July 2002, Ardara, County Donegal, Ireland.
27. V. Boyle, personal conversation, 25 August 2004, Miltown Malbay, County Clare, Ireland.
28. L. Ó Laoire, *On a Rock in the Middle of the Ocean: Songs and Singers, Tory Island, Ireland* (2005; Inverin, Conamara: Cló Iar-Chonnachta/Scarecrow Press, 2007), pp. 60–1.
29. Munnelly, recorded interview.
30. Munnelly, *The Mount Callan Garland*, pp. 120–1.
31. Munnelly, recorded interview.
32. Byrne, recorded interview, 20 July 2002.
33. K. Hayes, recorded interview, 21 July 2004, Coore, County Clare, Ireland.
34. K. McFadden, recorded interview, 9 August 2002, Bloody Foreland, County Donegal, Ireland.
35. McCarthy, recorded interview, no date.
36. Moulden, 'The Printed Ballad', p. 214.
37. Byrne, recorded interview, 20 July 2002.
38. Moulden, 'The Printed Ballad', p. 347.
39. Munnelly, recorded interview. Tom told me of one singer in north Clare whose daughter had computerized and bound his song collection: 'You meet a singer; not alone has he got them all beautifully bound, but there's an alphabetical index of every song and all that – I mean, never was collecting so easy!'
40. J. Callaghan, personal interview, 13 August 2004, Roslea, County Fermanagh, Ireland. Other singers have used emanuenses, including Eddie Butcher, who employed his wife Gracie for this task (Shields, 'Collecting "by Hand "', p. 63).
41. Shields, 'Literacy', pp. 158–9.
42. Byrne, recorded interview, 20 July 2002.
43. McCarthy, recorded interview, 28 November 1975.
44. Ó Laoire, *On a Rock in the Middle of the Ocean*, p. 62.
45. Ó Laoire, *On a Rock in the Middle of the Ocean*, pp. 57–9.
46. Henigan, 'Sean-Nós in America', p. 40.
47. Ong, *Orality and Literacy*, p. 11.
48. Shields, *Shamrock, Rose and Thistle*, p. 11.
49. W. Ong, 'Writing Is a Humanizing Technology', pp. 15.
50. Ong, *Orality and Literacy*, p. 95.
51. W. Foley, 'Literacy', p. 425.
52. W. Foley, 'Literacy', pp. 429–31.
53. D. R. Olson, 'Literacy as Metalinguistic Activity', p. 255.
54. See A. R. Lecours and M. A. Parente, 'A Neurological Point of View on Social Alexia', in D. R. Olson and N. Torrance (eds), *Literacy and Orality* (Cambridge: Cambridge University Press, 1991), pp. 236–50.
55. K. Thomas, 'The Meaning of Literacy in Early Modern England', in G. Baumann (ed.), *The Written Word: Literacy in Transition* (Oxford: Oxford University Press, 1986), p. 107.
56. Ó Laoire, *On a Rock in the Middle of the Ocean*, p. 63.
57. Ong dismisses this kind of list-making as 'a ready way of doing conspicuously what oral cultures have great difficulties in doing at all, namely, lining up a sizable assortment of

discrete elements in causal sequence': W. Ong, *Interfaces of the Word: Studies in the Evolution of Consciousness and Culture* (Ithaca and London: Cornell University Press, 1977), p. 258.
58. Shields, 'Literacy', p. 164.
59. 'That's when I was a young lad and trying to learn as many songs as I could. I said, "Will you teach me a few songs?" He was talkin' about that till he died – the memory I had: that I learned three songs in one night and remembered them' (A. Ó Duibheannaigh, recorded interview, 2 July 1979, Ranafast, County Donegal, Ireland).
60. See, for examples, Behan's 'Arkle', a horse-racing song in street-ballad style and almost indistinguishable from other ballads of the genre, in F. Harte (ed.), *Songs of Dublin* (1978, Dublin; Cork: Ossian Publications, 1993), pp. 20–1.
61. Moulden, 'The Printed Ballad', p. 231.
62. Shields, *Narrative Singing*, p. 189.
63. E. Montenyohl, 'Oralities (and Literacies): Comments on the Relationships of Contemporary Folkloristics and Literary Studies', in C. L. Preston (ed.), *Folklore, Literature and Cultural Theory: Collected Essays* (New York and London: Garland Press, 1995), p. 247.
64. H. Mayhew, *London Labour and the London Poor*, 3 vols (London: G. Woodfall, 1851), vol. 1, p. 275.
65. J. Ó Duibheannaigh, recorded interview, July 2001, Ranafast, County Donegal, Ireland.
66. Moulden, 'The Printed Ballad', pp. 273 and 285.
67. Shields, *Narrative Singing*, p. 107.
68. Moulden, 'The Printed Ballad', p. 278.
69. *Paddy's Resource: Being a Collection of Modern and Patriotic Songs, Toasts and Sentiments, Compiled for the Use of all Firm Patriots* (Philadelphia, PA: T. Stevens, 1796), p. 57.
70. Shields, *Narrative Singing*, 107.
71. D. Wilson, *United Irishmen, United States: Immigrant Radicals in the Early Republic* (Ithaca, NY and London: Cornell University Press, 1998), pp. 160–1.
72. Our historical understanding, however, is admittedly hampered by the lack of ethnographic records from before 1800 and the lack of consistent and inclusive (if still imperfect) ethnographic techniques until the last few decades. Despite the glimpses afforded us by the collections of Bunting, Petrie, Joyce and others and the accounts left by commentators like James Arbuckle, Patrick Kennedy, Crofton Croker and Gerald Griffin, our conclusions about whether certain songs were popular, however temporarily, for much of Ireland during the eighteenth century, must remain tentative.
73. See especially, 'A Mother', 'Clay', 'Two Gallants' and 'The Dead'.
74. J. Ó Duibheannaigh, personal interview, 6 October 2004.
75. Bronson, *The Ballad as Song*, p. 105.
76. Munnelly, *The Mount Callan Garland*, pp. 124–6.
77. Shields, *Narrative Singing*, p. 153.
78. Byrne, recorded interview, 20 July 2002. Packie's view on this particular song is shared by some outside the tradition, as well.
79. Byrne, personal interview, 20 August 2004. Compare this to Almeda Riddle's statement that 'I never change anything just to be changing, but I know that songs are supposed to make good sense' (Wolf, 'Folksingers and the Re-Creation of Folksong'). Compare also the view of Scottish singer Cameron Turriff, who felt that 'he could not "know" [a] song completely, or be able to sing it, until he had recovered every stanza from various sources' (J. Porter, 'The Traditional Ballad: Requickened Text or Performative Genre?' *Scottish Studies Review*, 4:1 (2003), p. 31).

80. Shields, *Narrative Singing*, p. 154.
81. Shields, *Narrative Singing*, p. 148.
82. Shields, 'Literacy', p. 154. David Mason Greene demonstrates the same kind of textual fidelity to a printed original in American oral tradition in his discussion of a British broadside 'apparently at the mercy of oral transmission for close to a hundred and fifty years, continuing in the main to adhere slavishly to a known printed prototype'. See Greene, '"The Lady and the Dragoon": A Broadside Ballad in Oral Tradition', *Journal of American Folklore* 70:277 (July-September, 1957), pp. 221–30.
83. Byrne, personal interview, 20 August 2004.
84. Henigan, 'Sean-Nós in America', p. 26. Phillips Barry describes a similar altercation in Waterford, at which two singers 'all but came to blows over the proper way to sing "The Old Beggar-Man"'. See P. Barry, 'The Part of the Singer in the Making of Folk Balladry', in M. Leach and T. P. Coffin (eds.), *The Critics and the Ballad* (1961, Carbondale, IL; London: Feffer and Simons, 1973), pp. 61–2.
85. S. Gwynn, *Irish Books and Irish People* (New York: Frederick A. Stokes, c. 1920), p. 57.
86. *Here Is a Health: Songs, Music and Stories of an Ulster Community*, coll. and ed. S. Corcoran (Belfast, Arts Council of Northern Ireland, 1986) [cassette and notes], notes, p. 9.
87. R. Finnegan, 'What Is Oral Poetry, Anyway?', pp. 263–4.
88. Olson, 'Literacy as Metalinguistic Activity', p. 253.
89. See Greene, '"The Lady and the Dragoon"'.
90. D. Buchan, *The Ballad and the Folk*, pp. 219 and 199.
91. Ó Laoire, *On a Rock in the Middle of the Ocean*, pp. 96–123.
92. McCarthy, recorded interview, 28 November 1975.
93. Byrne, recorded interview, 20 July 2002. Arkansas singer Neil Morris told John Quincy Wolf, that 'a singer doesn't deliberately change his songs. He may forget a word here and there and put in other words, but if he remembers a song as his parents sang it, he will not change it' (Wolf, 'Folksingers and the Re-Creation of Folksong').
94. Long, 'Ballad Singers', pp. 240–3.
95. Examples of this are legion. See H. Shields, 'Textual Criticism and Ballad Studies', in A. Clune (ed.), *Dear Far-Voiced Veteran: Essays in Honour of Tom Munnelly* (Miltown Malbay: The Old Kilfarboy Society, 2007), p. 291.
96. H. Shields, 'A History of the "Lass of Aughrim"', pp. 68–70. See also See Coffin, 'Mary Hamilton', pp. 245–56.
97. See Shields, *Shamrock, Rose and Thistle*, pp. 142–4.
98. Shields, *Narrative Singing*, p. 156.
99. Maguire and Morton, *Come Day, Go Day*, p.10.
100. H. Shields, '"The Proper Words"', p. 284.
101. The qualifications reflect the lack of certainty about the song's provenance: while Cinnamond claimed to have learned it from 'an old man that made baskets in the country', Shields believes it possible that he 'remade' the song text (Shields, '"The Proper Words"', p. 289).
102. Shields, '"The Proper Words"', pp. 290–1.
103. Quoted in Shields, '"The Proper Words"', p. 289.
104. Shields, '"The Proper Words"', p. 291.
105. Long, 'Ballad Singers', p. 238.
106. Shields, 'Collecting by Hand', p. 72.
107. Munnelly, recorded interview.

108. Ó Laoire, *On a Rock in the Middle of the Ocean*, pp. 66–70.
109. P. Ua Cnáimhsí, *Róise Rua: An Island Memoir*, trans. J. J. Keaveny (1988, Dublin; Mercier Press, 2009), p. 232.
110. D. Ní Chonaighle, 'Bailiúchán Bhairbre: Uncovering an Island Collection', Society for Musicology in Ireland Conference, Queen's University Belfast, 8 May 2004. See also D. Ní Chonghaile, '"Ag Teacht le Cuan": Irish Traditional Music and the Aran Islands', (PhD dissertation, National University of Ireland, Cork, 2010).
111. Atkinson, 'Folk Songs in Print', p. 461; and V. Gammon, 'Folk Song Collecting in Sussex and Surrey, 1843–1914', *History Workshop*, 10:1 (Autumn, 1980), p. 84.
112. Atkinson, 'Folk Songs in Print', pp. 471 and 468.
113. Musical variation is another matter. The concept of the fixed musical text is a post-Baroque convention.
114. See T. Pettitt, 'The Ballad of Tradition: In Pursuit of a Vernacular Aesthetic', in. T. Cheesman and S. Rieuwerts (eds), *Ballads into Books: The Legacies of Francis James Child* (Bern: Peter Lang, 1997), pp. 118 and 120.
115. E. Ives, '"How Got the Apples In?"', p. 36.
116. De Sola Pinto, *The Common Muse*, p. 15.
117. Maguire and Morton, *Come Day, Go Day*, p. xi.
118. Barry, 'The Part of the Singer', p. 63.
119. Ives, '"How Got the Apples In?"', p. 39.
120. There are a number of examples of even recently copyrighted songs that have variants in the oral tradition – including such recent popular hits as 'The Fields of Athenry'.
121. For examples, see D. Dugaw, 'Anglo-American Folksong Reconsidered: The Interface of Oral and Written Forms', *Western Folklore* 43:2 (1984), pp. 83–103; Greene, '"The Lady and the Dragoon"', pp. 221–30; and V. F. Bose, 'Volkslied-Schlager-Folklore' *Zeitschrift für Volkskunde* 63 (1967), pp. 40–78.
122. For an excellent discussion of this process at work in traditional ballads, see W. E. Richmond, 'Some Effects of Scribal and Typographical Error on Oral Tradition', in M. Leach and T. P. Coffin (eds), *The Critics and the Ballad* (1961, Carbondale, IL; London: Feffer and Simons, 1973), pp. 225–35.
123. Shepard, *The Broadside Ballad*, p. 48.

WORKS CITED

Abhráin Grádh Chúige Connacht: Being the Fourth Chapter of the Love Songs of Connacht, ed. D. Hyde (London, 1893, 3rd edn; repr., New York: Barnes and Noble, 1969).

Adams, J. R. R., 'The Poets Laureate of Donegal: Rural Rhymers of the Laggan in the First Decade of the 19th Century', *Ulster Folklife*, 34 (1988), pp. 68–75.

—, *The Printed Word and the Common Man: Popular Culture in Ulster, 1700–1900* (Belfast: Institute of Irish Studies, Queen's University of Belfast, 1987).

—, '"Swine-Tax and Eat-Him-All-Magee": The Hedge Schools and Popular Education in Ireland', in J. S. Donnelly and K. Miller (eds), *Irish Popular Culture, 1650–1850* (Dublin: Irish Academic Press, 1998), pp. 97–117.

Addison, J., R. Steele, and others, *Spectator Papers*, ed. G. Smith, 5 vols (1907, London; repr., J. M. Dent, 1950), vol. 1.

Akenson, D. H., *The Irish Education Experiment: The National System of Education in the Nineteenth Century* (London: Routledge and Kegan Paul, 1970).

Alexander, S., *A Practical Logical Essay on the Syntax of the English Language*, 2nd edn, (Liverpool: C. Bentham & Co., 1830).

Allingham, W., 'Irish Ballad Singers and Irish Street Ballads', *Ceol* 3:1 (1852; repr., 1967), pp. 2–20.

Amhráin Chearbhalláin, The Poems of Carolan, ed. T. Ó Máille (London: Irish Texts Society, 1916).

Amhráin Eoghan Ruaidh Ó Súilleabháin, ed. P. Ua Duinnín (Dublin, 1901).

Amhráin Mhuighe Seóla, ed. E. Bean Mhic Choisdealbha (1923; Bealdangan: Cló Iar-Chonnachta, 1990).

Amhráin Sheagháin Chláraigh Mhic Dhomhnaill, ed. P. Ua Duinnín (Dublin: Connradh na Gaedhilge, 1902).

Andersen, F. G. and T. Pettit, 'Mrs. Brown of Falkland: A Singer of Tales?', *Journal of American Folklore*, 92:363 (January–March, 1979), pp. 1–24.

Antaine Raiftearaí: Amhráin agus Dánta, ed. C. Ó Coighligh (Dublin: An Clóchomhar, 1987).

Around the Hills of Clare, rec. and ed. J. Carroll and P. McKenzie (Musical Traditions Records MTCD331–2, 2004) [CD and booklet].

Atkinson, D., 'Folk Songs in Print: Text and Tradition', *Folk Music Journal*, 8:4 (2004), pp. 456–83.

Bailey, N. *An Universal Etymological Dictionary* (J. Darby, etc.: London, 1928).

Barnard, T., 'Learning, the Learned and Literacy in Ireland, c. 1660–1760', in T. Barnard, D. Ó Cróinín and K. Simms (eds), *'A Miracle of Learning': Studies in Manuscripts and Irish Learning: Essays in Honour of William O'Sullivan* (Aldershot: Ashgate,1998), pp. 209–35.

Barry, P. 'Irish Folk-Song', in M. Leach and T. P. Coffin (eds), *The Critics and the Ballad* (1961; repr., Carbondale, IL: Southern Illinois University Press, 1973), pp. 59–76.

Ben-Amos, D., 'Toward a Definition of Folklore in Context', *Journal of American Folklore*, 84 (1971), pp. 3–15.

Binchy, D. A., 'The Background of Early Irish Literature', *Studia Hibernica*, 1 (1961), pp. 7–18.

Blankenhorn, V., *Irish Song-Craft and Metrical Practice Since 1600* (Lewiston, NY and Lampeter: Edwin Mellen, 2003).

Boase, R., *The Origin and Meaning of Courtly Love: A Critical Study of European Scholarship* (Manchester: University of Manchester Press, 1977).

The Book of Magauran: Leabhar Mhéig Shamhradháin, ed. L. McKenna (Dublin: 1947).

The Book of O'Hara: Leabhar Í Eadhra, ed. L. McKenna (1951; Dublin: Institute for Advanced Studies, 1980).

Bose, V. F., 'Volkslied-Schlager-Folklore' *Zeitschrift für Volkskunde* 63 (1967), pp. 40–78.

Bourke, A. (=Partridge, A.), 'More in Anger Than in Sorrow: Irish Women's Lament Poetry', in J. N. Radner (ed.), *Feminist Message: Coding in Women's Folk Culture* (Urbana, Chicago, IL: University of Illinois Press, 1993), pp. 160–82.

—, 'Performing, Not Writing: The Reception of an Irish Woman's Lament' in Y. Prins and M. Schreiber (eds), *Dwelling in Possibility: Women Poets and Critics on Poetry* (Ithaca, NY: Cornell University Press, 1997), pp. 132–46.

Boyle, V., personal conversation, 25 August 2004, Miltown Malbay, Co. Clare, Ireland.

Breatnach, P. A., 'Marbhna Aodha Ruaidh Uí Dhomhnaill', *Éigse*, 15:1 (Summer 1973), pp. 31–50.

—, 'Múnlaí Véarsaíocht Rithimiúil na Nua-Ghaeilge', in P. de Brún, S. Ó Coileáin and P. Ó Riain (eds), *Folia Gadelica* (Cork: Cork University Press, 1983), pp. 54–71.

—, 'Oral and Written Transmission of Poetry in the Eighteenth Century', *Eighteenth Century Ireland*, 2 (1987), pp. 51–72.

—, 'Form and Continuity in Later Irish Verse Tradition', *Ériu*, 44 (1993), pp. 125–38.

—, 'The Aesthetics of Irish Bardic Composition: An Analysis of *Fuaras Iongnadh, a Fhir Chumainn* by Fearghal Óg Mac an Bhaird', *Cambrian Medieval Celtic Studies*, 42 (Winter, 2001), p. 52.

Breatnach, R. A., 'The End of a Tradition: A Survey of Eighteenth Century Gaelic Literature', *Studia Hibernica*, 1 (1961), pp. 128–50.

—, 'A Musical Link between Dán and Amhrán', *Ceol: A Journal of Irish Music*, 4:2 (1981), pp. 102–9.

Brennan, B., *Máire Bhuí Ní Laoire: A Poet of Her People* (Cork: Collins Press, 2000).

Brennan, H., *The Story of Irish Dance* (1999, Dingle; Lanham, MD: Roberts Rinehart, 2001).

Brenan, M., *Schools of Kildare and Leighlin A.D. 1775–1835* (Dublin: M. H. Gill and Son, 1935).

Bromwich, R., 'The Keen for Art O'Leary: Its Background and Its Place in the Tradition of Gaelic Keening', *Éigse*, 5:4 (Winter 1947–8), pp. 236–52.

Bronson, B. H., *The Ballad as Song* (Berkeley and Los Angeles, CA: University of California Press, 1969), pp. 64–78.

Bruford, A., *Gaelic Folk-Tales and Mediaeval Romances: A Study of the Early Modern Irish Romantic Tales and their Oral Derivatives* (Dublin: Folklore of Ireland Society, 1969).

—, 'The Singing of Fenian and Similar Lays in Scotland', in H. Shields, *Ballad Research* (Dublin: Folk Music Society of Ireland, 1986), pp. 55–70.

—, 'Oral and Literary Fenian Tales', in B. Almqvist, S. Ó Catháin and P. Ó Héalaí, *The Heroic Process: Form, Function, and Fantasy in Folk Epic: The Proceedings of the International Folk Epic Conference, University College Dublin, 2–6 September 1985* (Dunleary: Glendale Press, 1987), pp. 25–65.

—, 'Song and Recitation in Early Ireland', *Celtica*, 21 (1990), pp. 61–74.

Brunvand, J., *The Study of American Folklore: An Introduction*, 2nd edn (New York: W. W. Norton, 1978).

Buchan, D., *The Ballad and the Folk* (London and Boston, MA: Routledge and Kegan Paul, 1972).

—, 'Oral Tradition and Literary Tradition', in D. Dugaw (ed.), *The Anglo-American Ballad: A Folklore Casebook* (New York: Garland, 1995), pp. 208–22.

Buckley, A. 'Musical Instruments in Ireland from the 9th to the 14th centuries: A Review of the Organological Evidence', in G. Gillen and H. White (eds) *Irish Musical Studies*, 1, (Blackrock: Irish Academic Press 1990).

Burke, W. P., *The Irish Priests in the Penal Times, 1660–1760* (Waterford: Irish University Press, 1968), pp. 394–6.

Byrne, P. M., recorded interview, 20 July 2002, Ardara, County Donegal, Ireland.

—, recorded interview, 20 August 2004, Ardara, County Donegal, Ireland.

—, personal inverview, 20 August 2004, Ardara, County Donegal, Ireland.

Cahill, E., 'The Native Schools of Ireland in the Penal Era', *The Irish Ecclesiastical Record*, 55 (1940), pp. 16–28.

Callaghan, J., personal interview, 13 August 2004, Roslea, County Fermanagh, Ireland.

Carleton, W., *Traits & Stories of the Irish Peasantry*, 2 vols (London: William Tegg, 1865).

—, *The Autobiography of William Carleton* (London: Downey, 1896); rev. edn, London: MacGibbon & Kee, 1968).

Carney, J., *Studies in Irish Literature and History* (Dublin: Dublin Institute for Advanced Studies, 1955).

—, 'Introduction', in E. Knott and G. Murphy (eds), *Early Irish Literature* (London: Routledge and Kegan Paul, 1966), pp. 1–17.

—, 'Three Old Accentual Irish Poems', *Ériu*, 22 (1971), pp. 23–80.

Carpenter, A. (ed.), *Verse in English from Eighteenth-Century Ireland* (Cork: Cork University Press, 1998).

Ceolta Gael 2, ed. M. Ó Baoill (Cork and Dublin: Mercier Press, 1986).

Chafe, W., and D. Tannen, 'The Relation between Written and Spoken Language', *Annual Review of Anthropology*, 16 (1987), pp. 383–407.

Chartier, R., *The Cultural Uses of Print in Early Modern France*, trans. L. D. Cochrane (Princeton, NJ: Princeton University Press, 1987).

Child, F. J. (ed.), *English and Scottish Ballads*, 8 vols (Boston: Little, Brown and Company, 1860), vol. 1.

— (ed.), *The English and Scottish Popular Ballads*, 5 vols (Boston, 1882–98; facs., New York: Dover Books, 1965), vol. 1.

Clendinning, K. 'The Armagh Bye-Election of 1753', *Review: Journal of the Craigavon Historical Society* 2:1, at http://www.geocities.com/craigavonhs/rev/clendinningarmaghelection.html [accessed 21 January 2007].

Coffin, T., 'Mary Hamilton and the Anglo-American Ballad as an Art Form', in M. Leach and T. P. Coffin (eds), *The Critics and the Ballad* (1961; Carbondale, IL: Southern Illinois University Press, 1973), pp. 245–56.

Cohane, M. E. and K. S. Goldstein, 'Folksongs and the Ethnography of Singing in Patrick Kennedy's *The Banks of the Boro*', *The Journal of American Folkore*, 109:434 (Autumn 1996), pp. 425–36.

Connell, P., *Parson, Priest and Master: National Education in Co. Meath, 1824–41* (Dublin: Irish Academic Press, 1995).

Connolly, S., 'Translating History: Brian Friel and the Irish Past', in A. J. Peacock (ed.), *The Achievement of Brian Friel*, Ulster Editions and Monographs, 4 (Gerrard's Cross: Colin Smythe, 1993), pp. 149–63.

—, '"Ag Déanamh *Commanding*": Élite Response to Popular Culture, 1660–1850', in James S. Donnelly, Sr, and Kerby A. Miller, *Irish Popular Culture* (Dublin: Irish Academic Press, 1998), pp. 173–200.

Cooke, H., *Henry Cooke's Centenary*, ed. R. Crawford and E. Dunlop (Draperstown, 1888; Ballymena: Braid Books, 1993).

Cathal Buí: Amhráin, ed. B. Ó Buachalla (Dublin: An Clóchamhar, 1975).

Cooper, D., 'Lámh Dearg: Celtic Minstrels and Orange Songsters', 1, *Celtic Cultural Studies, An Interdisciplinary Online Journal* (published online 1999), at http://www.celtic-cultural-studies.com/papers/01/cooper-01.html [accessed 1 March 2007].

Corkery, D., *The Hidden Ireland: A Study of Gaelic Munster in the Eighteenth Century* (1924; Dublin: Gill and Macmillan, 1996).

Crawford, T., 'Lowland Song and Popular Tradition in the Eighteenth Century', in A. Hook (ed.), *The History of Scottish Literature, Vol. 2: 1660–1880* (Aberdeen: Aberdeen University Press, 1987), pp. 123–41.

Croch Suas É, ed. M. Ó Conghaile (Bealdangan: Cló Iar-Chonnachta, 1986).

Croker, C., *The Keen of the South of Ireland*, Early English Poetry, Ballads and Popular Literature of the Middle Ages, vol. 30, (London, 1844; repr. New York: Johnson Reprint, 1965).

—, *Popular Songs of Ireland* (London: Henry Colburn, 1839).

Cullen, L. M., *The Hidden Ireland: Reassessment of a Concept* (1969, Cork; Dublin: Lilliput Press, 1988).

—, 'Patrons, Teachers and Literacy in Irish', in M. Daly and D. Dickson (eds), *The Origins of Popular Literacy in Ireland* (Dublin: Dept. of Modern History, Trinity College, 1990), pp. 15–44.

—, 'The Contemporary and Later Politics of *Caoineadh Airt Uí Laoire*', *Eighteenth-Century Ireland*, 8 (1993), pp. 7–38.

Dánta Aoghagáin Uí Rathaille: The Poems of Egan O'Rahilly, ed. and trans. P. S. Dinneen, The Irish Texts Society, 3 (London: D. Nutt, 1900).

Dánta Phiarais Feiritéir, ed. P. Muldowney (Aubane, Cork: Aubane Historical Society, 1999).

Davies, L. I., 'Orality, Literacy, Popular Culture: An Eighteenth-Century Case Study', *Oral Tradition*, 25:2 (2010), pp. 305–23.

De Brún, P., 'Caoine ar Mhac Fínín Duibh', *Éigse*, 13:3 (Summer 1970), pp. 221–4.

Delargy, J. H., 'The Gaelic Storyteller', *Proceedings of the British Academy*, 31 (1945), pp. 177–221.

De Rís, S., *Peadar Ó Doirnín: a Bheatha agus a Shaothar* (Dublin: Oifig an tSoláthair, 1969).

De Sola Pinto, V., and A. E. Rodway (eds), *The Common Muse* (London: Chatto and Windus, 1957).

Diarmuid na Bolgaighe agus a Chómhursain, ed. S. Ó Súilleabháin (Dublin: Oifig Díolta Foillseacháin Rialtais, 1937).

Doan, J. E., 'The Folksong Tradition of Cearball Ó Dálaigh', *Folklore*, 96:1 (1985), pp. 67–86.

Donoghue, D., 'Orality, Literacy, and Their Discontents', in *New Literary History*, 27.1 (1996), pp. 145–59.

Dorian, H., *The Outer Edge of Ulster: A Memoir of Social Life in Nineteenth-Century Donegal*, ed. B. Mac Suibhne and D. Dickson (Dublin: The Lilliput Press, 2000).

Dowling, P. J., *The Hedge Schools of Ireland*, (London and New York: Longmans, Green and Co., 1935).

—, *A History of Irish Education, A Study in Conflicts of Loyalty* (Cork: The Mercier Press, 1971).

Dugaw, D., 'Anglo-American Folksong Reconsidered: The Interface of Oral and Written Forms', *Western Folklore* 43:2 (1984), pp. 83–103.

Dumville, D., review of K. McCone, *Pagan Past and Christian Present in Early Irish Literature* (Maynooth, 2000), in *Peritia*, 10 (1996), pp. 389–98.

Edgeworth, M., *Castle Rackrent*, ed. George Watson (1964; Oxford and New York: Oxford University Press, 1999).

Eighteenth-Century Verse, ed. R. Lonsdale (1984; Oxford: Oxford University Press, 1987).

Fallon, P. K., *Printing, Literacy, and Education in 18th-Century Ireland: Why the Irish Speak English* (Lewiston, NY: Edwin Mellen Press, 2005).

The Field Day Anthology of Irish Writing: Irish Women's Writing and Traditions, ed. A. Bourke and others, 5 vols (Cork: Cork University Press, in association with Field Day; New York: New York University Press, 2002), vol 5.

Finnegan, R., *Oral Poetry: Its Nature, Significance and Social Context* (Cambridge: Cambridge University Press, 1977).

—, 'What Is Oral Literature, Anyway? Comments in the Light of Some African and Other Comparative Material', in J. M. Foley (ed.), *Oral-Formulaic Theory: A Folklore Casebook* (New York: Garland Publications, 1985), pp. 243–82.

—, *Literacy and Orality: Studies in the Technology of Communication* (Oxford: Blackwell, 1988).

Flower, R., *The Irish Tradition* (Oxford, 1947; Dublin: The Lilliput Press, 1994).

Foley, J. M. (ed.), 'Introduction', *Oral Tradition in Literature: Interpretation in Context* (Columbia, MO: University of Missouri Press, 1986), pp. 1–18.

—, *The Theory of Oral Composition: History and Methodology* (Bloomington, IN: University of Indiana Press, 1988).

—, *Traditional Oral Epic: The 'Odyssey', 'Beowulf', and the Serbo-Croatian Return Song* (Berkeley and Los Angeles, CA: University of California Press, 1990).

Foley, W. A., 'Literacy', in *Anthropological Linguistics: An Introduction* (Malden, MA: Blackwell Publishers, 1997), pp. 417–34.

Folksongs of Britain and Ireland, ed. Peter Kennedy (London: Cassell, 1975; London and New York: Oak Publications,1984).

Fox, A., *Oral and Literate Culture in England 1500–1700*, Oxford Studies in Social History (Oxford: Oxford University Press, 2000).

Friedman, A., *The Ballad Revival: Studies in the Influence of Popular on Sophisticated Poetry* (Chicago, IL: University of Chicago Press, 1961).

—, 'The Oral-Formulaic Theory of Balladry – A Re-Rebuttal', in J. Porter (ed.), *The Ballad Image: Essays presented to Bertrand Harris Bronson* (Los Angeles, CA: Center for the Study of Comparative Folklore and Mythology, University of California, 1983), pp. 215–40.

Friedman, A. (ed.), *The Viking Book of Folk Ballads of the English-Speaking World* (New York: The Viking Press, 1956).

Gagey, E. M., *Ballad Opera* (New York and London: Benjamin Blom, 1937).

Gammon, V., 'Folk Song Collecting in Sussex and Surrey, 1843–1914', *History Workshop*, 10:1 (Autumn, 1980), pp. 61–89.

Gillespie, R., 'Reading the Bible in Seventeenth-Century Ireland', in B. Cunningham and M. Kennedy (eds), *The Experience of Reading: Irish Historical Perspectives* (Dublin: Rare Books Group of the Library Association of Ireland, 1999), pp. 10–38.

Gillies, W. 'Music and Gaelic Strict-Metre Poetry', *Studia Celtica*, 44 (2010), pp. 111–34.

Glassie, H., *Passing the Time in Ballymenone: Culture and History of an Ulster Community* (Philadelphia, PA: University of Pennsylvania Press, 1982).

Goldsmith, Oliver, *She Stoops To Conquer, or The Mistakes of a Night*, 3rd edn (London: F. Newbery, 1773).

Goody, J., and I. Watt, 'The Consequences of Literacy' in J. Goody (ed.), *Literacy in Traditional Societies* (Cambridge: Cambridge University Press, 1968), pp. 27–68.

Greene, D. M., '"The Lady and the Dragoon": A Broadside Ballad in Oral Tradition'. *Journal of American Folklore*, 70:277 (July–September 1957), pp. 221–30.

Gwynn, E. J., 'An Irish Penitential', *Ériu*, 7 (1914), pp. 121–95.

Gwynn, S., *Irish Books and Irish People* (New York: Frederick A. Stokes, c. 1920).

Hall, S. C. *Ireland: Its Scenery and Character*, 3 vols (London, 1841–3), vol. 1.

Hall, S. C. *Hall's Ireland: Mr and Mrs Hall's Tour of 1840*, ed. M. Scott, 2 vols (cond. edn, London and Syndey: Sphere Books, 1984), vol. 2.

Harte, F. (ed.), *Songs of Dublin* (Dublin, 1978; Cork: Ossian Publications, 1993).

Havelock, E. A., *The Literate Revolution in Greece and its Cultural Consequences* (Princeton, NJ: Princeton University Press, 1982).

—, 'Orality and Literacy, an Overview', *Language and Communication*, 9:2–3 (1989), pp. 87–98.

Hayes, K., recorded interview, 21 July 2004. Coor, County Clare, Ireland.

Heaney, J., *Joe Heaney: The Road from Connemara* (Inverin: Cló Iar-Chonnachta Teo, 2000) [2-vol. CD set and booklet].

Henigan, J., '*Sean-Nós* in America: A Study of Two Singers', MA thesis, University of North Carolina at Chapel Hill, 1989.

Here Is a Health: Songs, Music and Stories of an Ulster Community, coll. and ed. S. Corcoran (Belfast, Arts Council of Northern Ireland, 1986) [audiocassette and booklet].

Hibernicus, *The Dublin Weekly Journal*, Saturday, 10 July 1725, pp. 57–8.

—, *The Dublin Weekly Journal*, Saturday, 17 July 1725, pp. 61–2.

Hogg, J., *Domestic Manners of Sir Walter Scott* (Stirling, 1909; repr., Folcroft, PA: Folcroft Library Editions, 1970).

Holmes, J. and L. Graham, *Chaste Muses, Bards and Sages*, Free Reed, FRR007 [LP and notes], notes, 1971.

Hudson, N., *Writing and European Thought, 1600–1830* (Cambridge and New York: Cambridge University Press, 1994).

—, '"Oral Tradition": The Evolution of an Eighteenth-Century Concept', in A. Ribeiro and J. G. Basker (eds), *Tradition in Transition: Women Writers, Marginal Texts, and the Eighteenth-Century Canon* (Oxford: Clarendon Press, 1996), pp. 161–76.

—, 'Challenging Eisenstein: Recent Studies in Print Culture', review of A. Johns, *The Nature of the Book* (Chicago, IL: University of Chicago Press, 2000), and others, in *Eighteenth-Century Life*, 26:2 (Spring 2002), pp. 83–95.

—, 'Constructing Oral Tradition: The Origins of the Concept in Enlightenment Intellectual Culture', in A. Fox and D. Woolf (eds), *The Spoken Word: Oral Culture in Britain, 1500–1850* (Manchester and New York: Manchester University Press, 2002), pp. 240–55.

Hustvedt, S. B., *Ballad Books and Ballad Men* (Cambridge, MA: Harvard University Press, 1930).

Irish Bardic Poetry, ed. O. Bergin, D. Greene and F. Kelly (Dublin: Dublin Institute for Advanced Studies, 1970).

The Irish Liber Hymnorum I, ed. J. H. Bernard and R. Atkinson, Henry Bradshaw Society Series, vols 13–14 (London: Henry Bradshaw Society, 1898), vol. 13.

Irving, W., *Oliver Goldsmith: A Biography* (London: John Murray, 1849).

Ives, E., '"How Got the Apples In?" Individual Creativity and Ballad Tradition', *The Folklore Historian*, 14 (1997), pp. 31–40.

Jackson, K. H., *The Oldest Irish Tradition: A Window on the Iron Age* (Cambridge: Cambridge University Press, 1964).

Joyce, P. W. (ed.), *Old Irish Folk Music and Songs: A Collection of 842 Irish Airs and Songs, Hitherto Unpublished* (London and New York: Longmans, Green and Co., 1909).

—, *English As We Speak It in Ireland* (London: Longmans, Green, & Co.; Dublin: M. H. Gill & Son, 1910).

Katz, R., and E. Katz, 'McLuhan: Where Did He Come From, Where Did He Disappear?' *Canadian Journal of Communication*, 23:3 (1998), at http://www.cjc-online.ca/index.php/journal/article/view/1046 [accessed 15 July 2008].

Kennedy, D., 'Education and the People', in R. B. McDowell, *Social Life in Ireland 1800–45* (Dublin: The Mercier Press, 1957), pp. 57–70.

Kennedy, P., *Evenings in the Duffrey* (Dublin: M'Glashan and Gill, 1869).

—, *The Banks of the Boro: A Chronicle of the County of Wexford* (Dublin, 1875; repr. Enniscorthy: Duffry Press, 1989).

Kiberd, D., *Irish Classics* (Cambridge, MA: Harvard University Press, 2001).

Kierse, S., *Education in the Parish of Killaloe* (Killaloe: Boru Books, 1987).

Knott, E., *Irish Classical Poetry*, 2nd edn (Dublin, 1957; 2nd and rev. repr., Cork: Mercier Press, 1973).

Koon, H., *Colley Cibber: A Biography* (Lexington, KY: University Press of Kentucky, 1986).

Lawless, E. J., 'Oral "Character" and "Literary" Art: A Call for a New Reciprocity between Oral Literature and Folklore', *Western-Folklore*, 44:2 (April 1985), pp. 77–96.

Lecours, A. R., and M. A. Parente, 'A Neurological Point of View on Social Alexia', in D. R. Olson and N. Torrance (eds), *Literacy and Orality* (Cambridge: Cambridge University Press, 1991), pp. 236–50.

Lerer, S. *Inventing English* (New York: Columbia University Press, 2007).

Lindahl, C., 'The Oral Aesthetic and the Bicameral Mind', *Oral Tradition*, 6:1 (1991), pp. 130–6.

—, 'The Oral Undertones of Late Medieval Romance', in W. F. H. Nicolaisen (ed.), *Oral Tradition in the Middle Ages*, Medieval & Renaissance Texts & Studies, 112 (Binghamton, NY: Medieval & Renaissance Texts & Studies, 1995), pp. 59–75.

Lloyd, G. E. R., *Demystifying Mentalities* (Cambridge: Cambridge University Press, 1990).

Long, E., 'Ballad Singers, Ballad Makers and Ballad Etiology', in D. Dugaw (ed.), *The Anglo-American Ballad, A Folklore Casebook* (New York: Garland, 1995), pp. 234–48.

Lord, A., *The Singer of Tales* (Cambridge, MA: Harvard University Press, 1960; New York: Atheneum, 1974).

Lysaght, P., '*Caoineadh os Cionn Coirp*: The Lament for the Dead in Ireland', *Folklore*, 108 (1997), pp. 65–82.

Mac a Liondain, P., *Dánta*, ed. S. Mag Uidhir (Dublin: An Clóchomhar, 1977).

Mac Cana, P., 'Irish Literary Tradition', in B. Ó Cuív (ed.), *A View of the Irish Language* (Dublin: Stationer's Office (1969), pp. 35–46.

—, '*Fianaigecht* in the Pre-Norman Period', in B. Almqvist, S. Ó Catháin and P. Ó Héalaí (eds), *Fiannaíocht: Essays on the Fenian Tradition of Ireland and Scotland* (Dublin: Folklore of Ireland Society, 1987), pp. 75–99.

McCarthy, M., recorded interview, with Jim Carroll and Denis Turner, 28 November 1975, London, England.

—, recorded interview, no date, London, England.

McCaughey, T. 'Performance of *Dán*', *Ériú*, 35 (1984), pp. 39–57.

McCone, K., *Pagan Past and Christian Present in Early Irish Literature*, Maynooth Monographs, 3 (Maynooth: An Sagart, 1990).

Mac Craith, M., *Lorg na hIasachta ar na Dánta Grá* (Dublin: An Clóchomhar, 1989).

Mac Cuarta, S., *Dánta*, ed. S. Ó Gallchóir (Dublin: An Clóchomhar, 1979).

Mac Eoin, G., review of D. A. Binchey (ed.), *Scéla Cano Meic Gartnáin* (Dublin: Dublin Institute for Advanced Studies, 1963) and C. O'Rahilly (ed.), *Cath Finntrágha* (Dublin: Dublin Institute for Advanced Studies, 1962), in *Studia Hibernica* 4 (1964), pp. 244–9.

Mac Eoin, G., review of E. Knott and G. Murphy, *Early Irish Literature* (London, 1966), in *Studia Hibernica*, 7 (1967), pp. 246–7.

Mac Grianna, S., *Ceoltaí agus Seanchas*, ed. I. Ó Searcaigh (Ranafast: Coiste Choláiste Bhríde, 1976).

McFadden, K., recorded interview, 9 August 2002, Bloody Foreland, County Donegal, Ireland.

McKibben, S., 'Angry Laments and Grieving Postcoloniality', in P. J. Mathews (ed.), *New Voices in Irish Criticism* (Dublin: Four Courts Press, 2000), pp. 215–23.

McManus, A., *The Irish Hedge School and its Books, 1695–1831* (Dublin: Four Courts Press, 2002.

Maguire, J., and R. Morton, *Come Day, Go Day, God Send Sunday: The Songs and Life Story, Told in His Own Words, of Traditional Singer and Farmer, John Maguire from Co. Fermanagh* (London: Routledge and Kegan Paul, 1973).

Marx, S. *Youth Against Age: Generational Strife in Renaissance Poetry* (New York: Peter Lang, 1985).

Mayhew, H., *London Labour and the London Poor*, 3 vols (London: G. Woodfall, 1851), vol. 1.

Moloney, C. (ed.), *The Irish Music Manuscripts of Edward Bunting: An Introduction and Catalogue* (Dublin: Irish Traditional Music Archive, 2000).

Montenyohl, E. L., 'Oralities (and Literacies): Comments on the Relationships of Contemporary Folkloristics and Literary Studies', in C. L. Preston (ed.), *Folklore, Literature and Cultural Theory: Collected Essays* (New York: Garland Press, 1995), pp. 240–56.

Moulden, J. (ed.), *Songs of the People: Selections from the Sam Henry Collection, Part One* (Belfast: Blackstaff Press, 1979).

— (ed.), *Songs of Hugh McWilliams, Schoolmaster, 1831* (Portrush: Ulstersongs, 1993).

—, 'The Printed Ballad in Ireland: A Guide to the Popular Printing of Songs in Ireland, 1760–1920', PhD dissertation, National University of Ireland, Galway, 2006.

Munnelly, T. (coll. and ed.), *The Mount Callan Garland: Songs from the Repertoire of Tom Lenihan* (Dublin: Comhairle Bhéaloideas Éireann, 1994) [2-vol. audiocassette set and booklet].

—, recorded interview, 15 July 2004, Miltown Malbay, County Clare, Ireland.

Murphy, G., 'Notes on Aisling Poetry', *Éigse*, 1 (1939), pp. 40–50.

—, *Early Irish Metrics* (1961; repr., Dublin: Royal Irish Academy, 1973).

—, 'Saga and Myth in Early Ireland', in E. Knott and G. Murphy (eds), *Early Irish Literature* (London: Routledge and Kegan Paul, 1966), pp. 95–194.

Murphy, J. A., 'O'Connell and the Gaelic World', in K. B. Nowland and M. R. O'Connell (eds), *Daniel O'Connell: Portrait of a Radical* (New York: Fordham University Press, 1985).

Murphy, M., 'The Ballad Singer and the Role of the Seditious Ballad in Nineteenth-Century Ireland: Dublin Castle's View', *Ulster Folklife*, 25 (1975), pp. 79–102.

Nagy, J. F., *The Wisdom of the Outlaw: The Boyhood Deeds of Finn in Gaelic Narrative Tradition* (Berkeley, CA: University of California Press, 1985).

—, 'Orality in Medieval Irish Narrative', *Oral Tradition*, 1–2 (1986), pp. 272–301.

—, 'Oral Tradition in the *Acallam na Senórach*', in W. F. H. Nicolaisen (ed.), *Oral Tradition in the Middle Ages*, Medieval and Renaissance Texts and Studies, 112 (Binghamton, NY: Medieval and Renaissance Texts and Studies, 1995), pp. 77–95.

—, *Conversing with Angels and Ancients: Literary Myths of Medieval Ireland* (Ithaca, NY: Cornell University Press, 1997).

Narasimhan, R., 'Literacy: Its Characterization and Implications', in D. R. Olson and N. Torrance (eds), *Literacy and Orality* (Cambridge: Cambridge University Press, 1991), pp. 177–97.

The New Oxford American Dictionary, ed. E. J. Jewell and F. Abate (Oxford: Oxford University Press, 2001).

Newell, W. W. 'The Study of Folklore', *Transactions of the New York Academy of Sciences*, 9 (1890), pp. 134–36.

Nic Éinrí, Ú. (ed.), *Canfar an Dán: Uilliam English agus a Chairde* (Dingle: An Sagart, 2003).

Ní Dhomhnaill, N., recorded interview, 27 June 1979, Ranafast, Co. Donegal.

Ní Chonaighle, D., 'Bailiúchán Bhairbre: Uncovering an Island Collection', paper, Society for Musicology in Ireland Conference (Queen's University Belfast, 8 May 2004).

Ní Dhonnchadha, M., 'Caoineadh ón Ochtú hAois Déag, Téacs agus Comhthéacs', in M. Ó Briain and P. Ó Héalaí (eds), *Téada Dúchais Aistí in Ómós don Ollamh Breandán Ó Madagáin* (Inverin, Conamara: Cló Iar-Chonnachta, 2002), pp. 189–221.

Ní Mhunghaile, L. 'The Intersection between Oral Tradition, Manuscript, and Print Cultures in Charlotte Brooke's *Reliques of Irish Poetry* (1789), in M. Caball and A. Carpenter (eds), *Oral and Print Cultures in Ireland* (Dublin: Four Courts, 2010), pp. 14–31.

Ní Uallacháin, P., *A Hidden Ulster: People, Songs and Traditions of Oriel* (Dublin: Four Courts Press, 2003).

Ní Urdail, M., *The Scribe in Eighteenth- and Nineteenth-Century Ireland: Motivations and Milieu* (Munster: Nodus Publikationen, 2000).

Nygard, N. O., 'Mrs. Brown's Recollected Ballads', in P. Conroy (ed.), *Ballads and Ballad Research* (Seattle, WA: University of Washington Press, 1978), pp. 68–87.

O'Boyle, S., *The Irish Song Tradition* (Dublin: Gilbert Dalton, 1976).

Ó Buachalla, B., 'The Making of a Cork Jacobite', in P. O'Flanagan and C. G. Buttimer (eds), *Cork History and Society* (Dublin: Geography Publications, 1993), p. 490.

—, *Aisling Ghéar: Na Stiobhartaigh agus an tAos Léinn 1603–1788* (Dublin: An Clóchomhar, 1996).

—, *An Caoine agus an Chaointeoireacht* (Dublin: Cois Life, 1998).

Ó Cadhla, L., *Amhráin ó Shliabh gCua* (Dublin: RTÉ 234, 2000) [CD and notes].

Ó Canainn, T. (ed.), *Down Erin's Lovely Lee: Songs of Cork* (Skerries: Gilbert Dalton, 1978).

Ó Ceallaigh, P., 'The Tunes of the Munster Poets (I)', *Ceol*, 1:1 (1963), pp. 11–13.

—, 'The Tunes of the Munster Poets (II)', *Ceol* 1:2 (1963), pp. 23–4.

Ó Ciosáin, N., *Print and Popular Culture in Ireland, 1750–1850* (Basingstoke:: Macmillan Press; New York: St. Martin's Press, 1997).

Ó Coileáin, S., 'Oral or Literary? Some Strands of the Argument', *Studia Hibernica*, 17–18 (1977–8), pp. 7–35.

—, 'The Irish Lament: An Oral Genre', *Studia Hibernica*, 24 (1988), pp. 97–117.

Ó Concheanainn, T., 'Moll Dubh an Ghleanna', *Éigse*, 11:4 (Autumn 1966), pp. 253–85.

O'Connell, Mrs J. Morgan. *The Last Colonel of the Irish Brigade: Count O'Connell and Old Irish Life at Home and Abroad 1745–1833*, 2 vols (London: Kegan Paul, Trench, Trübner & Co., 1892).

O'Connor, F., *A Short History of Irish Literature* (New York: G. P. Putnam's Sons, 1967).

Ó Cróinín, D. (ed.), *The Songs of Elizabeth Cronin, Traditional Singer* (Dublin: Four Courts, 2000).

Ó Crualaoich, G., 'The "Merry Wake"', in J. S. Donnelly and K. A. Miller (eds), *Irish Popular Culture* (Dublin: Irish Academic Press, 1998), pp. 173–200.

—, *The Book of the Cailleach: Stories of the Wise Woman Healer* (Cork: Cork University Press, 2003).

Ó Cuiv, B., 'An Era of Upheaval', in *Seven Centuries of Irish Learning 1000–1700* (Cork: Mercier, 1971), pp. 115–27.

O'Curry, E., *On the Manners and Customs of the Ancient Irish*, 3 vols (Dublin: Kelly, 1873), vol. 1.

O'Daly, J. (ed.), *Poets and Poetry of Munster* (Dublin: John O'Daly, 1860).

Ó Dónaill, N. (ed.), *Foclóir Gaeilge-Béarla* (Dublin: Oifig an tSoláthair, Rialtas na hÉireann, 1977).

O'Donovan, J. *The Journal of the Kilkenny and South-East of Ireland Archeological Society*, New Series, 2 (Dublin: The University Press, McGlashan and Gill, 1858–9; Dublin: Royal Society of Antiquaries of Ireland, 1997).

Ó Drisceoil, C., *The Spoons Murder and Other Mysteries* (Dublin: Craft Recordings, 2006) [book and CD].

Ó Duibheannaigh, A., recorded interview. 2 July 1979, Ranafast, County Donegal, 1979.

Ó Duibheannaigh, J., recorded interview, 25–26 July 2001, Ranafast, Co. Donegal, Ireland.

—, personal interview, 6 October 2004, Ranafast, County Donegal, Ireland.

Ó hAilín, T., 'Caointe agus Caointeoirí', i, *Feasta*, 23:10 (Eanáir 1971), pp. 7–11.

—, 'Caointe agus Caointeoirí', ii, *Feasta*, 23:11 (Feabhra 1971), pp. 5–9.

Ó hÁinle, C., 'An Ceol san Fhilíocht Chlasaiceach', in P. Ó Fiannachta (ed.), *An Ceol i Litríocht na Gaeilge*, Léachtaí Cholm Cille, 7 (Maynooth: An Sagart, 1976), pp. 31–57.

Ó Hógáin, D., 'Folklore and Literature: 1700–1850', in M. Daly and D. Dickson (eds), *The Origins of Popular Literacy in Ireland* (Dublin: Dept. of Modern History, Trinity College and Department of Modern Irish History, University College Dublin, 1990), pp. 1–13.

Ó hUiginn, R., 'The Background and Development of *Táin Bó Cúailnge*', in J. P. Mallory (ed.), *Aspects of the Táin* (Belfast: Universities Press, 1992), pp. 29–67.

O'Keeffe, J., *The Agreeable Surprise: A Comic Opera, in Two Acts*, 4th edn (London: 1795), p. 6.

Ó Laoire, L., *On a Rock in the Middle of the Ocean: Songs and Singers, Tory Island, Ireland* (2005; Inverin: Cló Iar-Chonnachta, in association with Scarecrow Press, 2007).

Ó Lochlainn, C., *More Irish Street Ballads* (Dublin, 1965; repr., London: Pan Books, 1978).

Olson, D. R., 'Literacy as Metalinguistic Activity', in D. R. Olson and N. Torrance (eds), *Literacy and Orality* (Cambridge: Cambridge University Press, 1991), pp. 251–70.

Ó Madagáin, B., 'Ceol an Chaointe', in B. Ó Madagáin (ed.), *Gnéithe den Chaointearacht* (Dublin: An Clóchomhar, 1978), pp. 30–52.

—, 'Irish Vocal Music', in R. O'Driscoll (ed.), *The Celtic Consciousness* (Portlaoise, 1981; New York: Braziller, 1982), pp. 311–32.

—, 'Functions of Irish Music', *Béaloideas*, 53 (1985), pp. 130–216.

—, 'Song for Emotional Release in the Gaelic Tradition', in P. E. Devine and H. White (eds), *Irish Musical Studies*, 4 (Dublin: Four Courts Press, 1996), pp. 254–75.

—, 'Coibhneas na Filíochta leis an gCeol, 1700–1900', P. Riggs, B. Ó Conchúir and S. Ó Coileáin (eds.) in *Saoi na hÉigse: Aistí in Ómós do Sheán Ó Tuama* (Dublin, 2000), pp. 83–104.

—, *Caointe agus Seancheolta Eile: Keening and Other Old Irish Musics* (Inverin: Cló Iar-Chonnachta, 2005).

Ó Muirgheasa, É. (ed.), *Chéad de Cheoltaibh Uladh* (Dublin, 1915; rev. edn, Newry: Ó Casaide, 1983).

— (ed.), *Dhá Chéad de Cheoltaibh Uladh* (1934; repr., 3rd edn, Dublin: Office of Government Publications, 1974).

Ó Muirí, L. (ed.), *Amhráin Chúige Uladh* (Dundalk, 1927; Dublin: Gilbert Dalton, 1984).

Ó Muirithe, D. (ed.), *An tAmhrán Macarónach* (Dublin: An Clóchomhar, 1980).

—, '"Tho' Not in Full Stile Compleat": Jacobite Songs from Gaelic Manuscript Sources', *Eighteenth Century Ireland*, 6 (1991), pp. 93–103.

—, '"Of English Fayre I Am Scarce Indeed": Amhráin Ghaeilge agus a nAistritheoirí ca. 1700–1800', in *Leachtaí Cholm Cille*, 29 (1999), pp. 138–60.

Ong, W. J., *Interfaces of the Word: Studies in the Evolution of Consciousness and Culture* (Ithaca, NY: Cornell University Press, 1977).

—, *Orality and Literacy: The Technologizing of the Word* (New York, 1982; repr., London: Routledge, 2000).

—, 'Writing Is a Humanizing Technology', *ADE Bulletin*, 74 (Spring 1983), pp. 13–16.

—, 'Writing Is a Technology that Restructures Thought', in G. Baumann (ed.), *The Written Word: Literacy in Transition* (Oxford: Clarendon Press, 1986), pp. 23–50.

Opie, I. and P. (eds), *The Oxford Dictionary of Nursery Rhymes* (1951; 2nd edn, Oxford: Oxford University Press, 1997).

Oring, E., 'On the Concept of Folklore', in E. Oring (ed.), *Folk Groups and Folklore Genres* (Logan, UT: Utah State University Press, 1986), pp. 1–22.

Ó Súilleabháin, S., 'The Keening of the Dead', in *Irish Wake Amusements*, 4th repr., (1967, Dublin, 1961; Dublin: Mercier Press, 1979), pp. 130–45.

—, 'Irish Oral Tradition', in B. Ó Cuív (ed.), *A View of the Irish Language* (Dublin: Stationery Office, Rialtas na hÉireann, 1969), pp. 47–56.

O'Sullivan, D., 'A Courtly Poem for Sir Richard Cox', *Éigse*, 4 (1943–4), pp. 284–7.

—, *Songs of the Irish: An Anthology of Irish Folk Music and Poetry with English Verse Translations* (New York, 1960; Dublin and Cork: Mercier Press, 1960).

Ó Tuama, S., *An Grá in Amhráin na nDaoine: Léiriú Téamúil* (1960; Dublin: An Clóchomhar, 1978).

— (ed.), *Caoineadh Airt Uí Laoghaire* (1961; Dublin: An Clóchomhar, 1993).

—, 'Gaelic Culture in Crisis: The Literary Response 1600–1850', in T. Bartlett, C. Curtin and others (eds), *Irish Studies: A General Introduction* (Dublin: Gill and MacMillan, 1988), pp. 28–43.

—, 'The Lament for Art O'Leary', in *Repossessions* (Cork: Cork University Press, 1995), pp. 78–100.

—, 'Love in Irish Folksong', in *Repossessions* (Cork: Cork University Press, 1995), pp. 134–58.

Ó Tuama, S. (ed.) and T. Kinsella (contrib.) *An Duanaire 1600–1900: Poems of the Dispossessed*, repr. 1985 (1981; Mountrath: The Dolmen Press).

Paddy's Resource: Being a Collection of Modern and Patriotic Songs, Toasts and Sentiments, Compiled for the Use of all Firm Patriots (Philadelphia, PA: T. Stevens, 1796).

Partridge, A. (=Bourke, A.), 'Caoineadh na dTrí Muire agus an Chaointeoireacht', in B. Ó Madagáin (ed.), *Gnéithe den Chaointeoireacht* (Dublin: An Clóchomhar, 1978), pp. 67–81.

—, 'Wild Men and Wailing Women', *Éigse*, 18:1 (1980), pp. 25–37.

— '"Is Beo Duine tar éis a Bhuailte": Caoineadh Magaidh as Béara', *Sinsear*, 3 (1981), pp. 70–6.

Pattanayak, D. P., 'Literacy: An Instrument of Oppression', in D. R. Olson and N. Torrance (eds), *Literacy and Orality* (Cambridge: Cambridge University Press, 1991), pp. 105–8.

Peadar Ó Dornín: Amhráin, ed. B. Ó Buachalla (Dublin: An Clóchomhar, 1970).

The Petrie Collection of the Ancient Music of Ireland, ed. D. Cooper and L. Ó Laoire (Cork: Cork University Press, 2002).

Pettitt, T. 'The Ballad of Tradition: In Pursuit of a Vernacular Aesthetic', in. T. Cheesman and S. Rieuwerts (eds), *Ballads into Books: The Legacies of Francis James Child* (Bern: Peter Lang, 1997).

Phillips, J., *The New World of Words; or Universal English Dictionary*, 6th edn (London, 1706).

Pincombe, M., and C. Shrank (eds), *The Oxford Handbook of Tudor Literature: 1485–1603*, (Oxford: Oxford University Press, 2009).

Pinkerton, J., 'A Dissertation on the Oral Tradition of Poetry', *Select Scottish Ballads*, Vol. I (London: J. Nichols, 1783).

Poems on the O'Reillys, ed. J. Carney (Dublin: The Dublin Institute for Advanced Studies, 1950).

Porter, J., 'The Traditional Ballad: Requickened Text or Performative Genre?' *Scottish Studies Review*, 4:1 (2003).

Raby, F. J. E., *A History of Secular Latin Poetry in the Middle Ages*, 2 vols (1934; Oxford: The Clarendon Press, 1957), vol. 1.

Raven, D. 'How Not to Explain the Great Divide', *Social Science Information* 40:3 (2001), pp. 373–409.

Reay, B., *Popular Cultures in England 1550–1750*, Themes in British Social History (New York: Longman, 1988).

Richmond, W. E., 'Some Effects of Scribal and Typographical Error on Oral Tradition', in M. Leach and T. P. Coffin (eds), *The Critics and the Ballad* (Carbondale, IL: Southern Illinois University Press, 1961; London: Feffer and Simons, 1973), pp. 225–35.

Róise na nAmhrán: Songs of a Donegal Woman (Dublin: RTÉ 178, 1994) [CD and notes].

Rosenberg, B., 'The Complexity of Oral Tradition', *Oral Tradition*, 2:1 (1987), pp. 73–90.

—, *Can These Bones Live? The Art of the American Folk Preacher* (rev. edn, Urbana and Chicago, IL: University of Illinois Press, 1988).

Ross, J., 'The Sub-Literary Tradition in Scottish-Gaelic Song Poetry', part 2, *Éigse*, 8:1 (Autumn 1955), pp. 1–17.

Rubsamen, W. H. (ed.), *Irish Ballad Operas and Burlesques II* (facs., New York and London: Garland, 1974).

Shepard, L., *The Broadside Ballad: A Study in Origins and Meaning* (London, 1962; Hatboro, PA: Legacy Books, 1978).

—, *The History of Street Literature* (Newton Abbot: David and Charles, 1973).

Shields, H. 'Singing Traditions of a Bilingual Parish in North-West Ireland', *Yearbook of the International Folk Music Council*, 3 (1971), pp. 109–19.

—, '"The Proper Words": A Discussion on Folk Song and Literary Poetry', *Irish University Review*, 5 (1975), pp. 274–91.

—, *Shamrock, Rose and Thistle: Folk Singing in North Derry* (Belfast: Blackstaff Press, 1981).

—, 'Literacy and the Ballad Genre in Ireland', *Aspecten van het Europese Marktlied: 12d Internationale Volksballadenconferentie, 1981* (Brussels: Centrum voor Vlaamse Volkscultur, 1982), pp. 151–65.

—, 'Impossibles in Ballad Style', in J. Porter (ed.), *The Ballad Image: Essays Presented to Bertrand Harris Bronson* (Los Angeles, CA: Center for the Study of Comparative Folklore and Mythology, University of California, 1983), p. 192.

—, *Oliver Goldsmith and Popular Song in 18th-Century Dublin* (Dublin: Folk Music Society of Ireland, 1985).

—, 'Ballads, Ballad-Singing and Ballad-Selling', in *Popular Music in 18th-Century Dublin* (Dublin: Folk Music Society of Ireland and Na Píobairí Uillean, 1985), pp. 24–31.

—, 'Collecting Songs "by Hand"', 1954–1966', *Irish Folk Music Studies: Éigse Cheol Tíre*, 5–6 (1986), pp. 61–76.

— (ed.), *Old Dublin Songs* (Dublin: Folk Music Society of Ireland, 1988).

—, 'A History of "The Lass of Aughrim"', in G. Gillen and H. White (eds), *Musicology in Ireland*, Irish Musical Studies, 1 (Dublin: Irish Academic Press, 1990), pp. 58–73.

—, 'Printed Aids to Folk Singing, 1700–1900', in M. Daly and D. Dickson (eds), *The Origins of Popular Literacy in Ireland* (Dublin, 1990), pp. 139–52.

—, *Narrative Singing in Ireland: Lays, Ballads, Come-All-Yes and Other Songs* (Blackrock: Irish Academic Press, 1993).

—, 'Textual Criticism and Ballad Studies', in A. Clune (ed.), *Dear Far-Voiced Veteran: Essays in Honour of Tom Munnelly* (Miltown Malbay: The Old Kilfarboy Society, 2007), p. 291.

Shields, H., and T. Munnelly, 'Scots Ballad Influences in Ireland', *Ceol Tíre* (October 1979), pp. 3–22.

Simms, K., 'The Poet as Chieftain's Widow: Bardic Elegies', in D. Ó Corráin, L. Breatnach and K. McCone (eds), *Sages, Saints and Storytellers: Celtic Studies in Honour of Professor James Carney*, Maynooth Monographs, 2 (Maynooth: An Sagart, 1989), pp. 400–11.

—, 'Literacy and the Irish Bards', in H. Pryce (ed.), *Literacy in Medieval Celtic Societies* (Cambridge: Cambridge University Press, 1998), pp. 238–58.

Slotkin, E., 'Medieval Irish Scribes and Fixed Texts', *Éigse*, 17:4 (Winter 1978–9), pp. 437–50.

Songs of Aran, coll. Sydney Robertson Cowell (Folkways Records, FW 04002,1957) [CD and notes].

Stanyhurst, R., *Translation of the First Four Books of the Aeneis of P. Vergilius Maro: With Other Poetical Devices Thereto Annexed, 1582*, ed. E. Arber (Westminster: Archibald Constable & Co., 1895).

Thomas, K., 'The Meaning of Literacy in Early Modern England', in G. Baumann (ed.), *The Written Word: Literacy in Transition* (Oxford: Oxford University Press, 1986), pp. 97–131.

Thomson, D., *An Introduction to Gaelic Poetry* (New York: St. Martin's Press, 1974).

Travis, J., *Early Celtic Versecraft* (Ithaca, NY: Cornell University Press, 1973).

Tunney, P., *The Stone Fiddle* (Dublin: Gilbert Dalton, 1979).

Ua Cnáimhsí, P., *Róise Rua: An Island Memoir*, trans. J. J. Keaveny (Dublin, 1988; Mercier Press, 2009).

Ward, E., *Wine and Wisdom: or, the Tipling Philosophers. A Lyrick Poem* (London: J. Woodward in Scalding-Ally over-against Stocks-Market, 1710).

Wenham, L. P., *Frances L'Anson, The Lass of Richmond Hill* (Richmond, North Yorkshire: L. P. Wenham, 1986).

Whelan, K., *The Tree of Liberty: Radicalism, Catholicism and the Construction of Irish Identity 1760–1830* (Notre Dame, IN: University of Notre Dame Press, 1996).

—, 'The Cultural Effects of the Famine', in J. Cleary and C. Connolly (eds), *The Cambridge Companion to Modern Irish Culture* (Cambridge: Cambridge University Press, 2005), pp. 137–54.

Whitfield, N. 'Lyres Decorated with Snakes, Birds and Hounds in *Táin Bó Fraích*', in P. Harbison and V. Hall, *A Carnival of Learning: Essays to Honour George Cunningham* (Roscrea: Cistercian Press, 2012).

Wilgus, D. K., 'Irish Traditional Narrative Songs in English: 1800–1916', in D. J. Casey and R. E. Rhodes (eds), *Views of the Irish Peasantry 1800–1916* (Hamden, CT: Archon Books, 1977), pp. 107–28.

Williams, N. (ed.), *Riocard Bairéad: Amhráin* (Dublin: An Clóchomhar, 1978).

—, 'Gaelic Texts and English Script', in M. Caball and A. Carpenter (eds), *Oral and Print Cultures in Ireland, 1600–1900* (Dublin: Four Courts Press, 2010).

Wilson, D., *United Irishmen, United States: Immigrant Radicals in the Early Republic* (Ithaca, NY and London: Cornell University Press, 1998).

Wolf, J. Q., 'Folksingers and the Re-Creation of Folksong' *Western Folklore* 26:2 (April 1967), at http://web.lyon.edu/wolfcollection/re-creation.htm [accessed 15 August 2011].

World Library of Folk and Primitive Music, v. 2: Ireland, track 28 (Rounder 1742, 1998) [CD and notes].

Wood, R. *An Essay on the Origianl Genius and Writings of Homer* (London: H. Hughs, 1775).

Yeats, G., 'The Rediscovery of Carolan', in B. Harris and G. Freyer (eds), *Integrating Tradition: The Achievement of Seán Ó Riada* (Ballina/Chester Springs, PA: Irish Humanities Centre/Dufour Editions, 1981).

—, *The Harp of Ireland: The Belfast Harpers' Festival, 1792 and the Saving of Ireland's Harp Music by Edward Bunting* (Dalkey: Belfast Harpers' Bicentenary, 1992).

Zimmermann, G. D., *Songs of Irish Rebellion: Political Street Ballads and Rebl Songs 1780–1890* (Hatboro, PA: Folklore Associates, 1967).

—, *The Irish Storyteller* (Dublin: Four Courts Press, 2001).

Zumthor, P., *Histoire Littéraire de la France Médiévale* (1954; Génève: Slatkine Reprints, 1973).

Archives Consulted:

British Library, Early Printed Books, London, England

Linen Hall Library, Belfast, Ireland

Queen's University, Special Collections, Belfast, Ireland

Trinity College Library, Early Printed Books, Dublin, Ireland

Royal Irish Academy, Dublin, Ireland

Ulster Museum, Belfast, Ireland

INDEX

Acallam na Senórach, 21–2
Addison, Joseph, 4–5, 153, 156
Aeneid, The, 18, 145
aesthetics, 58–63, 183–6
    community, 189–90, 198, 200–5
    individual, 59–60, 204–5
    oral/vernacular, 195–204
    role of melody, 52, 195
    see also brí
agallamh beirte, 94, 98
aisling (*aislingí*), 2, 127–30, 134, 138, 143, 149, 168
    allegorical/political, 41–4, 45, 122–4
    love (fairy), 41, 124–5
    and *reverdie, pastourelle*, 124–5
    see also hedge schoolmaster song
'Aithreachas Chathail Bhuí', 81, 86
Allingham, William, 172, 203
amhrán (song-poetry) *see* metres, Irish, accentual
'Amhrán Iomartha', 81, 91
Amman, Conrad, 5
'Anach Cuain', 90, 182
'Ancient Philosophers Vindicated against Tipling, The', 162
Arbuckle, James *see* Hibernicus
Arnold, Matthew, 50
athláech theory, 19–20, 24
    see also multiforms; transitional texts
Atkinson, David, 203

Baggott, James, 122
Bailey, Nathan (*Dictionary*), 152
Bairéad, Riocard, 45, 122, 159
ballads, broadside (printed narrative), 151–4, 168, 169, 176, 177, 182, 184, 194, 200, 204

ballads, Child ('oral'/'traditional'), 165, 176, 181, 183, 202, 203
    and oral-formulaic theory, 10–11, 13, 63
ballads, parlour, 59, 181–2, 183, 202–3, 204, 205
ballads, printed
    and Victorian diction, 185–6, 196
    broadside *see* ballads, broadside
    definitions, 151–3
    distribution and availability of, 154–5, 158–61, 165–8, 173–8
    Irish linguistic influence on, 169–71
    influence of Irish verse forms on 138–9, 168–9, 171, 186
    localization of, 189, 200
    market for, 155–6, 162, 164–5, 167
    naturalization of, 168–73, 176–8
    see also diction
ballads, printed, genres
    American minstrel, 182
    cante-fables, 182
    drinking, 153, 162–3, 164, 166, 169, 182, 185
    Dublin slang songs, 166, 167
    elegies, 161–2
    hunting, 141–2, 155, 162, 166, 169, 172
    hybrid, 142–4
    macaronic, 170
    music hall, 177, 182, 197, 202, 203, 205
    narrative *see* ballads, broadside
    pleasure garden (Vauxhall), 141–3, 163, 166, 177, 196
    political *see* topical
    sporting, 121, 153, 162, 168, 182
    topical, 158–60, 163, 167, 196
    theatre, 153, 163–6, 167

topical, 153, 155–6, 158–62, 163, 167, 196
translations, 171, 182
'ballad/ballet books', 152, 190–2
ballad opera, 162–3, 170
ballad printers, 154–5, 158, 167, 169, 173, 175, 176
ballad-singers/sellers
    accounts of, 154–5, 173–5, 195
    twentieth century, 187, 190, 197
    see also McCarthy, Mikeen
'Banks of the Lee, The', 186
barántas, 31
bard, 23, 27–30, 37, 42, 50
bardic poetry
    composition of, 30
    decline of, 27, 31–40
    loss of patronage for, 33, 37–8
    performance of, 27–31
    schools/training, 22, 30–1, 35, 120
bardism, 4–5
Barry, Phillips, 204
bean chaointe, 86, 90
Bean Mhic Grianna, Róise, 51
Behan, Dominic, 194
Ben-Amos, Dan, 12
beochaoineadh, 90
Bernstein, Basil, 10, 95, 203
'Bhean Chaointe, An', 86, 90
'Blackbird, or the Flower of England flown, The', 123, 156, 171, 177
Blankenhorn, Virginia, 31, 32, 40, 53, 76
Blair, Hugh, 14
'Blaris Moor', 123
Blathmac, 84
'Blind Beggar's Daughter of Bednal Green, The', 153, 167, 190, 197
Book of Magauran, The, 85
Book of O'Hara, The: Leabhar Í Eadhra, 85
'Bottle, The', 169
Bourke, Angela, 76, 91, 102, 104, 106,
Boyle, Vincie, 188
'Boys of Mullaghbawn, The', 123, 139
Breatnach, Pádraig A., 29–30, 31–2, 33, 46, 53, 70, 100
Breatnach, R. A., 39
brí ('significance'), 197
'Brighid Ní'c Fheorais', 126

Bromwich, Rachel, 183, 91
Brooke, Charlotte, 22
Brownlow, William, 159
Bruford, Alan, 16, 19, 20, 22–3, 24–5, 32, 58, 98
Buchan, David, 10, 13, 63, 151, 192, 199, 203
Buile Suibhne, 76
'Bumper Squire Jones', 140, 163
'Bunnán Buí, An', 45, 54–6
Bunting, Edward, 77–8, 80–1, 176
Burns, Robert, 51, 163, 167, 171, 196–7
Butcher, Eddie, 59, 184, 197, 201, 204
Butcher, Robert, 198
Byrne, Packie Manus, 59, 188–91, 197, 199, 201–2, 204

caoine, 83
    see also *caoineadh*
caoineadh (*caointe*), 2, 65, 70–91
    accounts of, 71–4, 76–82, 84, 92–4
    and oral-formulaic theory, 94–103
    as women's genre, 71–2, 74
    beochaoineadh, 90
    conflict, expressed in, 74, 76, 84–5
    features of, 73–6
    improvisation in, 78, 83–4, 91–2
    literary keens, 84, 106–8
    memorization of, 93–4, 97, 100
    motifs of, 74–6, 83
    musical features of, 76–83
    nomenclature for, 70, 83, 100
    performance of, 71–2, 74, 76–84, 93, 95–8, 99–102, 109–10
    reconstructions of, 65, 72–3, 76, 198
    refrain/*gol/caoinan*, 78, 83
    and elegiac tradition, 82–6, 106–10
    and *geltacht* poetry, 76
    rosc, 76
    sound recordings of, 65, 70, 73, 76, 78
    see also *crónán*; death-song; *marbna*
Caoineadh Airt Uí Laoghaire, 65, 76, 90, 91–108
    and oral-formulaic theory, 94–103
    antecedents, 100, 103–4
    historical background, 91, 105
Caoineadh Dhiarmada Mhic Eoghain na Toinne, 95

'Caoineadh na dTrí Muire', 76, 81, 90–1
'Caoineadh Uí Cheallaigh Chluain Leathaní', 87–9
Carey, Henry, 158
Carleton, William, 115, 116, 119
Carney, James, 16-19, 24, 32, 83
Carolan, Turlough, 29, 32, 58, 82, 126, 140, 159
'Castlehyde', 130–1, 177
'Cavalcade: A Poem On the Riding the Franchises, The', 140
ceart, 199–200
   see also fixed text
'Ceo Draíochta, An', 41, 45
chapbooks, 112, 123, 141–2, 147–8, 154, 166, 167, 172, 175, 197
   bibliographic features, 152–3
   see also eight-page songbooks
Charms of Melody, The, 163, 170, 181
'Chevy Chase', 153, 155, 156, 158, 159, 167
Child, Francis James, 151, 152
   English and Scottish Popular Ballads, The, 47, 152
'Children in the Wood, The' ('Babes in the Wood'), 153, 155, 158
Cinnamond, Robert, 201, 204
Coffey, Charles,
   Beggar's Wedding, The, 163, 170
Coffin, Tristram, 53, 58
cóiriú catha see runs
'Colleen Rue, The', 120–1, 138–9, 177–8
Colman, George, 170
Colum, Padraic, 44, 59, 201–2, 204
community singing traditions, 183–205
   communication, 195, 204–5
   aesthetics, 195–200, 202, 204–5
   performance contexts, 187, 190, 195, 199, 204–5
   oral transmission, 194–5
   repertoire, 183–6, 188–90, 196–7, 201–4
   variation in, 198–201, 203–5
   see also singers, aesthetics
conchlann, 69
conflictus, 2, 128-30, 185
Connolly, Sean, 38, 44, 117, 146, 147, 165, 178
Connors, Mickey, 177, 183
Cooke, Henry, 115

Corkery, Daniel, 32, 37, 41, 43, 44, 50–1
'Cottage Boy, The', 141
'Cottage Maid, The', 112, 121, 149
'Cottager's Daughter, The', 142–3
Cotter, James, 100
   elegy for, 103, 161
courts of poetry, 30–1, 38, 100, 122
   see also Prior, Anna
Cowell, Sidney Robertson, 78
Cox, Sir Richard, 103, 120, 154
Cox, Watty, 115
Croker, Crofton, 72, 78, 93–4, 109, 121, 131, 143, 145, 150
crónán, 80
Cronin, Elizabeth, 183
Crowley, Jimmy, 185
'Cruise of the Calabar, The', 184
cruit, 29, 33
   see also harp accompaniment
cruitire, 28–9
   see also harp accompaniment; harpers
Cú Chulainn, 84
cúirteanna filíochta see courts of poetry
Cullen, Louis, 36, 37–8, 40, 43, 44, 95, 103–4, 105, 108, 112, 117
cultural nexuses, 198
   courts of poetry/taverns, 38, 44, 100
   dance, 38
   hedge schools, 44, 146–7
   manuscripts, 22, 38–40
   printed ballads, 166
   theatre, 165

Davis, Thomas, 195
Dawson, Sir Arthur, 140
death-song, 66, 86–91, 100, 109
   and *caoineadh*, 86,
   and *marbhna*, 87–91
   used in context of wakes, 81, 86, 91
   see also caoineadh; *marbhna*
De Búrca, Angela *see* Bourke, Angela
De Montbret, Coquebert, 113
De Noraidh, Liam, 77, 92
Deorchaoineadh na hÉireann, 98
Derricke, John, 27–8
'Deus Meus Adiuva Me', 102
Dibdin, Charles, 166, 178

diction, 3, 35, 44, 97, 149, 201, 204
   in eighteenth-century English song, 140, 184, 204
   in eighteenth-century song, 44, 48–51, 53, 56–7, 61
   in hedge schoolmaster song, 136–9, 140, 143, 149, 150, 185
   in nineteenth-century song, 185–6, 196
   in printed ballads, 168, 182, 185
   see also folksong; linguistic registers
Dinneen, Patrick, 32, 40, 41, 80, 102
'Discussion between Church and Chapel, A', 128–9
'Donncha Bán', 89, 90
Dorian, Hugh, 147
'Do Tharlaigh Inné Orm', 49, 137
Dowling, Patrick J., 113, 117, 120, 121
duanairí (*duanaire*), 30, 31, 38, 39, 40
   see also manuscript tradition, 17th-19th century
'Dublin Baker, The', 168
Duffy, Charles Gavin, 148–9, 150
dúnadh, 70
Dunton, John, 155, 165
D'Urfey, Thomas, 153, 160

Edgeworth, Maria, 165
'Easter Snow', 148
'Eibhlín, a Rúin', 47, 48–9, 163
eighteenth-century Irish-language poets
   as scribes, 31, 38, 39, 40, 53–5, 58
   audience, 34–40, 43–6
   status, 35, 37–8, 170
   transmission of poetry, 30–1, 37–40
eight-page songbooks, 152–3, 166–70, 72–5, 176, 178
   bibliographic features, 166–7
   contents of, 162, 166–72
   cost of, 175
   markets for, 155–6, 158, 162, 164–7
   see also chapbooks
Eisenstein, Elizabeth, 11
elegies *see marbhna*; ballads, printed, genres
'emotional core', 53, 58, 200
   see also 'lyric intensity'
English, Uilliam, 3, 47, 49, 137
'Eóin Búrcach', 87, 90
'Erin's Green Shore', 122

'Excellent New Song Upon His Grace Our good Lord Archbishop of Dublin, An', 158
'Excellent New Song Upon the Late Grand-Jury, An', 159

'Fáinne Geal an Lae', 140
Farquhar, George, 46
Feiritéar, Piaras, 125
Ferguson, Adam, 5
Fiannaíocht, 15, 20–4
   see also lays, Fenian
filí (*file*), 19, 27–9, 33, 37,
Filidhe na Máighe (*The Poets of the Maigue*), 102
'Fill a Rún', 90
Finnegan, Ruth, 3, 6, 9, 11, 12, 97
fixed ('correct') text, 6–7, 11, 13, 18–20, 53, 63, 98, 199–201
   see also ceart
Flight of the Earls, 35
Flight of the Wild Geese, 35
'Flower of Tyrone, The', 134
Foley, John Miles, 7, 97, 109
folklore
   definitions of, 12–13
folksong, 1, 3, 78, 94–9, 201–2, 203
   and anonymity, 1, 47, 51, 63
   and melody, 52
   diction, 48–51, 53, 56–7, 201–4
   floating verses in, 51
   immediacy of, 53
   influence of literary tradition on, 61–2
   lyric vs. narrative in, 47, 52, 58, 95, 98
   stock phrases in, 51–2
   stylistic traits of, 45–7, 48–50, 53, 59
   variation in *see* variation, main entry
   vs. literary poetry, 47–63, 94-9
formula (oral) in, 17–8
   definition of, 6
   ballad commonplaces as formulae, 10, 13, 192
   runs, 18, 22
   in *caointe*/keens, 74, 87, 95–7, 104, 106, 107
   see also community singing traditions; song-types, French; song-types, Irish; *údar an amhráin*

Foster, Stephen, 182
Friedman, Albert, 5, 10, 101, 153

Garrick, David, 166
Gay, John
   Beggar's Opera, The, 46, 163
   'Sweet William's Farewell to Black-Eyed Susan', 167
   "'Twas When the Seas Were Roaring', 153, 176
Gerould, Gordon, 151, 203
'Ghéag dá dTug Mé Grá Di, An', 137
Gibbon, Edward, 5
'Gobbio, The', 172
'Goblet of Wine, The', 169
'goddess routine', 41–3, 124–5
Goldsmith, Oliver, 5, 140
   as ballad composer, 155, 164–5, 178
   'Deserted Village, The', 118
   She Stoops to Conquer, 164
Gormlaidh (daughter of Brian Mág Shamhradháin), 126
Gormlaith (queen), 84, 108
Graham, Len, 145
'Green Linnet, The', 123
Grey, Thomas, 4
Griffin, Gerald, 177-8
'Groves of Blarney, The', 131
Grundtvig, Svend, 154

Haicéad, Pádraigín, 34, 125
Hall, Mr and Mrs Samuel, 83, 92, 94, 148
Hanna, Geordie, 145
harp accompaniment, 28–9, 32, 38
harpers, 29, 32, 38, 50, 66, 77, 82, 137, 140, 178
   see also cruitire
Havelock, Eric, 7–8
Hayes, Kitty, 189
Heaney, Joe, 202
Heath, Shirley Brice, 10, 193
Hebrides (psalm-singing), 78, 80
hedge schoolmasters
   political activities of, 122–3
   as poets, 118
   qualifications of, 117
   reputation of, 117–9
   use of Latin by, 118–21, 128, 132
   use of classical allusion by, 120–1

hedge schoolmaster song
   aisling, 122, 124–5, 127–30, 138, 143–4
   conflictus/altercatio, 2, 128–30, 185
   female praise songs, 125, 127–8,
   macaronic songs, 127, 129, 134–8, 146
   parodies of, 112, 127–8, 131, 137, 146
   pastourelle, 125, 127, 128-9, 143, 169, 182, 197
   place-praise songs, 130–1
   reverdie, 124–5, 127, 128, 130–1, 138–9, 143, 169
   reverdie léannta, 124–5, 128, 149
   translations by, 134–5
   use of classical allusion in, 120–8, 134–8, 142–5, 146–8
   use of Hiberno-English in, 136, 142
   use of Irish verse forms in, 138–9
   use of Latinate English in, 119, 120–1, 136, 138, 143
   see also diction
hedge schools
   and charter schools, 116
   curriculum in, 116–8
   classical education in, 113, 117, 118
   definition of, 115–16
   descriptions of, 113, 115–16
   English, taught in, 117
   history of, 112–19
   standard of education available in, 117
   use of chapbooks in, 112, 123, 131
Hibernicus, 156–8, 160–1, 168, 176
Hiberno-English, 136, 142, 171, 184
Hogg, James, 151
Homer, 4-6, 121, 125, 185, 194
Hook, James, 142, 143
Hudson, Nicholas, 4, 5
Hyde, Douglas, 52
   Love Songs of Connacht, The, 58

Imtheachta Aeniasa, 18
improvisation, 15, 22, 31, 52, 59, 78, 83–4, 91–2
   see also caoineadh; oral-formulaic theory
'Independent Man, The', 46, 159
'Ireland's Warning', 58
Irish Folklore Commission, 72, 86, 92, 194
'It's Pretty to Be in Ballinderry', 80
Ives, Edward, 13, 59, 204

Jeffreys, Arabella, 131
Johnson, Samuel, 5,164
Joyce, James, 197
Joyce, Patrick W., 70, 86, 92–4, 112, 116, 118, 131
  English As We Speak It in Ireland, 171

Keane, Francis, 93
Keane, Sarah and Rita, 183
keens *see caoineadh*
Kennedy, Patrick, 3, 80, 149, 178, 183, 197
  Banks of the Boro, The, 176–7
  Evenings in the Duffrey, 72, 176–7
'Kilruddery Hunt, The' ('The Kilruddery Fox Chase), 162, 169
Koran, 11
Knott, Eleanor, 32, 35, 44

Labov, William, 9, 10
laments *see caoineadh*; death-song; *marbhna*
'Lament for Diarmaid Uí Laoghaire', 68
'Lament for John Burke', 108
Lament for the Sons of Uisneach, 84
Lamont, Aeneas, 175
laoithe see lays, Fenian
'Larry's Ghost', 166
'Lass of Richmond Hill, The', 143
lays, Fenian/heroic, 15, 17, 23, 27, 33, 44, 54, 70, 80–2, 108
Lenihan, Tom, 146, 183, 188–9, 197, 202
Liber Hymnorum, 33
linguistic registers, 10, 195, 203
  see also Atkinson, David; Bernstein, Basil
'Líontar Dúinn an Cruiscín', 59
literacy, 3, 5, 9–11, 30, 39, 150, 153, 175, 192–4
  and cognition, 7–10, 191–3
  and Greek culture, 7, 9
  and hedge schools, 113, 123
  and logic, 7–10
  and oral tradition, 63, 110
  in eighteenth-century England, 12
  learning/retention of songs, 190, 194
  spread of, 2, 19, 22, 30, 36, 123, 134, 148, 153, 170, 175, 195
Lloyd, Seón, 134
Long, Eleanor, 13, 59, 200

Lord, Albert, 6–8, 10–11, 17–18, 62, 94, 97, 101, 151
  see also oral-formulaic theory; *The Singer of Tales*
'Lord Randall', 47, 51
'Lovers' Meeting, The', 144–5
'lyric intensity', 52–3
  see also 'emotional core'
lúibíní, 22
Lysaght, Ned, 139–40

Mac a Liondain, Pádraig, 126, 137–8
Mac an Bhaird, Fearghal Óg, 30, 66
macaronic song, 46, 127, 129, 134–8, 146, 169, 170
McCafferty, Joe, 191, 194
Mac Cana, Proinsias, 20, 23, 24, 34, 44, 50, 76
Mac Carthaigh, Eoghan an Mhéirín, 42, 47, 124
McCarthy, Mikeen, 187, 190–1, 197, 199
McClafferty, Teresa, 202
'Mc. Clure's Rambles', 169
Mac Craith, Andrias, 137
Mac Cuarta, Séamus Dall, 29, 31, 33, 46, 85, 126
Mac Cumhaigh, Art, 2, 41, 46, 129, 135
Mac Domhnaill, Seán Clárach, 31, 37, 42, 46, 90, 125, 127
Mac Gabhann, Pádraig, 137
Mac Gearailt, Piaras, 37
Mac Giolla Fhiondáin, Pádraig, 29, 30
Mac Giolla Ghunna, Cathal, 45-6, 54, 81
  see also 'An Bunnán Buí'
Mac Grianna brothers (Seán Bán and Séamus), 101, 194
Mac Grianna, Seán Bán, 2, 52, 53–4, 59, 62, 100–1, 194
McLuhan, Marshall, 7–8, 9, 11, 12, 109, 192
MacNally, Leonard, 143
Macpherson, James, 4
Mac Ruairí, Éamonn, 188, 191, 193
McWilliams, Hugh, 147
Maguire, John, 184, 186, 201
Mallet, David, 186
  see also 'William and Margaret'
'Man in Love, A', 147

manuscript tradition
  and *caoineadh*, 81–6, 87–91, 100, 107–09
  and *marbhn*a, 66–70, 94
  and oral tradition, 2, 17, 22, 24–5, 53–60
  and reading aloud, 22, 24, 27, 39, 53
  Medieval, 15–6, 18–21, 33, 35, 36, 38
  17th-19th century, 30, 31, 36, 38–40, 44, 47, 53–60, 64, 65, 73, 78, 80, 83–4, 97–8, 100–2, 105–6, 108, 109, 111, 117, 122, 134, 146–7, 150, 166, 167, 190–2, 194
  motifs of , 66, 75
  musical features of, 81–3, 90
  performance of, 66
  personal, 66–7, 84, 89
  poetic features of, 66–70
  'tAbhránuíghe, An', 40
  see also *athláech* theory; *caoineadh*; death-song; *duanairí*; multiforms; scribal tradition; transitional texts
Marbhna Aodha Ruaidh Uí Dhomhnaill, 66
Marbhna Mhic Fínín Duibh, 70, 81, 82, 94, 108
Marquis of Clanrickarde, 28
'Má Théid Tú 'un Aonaigh', 81, 86, 91
Mayhew, Henry, 195
Meillet, Antoine, 6
Merriman, Brian, 118
metres, Irish, accentual (*amhrán*) 27, 31–40
  caoineadh, 68–9, 83, 88, 90, 91, 94, 98–9
  ochtfhoclach, 138–9, 168, 186
  origins of, 32–4
  rise of, 27, 31–40
  rosc, 76
metres, Irish, syllabic/mixed, 22–3, 24, 31–2, 34, 35–7, 39–40
  dán díreach, 23, 66
  decline of, 31–40
  deibhidhe, 66
  rannaíocht mhór, 67
  trí rann agus amhrán, 31
  see also *dúnadh*; *conchlann*
metres, English
  ballad, 152
  broadside ballad, 152, 168, 169, 171, 184
Milliken, Alfred, 131
'Miltown Fourteen, The', 146
Miltown Malbay, County Clare, 196–7

miscellanies, 3, 152–3, 158, 162–3, 170, 181, 195, 196
  see also *The Charms of Melody*; *Paddy's Resource*; *Pills to Purge Melancholy*; and *The Tea-Table Miscellany*
'Misses Limerick, Kerry and Clare', 185
'Mná na hÉireann', 47, 49, 51
'Moll Dubh an Ghleanna', 56–8, 60
'Molly Astore', 141
'Molly Maguires, The', 184
Moore, Thomas, 196–7
Moulden, John, 166–7, 168, 171–2, 175, 183, 190, 194–6
'Mount Taragh's Triumph', 155
'Mudion River', 112, 131
multiforms, 18–20, 98
Munnelly, Tom, 14, 187, 189, 191, 196, 202
Murphy, Gerard, 16–17, 19, 23–4, 32, 43, 50
'My Laddie Can Fight and My Laddie Can Sing', 137, 176

Nagy, Joseph Falaky, 15–16, 18–21, 23, 24, 29
Na Ráithíneach, Seán, 69–70, 82, 94
Nash, James, 120
Nation, The, 196
'New Song on the Beauties of Dunganstown, A', 131
'New Tractor, The', 184
Neoclassicism, 121–2, 139–45, 158, 163, 169, 171
New World of Words, The, 152
Ní Chonaill, Éibhlín (Dubh), 65, 91, 95, 103–6
Ní Chonaill, Máire (Dubh), 105
Ní Chonghaile, Bairbre (Quinn), 202
Nic Cuarta, Peig, 85
Nic Ruairí, Kitty, 191
Ní Dhomhnaill, Máire Chonnachtach, 100
Ní Dhomhnaill, Neilí, 101
Ní Dhonnagáin Máire, 86
Ní Laoghaire, Máire (Bhuí), 46, 87, 108, 109, 194
Ní Liaghain, Siobhán, 85
Ní Reachtagáin, Máire, 108
Ní Uallacháin, Pádraigín, 46, 52, 80, 83, 86
'North Country Beauty, The', 126, 147

O'Brien, John (lament for), 95, 98–9
Ó Bruadair, Dáibhí, 34–5, 37, 46, 154
Ó Buachalla, Breandán, 54
   aisling, 41, 43–4
   caoineadh, as literary form, 94, 97–104, 108, 109
   caoineadh, as metre, 68–9, 76
Ó Cadhla, Labhrás, 77, 78, 90, 92
Ó Coileáin, Seán, 15, 17–19, 24, 75, 76, 91, 93–6, 101, 102, 104, 108
O'Connell, Daniel, 72, 105, 122, 123, 156, 185
O'Connell, Mrs Morgan J., 105
O'Conor, Charles, 58
Ó Crualaoi, Pádraig, 100
Ó Crualaoich, Gearóid, 72, 86, 110
O'Curry, Eugene, 78, 82, 92
Ó Dálaigh, Cearbhall, 29, 48
Ó Dálaigh, Donnchadh Mór, 29
O'Daly, John, 58, 86
Ó Dóirnín, Peadar, 2, 46, 47, 49, 51, 52, 118, 127–8, 137, 159
O'Donovan, John, 73, 92, 95, 98
Ó Drisceoil, Con 'Fada', 146
Ó Duibheannaigh, Aodh, 52, 194
Ó Duibhannaigh, John, 59, 92, 101, 195, 197
Ó Gealacáin, Peadar, 135
Ó Gormáin, Muiris, 127–8
Ogle, George, 141, 166, 177
O'Grady, Standish, 22
Ó hAilín, Tomás, 74, 91, 92
Ó hEódhusa, Eochaidh, 34
Ó hUiginn, Ruairí, 16
Ó hUiginn, Tádhg Dall, 29, 85
O'Kearney, Nicholas, 30
O'Keeffe, John, 163, 166
   Agreeable Surprise, The, 118, 120, 141
'Ólaim Puins is Ólaim Tae', 47
Ó Laoire, Lillis, 188, 191, 193, 198–9, 202
Ó Lochlainn, Colm
   Irish Street Ballads, 182
   More Irish Street Ballads, 187
Ó Longáin, Mícheál Óg, 122
Ó Macháin, Pádraig, 30
Ó Mathúna, Donncha, 134
Ó Muirgheasa, Énrí, 54, 83, 100, 171
Ó Muirí, Lorcán, 54, 55, 57
Ó Muirithe, Diarmaid, 134–5, 140

Ong, Walter J., 7–8, 12, 191–3
Orality Studies, 3–14
oral-formulaic theory, 4, 6–7, 10, 12, 13, 17–9, 24, 62, 94–103
   see also re-creation; variation
orality/oral culture
   as primitive, 5–8
   primary, 7–9, 109
   and iterary hypothesis, 7–9
   residual, 191–4
oral tradition
   and Homeric composition, 4–5
   as theological concept, 3–4
   stability in, 10–11, 18–19, 29, 31, 97, 198–200
   see also oral-formulaic theory
Ó Rathaille, Aogán, 2, 32, 33, 35, 40, 41–2, 46, 68–9, 80, 125–6, 138
Oriel (southeast Ulster), 39, 46, 70, 72 80, 81–2, 83, 86
Orr, James, 171
Ó Sé, Diarmuid (na Bolgaighe), 100
   Marbhna Mhic Fínín Duibh, 70, 94
   Tuireamh Mhic Fínín Duibh, 106
Ossian *see* MacPherson, James
Ossianic poetry *see* lays, Fenian
Ó Súilleabháin, Donncha, 137
Ó Súilleabháin, Eoghan (Rua), 3, 32, 34, 35, 40, 41–4, 46, 47, 112, 118, 124, 132–3, 137
Ó Súlleabháin, Seán, 50, 61, 92
Ó Súilleabháin, Tadhg Gaelach, 33, 47
Ó Súilleabháin, Tomás Rua, 46, 100
O'Sullivan, Morty Oge, 108
Ó Tuama, Seán (18th-century poet), 87, 90, 141
Ó Tuama, Seán (20th-century scholar), 31–2, 41, 43, 47–8, 50, 62, 97, 103–6, 124–5, 127
'Over the Hills and Far Away', 46, 165

'Paddy's Panacea', 146
Paddy's Resource, 163, 195, 196
Pairlement Chloinne Tomáis, 38
Palmerston, Lord, 113
paragraph form, 69, 76, 83
Parry, Milman, 6–7, 8, 17, 97

pastoral poetry, 141–4, 169, 153, 158, 163, 166, 167, 169, 196
pastourelle see song-types, French
'Patriot Queen, The', 122
'Pearlha Nhe Kilthee Bawne', 170–1
Penal Laws, 30, 113–16
Percy, Thomas 152, 164
  Reliques of Ancient English Poetry, 4
performance 1, 3, 6–9, 12–13, 16
  as communication, 195, 204–5
  centrality of, 9, 204–5
  contexts, 22, 38, 44, 154–5, 186–7, 190, 195, 199, 204–5
  at wakes, 22, 46, 65, 70, 72, 74, 81, 86, 91–3, 98
  see also community singing traditions
  reading aloud, 22, 24, 27, 39, 53, 176
  theory, 13
  see also bardic poetry; *caoineadh*; *marbhna*; oral-formulaic theory
Pills to Purge Melancholy, 153, 166
Pilson, Aynsworth, 172–3
Playford, Henry/John, 153, 160
Pope, Alexander, 140, 161
'Preab san Ól', 45, 138, 159
Prior, Anna, 31

Raiftearaí, Antáine, 46, 87, 88–9, 90, 109, 182, 194
Ramsay, Allan, 156
  Gentle Shepherd, The, 141
  Tea-Table Miscellany, The, 153, 162, 163
Ranafast, County Donegal, 59, 92, 101, 194
re-creation, 59–63, 200–1, 203–5
  see also improvisation; variation
Recruiting Officer, The, 46
Reynolds, Joshua, 164
reverdie see song-types, French
reverdie léannta, 124-5, 128, 149
Riddle, Almeda, 203
Rigveda, 11
'Rodney's Glory', 46
romances, medieval, 15, 20–4
  see also lays, Fenian
rosc, 76
Rosenberg, Bruce, 11, 97, 101
Rousseau, Jean-Jacques, 4
runs, 18, 22, 149
  see also formula

'Sagart na Cúile Báine', 87–8
sagas, medieval Irish, 15, 16–20, 84
  and oral-formulaic theory, 17–19, 24
  and multiforms, 18–20
'Saxaibh na Séad', 43
scribal tradition, 95, 97-8, 116
  Medieval, 16, 19-20, 24, 30, 31
  17th-19th-century *see* manuscript tradition, 17th-19th century
scribes, 31, 38, 39, 40, 53–5, 58, 98, 113, 122, 127, 134, 135, 137, 138
Scribner and Cole, 9, 193
'Seán Ó Duibhir an Ghleanna', 44, 171
'Sewball', 168
'Shannon Scheme, The', 185
Shepard, Leslie, 205
Sheridan, Richard Brinsley, 163
Sheridan, Thomas, 5, 140, 163
Sheil, John, 175
Shields, Hugh, 13, 23, 43, 44, 52–3, 61, 108, 139, 149, 153, 155, 160, 166, 170, 172, 181–2, 184, 191–2, 194,195, 196, 197-8, 200–2
Sigerson, George, 44
singers
  aesthetics, 59-63, 109, 145-50, 195-205
  and literacy, 188-9, 190-1, 193-4
  and written sources, 188-92, 201, 203
  see also community singing traditions; re-creation
Singer of Tales, The, 6
  see also Lord, Albert; Parry, Milman
Smyth, Thomas, 28
song-types, French
  carole, 46, 47,
  chanson de malmarieé, 47
  pastourelle, 47, 124, 125–6, 127–8, 143, 169, 182, 197
  reverdie, 43, 47, 124–5, 127–9, 130, 131, 138, 169
  see also reverdie léannta
song-types, Irish
  aisling see main entry
  ballads *see* main entry
  crosántacht, 30
  death-song *see* main entry
  drinking, 44–5, 141–2, 153, 162–4, 166, 169, 182, 185

hedge schoolmaster *see* main entry
Jacobite, 41–4, 46, 122, 123, 156, 176
lullaby, 43, 46, 94, 98, 99
lúibíní, 22
macaronic *see* main entry
narrative *see* ballads
   see also caoineadh; *marbhna*
'Sorrowful Lamentation, A', 185
'Spealadóir, An', 132–3
Spectator, The, 153
Spenser, Edmund, 28
spéirbhean, 41, 61–2, 130
sráidéigse, 34, 154
Stanyhurst, Richard, 145
Suil Dhuv, the Coiner, 177–8
'Sweet William's Farewell to Black-Eyed Susan', 167
Swift, Jonathan, 140, 156, 158–9, 160

'Tá Daoine a' Rádh', 171
'Tagra an Dá Theampall', 129–30
Táin Bó Fraích, 16
'Tá Mé 'mo Shuí', 138
Tea-Table Miscellany, The, 153, 158, 162–3
'Terry O'Brien's Adventure', 170
'Thugamar Féin an Samhradh Linn', 46
Tipling Philosophers, The, 162, 164, 166, 169
Tory Island, County Donegal, 198–9, 202
traditional song *see* folksong
transitional texts, 19–20
   see also athláech theory; multiforms
translations
   of Child ballads, 47, 51
   of Irish-Gaelic songs, 171, 134–5, 182
'Trial of John Twiss, The', 184
tuireamh see marbhna
Tuireamh Mhic Fínín Duibh, 106, 108
tune family, 77
Tunney, Paddy, 59, 145, 183
'Turf and Reading-made-easy, The', 133–4
''Twas When the Seas Were Roaring', 153, 176

údar an amhráin, 52, 61, 198
'Úna Bhán', 89
'Under an Arbour of a Wide-Spreading Fagus', 112, 137
United Irishmen, 122-3, 196
'Úr-chill an Chreagáin', 41, 45, 54, 129, 135

variation, 2, 11, 13, 16, 18–22, 24, 53–60, 77–8, 95–100, 151, 198–201, 203–5
   abbreviation/compression, 54, 58–60, 200
   and creativity, 18–9, 59–62, 200, 202–5
   inflation, 54
   localization, 54, 56-7
   see also improvisation; re-creation
Vauxhall songs *see* ballads, printed, genres
vernacular song *see* folksong
verse forms, Irish (non-song)
   agallamh beirte, 94, 98
   barántas, 31
Vico, Giambattista, 4, 5

Walker, Joseph Cooper, 58, 77
Ward, Ned (Edward) *see* 'The Tipling Philosophers'
Wardlaw, Lady, 156
Wedding of Pritty Miss S—ally, The, 160
Wexford (County), 3, 149, 176–8, 197
   see also Kennedy, Patrick
Whelan, Kevin, 74, 113, 123, 146
'Wild Sports of O'Sullivan, The', 132–3
'William and Margaret', 153, 158, 159–60
'Willy Reilly and his Cooleen Bawn', 169
Wolf, Friedrich August, 4, 5
   Prolegomena ad Homerum, 4
Wolf, John Quincy, 13, 59-60
Wood, Robert, 4, 5

Yeats, Gráinne, 32
Yeats, W. B., 2
Young, Arthur, 115